MENANDER

II

LCL 459

MENANDER

VOLUME II

EDITED AND TRANSLATED BY

W. G. ARNOTT

HARVARD UNIVERSITY PRESS
CAMBRIDGE, MASSACHUSETTS
LONDON, ENGLAND
1996

ISBN 0–674–99506–6
Library of Congress Catalog Card Number 80–154351

*Typeset in ZephGreek and ZephText
by Chiron, Inc, North Chelmsford, Massachusetts.
Printed in Great Britain by St Edmundsbury Press Ltd,
Bury St Edmunds, Suffolk, on acid-free paper.
Bound by Hunter & Foulis Ltd, Edinburgh, Scotland.*

CONTENTS

PREFACE

The delay in the appearance of this second volume of the Loeb Menander, which is entirely the responsibility of its editor and translator, has nevertheless made possible some substantial benefits. Menandrean papyri have continued to be published in the last sixteen years, and this volume can accordingly include more of *Kitharistes* and *Misoumenos* than would have been available earlier, together with new scraps of *Leukadia*, which illuminate that play's unusual opening.

The principles followed in the first volume and sketched out in its preface are here continued, but there is one minor adjustment which seems to be advisable. In my translation, on the advice of some reviewers, I now generally avoid the literal translation of oaths and attempt to substitute more modern and idiomatic phrases.

The line-numbering used for *Kolax* and particularly *Misoumenos* in previous editions has become unwieldy, and new schemes are adopted here; the one for *Misoumenos* I have sought to justify in *Zeitschrift für Papyrologie und Epigraphik*, 110 (1996), 27. It avoids the addition of letters and stars to some of the numbers, and should σὺν θεῷ continue to prove serviceable if in the future further portions of text surface from the Egyptian sands.

PREFACE

The text and apparatus of each play in this volume are based, as before, on a study of good photographs of the papyri wherever possible. Unpublished photographs of the two Berlin papyri of *Misoumenos* and of the Oxyrhynchus papyrus of *Perinthia* have been supplied to me; due acknowledgement is made below. No photograph has ever been published of the papyrus of *Koneiazomenai* now in Tbilisi; here I have been compelled to rely on the full reports of G. Zereteli and A. Körte; the bibliographical details of its first edition in 1909 are now given fully and correctly for the first time.

I should like to supplement those acknowledgements of help, advice and useful information received from institutions and colleagues which are listed in the preface to the first volume by thanking here the Bodleian Library in Oxford for supplying a photograph of *P. Oxyrhynchus* 855 of Menander's *Perinthia*, Dr Colin Austin for making available to me his photographs of *P. Berlin* 13281 and 13932 of *Misoumenos* and for other helpful information, Dr Revell Coles, Dr M. Gronewald, Professor E. W. Handley, Dr Malcolm Heath, Professor G. Paduano and Dr W. Stockert for advice, publications and helpful information, and above all Mrs Philippa Goold, whose courteous assistance as subeditor and proof-reader has been invaluable. It is sad that the names of Charles Brink, Konrad Gaiser, Harry Sandbach and Günther Zuntz can no longer be added to the above list; here death has robbed us of both scholarship and true friendship.

Leeds   W. Geoffrey Arnott
January 1996

viii

Supplement to the Bibliography in Volume One

Editions

(b) The monostichs. See also Rudolf Führer, *Zur slavischen Übersetzung der Menandersentenzen* (Königstein 1982).

(d) Complete editions of the papyri of Menander known today. F. H. Sandbach (text: 2nd edition, Oxford 1990, with an appendix containing *inter alia* the new fragments of the fourth act of *Epitrepontes*, the first act of *Misoumenos* and fr. 1 of *Kitharistes*). I have not myself seen the editions of I. Zacharopolos (Athens, undated but in the 1970s) and A. Ramírez Trejo, I (Mexico City 1979).

(e) Selections from the papyri. Guido Paduano (Milan 1980: *Asp., Dysk., Epit., Perik., Sam.*).

(f) Single plays.

Aspis. No complete edition, but a commentary on vv. 1–163 by A. H. Groton (Diss. University of Michigan 1982, available on microfilm).

Dyskolos. M. de Fátima de Sousa e Silva (Coimbra 1976). Stanley Ireland (Warminster 1995).

Epitrepontes. Francesco Sisti (Genoa 1991).

Misoumenos. Francesco Sisti (Genoa 1986).

Perikeiromene. Mario Lamagna (Naples 1994).

Samia. J. Thomsen (Copenhagen 1977). H. Offermann (Stuttgart 1980). D. Bain (Warminster 1983).

Sikyonioi. A. M. Belardinelli (Bari 1994, defending the plural form of the title).

BIBLIOGRAPHY

? *Hydria.* Konrad Gaiser, *Menanders 'Hydria'* (*Abhandlungen der Heidelberger Akademie der Wissenschaften, Philologisch-Historische Klasse*, 1/1977), identifying the extensive papyrus fragments of the 'Strobilos comedy' (no. 244 in Colin Austin, *Comicorum Graecorum Fragmenta in Papyris Reperta*, Berlin 1973, pp. 252–265) as Menander's *Hydria*, but see R. L. Hunter, *Classical Review*, 29 (1979), 209–211 and Jürgen Blänsdorf, *Göttingische Gelehrte Anzeigen*, 232 (1950), 42–66.

Photographs

The Cairo Codex of Menander (P.Cair. J. 43227) (Institute of Classical Studies, London 1978), with a preface by Ludwig Koenen, contains new and clearer photographs of this papyrus, prepared under the supervision of H. Riad and Abd el-Kadr Selim.

Bibliographies

(b) After 1958

(i) *Dyskolos.* J. M. Jacques, *L'Information littéraire* (Paris), 35 (1983), 168–172.

(ii) and (iii) General surveys. F. Uebel, *Archiv für Papyrusforschung*, 21 (1974), 171, 191–202, and 22/23 (1974), 363–365. L. V. Pavlenko, *Vestnik Drevnej Istorii* (Moscow), 2/140 (1977), 154–159.

A. Blanchard, *Revue des Études Grecques*, 94 (1981), 496–501. H. J. Mette, *Lustrum*, 25 (1983), 15–30, and 27 (1985), 27–31. W. Luppe, *Archiv für Papyrusforschung*, 27 (1980), 233–234, 236–238 and 250, and 38 (1992), 78–82, 84.

HEROS
(THE GUARDIAN SPIRIT)

INTRODUCTION

Manuscript

C = *P. Cairensis* 43227, part of a papyrus codex described
more fully in the introduction to *Epitrepontes*. *Heros*
seems to have been the second of the five or more plays
originally contained in the codex.[1] Extant in C are a met-
rical hypothesis and cast-list to the play, its first 52 lines
(some of them damaged), and a series of scraps (with text
on both sides) which have been assembled to form three
fragments, two of which certainly and the third possibly
derive from a later stage in the play. First edition:
G. Lefebvre, *Fragments d'un manuscrit de Ménandre*
(Cairo 1907); the same editor's *Papyrus de Ménandre*
(Cairo 1911), with a revised text, contains photographs, as
does *The Cairo Codex of Menander (P.Cair. J. 43227)* (In-
stitute of Classical Studies, London 1978).

Fragments 1–8 are definitely, and 9–10 doubtfully,

---

[1] This can easily be inferred from the fact that the sheet of
papyrus containing the opening of the *Heros* is numbered $\kappa\theta$
(= 29) on its first side and λ (= 30) on its second. Each extant
side of C contains from 33 to 38 lines, averaging 35.75. Accord-
ingly there was room before the *Heros* for one play of about 950
to 990 lines, prefaced perhaps, like the *Heros*, by a hypothesis
and cast-list.

assigned quotations from a multitude of sources. See vol. I pp. xxiv–xxv.

This text, like the Bodmer codex of the *Dyskolos*, is prefaced by a 12-line metrical hypothesis and a list of characters arranged presumably in order of their appearance on the stage. Unlike the Bodmer codex, however, the Cairo papyrus does not add a didascalic notice (the *Heros* accordingly cannot be dated[1]), and its hypothesis is not foisted upon the Hellenistic scholar Aristophanes of Byzantium. The plot summaries that such verse hypotheses contain are often found to be inaccurate over details when these can be checked against completely preserved texts of tragedy or comedy, and there is at least one statement in the hypothesis of *Heros* that arouses suspicion. The man who reared the twins is said to have given them to their true father as a security for a loan (hyp. 3–4); this seems to be a distortion of the true facts, if Daos' version of the events (not admittedly a wholly accurate one,

---

[1] The text of the play fragments themselves provides no tangible clues to the date. A plausible supplementation at line 46 puts Gorgias on a visit to the island of Lemnos, and this probably rules out the period 314 to 306 B.C., when the island was lost to Athens. At line 30 there is a reference to a recent famine, but the comedy of Menander's age is so full of references to the high price of food and the consequent hardships of the poor that we are driven to assume that famine was a regular visitor to Attica between 324 and 291 B.C. The modern historian, however, is here hindered by the inadequacy of our ancient sources. Cf. W. S. Ferguson, *Hellenistic Athens* (London 1911), 50 f., 64 f. (Lemnos), 66 f. and 133 (famine), and Peter Garnsey, *Famine and Food Supply in the Graeco-Roman World* (Cambridge 1988), 154–164.

either!) in the first scene is to be believed. Daos says there that the foster-parent died seriously in debt to Daos' master, and the twins thereafter began to work off the debt as employees of the creditor.

Even so, judicious combination of the information provided by the *Heros* hypothesis with the cast-list and with the clues scattered about the dramatic fragments, particularly those of the expository opening scene, allows us a fairly clear picture of the antecedent events on which the plot is based, and a reasonable idea about the two major elements in the dénouement.

Eighteen years before the action of the play begins (cf. line 94), a man raped a woman, who then bore twins, a boy and a girl. The raper later married the woman without realising that she had previously been his victim. The cast-list enables us to identify the raper as Laches and his wife as Myrrhine (cf. also line 72). The twins were called Gorgias and Plangon (24–25); of them only Gorgias has a speaking part in the play. When they were still babies Myrrhine gave them to a freedman shepherd named Tibeios from the village of Ptelea, the scene of the play. This shepherd pretended that the twins were his own children (23 ff.), and this may have been what the twins themselves were brought up to believe. Tibeios eventually died, having got heavily in debt to Laches, his former master. When the play opens the twins are working for the creditor in order to pay off Tibeios' debt. The inaugural complication is caused by Plangon's situation. She in her turn has been raped by a young neighbour, identifiable from the cast-list as Pheidias, and she is pregnant. Daos, a slave in Laches' house, is in love with Plangon and wishes to set up house with her.[1] Laches has given his consent, and only his temporary absence from Athens holds up the union between Gorgias' sister and Daos, who is willing to pretend that Plangon's expected child was fathered by himself. These plans appal Myrrhine, who was probably the only person in the house aware of the twins' relationship to her. Apparently, however, Myrrhine was as ignorant of the true identity of her own ravisher as she was of Plangon's (hyp. 9).

The hypothesis refers to the play's double dénouement (hyp. 10–12). Laches and Myrrhine discover that they are the joint parents of Gorgias and Plangon; and Plangon, now the acknowledged free daughter of Athenian citizens, is able to marry Pheidias.[2] Some brief passages

---

[1] So far as Daos knew, Plangon was the daughter of the freedman Tibeios, and the status of a freedman's children, especially those born before he was freed, was equivocal. When Daos says that Plangon was 'in a way' a slave (line 20: line 6 of the hypothesis is less subtle), he means simply that her status was not so different from his own that a settled relationship between them was unthinkable. Slaves were allowed to live together with members of their own class or with the children of freedmen in relationships which doubtless could last as long as those of formal marriage, but marriage itself was limited in Attica to free citizens. Cf. A. R. W. Harrison, *The Law of Athens*, I (Oxford 1968), 21–29, 177, 184–186, and D. M. MacDowell, *The Law in Classical Athens* (London 1978), 87.

[2] Menander's comedy avoids sentimentality. Daos' infatuation for Plangon may have been handled very sympathetically in the play's opening scene, but Daos was a slave and Plangon the daughter of free Athenian citizens. Furthermore Pheidias, who had fathered Plangon's child, was a free (and probably wealthy) young Athenian. In a civilisation which valued property, citizen-

from the scene in which Laches and Myrrhine make their discovery appear to be preserved in a series of scraps from the Cairo codex, but they are tantalisingly mutilated, and in the absence of further evidence it would be unprofitable to speculate overmuch about the details of the dénouement or of the earlier plot structure. Daos may at one point have sought to justify to Myrrhine his love for Plangon (cf. fr. 2). The cast-list testifies to the appearance later in the play of two slaves named Sangarios and Sophrone. The latter name is elsewhere in comedy given to aged nurses (Men. *Epit.*; Terence, *Eunuchus, Phormio*; cf. [Aristaenetus], *Ep.* 1. 6), and if Sophrone had been the go-between at the time when Myrrhine disposed of her baby twins to Tibeios, her role in their subsequent recognition of their parents may have been important.

The cast-list contains one further name of interest. After the opening scene between Getas and Daos, the exposition was apparently continued in a prologue speech delivered by the play's title figure, the 'guardian spirit' of my translation. These spirits, or 'heroes' as they are often called, played an important part in Greek popular religion.[1] They came half way between gods and

ship, and formal marriage between free-born citizens, the only conventionally acceptable resolution of the plot would be a wedding between Pheidias and Plangon.

[1] The standard account is L. R. Farnell, *Greek Hero Cults and Ideas of Immortality* (Oxford 1921, reprinted 1970). Cf. also M. P. Nilsson, *Greek Popular Religion* (New York 1940), 18–21, W. K. C. Guthrie, *The Greeks and Their Gods* (London 1950), 231–235, and Walter Burkert, *Greek Religion* (transl. J. Raffan, Oxford 1985), 203–208.

humans. Many of them were the spirits of dead cele-
brities—real and fictional—who were believed to guide
from their tombs the fortunes of cities, tribes, demes and
individuals in public and private affairs. Such a spirit was
aptly chosen to deliver the prologue in a comedy of this
kind. None of the human figures possessed all the back-
ground information essential to the exposition. And one
of the functions of these guardian heroes was that of help-
ing men and women unhappily wounded by love.

[Η]Ρ[ΩΣ Μ]ΕΝΑΝΔΡΟΥ

(Η ΥΠΟΘΕΣΙΣ)

ἄρρεν <τε> θῆλύ θ' ἅμα τεκοῦσα παρθένος
ἔδωκεν ἐπιτρόπῳ τρέφειν· εἶθ' ὕστερον
ἔγημε τὸν φθείραντα. ταῦτα δ' ὑπέθετο
ὁ τρέφων πρὸς αὐτὸν ἀγνοῶν. θεράπων δέ τις
5   ἐνέπεσεν εἰς ἔρωτα τῆς νεανίδος
ὁμόδουλον εἶναι διαλαβών. γείτων δέ τις
προηδικήκει μετὰ βίας τὴν μείρακα.
τὴν αἰτίαν ἐφ' ἑαυτὸν ὁ θεράπων στρέφειν
ἐβούλετ'· οὐκ εἰδυῖα δ' ἡ μήτηρ ἄγαν
10   ἐδυσχέραινε. καταφανῶν δὲ γενομένων
εὗρεν μὲν ὁ γέρων τοὺς ἑαυτοῦ γνωρίσας,
ὁ δ' ἠδικηκὼς ἔλαβε τὴν κόρην θέλων.

Title and hypothesis taken from the Cairo papyrus.

Title   Suppl. ed. pr.

Hypothesis   1 Corr. Wilamowitz: αρρεντεκουσαπαρθενοσθη-
λυθ'αμα C.   2 Corr. several: επιτροφω C.

8

THE GUARDIAN SPIRIT BY MENANDER

(HYPOTHESIS)

A maiden bore twin babies, boy and girl.
She gave them to a guardian to rear,
And later married her seducer. Unawares
Their foster-father pawned them for a loan
To him.[a] A servant deemed the girl a slave   5
Like him, and fell in love with her. A neighbour
Had previously forced the maid. The servant
Desired to focus blame upon himself.
The mother didn't know the truth, and was
Exceedingly displeased. The facts came out.   10
The old man found and recognised his own.
The violator gladly took the girl.

[a] 'Him' must be the seducer mentioned in line 3. The statement appears to be inaccurate: see the introduction to *Heros*.

ΤΑ ΤΟΥ ΔΡΑΜ(ΑΤΟΣ) ΠΡΟΣΩΠΑ

Γέτας
Δᾶος
Ἥρως θεός
Μυρρίνη
Φειδίας
Σωφρόνη
Σαγγάριος
Γοργίας
Λάχης

Cast-list, as it appears in the Cairo papyrus.

Getas, a slave probably in Pheidias' household
Daos, a slave in Laches' household
The guardian spirit, a local divinity who spoke the
    prologue
Myrrhine, the wife of Laches
Pheidias, a young man, the ravisher of Gorgias'
    twin-sister
Sophrone, probably Myrrhine's old nurse
Sangarios, a slave probably in Laches' or Pheidias'
    household
Gorgias, the son of Myrrhine
Laches, an old man

The cast-list in the Cairo papyrus does not mention any mute characters, who in this play may have included Plangon, Gorgias' twin-sister. Nor does it refer to the chorus, who may have performed the customary entr'actes in the guise not of the conventional tipsy revellers, but of huntsmen from Athens (see on fr. 1, below).

11

ΗΡΩΣ

(*SCENE: Ptelea, a small but wealthy village whose precise location in Attica is still a little uncertain. It is most likely to have been about 2½ miles west-north-west of Athens in the Kephisos valley at the edge of the Aigaleos hills, less than half a mile north of the Sacred Way from Athens to Eleusis. A less likely site is on the other side of the Aigaleos hills, in the eastern part of the Thriasian plain.[a] A street in the village, backed by two houses; one belongs to Laches and his family, the other to Pheidias.*)

ΓΕΤΑΣ

κακόν τι, Δᾶέ, μοι δοκεῖς πεποηκέναι
παμμέγεθες· εἶτα προσδοκῶν ἀγωνιᾷς
μυλῶνα σαυτῷ καὶ πέδας· εὔδηλος εἶ.
τί γὰρ σὺ κόπτεις τὴν κεφαλὴν οὕτω πυκνά;
5   τί τὰς τρίχας τίλλεις ἐπιστάς; τί στένεις;

In the apparatus to this play, those corrections and supplements whose author is not named were made by the ed. pr., G. Lefebvre, *Fragments d'un manuscrit de Ménandre* (Cairo 1907).

[a] Cf. J. S. Traill, *The Political Organisation of Attica* (*Hesperia.* Supp. Vol. 14, 1975), 49, and Eugene Vanderpool, *Hesperia*, 35 (1966), 280. Ernst Meyer's entry in *RE* xxiii (1959), 1478 f., now needs revising.

[b] The punishment that slaves feared most was that of being

HEROS

(The Guardian Spirit)

(The play opens with a conversation between the two slaves Getas and Daos. Daos may have entered first, probably from Laches' house or by the entrance to the spectators' right which was conventionally assumed to lead to the city of Athens. Daos appears to be in great distress. A moment later Getas enters, probably by the entrance on the spectators' left, assumed to lead into the country. He is carrying a bundle of wood, which he puts down to talk to Daos.)

GETAS

You look as if you've done a terrible
Crime, Daos! You're distressed. Expecting to
Be sent quern-pushing in leg irons?[b] Can't
Be doubted—otherwise, why smack your scalp
So much, why stand and tear your hair out, why   5
Whimper?

sent to work in a flour mill, where they had the laborious and monotonous task of pushing a saddle-quern backwards and forwards all day long, often with their feet fettered (Plautus, *Mostellaria* 15–19, Terence, *Phormio* 249). See L. A. Moritz, *Grain-Mills and Flour in Classical Antiquity* (Oxford 1958), 34 ff. and 67.

ΔΑΟΣ

οἴμοι.

ΓΕΤΑΣ

τοιοῦτόν ἐστιν, ὦ πόνηρε σύ.
εἶτ᾽ οὐκ ἐχρῆν, κερμάτιον εἰ συνηγμένον
σοὶ τυγχάν]ει τι, τ[ο]ῦτ᾽ ἐμοὶ δοῦναι τέως
εἰ συγκυκᾷς] τὰ κατὰ σεαυτὸν πράγματα;
10 φιλῶ σε, Δᾶε, καὶ σ]υνάχθομαί γέ σοι
εἰ προσδοκᾷς λυπ]ηρά.

ΔΑΟΣ

σὺ μὲν οὐκ οἶδ᾽ ὅ τι
ληρεῖς· ἐγὼ γὰρ συμπ]έπλεγμαι πράγματι
ἀπροσδοκήτῳ καὶ δι]έφθαρμαι, Γέτα.

ΓΕΤΑΣ

πῶς γάρ, κατάρατε;]

ΔΑΟΣ

μὴ καταρῶ, πρὸς <τῶν> θεῶν,
15 βέλτιστ᾽, ἐρῶντι.]

ΓΕΤΑΣ

τί σὺ λέγεις; ἐρᾷς;

ΔΑΟΣ

ἐρῶ.

6 οιμμοι C.   8–15 A large tear has removed the opening 9 to
16 letters of these lines. Plausible supplementation is well-nigh
impossible; the text printed here is merely *exempli gratia*, in
order to provide the reader with a continuous text.   8 σοὶ
τυγχάν]ει suppl. Körte.   9–10 Suppl. Arnott (in 10 after van

14

DAOS

Oh dear!

GETAS

         It's something like that, you
Poor thing . . . So shouldn't you have given me
Your savings—any you've perhaps amassed,
[If you're mismanaging] your own affairs?
[I like you, Daos, and] I sympathise   10
[If] troubles [lie ahead].

DAOS

         [Your drivelling]
Defeats me. Getas, I'm entangled in
Something [surprising—and] it's shattered me!

GETAS

[Damn you, how's that?]

DAOS

         [Dear fellow], by the gods,
Don't *damn* [a lover]!

GETAS

(*pricking up his ears*)

         What's that? You in love?   15

DAOS

I am.

Leeuwen, who suggested ἐπεὶ φιλῶ σε καὶ], and ed. pr., who
suppl. σ]υνάχθομαι).   11 Suppl. van Herwerden.   12 λη-
ρεῖς suppl. Croiset, ἐγὼ γὰρ Sandbach (ἐγὼ δὲ van Leeuwen),
συμπ]έπλεγμαι Leo.   13 ἀπροσδοκήτῳ καὶ suppl. Sand-
bach, δι]έφθαρμαι Croiset.   14 Suppl. Körte. προσθέων C:
corr. Leo.   15 Suppl. van Leeuwen.

MENANDER

ΓΕΤΑΣ

πλέον δυοῖν σοι χοινίκων ὁ δεσπότης
παρέχει. πονηρόν, Δᾶ᾽· ὑπερδειπνεῖς ἴσως.

ΔΑΟΣ

πέπονθα τὴν ψυχήν τι παιδίσκην ὁρῶν
συντρεφομένην, ἄκακον, κατ᾽ ἐμαυτόν, ὦ Γέτα.

ΓΕΤΑΣ

20   δούλη ᾽στιν;

ΔΑΟΣ

οὕτως, ἡσυχῇ, τρόπον τινά.
ποιμὴν γὰρ ἦν Τίβειος οἰκῶν ἐνθαδὶ
Πτελέασι, γεγονὼς οἰκέτης νέος ὤν ποτε.
ἐγένετο τούτῳ δίδυμα ταῦτα παιδία,
ὡς ἔλεγεν αὐτός, ἥ τε Πλαγγών, ἧς ἐρῶ—

ΓΕΤΑΣ

25   νῦν μανθάνω.

ΔΑΟΣ

—τὸ μειράκιόν θ᾽, ὁ Γοργίας.

ΓΕΤΑΣ

ὁ τῶν προβατίων ἐνθάδ᾽ ἐπιμελούμενος
νυνὶ παρ᾽ ὑμῖν;

16–17 Adesp. fr. 444 Kock   21 See Men. fr. 1075 Kock

16 πλέον δυοῖν σοι χοινίκων Choeroboscus, *Scholia in Theo-dosii Canones*, i. 293. 30 Hilgard:]χοινικων C.   25–26 Change of speaker after Γοργίας indicated by ed. pr. (no dicolon is now visible in C at this point).   27 ὑμῖν Leo: ημιν C.

16

HEROS

GETAS
Your master's more than doubled your
Grain ration.[a] That's bad, Daos. Overfed,
Perhaps?

DAOS
My heart throbs when I see her. She
Grew up with me, she's pure, and, Getas, she's
My class!

GETAS
A slave?

DAOS
Yes—nearly . . . in a way. 20
You see, there was a shepherd living here
In Ptelea, he'd been a slave when young,
Tibeios, who'd got these twin children—that's
What he himself said—Plangon, she's the girl
I worship, . . .

GETAS
Now I see!

DAOS
. . . and Gorgias, 25
The boy.

GETAS
The one you've now got here, in charge
Of the sheep?

[a] Literally, 'Your master provides you with more than two
choinikes (sc. of grain each day).' The normal ration that an
Athenian master allowed his slave seems to have been much less
than this—possibly only one *choinix* (= about one litre) a day.
Compare also fr. 10 of *Heros*.

17

ΔΑΟΣ

οὗτος. ὢν ἤδη γέρων
ὁ Τίβειος ὁ πατὴρ εἰς τροφήν γε λαμβάνει
τούτοις παρὰ τοὐμοῦ δεσπότου μνᾶν, καὶ πάλιν—
30 λιμὸς γὰρ ἦν—μνᾶν· εἶτ' ἀπέσκλη.

ΓΕΤΑΣ

τὴν τρίτην
ὡς οὐκ ἐπεδίδου τυχὸν ὁ δεσπότης ὁ σός.

ΔΑΟΣ

ἴσως. τελευτήσαντα δ' αὐτὸν προσλαβὼν
ὁ Γοργίας τι κερμάτιον ἔθαψε καὶ
τὰ νόμιμα ποιήσας πρὸς ἡμᾶς ἐνθάδε
35 ἐλθὼν ἀγαγών τε τὴν ἀδελφὴν ἐπιμένει
τὸ χρέος ἀπεργαζόμενος.

ΓΕΤΑΣ

ἡ Πλαγγὼν δὲ τί;

ΔΑΟΣ

μετὰ τῆς ἐμῆς κεκτημένης ἐργάζεται
ἔρια διακονεῖ τε.

31 Corr. Arnott: απεδιδου C.

---

[a] 100 drachmas.
[b] The funeral took place before sunrise on the third day after
death. The 'normal ceremonies' mentioned here would include
the dinner in memory of the dead man directly after the funeral,

DAOS

That's the man. When he grew old,
Their father—this Tibeios—borrowed from
My master for their keep one mina,[a] then
Another. Life was hard. It killed him.

GETAS

When   30
Your master wouldn't lend him number three,
Perhaps?

DAOS

Maybe. He died, and Gorgias
Borrowed some more cash for the funeral,
The normal ceremonies.[b] After that
He came to us here with his sister, and   35
He's stayed, while working off the debt.[c]

GETAS

And Plangon?

DAOS

She spins and weaves wool with my mistress, and
Works as a servant.

a rite at the tomb on the ninth day after burial, and a further rite
to mark the end of the period of mourning. See D. C. Kurtz
and John Boardman, *Greek Burial Customs* (London 1971),
142–161, and Robert Garland, *The Greek Way of Death* (London
1985), 21–27.

[c] Tibeios had presumably contracted to repay the loan by
working for Laches without pay for a fixed time, and when he
died before the stipulated amount of work had been completed,
the duty of fulfilling the contract devolved on Gorgias and Plan-
gon, who passed for his children. Cf. the Gomme-Sandbach
Commentary, on *Heros* 36.

ΓΕΤΑΣ

παιδίσκη;

ΔΑΟΣ

πάνυ,

Γέτα—καταγελᾷς.

ΓΕΤΑΣ

μὰ τὸν Ἀπόλλω.

ΔΑΟΣ

πάνυ, Γέτα,

40   ἐλευθέριος καὶ κοσμία.

ΓΕΤΑΣ

τί οὖν σύ; τί

πράττεις ὑπὲρ σαυτοῦ;

ΔΑΟΣ

λάθρᾳ μέν, Ἡράκλεις,

οὐδ' ἐγκεχείρηκ', ἀλλὰ τῷμῷ δεσπότῃ

εἴρηχ', ὑπέσχηταί τ' ἐμοὶ σ[υνοικιεῖν

αὐτὴν διαλεχθεὶς πρὸς τ[ὸν ἀδελφόν.

ΓΕΤΑΣ

[λαμπρὸς εἶ.

43 Suppl. Croiset.   44 τ[ὸν ἀδελφόν suppl. ed. pr., (Γετ.)
λαμπρὸς εἶ Wilamowitz.

---

[a] If the interpretation suggested here is correct (see *Classical*

GETAS

(*leering*)

Serves you, does she?[a]

DAOS

(*innocently*)

Yes,

Getas. You're laughing!

GETAS

By Apollo, no I'm not!

DAOS

She's really decent, Getas, well-behaved.

GETAS

And you—   40

How are you pushing *your* claims?

DAOS

Heracles,

No monkey business—haven't even tried it! No,
I told my master, and he's promised she
[Can join] me, once he's seen [her brother].

GETAS

[You're]

[In clover!]

Quarterly, 18, 1968, 225–226), Getas makes a coarse pun here
which is difficult to translate effectively. The word rendered by
'Serves you, does she?' is παιδίσκη, which often means simply 'a
girl' (cf. line 18), but in current usage had become a euphemism
first for a slave girl and then for a prostitute. Getas asks with
apparent innocence, 'A girl?' Daos' immediate reaction, 'Yes',
comes before he has had time to appreciate Daos' equivocation,
and Getas bursts out laughing at the success of his verbal trick.

ΔΑΟΣ

45 τί λαμπρός; ἀποδημεῖ τρ[ίμηνος ἐπί τινα
πρᾶξιν ἰδίαν εἰς Λῆμ[νον· ἄμφω δ' ἐλπίδος
ἐχόμεθα τῆς αὐτῆς [
σώζοιτο.

ΓΕΤΑΣ
χρηστὸς [οὗτος

ΔΑΟΣ (?)

[

ὄνησις εἴη.

ΓΕΤΑΣ (?)
πολυπ[
50 φρονεῖς· ἐγὼ γὰρ κλι[
θύσαιμ' ἀνόνητο....[
52 ᾧ ξυλοφορῶ [

(Eight further shreds of the Cairo papyrus have been skil-
fully fitted together into three fragments with text on both
sides: γ0, δεζ, and θη. Fragment γ0 comes from the bot-
tom of a page; it contains an address to a Myrrhine and a
reference to a shepherd in two successive lines (here
72–73), and its subject matter suits what is known of the
plot of the *Heros* very well. Its attribution to this play
seems certain. Fragment δεζ can be assigned to the
Heros with even greater confidence, for two of its broken

45 τρ[ίμηνος suppl. Sudhaus, ἐπί τινα Croenert, Leo.
46 Λῆμ[νον suppl. Croenert, Leo, ἄμφω Arnott, δ' ἐλπίδος
Sonnenburg.   48 Suppl. Arnott (οὑτοσί Sudhaus).

22

DAOS

Clover? *He's* away in Lem[nos] —   45
[Three months on] private business. [Both of us]
Cherish the same [hopes. My one prayer's for]
His safe [return].

GETAS

A good man, [Laches   ]

DAOS (?)

[   ]

I hope it's fruitful.

GETAS (?)

Much [
You're sensible. You see, I [50
I'd sacrifice in vain [
For whom I carry wood [52

---

lines (76–77) tie with a quotation made from this play by
Stobaeus (*Eclogae* 4. 40. 13 = fr. 211 Kock). The other
side of δεζ (the verso or vertical-fibres side) contains the
end of one act and the beginning of the next. Fragment
θη, on the other hand, is a maverick; although editors of
Menander print it alongside γ0 and δεζ as part of the
Heros, nothing in the few words preserved on it supports
its attribution to this play.

Furthermore, even if all three fragments do belong to
the same play, their relative placing must be considered
uncertain. Fragment δεζ (verso) contains the beginning
of an act. The most plausible speaker of the opening
words in this new act is Laches; of the characters in this

play, only he can talk of 'giving' a girl to a 'bridegroom' (56). In the cast-list prefaced to the text of the opening scene, Laches' name comes last: he was, therefore, the last of the characters to be seen on the stage. This is not surprising if he was supposed to be on a visit to Lemnos when the play opens (45–46). Yet his words at this act opening do not look like those of a character just now making his first entry, newly arrived from abroad (contrast *Aspis* 491 ff.). If Laches returned home in the third or fourth act, the new act that begins on fr. δεζ will be either the fourth or the fifth act, with the balance of probability perhaps in favour of the fifth. But does the recto (or horizontal-fibres) side of δεζ precede or follow the verso? And where does fr. γ0 come in relation to δεζ? Neither question can be answered with complete confidence. If γ0 and δεζ belong to the same sheet of papyrus—and this has never been objectively established, although it is assumed to be true by virtually all modern editors of Menander[1]—it follows that δεζ precedes γ0 (which comes from the foot of the page), but the vertical space between the two fragments could be anything from 1 to 19 lines (on a hypothetical 37-line page). If the contents of the fragments are then considered, it becomes a plausible supplementary assumption that the verso comes before the recto. The argument for this is circumstantial. The speakers in fr. δεζ and γ0 on the verso side seem to be Laches and Myrrhine. They begin with reference to Plangon's betrothal to Daos (δεζ v. 2 = 56), and continue with Laches' observation that something—quite possibly his reaction to news about Plangon's baby—is causing Myrrhine to be flustered and perspire (γ0 v. 8 = 72). Laches may now have begun to wonder why Myrrhine

*(The references in the mutilated lines 51 and 52 to 'sacri-
ficing' and 'carrying wood' are obscure. Is Getas perhaps
bringing brushwood that he has collected as fuel for a sac-
rifice planned by his master (Pheidias probably)? If he is,
the purpose of that sacrifice cannot be established,
because the Cairo papyrus leaf ends at this point, leaving
us in ignorance about most of the developments in this
and the succeeding acts. Fragment 10 (see below) may be
a further short extract from the opening scene, but it adds
nothing to our knowledge of the plot. After the two slaves
make their exits at the end of this scene, the guardian
spirit from whom the play takes its title enters to deliver
the prologue; this may safely be inferred from the cast-list.*

*The hypothesis (lines 10–12) mentions the two major
elements in the dénouement: Laches' discovery that he is
the father of Myrrhine's twin children, and Pheidias'
union with Plangon. A few rays of light are shed on
Menander's management of Laches' discovery by a small
group of papyrus shreds from the Cairo codex. These
pose a series of papyrological and other problems which
are discussed on pages 22, 23, 24 and 26. It is a working
but unverifiable hypothesis that two of these fragments
(δεζ and γ0) provide four brief snatches of text (these
shreds, like all the remains of the Cairo codex, carry*

---

[1] In recent times F. H. Sandbach (*Gnomon*, 19, 1967, 766,
and *Commentary*, 393–396) has sounded a desirable note of cau-
tion.

was so concerned about Plangon's misfortune (see the discussion on pages 25, 27 and 29). The recto side would then provide a natural continuation of this agitated conversation, with Myrrhine first lamenting her misfortune, secondly being questioned about the rape that led to her own pregnancy (δεζ r. 3–6 = 76–79), and finally being compelled to recall the circumstances surrounding that event eighteen years ago (γ0 r. 5 = 94). As this arrangement of frs. γ0 and δεζ makes dramatic as well as papyrological sense, it has been adopted in this edition, but only as a working hypothesis, not as a proven solution.)

(a) *Cairo fragments* δεζ *and* γ0, *in their provisionally accepted order*

δεζ verso

53
$$]\epsilon\lambda οιμ' \ ω[$$
$$]\iota[.]\sigma οι[...] \ τοῦτο \ τ[$$

ΧΟ Ρ [ΟΥ

ΜΕΡΟΣ Ε΄ (or less probably Δ΄)

ΛΑΧΗΣ

55
$$\hat{ω} \ Ἡρά]κλεις, \ ἔα \ μ'· \ ἁμαρ[τάνειν \ δοκῶ$$
$$εἰ \ νῦν] \ δίδωμι \ νύμφ[ίῳ \ τὴν \ Πλαγγόνα;$$
57
$$]μα[$$

55–56 ὦ Ἡρά]κλεις suppl. Jensen, the rest (tentatively and *exempli gratia*) Arnott after ideas by Robert and Sandbach.

*text on both sides of the sheet) which derive from the end
of one act and the opening scene of the next. This new act
is most probably the play's final act,*[a] *and its opening
scene a tense dialogue between Laches and Myrrhine
which gradually leads Laches to the discovery that Gorgias and Plangon are his own children. The four snatches
of text, in their probably correct sequence, but see the discussion on the facing pages, are:)*

(a) *Cairo fragments* δεζ *and* γ0, *in their provisionally
accepted order*

Fr. δεζ verso

*(This fragment begins with two mutilated lines which
close an act, but there is no clue to the identity of the
speaker or speakers, and virtually nothing is coherent
enough for translation (line 54 reveals the word* this). *The
opening two lines of the new act, however, can be tentatively restored to provide part of a speech addressed by
Laches to Myrrhine as they come on to the stage in
mid-conversation:*)

ACT V (or less probably IV)

LACHES

Don't nag me! [Hera]cles! [You think I'm wrong]	55
[In] giving [Plangon to] a husband now?	56

(Clearly Laches, having returned from his private busi-

[a] The possibility that it was the fourth cannot, however, be
entirely ruled out.

A gap of between 1 and 19 lines, then

γ0 verso

65   [.]...σι.ο[
      τούτῳ. : πο[
      μᾶλλον δι. [
      τὴν Θρᾷττα[ν

*ness in Lemnos which kept him outside the dramatic
action in the play's opening two or three acts, has immedi-
ately confirmed the promise he made earlier (cf. lines
42–44) that Daos should be allowed to set up house with
Plangon. And Myrrhine, with her secret knowledge that
she is Plangon's mother, has been opposing Laches' inten-
tion, without being able to reveal her true reasons. After
fr. δεζ (verso) there is a gap of between one and nineteen
lines before the next shred of text, on fr. γ0 (verso).)*

Fr. γ0 verso

*(Of the first four lines of this fragment only the opening
letters are preserved, but even though little here makes
sense when translated (66 To this or With this, followed
by a change of speaker; 67 Rather; 68 Thratta or The
Thracian woman), the paragraphi placed under lines 66,
67 and 68, together with the dicolon in 66, indicate that
originally these lines must have contained lively dialogue.
The speakers were presumably Laches and Myrrhine;
what were they discussing? If 'Thratta' or 'The Thracian
woman' (66) was Tibeios' widow, as has been suggested,
she may have been living with Plangon in Laches' house
after her husband's death. It is possible that Laches has
suddenly discovered that Plangon is having or more prob-
ably has just had a baby (the birth may well have taken
place during the play). If so, Laches may here be
announcing his decision to expel Plangon along with the
baby and Tibeios' widow from his house, in exactly the
same way as Demeas expels Chrysis and the baby from his
house in the Samia. This hypothesis at any rate would
allow us to make tolerable sense of the ensuing five lines of
this fragment, which are a well-preserved puzzle.)*

ΜΥΡΡΙΝΗ

σὺ τάλαινα.

ΛΑΧΗΣ

τί; φ[α]νερῶς γε, νὴ Δί', ὦ γύναι —
70 ἐς κόρακας.

ΜΥΡΡΙΝΗ

ἐξέστηκας· οἷα γὰρ λέγεις.

ΛΑΧΗΣ

ἃ καὶ ποήσω καὶ δέδοκταί μοι πάλαι —
ἱδρώς, ἀπορία· νὴ Δί', εὖ γ', ὦ Μυρρίνη,
73 ἐπ' ἐμαυτὸν ἔλαβον ποιμέν', ὃς βληχώμενον

A gap of up to 21 lines, then

δεζ recto

74   ]οντρ[
75   ὡς γ]ὰρ ἀνδριὰ[ς

69 Text established by Sudhaus, part-division and assignments
by Webster: ταλαιναφ[.]νερως C, with τι: misplaced at the end
of the line, at one letter's interval after γυναι.   70 Division of
speakers after κόρακας suggested by Körte (C places its dicolon
after εξεστηκας in error).   72 απορια· or απορια: C.   75 ὡς
γ]ὰρ suppl. Sudhaus, ἀνδριὰ[ς Körte.

MYRRHINE

(thinking of Plangon)
Poor girl!

LACHES

What? Wife, It's obvious, I swear —   69
To hell with them!

MYRRHINE

You're crazy! What a thing to say!   70

LACHES

My mind was made up long ago, I'm going
To do it! *(to himself)* Sweating, nonplussed! Myrrhine,
    by Zeus,
I well deserved a shepherd with a bleating   73

*(The fragment closes, as it opens, in mystery. Laches'
threat to expel Plangon has caused Myrrhine, her mother,
to break out in perspiration. When the fragment breaks
off, Laches is in the middle of a bitter joke about his shep-
herd, for the word translated 'bleating' (βληχώμενον) is
used in Greek to describe the sounds made by both sheep
and babies. After fr. γ0 (verso), there is a further gap of
between one and 21 lines before the next shred of text, on
fr. δεζ recto.)*

Fr. δεζ recto

*(The first line of this fr. yields only four unintelligible let-
ters, but thereafter something can be made out of the dia-
logue even where the lines are mutilated. The speakers,
on the assumption that frs. δεζ and γ0 belong to the same
leaf of text, are still Laches and Myrrhine. At line 75 we
appear to have* [like] *a statue, part of a remark which*

31

ΜΥΡΡΙΝΗ

ὡς οἰκτρόν, ἢ τοιαῦτα δυστυχῶ μόνη,
ἃ μηδὲ πιθανὰς τὰς ὑπερβολὰς ἔχει.

ΛΑΧΗΣ (?)

] πάθος ἡ γνώμη σφό[δρα.
ἀλλ᾿ ἠδίκηκε]ν ἐκ βίας σέ τις ποτέ;

ΜΥΡΡΙΝΗ

80   γά]ρ.

ΛΑΧΗΣ (?)

ὑπονοε[ῖ]ς ὅστ[ις

81   ]τιγημ[

A gap of up to 21 lines, then

γ0 recto

90   ]ι γε σύ
                      ]ς ὅτι
                      ]ρέστατον

76–77 The full text is preserved by Stobaeus, *Eclogae* 4. 40. 13:
]ιαυτα[. . . .]υχωμο[,]ασυ[. .]ρβολαζεχ[C.   76 τοιαῦτα
Hirschig (and C? Before]ιαυτα in C there is space for only 12
letters): τὰ τοιαῦτα mss. of Stobaeus.   79–80 Suppl. Sud-
haus.   91 Or ὅ τι.

32

doubtless Laches made about the appearance of Myr-
rhine, petrified now by the direction which the conversa-
tion is taking. The next five lines are better preserved.)

MYRRHINE

How poignant! I alone must suffer blows   76
So bad that no one could imagine worse!

LACHES

Grit's the best [antidote to] tragedy.
[But] did a man [misuse] you once, by force?

MYRRHINE

[Yes. He was drunk.]

LACHES

Any idea who [he was]?   80

(Here the fragment breaks off, apart from a few incompre-
hensible letters in line 81. The conversation has now
moved on to the occasion when Myrrhine was raped.
Why does Myrrhine consider her bitter experiences
exceptional (lines 76–77)? Presumably because she is
thinking not only of her own rape years ago, but also of
her daughter Plangon's recent parallel experience; but the
loss of the preceding context makes this an uncertain spec-
ulation. Lines 78–80 lead the conversation towards its
final climax, but a gap now intervenes of between one and
21 lines, before we come to fr. γ0 (recto).)

Fr. γ0 recto

(Of this fragment's first four lines only the end letters sur-
vive, and assignment to speakers is impossible. Line 90
yields you, *91* that *or* what. *From the end of 93 a fuller,*
but not undamaged, passage is preserved.)

ΛΑΧΗΣ (?: it is unclear where this speech begins)

π]ρῶτον λέγε.

ἔ]τη 'στιν ὀκτὼ καὶ δέκ';

ΜΥΡΡΙΝΗ

οὐ[κ] ἔστιν μόνη

95   ....].αὐτ᾿· ἔστω δὲ τοῦτ', εἰ σοὶ δοκεῖ.

ΛΑΧΗΣ

ἀσαφὲ]ς τὸ πρᾶγμα γίνεται. πῶς λανθάνει

97   ὁ π]ρ[οσ]πεσών σε; πῶς δ' ἀπέλ[ι]πε; πηνίκ[α

94 Or μόνη.   95 Corr. Sudhaus: συδοκει (possibly, but not certainly, followed by a dicolon) C.   96 Suppl. Körte.   97 ὁ π]ρ[οσ]πεσών suppl. Jensen, ἀπέλ[ι]πε deciphered and suppl. Sandbach.

(b) *Cairo fragment θη, doubtfully assigned to this play*

(If the maverick fragment θη derives from the same page or the same scene as δεζ and γ0, nothing in it helps to establish its position relative to the other two fragments. It may, on the other hand, derive from another scene in the *Heros*, or even from another play in the Cairo codex. Accordingly, it is printed here separately from δεζ and γ0, and given a new line-numbering, with the traditional one of editions such as Körte's and Sandbach's added in brackets.)

LACHES (?: *the opening words are lost*)
                              ] tell me first.   93
It's eighteen years ago?

MYRRHINE
                    There's more than one
                    ] But drop the subject, please.   95

LACHES
The puzzle's [worse] now. How did this assailant
Avoid your seeing him? How did he leave you? When   97

(*Here the fragment breaks off in mid-question, and the
final details which led Laches to identify himself as the
unknown assailant are lost to us.*

*The above discussion of these four fragments rests on
the assumption that they all come from the same scene. It
cannot be stated too often, however, that it is only an
assumption, and that other interpretations, based perhaps
on less economical hypotheses, cannot be excluded. If the
two scraps* δεζ *and* γ0 *do not come from the same papyrus
leaf, for example, they could derive from different scenes;*
γ0 *from the conversation between Myrrhine and Laches,
but* δεζ *from a different conversation between Myrrhine
and another character such as Sophrone her nurse.*)

(b) *Cairo fragment* θη, *doubtfully assigned to this play*

(*A third scrap of papyrus from the Cairo codex, fragment*
θη, *is thought by many scholars to belong to the same leaf
as frs.* δεζ *and* γ0, *but no evidence for this belief has ever
been advanced other than subjective impression. Thus fr.*
θη *may be part of the climactic scene between Myrrhine
and Laches discussed above, but it may equally well*

$\theta\eta$ verso

101   ].....[.]$\rho\eta\nu$
       ]. ὅτι τῆς πολλῆς .[
(60 Kö, S)   ]ε..[.] ἄσωτο[
       κ]αὶ συνδοκ[εῖ
105   λέ]γει δ' αὐτῷ πόθ[εν
(63)   .[.]. τινα
107   ]ονκ[

$\theta\eta$ recto

108   ..]ρ[
(83)   <u>ἠσχύν[ε]θ' οὗτο[ς</u>
110   <u>'Αλέας 'Αθάνας [</u>
(85)   .]υ δῆτα· καὶ μ[
      <u>ἐ]λθεῖν ἐκει[</u>
      νὴ τὸν Ποσ[ειδῶ
(88)   <u>λαβεῖν .δ.[</u>
115   ἐλθ[

110 Kock fr. 967

104 κ]αὶ deciphered and suppl. Arnott, συνδοκ[εῖ Sudhaus.
105 Suppl. Jensen.   110 = Euripides, *Auge*, line 1 (see Ludwig Koenen, *Zeitschrift für Papyrologie und Epigraphik*, 4 (1969), 7–11.   111 Either σ]ὺ (ed. pr.) or ο]ὐ (Körte).

derive from another scene of the Heros *or indeed from a scene of one of the other plays in the Cairo codex. The two bits of text that it contains are very scrappy and generally—apart from one phrase (θη recto, line 3 = 110 in this edition)—uninformative.)*

Fr. θη verso

(This side contains the ends—or near-ends—of seven lines. A few words here and there are intelligible (that of much 102, a profligate man 103, it's agreed 104, tells him from where 105, some 106), but nothing emerges to identify speaker(s) or situation.)

Fr. θη recto

(The beginnings of eight lines, with paragraphi below the second, third, fifth and seventh. The speakers in the dialogue cannot be identified, but one of them must be male, since he swears by Posidon (113), an oath confined to men. The following words and phrases are translatable: speaker A, He was ashamed (109); speaker B, "Of Alea Athena" (110); A, You or No, followed by certainly; and [   ] / Came there (or He came) (111–112); A again (after a lost interjection by B?), or a new character C, Yes by Posidon [   ] / Took (113–14), B (?), Came (115). It is possible—no more than possible—that a rape is being discussed. The key phrase is "Of Alea Athena" in line 110, where the name Athena is spelled not in the normal Attic way but in the Doric form favoured by Greek tragedy. It seems likely therefore that the speaker is here quoting from tragedy, very possibly the opening words of Euripides' Auge, which appear to have run "Of Alea Athena

37

MENANDER

*　　*　　*

Eight fragments of Ἥρως, *quoted by ancient authors*

1 (8 Körte)

The *Lexicon Sabbaiticum* (edited by A. Papadopoulos-Kerameus (St Petersburg 1982), p. 4), with the heading Μένανδρος Ἥρωι·

> νῦν δὲ τοῖς ἐξ ἄστεως
> κυνηγέταις ἥκουσι περιηγήσομαι
> τὰς ἀχράδας.

---

[a] The goddess Athena was worshipped with the cult-title of Alea (the meaning of Alea is uncertain: it may be connected with ἀλέα = 'warmth', or with the name of Aleos the Arcadian hero) in several parts of the Peloponnese, but especially in Tegea. Here her shrine was founded, according to legend, by this same Aleos, king of Tegea, and his daughter Auge was Athena's priestess there at the time of her violation by Heracles. Cf. especially, L. R. Farnell, *Cults of the Greek States*, I (Oxford 1896), 274–276.

38

here's the gold-rich house" (cf. L. Koenen, ZPE 4, 1969, 7 ff.). In Euripides' Auge the heroine may have recalled how she was ravished by Heracles while she was washing Athena's robe at a spring, probably within the precincts of the temple of Athena at Tegea. Under what circumstances is Euripides' opening line most likely to have been quoted in a play by Menander? It is hard to know, but a woman might have recalled or hinted at the illustrious precedent of Auge and Heracles, if she had herself been raped in similar circumstances, possibly in a temple precinct, but not necessarily that of Alea Athena in Tegea, the legendary site of the Auge myth.[a] If fr. θη does after all derive from the Heros, that woman is most plausibly to be identified as Myrrhine. But too many women were raped in too many plays of Menander for this identification to be more than speculative.)

*   *   *

Eight fragments of Heros, quoted by ancient authors

1

Lexicon Sabbaiticum: Menander in *Heros*,

But now I'll guide

The huntsmen coming from the city round
The wild pear trees.

The identity of the speaker is uncertain, but these lines sound like an excuse for removing him or her off stage at the end of a scene. Could the huntsmen referred to here have been the chorus, replacing the more usual group of tipsy young men? In that case this fragment would come from the closing lines of the first act, since the arrival of the chorus is mentioned only there in the surviving work of Menander.

MENANDER

2 (1 Kö, 209 Kock)

Stobaeus, *Eclogae* 4. 20a. 21 (περὶ Ἀφροδίτης), with the heading Μένανδρος Ἥρωι·

ΔΑΟΣ (?)

δέσποιν᾽, ἔρωτος οὐδὲν ἰσχύει πλέον,
οὐδ᾽ αὐτὸς ὁ κρατῶν <τῶν> ἐν οὐρανῷ θεῶν
Ζεύς, ἀλλ᾽ ἐκείνῳ πάντ᾽ ἀναγκασθεὶς ποεῖ.

2 τῶν om. mss. of Stobaeus, suppl. Grotius.   2–3 Ms. A omits θεῶν and transposes to ἀναγκασθεὶς πάντα.

3 (2 Kö, 210 K)

Stobaeus, *Eclogae* 4. 29d. 60 (περὶ εὐγενείας) quotes the whole fragment with the heading Μένανδρος Ἥρωι. Line 2 became proverbial, and is cited without play-title in ancient and Byzantine collections of the monostichs ascribed to Menander (line 19 of the 4th-century A.D. *P.Bouriant* 1, first published by P. Jouguet and P. Perdrizet, *Studien zur Palaeographie und Papyruskunde* (Leipzig), 6 (1906), 148 ff. = *Pap.* II. 19 Jäkel; line 768 of the Byzantine collections in Jäkel, cf. W. Mayer, *Sitzungsberichte Munich* (1890) 366).

ἐχρῆν γὰρ εἶναι τὸ καλὸν εὐγενέστατον,
τὸν ἐλεύθερον δὲ πανταχοῦ φρονεῖν μέγα.

2 δὲ Bentley: δὲ δεῖ mss. of Stobaus, δεῖ *P.Bouriant*, ἀεὶ ms. K of the monostichs.

4 (3 Kö, 212 K)

Athenaeus 10. 426bc: ἔδοξε πᾶσι λέγειν περὶ τῶν κράσεων τῶν παρὰ τοῖς ἀρχαίοις. καί τινος εἰπόντος ὅτι Μένανδρος ἐν Ἥρωι ἔφη·

χοῦς κεκραμένου
οἴνου· λαβὼν ἔκπιθι τούτου.

2

Stobaeus ('On Aphrodite'): in Menander's *Heros*,

DAOS (?)

There's nothing, mistress, with more power than love —
Not even Zeus himself, who rules the gods
In heaven. Love controls his every action.

*The speaker is a slave addressing his or her mistress.
Although a case might be made for assigning the lines to the
nurse Sophrone, their most plausible context must be a
speech by Daos to Myrrhine in which the slave defends his
love for Plangon. A speech with a similar justification was
made in Euripides' first Hippolytus (fr. 431 Nauck[2]). The
theme of the universal power of love, however, is a common-
place in Greek literature (see Barrett's note in his edition of
Euripides' Hippolytus, on 1277–80).*

3

Stobaeus ('On Nobility'): in Menander's *Heros*,

For virtue should be true nobility,
And free men everywhere show dignity.

*On v. 2 see the opposite page. These high-sounding plati-
tudes are too unspecific to be assigned to a particular speaker
or context.*

4

Athenaeus: They all agreed to discuss the dilutions of wine
with water among the ancients. One of them noted that
Menander had said in *Heros*,

Five pints of wine,
Diluted. Take this, drink it up.

Could this have been said towards the end of the play, at a

MENANDER

5 (4 Kö, 213 K)

Photius (α 1548 Theodoridis) and the *Suda* (α 1950 Adler) s.v. ἀναλυθῆναι· τὸ καθαρμῷ τινι χρήσασθαι φαρμάκων. Μένανδρος Ἥρωι·

ἐπεφαρμάκευσ᾽, ὦ γλυκύτατ᾽, ἀναλυθεὶς μόλις.

Lemma φαρμάκων *Suda*, φαρμάκῳ Photius (-κω ms. z). Ἥρωι *Suda*, Ἥρωσι ms. b of Phot. (quotation of Menander omitted by z).
Fragment ἐπεφαρμακεύσω b of Phot., -κευσο A of *Suda*, -κευσον other mss. of *Suda*: corr. Arnott.

6 (5 Kö, 214 K)

Ammonius, Περὶ ὁμοίων καὶ διαφόρων λέξεων (p. 249 Nickau): ἴσθι καὶ γίνωσκε διαφέρει . . . καὶ Μένανδρος ἐν Ἥρωι·

εὖ ἴσθι, κἀγὼ τοῦτο συγχωρήσομαι.

7 (6 Kö, 215 K)

Choeroboscus, *Scholia in Theodosii Canones* (1. 410. 15–17 Hilgard): ἀπὸ δὲ τοῦ θηλυκοῦ τοῦ ἡ παῖς γίνεται ἡ παι-δίσκη . . .·

τῶν <δὲ> παιδισκῶν τινι
δούς,

---

[a] A diminutive: on its meaning see also my note on *Heros* 38.

party celebrating the betrothal or wedding of Pheidias and Plangon?

5

Photius and the *Suda* defining ἀναλυθῆναι: to practise purgation of drugs (or poisons). Menander in *Heros*,

> My dearest, you'd been drugged, and barely purged!

A puzzling line. In Menander's comedies, only women use the expression translated here as 'My dearest', and so the speaker is likely to have been Myrrhine or Sophrone. It is hard to think of a convincing context, if the words are to be taken literally. Could Myrrhine have been speaking metaphorically to Laches, who had either relapsed into an abnormal state after initial recovery from it, or just now recovered from a previous abnormal state? Both interpretations are possible; as it stands, without further context, the line is ambiguous.

6

Ammonius: ἴσθι (be certain) and γίνωσκε (make certain) are different . . . Menander in *Heros*

> Be certain—I shall go along with that!

Speaker and context are unknown. The Greek can mean either 'I too shall' or 'and I shall'.

7

Choeroboscus: the word παιδίσκη[a] (girl) is formed from the feminine use of παῖς (child) . . . ,

> Giving to
> One of the girls.

παρὰ τῷ Μενάνδρῳ ἐν τῷ Ἥρωι.

δὲ om. mss., suppl. Meineke.

8 (7 Kö, 216 K)

Choeroboscus, *Scholia in Theodosii Canones* (1. 176. 39–177. 1 Hilgard): ὁμόφωνός ἐστιν ἡ κλητικὴ τῇ εὐθείᾳ, οἷον ὁ δυστυχής, ὦ δυστυχής, ὡς παρὰ Μενάνδρῳ ἐν τῷ Ἥρωι·

   ὦ δυστυχής, εἰ μὴ βαδιεῖ

βαδιῆς mss.: corr. Schneidewin.

*Two further fragments, whose attribution
to Ἥρως is very uncertain*

9 (9 Kö, 868 K)

The Συναγωγὴ λέξεων χρησίμων (Bekker, *Anecdota Graeca* 1. 454. 7): ἀστεῖος καὶ ἀστικός, διττῶς. Μέναν-δρος †προ†ποιήσεις ἀστικὸν σαυτὸν πάλιν.

Μένανδρος Ἥρωι· ποήσεις conj. Toup, but Meineke's Μέναν-δρος· πάτερ, ποήσεις is no less plausible.

10 (10 Kö, 345 K)

Hermias' commentary on Plato, *Phaedrus* 230e (p. 33. 11 ff. Couvreur): οἱ μὲν γὰρ ὑπέλαβον ἁπλῶς φαῦλον τὸ ἐρᾶν,

HEROS

In Menander in the *Heros*.
Speaker and context are unknown.

8

Choeroboscus writes: the vocative sounds the same as the
nominative, e.g. ὁ δυστυχής (the poor fellow), ὦ δυστυχής
(poor thing!), as in Menander in the *Heros*,

Poor thing, if you don't go . . .

Speaker and context are unknown.

*Two further fragments, whose attribution
to Heros is very uncertain*

9

The *Collection of Useful Terms*: ἀστεῖος and ἀστικός have
two meanings (sc. 'urban' and 'urbane'). Menander in *Heros*
(?),

You'll make yourself a city man again.

*Here 'in Heros' is an uncertain attempt at correcting a cor-
rupt text; another conjecture would yield the sense: 'Menan-
der,*
Father, you'll make yourself . . .'.

10

Hermias of Alexandria's commentary on Plato's *Phaedrus*:
Some assumed that being in love was simply vulgar, like . . .

ὡς ... ὁ εἰπὼν "πλήρει γὰρ ὄγκῳ γαστρὸς αὔξεται
Κύπρις" (TrGF 2. 67 F 186), καὶ "οὐπώποτε {φησίν} (del.
Couvreur) ἠράσθης, Γέτα;" "οὐ γὰρ ἐνεπλήσθην", φησίν.

(ΔΑΟΣ ?)

οὐπώποτ᾽ ἠράσθης, Γέτα;

ΓΕΤΑΣ

οὐ γὰρ ἐνεπλήσθην.

Fragment 10 was tentatively assigned by Leo to the opening
scene of *Heros*, shortly after v. 52. Characters named Getas,
however, appear in other comedies by Menander (e.g. *Dyskolos,
Misoumenos, Perinthia*), and Meineke's suggestion that this fr.
might derive from *Misoumenos* (see fr. 12 there) is no less attrac-
tive.

the man who said 'The bulk of a full maw makes passion grow',[a] and

(DAOS ?)
Were you never in love, Getas?

GETAS
No, for I never ate my fill.

So he says.

Hermias does not name the author of the second passage quoted, and its attribution to Heros is very uncertain. It could derive from a lost portion of the initial dialogue between Getas and Daos, or from another play (see also Misoumenos fr. 12).

[a] A line from an unidentified lost tragedy or satyr play (fr. adesp. 106 Snell–Kannicht).

THEOPHOROUMENE
(THE DEMONIAC GIRL)

INTRODUCTION

Manuscripts

F = (i) *PSI* 1280, part of a papyrus roll from Oxyrhynchus written in the late first, or the first half of the second, century A.D. It contains one column of text little damaged (lines 16–30) and the line-endings from the previous column (1–15). First edition: M. Norsa and G. Vitelli, *Annali della r. scuola normale superiore di Pisa* (*Lettere*, etc.), 4 (1935), 1–3. A photograph appears in M. Norsa, *La scrittura letteraria greca dal secolo IV A.C. all' VIII D.C.* (Florence 1939–48), plate 9D (mislabelled as *PSI* 1285).

(ii) another papyrus in Florence, as yet unnumbered, part of a wider papyrus roll of unknown provenance dating from either the first century B.C. or the following century. It preserves the right-hand edge of one column (here lines 31–57) and indistinct traces from the beginning of the next. First edition: Vittorio Bartoletti, *Dai papiri della società italiana* (Florence 1965), 9 ff., with a photograph, but misidentified as 'hymns to Cybele'; the highly convincing argument for its attribution to the *Theophoroumene* was set out by E. W. Handley, *Bulletin of the Institute of Classical Studies*, 16 (1969), 95–101.

Fragments 1 to 8 are quotations from a variety of sources. See the introduction to vol. I, xxiv–xxv.

THEOPHOROUMENE

Pictorial Evidence

A mosaic of the third century A.D. from the 'House of
Menander' at Mytilene in Lesbos. It is inscribed ΘΕΟ-
ΦΟΡΟΥΜΕΝΗΣ Μ(ΕΡΟΣ) Β (*Theophoroumene*, Act
II) and portrays a scene in which three named men and a
boy are involved. On the left a young man (identified as
ΛΥΣΙΑΣ, Lysias), dressed in a long tunic and cloak and
wearing a garland of green leaves, seems to be playing
cymbals. His right foot is raised from the ground as if he
is beating time with it. In the centre stands a slave
(named on the mosaic ΠΑΡΜΕΝΩΝ, Parmenon) in sim-
ilar costume but ungarlanded and with a narrow scarf or
stole round his neck and over his left arm. Another young
man (identified as ΚΛΕΙΝΙΑΣ, Kleinias) stands on the
right, dressed and garlanded like Lysias but with a more
sumptuous cloak coloured purple. In his right hand he
holds a round yellow object, perhaps intended to be cym-
bals or a tambourine. In front of him stands an unnamed
boy in a knee-length dark-green tunic, carrying in his
hands what seems to be a single yellow pipe. The inter-
pretation of this picture and its relation to the famous
Dioscurides mosaic of musicians on the one hand, and to
the papyrus fragments of the *Theophoroumene* on the
other, are discussed below. Standard publication of the
mosaic: L. Kahil and others, *Les Mosaïques*, 46 ff. and
colour plate 6.

Twelve circular lead tokens found in Athens, each bearing
the inscription ΘΕΟΦΟΡΟΥΜΕΝΗ and a picture of
three masks (free maiden; slave; young man) which rest
on cylindrical altars. The free maiden was presumably
the demoniac girl of the title, the slave Parmenon, and
the young man either Kleinias or Lysias. These tokens

date from the middle of the third century A.D., and were presumably entrance tickets or souvenirs of a contemporary performance in the Theatre of Dionysus. First publications: I. N. Svoronos, *Journal International de l'Archéologie Numismatique* (Athens), 3 (1900), 319 ff.; M. Crosby, *The Athenian Agora, X: Weights and Tokens* (Princeton 1964), p. 122 (L 329 a–f) and plate 30. There are illustrations also in L. Kahil and others, *Les Mosaïques*, plate 25; and A. Pickard-Cambridge, *The Dramatic Festivals of Athens*, 2nd edition revised by J. Gould and D. M. Lewis (Oxford 1968), fig. 140 (text p. 271 and n. 6).

The identification and interpretation of the remains from Menander's *Theophoroumene*—both textual and pictorial—are linked closely together. So many problems and mysteries, however, surround this material that we are still a long way from final solutions. The views expressed here were in the main pioneered by E. W. Handley, whose work on the play (*B.I.C.S.* 16, 88–101) advances our knowledge considerably at many points.

When the fragment of papyrus roll later catalogued as *PSI* 1280 was first published in 1935, its attribution to Menander's *Theophoroumene* was probable rather than certain. The text coincided with no previously known quotations from the play, but the aorist imperative form παράστα ('stand beside', occurring in line 28) was cited only from Menander by ancient lexica (cf. *Dis Exapaton*, fr. 3), and the reference to a girl who is demoniac (θεοφορεῖται, 25) matched well the title Θεοφορουμένη, which was attested in comedy for Menander alone, although his prolific elder contemporary Alexis was the author of a Θεοφόρητος ('The Demoniac Man'). Qualms were at first felt about saddling Menander with the offensive coarseness of ἱππόπορνε ('bloody whore', 19), but such indelicacies, in the mouths of cooks and slaves at least, are not avoided by Menander.[1] Probability, however, was turned into certainty by the discovery of the Mytilene mosaic, which identified the two young men named in *PSI* 1280 (Lysias, 8, 23, 29; Kleinias, a virtually certain supplement at 14) as characters appearing in a second-act scene of the *Theophoroumene*.

Welcome though this confirmation was, it still leaves many of the details of the text of *PSI* 1280 totally mysterious. The second half of its well-preserved column (lines 23b–30) is a dialogue between Lysias and another man (probably, but not certainly, Kleinias), in which Lysias takes the initiative. He suggests that an experiment should be mounted to see whether the heroine of the play's title is really possessed or only pretending. An attendant is to play an appropriate tune on the pipes (28) while Lysias and his companion stand by the doors of an inn. If the girl is really possessed she will be drawn out by the music. Kleinas welcomes the prospect of her appearance (30).

It is tempting to identify Lysias' order to the piper to begin playing as the incident captured on the Mytilene mosaic. There the piper is represented as a boy with a young pert face and bare legs.[2] He clasps what seems to be a single pipe in both hands, his gaze fixed on Lysias and

[1] E.g. *Dysk.* 462 (κινητιᾶν), 892 (λαικάσει), *Pk.* 485 Sandbach (λαικάστρια).

[2] The knee-length tunic rather than the size of the figure here indicates juvenility. On the Mytilene mosaics adults may be drawn on a dwarfish scale if their dramatic roles are insignificant (see the introduction to *Epitrepontes*, vol. I, p. 382).

Parmenon. Lysias is already clashing cymbals and apparently beating time with his right foot, while Kleinias clutches to his side a small yellow cymbal or tambourine, although this object is too badly portrayed for any precise identification.

Such a linkage between the text of *PSI* 1280 and the mosaic, however, solves some problems only to pose others. Parmenon is present on the mosaic, for example, but there is no cast-iron evidence that he is present on the stage, let alone says anything, in the papyrus text. The puzzling speech that extends from before line 16 to 23a seems to report a conversation containing the coarse word discussed above, and such language in Menander normally comes from cooks or slaves, not free men.[1] But if Parmenon was the speaker here, on stage with Kleinias and Lysias, he must have been engineered off stage by Menander before the demoniac girl made her appearance. Menander's plays were written so that they could be performed with a cast of three actors, and the character who played Parmenon in this scene would have to double as the girl in the next, since Kleinias and Lysias appear to have been present in both scenes.

A further puzzle is set by the existence of what may be a variant version of the scene on the Mytilene mosaic. The best-known example of this version is a mosaic by Dioscurides of Samos now in the National Museum of Naples (inv. 9985; NM2 in T.B.L. Webster, *Monuments Illustrating New Comedy*, 2nd edition, *B.I.C.S. Supplement* 24, London 1969; colour photographs in e.g. Kahil

---

[1] But it is not certain that the man who used the word was a slave, any more than the person who reported his remark: see below.

and others, *Les Mosaïques*, plate 6; A. Maiuri, *Roman Painting*, Geneva 1953, p. 96), although a copy exists in a wall-painting from Stabiae (now also in the National Museum of Naples, inv. 9034; NP 54 Webster[2]); a series of at least eight pyxides and a *lebes gamikos* from Centirupe dating from the mid-third century B.C. seem to carry this or a closely related scene, thus confirming that the original picture from which the mosaics derive was a work of the first half of the third century (E. Simon, *Menander in Centuripe, Sitzungsberichte Frankfurt* 25.2, 1989, and *Dioniso*, 59, 1989, 45–63); and several terracotta statuettes from Myrina appear to be modelled on the two male musicians in the Dioscurides mosaic (young man with castanets, MT 15 Webster[2], figured in M. Bieber, *History of the Greek and Roman Theater*, 2nd edition, Princeton 1961, fig. 342; young man striking tambourine, MT 1 a–c Webster[2], figured in Bieber, fig. 341, where the loss of the musical instrument from the three fragile surviving examples has sometimes led to their misidentification). The Dioscurides mosaic, made originally for a Pompeian villa in the second century B.C., is over 400 years earlier than the one in Mytilene and incomparably superior in quality. It also contains four figures, three with musical instruments, but the differences from its later counterpart are striking. The arrangement of the figures is a mirror-image reversal of that in the Mytilene mosaic, in the same way that a second Dioscurides mosaic from that same Pompeian villa reverses another Mytilene mosaic portraying the opening of Menander's *Synaristosai* (cf. Kahil and others, *Les Mosaïques*, 41 ff. and plate 5). Thus the boy in the Dioscurides mosaic of the musicians stands on the extreme left of the group. The differences do not end there, however. The slave Parmenon is absent from Dioscurides' picture, the cymbalist moves from the left-hand side to the centre, the boy lacks his single pipe, a woman with a *hetaira* mask drawn to the same scale as her male companion stands on the left of the picture playing double pipes, while the man on the right is beating a tambourine. These changes are striking; what is their significance? The Dioscurides mosaic almost certainly portrays a scene from Greek comedy. Its figures are drawn moving about a raised stage, with a doorway behind them to the right, and its companion piece from that Pompeian villa incontrovertibly presents a scene from a Menandrean comedy. Accordingly three interpretations of the Dioscuridean musicians seem possible. They could be characters in an unidentified comedy, probably by Menander. They could belong to the *Theophoroumene*, but to a different scene where the two young men cavorted alone with a boy and a female piper. Or they could be involved in a later stage of the scene portrayed on the Mytilene mosaic, after Parmenon has departed and before the demoniac girl has entered. The last interpretation is perhaps the most attractive, but a firm decision would be premature in the present state of the evidence.

What happened next in the play? Here the second Florence papyrus, badly damaged as it is, may provide some clues. When this papyrus was first discovered, its text was first identified as hymns to Cybele, then as part of a mime; its attribution to the *Theophoroumene* cannot be considered absolutely certain so long as no exact ties with known extracts from the play emerge, but the circumstantial argument is very plausible indeed. This papyrus contains 27 line ends,[1] partly in the iambic metre and Attic dialect of New Comedy (31–35, 42–49, 51, 53–55, 57), and partly in dactylic hexameters written in a conventional lyric style and addressed mainly to the goddess Cybele and the Corybantes who attend her (36–41, 50?, 52, 56). If this papyrus derives from the scene in the *Theophoroumene* directly following that in *PSI* 1280 and the Mytilene mosaic, the possessed girl appears now to be on stage with Lysias and Kleinias, first engaging in conversation with them in the normal dialogue metre of iambic trimeters (at lines 34–35 she seems to tell her partners to assist in her ritual), and then breaking out into sung[2] hexameters in praise of the divinities associated with demonianism in antiquity. By this means presumably the girl sought to prove that she was possessed.

Here our papyrus breaks off, and darkness closes in. The further developments of the *Theophoroumene* are as obscure to us as are the plot's antecedents. Was the heroine of the title genuinely possessed (cf. lines 23 f.) or only pretending? Since Menander's comedies are full of shams—a fake corpse in the *Aspis*, a fake apparition in the *Phasma*, even a fake male demoniac in the *Hiereia*—the latter is the more likely situation. But if the girl was faking, what was her reason? Was it an excuse to enable her to go out of doors unchaperoned (cf. lines 21 ff.)?

[1] I ignore here the two puzzling mutilated lines (prose? dactyls?) inserted by the scribe in smaller letters between lines 41 and 42. These are discussed *ad loc.*

[2] Sung, not declaimed. A scholiast on Euripides, *Andromache* 103 mentions in passing that a portion of the *Theophoroumene* was actually sung. Cf. the critical apparatus on lines 36–41.

This was normally impossible for respectable free girls. But if so, why did she need to go out of doors? This may be partly but mysteriously explained by her reported claim, in the difficult passage which opens the preserved column of *PSI* 1280, that 'they've filched my presents' (17 f.). We cannot identify the filchers, but the presents might have been tokens, recovered in the end and leading to a recognition scene. We cannot safely identify either the person who insulted her so coarsely at line 19, although her father or guardian would be the most plausible candidate. Nor do we know the relationship of Lysias and Kleinias to the girl, although Kleinias' remark (if it is Kleinias who speaks here) that the girl's appearance would be 'a splendid sight' (30) may imply that he had fallen in love with her, perhaps having originally seen her on a previous demoniac expedition. Fragment 1 introduces a further character, an old man called Kraton, who complains eloquently about the undeserved success of social inferiors. There is no evidence to support the view that he was the girl's father or alternatively related to Kleinias or Lysias, although the economy of Menandrean plots makes one of these possibilities very likely. And finally, what was the reason for having an inn as one of the stage buildings (28 f.)? Was this the scene of the incident narrated in 16 ff.? Questions abound, answers are few.

The line-numbering in this edition differs to some extent from that of Sandbach's Oxford Text (*Menandri Reliquiae Selectae*, Oxford 1972); lines 1–30 agree with those so numbered in his and other editions, but the second Florence fragment is here numbered sequentially

31–57, with Sandbach's non-sequential numbering in brackets.

No hypothesis, didascalic notice or cast-list survives for this play. Its date of production is therefore unknown and unguessable.

Dramatis personae, so far as they are known:

Parmenon, a slave
Kleinias, a young man, perhaps in love with the demoniac girl
Lysias, another young man [1]
A free girl who either is demoniac or pretends to be so
Kraton, an old man, father perhaps of one of the younger free characters

In the lost parts of the play some other characters doubtless had speaking roles, but their identities and relationships cannot be surmised. A piper appears to be involved in the action at lines 27 ff. A chorus, probably of tipsy revellers, would have performed the entr'actes.

[1] See also Marina Pagliardini, "Sulla *Theophoroumene* di Menandro", *Atene e Roma*, 27 (1982), 118.

ΘΕΟΦΟΡΟΥΜΕΝΗ

(The texts of the two Florence papyri appear to derive from the play's second act. First comes *PSI* 1280. Of its first column, only the line ends are preserved:]ρετωι: 1,]ποιει 2,]ω λέγω 3,] 4,]ων 5,].ποῶν 6, οἱ]κίαν: 7,]. Λυσία: 8,] 9,]πολαβεῖν 10,]ουν ἔχει 11, ἀλα]ζο-νεύεται 12,]ραν ποτε 13,] Κλει[ν]ία 14.)

In the apparatus to lines 1–30 of this play, those supplements whose author is not named were made in the ed. pr. by M. Norsa and G. Vitelli, *Annali della r. scuola normale superiore di Pisa* (*Lettere*, etc.), 4 (1935), 1 ff.   7 Suppl. Körte.   10 Either ὑ]πο- or ἀ]πολαβεῖν.   14 Suppl. Webster.

[a] The suggestion offered in my translation assumes that Parmenon began a narrative to Kleinias (cf. 14) well before line 15, alleging that the demoniac girl's fits of possession were faked. Several details, however, are still very obscure. Did Parmenon see the girl in the street or elsewhere (e.g. in the inn)? Who was the man who addressed the girl so offensively in lines 18–23? What were the objects that Parmenon filled up (16 f.: if wine-

THEOPHOROUMENE

(The Demoniac Girl)

(SCENE: Uncertain, possibly a street in Athens backed by two or three buildings. One of these is an inn; the second is probably the house where the girl of the title lives; if there was a third, its residents cannot now be identified.)

(The remains of the two Florence papyri belong in all probability to the second act. From the first one (PSI 1280) we have a fragment of a scene in which Lysias, Kleinias, and probably also the slave Parmenon take part. Only a few letters survive from the ends of this papyrus' opening fifteen lines, with indications of change of speaker at the close of lines 1, 7, and 8. A few words can be translated: do or does 2, I say 3, doing 6, house (?) 7, an address to Lysias *8 before the change of speaker, to take up or from 10, he has 11, he's or (perhaps more probably, with reference to the demoniac girl) she's a humbug 12, once 13, and an address to* Kleinias *14. Continuous text begins at the end of line 15, although the interpretation of lines 15–17 is still an unsolved mystery.*[a]*)*

cups, the venue may have been the inn)? And what were the presents that the girl had lost? Cf. my introductory notes on the *Theophoroumene*.

ΠΑΡΜΕΝΩΝ (?)

15   ] ἐξηπ[ί]στατο.

ΚΛΕΙΝΙΑΣ (?)

τάχ' [ἂν] καταστάξαντες; οἶδ'.

ΠΑΡΜΕΝΩΝ (?)

               ἀπ' ὀμμ[άτων
ἔπλησα. "τἀμὰ δῶρ'· ἀκούεις;" ἡ κόρη,
"τὰ δῶρα," φησί, "τἀμὰ μ' ἐξείλονθ'." ὁ δέ,
"τί [δ'] ἔλαβες, ἱππόπο[ρ]νε; τὸν δὲ δόν[τα σοι
20 πόθεν οἶσθα τοῦτον; τί δέ; νεανίσκο[ν κόρῃ;
ἢ σὺ τί λαβοῦσα στέφανον ἔξω περιπατ[εῖς;
μαίνει; τί οὖν οὐκ ἔνδον ἐγκεκλειμ[ένη
μαίνει;"

ΚΛΕΙΝΙΑΣ (?)

φλυαρεῖς. [τ]οῦτό γ' αὐτό, Λυσία,
οὐ προσποεῖται.

ΛΥΣΙΑΣ

πεῖραν ἔξεστιν λα[βεῖν·
25 εἰ θεοφορεῖται ταῖς ἀληθείαισι γάρ,

15–16 Supplementation and interpretation here are hazardous
in the extreme, and the printed text is merely a shot in the dark.
15 ἐξηπ[ί]στατο Arnott:]εξιπ[.]στατο[F, apparently.
16 τάχ'—οἶδ' assigned to Kleinias by Arnott (F has no dicolon

PARMENON (?)

(*in mid-speech*)

]she really knew [her part].   15

KLEINIAS (?)

(*commenting on the demoniac girl's appearance?*)

Tears flooding down, perhaps (?). I know.

PARMENON (?)

(*continuing his narrative*)

I filled
Them unobserved. "My presents—do you hear? —
They've filched my presents," said the girl. "What gifts,
You bloody whore?" said he. "How do you know
The man who gave them? What! A lad, [and to]   20
[A girl]! Why are you out of doors here, with
That garland? Are you mad? Why not be mad
Locked up indoors?"

KLEINIAS (?)

That's nonsense.—Lysias,
This thing—she's *not* pretending!

LYSIAS

We can test
Her. If she's really a demoniac,   25

---

after οιδ, but a one-letter space between οι and δ may be a mis-
placed indication of change of speaker). ἂν suppl. Arnott.
20 κόρη tentatively suppl. Handley.   22–23 τί οὖν—μαίνει
(23) continued to the same speaker (Parmenon?) by Handley (22
μαινει:τιουν F).

νῦν εἰς τὸ πρόσθεν ἐνθάδ' ἐκπηδή[σεται.
μητρὸς θεῶν, μᾶλλον δὲ κορυβάντ[ων σύ μοι
αὔλει. παράστα δ' ἐνθαδὶ πρὸς τὰς θύρας
τοῦ πανδοκείου.

KΛΕΙΝΙΑΣ (?)

νὴ Δί', εὖ γε, Λυσία,

30   ὑπέρευγε· τοῦτο βούλομαι. καλὴ θέα . . .

(Here *PSI* 1280 breaks off. If the second, as yet unnum-
bered, Florence papyrus is rightly attributed to the *Theo-
phoroumene*, as seems most likely, its text must follow at a
short interval—probably fewer than 20 lines—after the
close of *PSI* 1280. When this second papyrus fragment
opens, the demoniac girl is in mid-speech.)

KOPH

31   ] καὶ τὸ χρυσίον
                            ] θάλατταν ἐκχέον
(3 Sa)   ]το προσφιλὲς
                    τοῖ]ς παροῦσι δ' ἅμα λέγω
35   πά]ντες ἐπολολύξατε.

26 Suppl. Maas.   27 Suppl. Handley *exempli gratia*.
30 ὑπέρευγε Norsa, Vitelli: υπερευ F.   31–57 The papyrus
fragment containing these lines was assigned to this character,
scene and play by Handley.   34–35 Suppl. Pavese.

---

[a] The 'Gods' Great Mother' is Cybele, a Phrygian goddess
whose cult was established in Athens already by the fifth century
B.C. The Corybantes were demons from Asia Minor associated
with her worship, and votaries of the religion went into orgiastic
trances which were popularly identified as possession by the
Corybantes. These trances, which were induced by the rhythmi-

[She'll] now skip out in front here. (*To the piper*) Pipe
a 'Gods'
Great Mother'—no, a Corybantic tune.[a]
(*To Kleinias*) You stand beside me here, just by the
    door
Of the hotel.

(*The piper plays his tune, while Kleinias retires with
Lysias into the background by the side of the inn's
double doors.*)

KLEINIAS (?)
    Fine, Lysias—superb,
I swear! Just what I want! A splendid sight . . .   30

(*At this point PSI 1280 breaks off. If the second Florence
papyrus is rightly assigned to the Theophoroumene, its 27
line-endings must come shortly—probably within 20
lines—after the close of PSI 1280. Parmenon has now
been engineered off the stage, and the girl has entered,
doubtless in response to the wild pipe music that Lysias
has organised for her benefit.*)

THE GIRL (?)
(*speaking ecstatically*)
          ] and the gold   31
          ] debouching [in the] sea
          ] agreeable
          ] I bid those present too
          ] you must all raise your voices!   35

cal beating of cymbals and drums, wild pipe music and furious
dancing, were characterised by palpitations and violent weeping
(cf. lines 15 f., if my interpretation there holds water). See espe-
cially E. R. Dodds, *The Greeks and the Irrational* (Berkeley and
Los Angeles 1951), 77–80.

(Here the girl begins to sing in lyric dactylic hexameters.)

(7)

40

] βασίλεια μεγίστα,
]μοι καὶ σεισικάρηνοι
κ]ορύβαντές θ᾽ ἀδυπρόσωποι.
θυ]σίαν κλειτάν θ᾽ ἑκατόμβαν
] θεά, Φρυγία βασίλεια
]α τύμπανα, μᾶτερ ὀ[ρεία.

(The next eight lines revert to the metre and dialect of normal comic dialogue. It is perhaps most likely that the girl continues, but now in a normal speaking voice. But an intervention by Lysias or Kleinias, or even dialogue involving two or three characters, cannot be ruled out.)

(12)

45

]θορυβοῦντες οὔτε [
]ους σαυτῷ πόε[ι
κ]ατὰ χώραν λαβὲ
]ον ἐπιτίθει τε πῦ[ρ
τὴν θ]εὸν γὰρ βούλομαι

36–41, 50, 52, 56 A scholiast on Euripides, *Andromache* 103 refers to τὰ ἐν Θεοφορουμένῃ ᾀδόμενα.   38–39 Suppl. Bartoletti.   39 The papyrus offers κλειναν as a variant reading. 41 Suppl. Bartoletti.   41–42 Between these lines is written in smaller letters] στέφαν(ον) ἐχέτω (or ἔχε τῷ) [.]. .λακιτω [/] παρὰ χεῖρα θα.λει[..]. Are these remains of a prose stage-direction, or of dactylic hexameters?   43–44 Suppl. Bartoletti.   45 Suppl. Handley, Lloyd-Jones.   46 Suppl. Handley.

(It is hard to make coherent sense of the above remarks. The girl may have entered the stage not long before line 31, and then launched into a poetical description of Phrygia, the home of Cybele, and the gold-bearing river Pactolus which flows not far to the south of Phrygia. At 34 the girl evidently turns to Lysias and Kleinias, and asks them to join in her act of worship. From 36 to 41 she sings a hymn to Cybele, the 'goddess, queen of Phrygia.')

    ] queen almighty
    ] and with heads atremble
    ] and sweet-faced Corybantes
    ] sacrifice and hecatomb of splendour
    ] goddess, queen of Phrygia,   40
    ] tambourines, O [mountain] mother.[a]

(The words of the above hymn are clearly a series of invocations to Cybele and the Corybantes, with accessory references to the sacrifices and the tambourines associated with this goddess's worship. Then follow eight lines in the metre and dialect of normal comic dialogue.)

    ] clamouring nor [
    ] make for yourself
    ] in place pick up
    ] and ignite   45
    ] for I'd like [the] god[dess]

[a] Between lines 41 and 42 the scribe inserts in smaller letters two lines of Greek, now badly mutilated, which may be partially translated '[ ] take (or let her/him take) a garland [ ] / [ ] to her/his hand [ ].' This may be a stage direction, referring to the girl's actions before she begins her song, or alternatively (but perhaps less probably) two dactylic hexameters which the scribe had inadvertently omitted at the beginning of the girl's song.

(17)

$$]\gamma\epsilon\varsigma. \ a\check{v}\lambda\epsilon\iota \ \delta\grave{\eta} \ \sigma\acute{v} \ \mu o\iota.$$
$$\epsilon\check{v}\mu]\epsilon\nu\grave{\eta}\varsigma \ \gamma\acute{\iota}\nu o\iota o \ \delta\grave{\epsilon}$$
$$]\mu\acute{\epsilon}\nu o\iota\varsigma \ \acute{a}\epsilon\acute{\iota}.$$

(The final eight lines mix lyric hexameters (50 ?, 52, 56) with iambics (51, 53–55, 57). The girl doubtless sings the hexameters, but the speaker or speakers of the iambics cannot certainly be identified. Perhaps the girl is again the likeliest candidate.)

50

$$\chi]a\hat{\iota}\rho', \ "A\gamma\gamma\delta\iota\sigma\tau\iota,$$
$$\mu]\epsilon\tau\grave{a} \ \kappa\upsilon\mu\beta\acute{a}\lambda\omega\nu$$

(22)

$$].\rho \ \acute{o}\lambda o\lambda\upsilon\gamma\mu\hat{\omega}\nu$$
$$] \ \mu\hat{\eta}\tau\epsilon\rho \ \theta\epsilon\hat{\omega}\nu,$$
$$"A\gamma\gamma\delta]\iota\sigma\tau\iota \ \Phi\rho\upsilon\gamma\acute{\iota}a \ K\rho\eta\sigma\acute{\iota}a$$

55

$$\delta]\epsilon\hat{\upsilon}\rho o \ \kappa\upsilon\rho\acute{\iota}a$$

(26)

$$]\nu a\pi a\varsigma \ \beta a\sigma\acute{\iota}\lambda\epsilon\iota a$$

57

$$]a \ \Lambda\upsilon\delta\acute{\iota}o\upsilon\varsigma$$

(At this point the papyrus breaks off.)

*   *   *

48 Suppl. Handley.   50–51, 54–55 Suppl. Bartoletti.

---

[a] Angdistis or Agdistis was an Asiatic goddess often identified with Cybele. She derives her name from Mount Agdos near the ancient city of Pessinus in Phrygia.

[b] Rhea, the Cretan mother goddess, was also identified with Cybele. Cf. fr. 8 below.

] You pipe for me
] may you favour (?) me
] always so remain (?).

(The speaker or speakers of lines 42 to 49 cannot be established with any certainty. The most plausible hypothesis perhaps is that the girl here interrupts her hymn in order to address the bystanders. First she asks Lysias or Kleinias to pick something up—possibly a torch—and to ignite something else—possibly incense on an altar—in furtherance of her act of worship. Then, as she prepares to resume her hymn, she tells the piper to begin piping again, and she subjoins a prayer, probably to Cybele.

The final eight lines of the papyrus, 50 to 57, are a mixture of sung hymn lines (50?, 52, 56) and spoken comic iambics (51, 53–55, 57). The girl almost certainly sings the former, but it is impossible now to be sure who speaks or speak the interlarded iambics. The girl may again be the likeliest candidate.)

] O hail, Angdistis![a]   50
] with tambourines.
  ] joyful shouting.
] O mother of the gods,
Angd]istis, Phrygian, Cretan too[b] —
] here supreme.   55
] queen [in] tree-clad valleys.
] Lydian[c]

*   *   *

[c] Lydia, in western Asia Minor, was closely associated with the cult of Cybele.

MENANDER

*Eight fragments quoted from Θεοφορουμένη
by ancient authors*

1 (1 Körte, 223 Kock)

Stobaeus, *Eclogae* 4. 42. 3 (περὶ τῶν παρ᾽ ἀξίαν εὐτυχούν-
των) cites the whole fragment with the heading Μενάνδρου
Θεοφορουμένης (so ms. S: -μένου mss. MA). Line 2 was fit-
ted into a witticism by Vespasian according to Suetonius,
Vesp. 23, who does not identify the source. Lines 16–17 are
cited with the author's name alone by the scholiast on Euripi-
des, *Hippolytus* 426. The first six words of line 16 are quoted
also by Athenaeus 6. 248d, inaccurately but with an ascrip-
tion to Menander. Lines 18–19 are cited by Plutarch,
Moralia 739f (*Quaest. Conv.* 9. 5) simply as τὰ τοῦ κωμικοῦ
γέροντος.

ΚΡΑΤΩΝ

εἴ τις προσελθών μοι θεῶν λέγοι, "Κράτων,
ἐπὰν ἀποθάνῃς, αὖθις ἐξ ἀρχῆς ἔσει·
ἔσει δ᾽ ὅ τι ἂν βούλῃ, κύων, πρόβατον, τράγος,
ἄνθρωπος, ἵππος. δὶς βιῶναι γάρ σε δεῖ·
5 εἱμαρμένον τοῦτ᾽ ἐστίν· ὅ τι βούλει δ᾽ ἑλοῦ·"
"ἅπαντα μᾶλλον," εὐθὺς εἰπεῖν ἂν δοκῶ,
"πόει με πλὴν ἄνθρωπον· ἀδίκως εὐτυχεῖ
κακῶς τε πάττει τοῦτο τὸ ζῷον μόνον.
ὁ κράτιστος ἵππος ἐπιμελεστέραν ἔχει
10 ἑτέρου θεραπείαν. ἀγαθὸς ἂν γένῃ κύων,
ἐντιμότερος εἶ τοῦ κακοῦ κυνὸς πολύ.
ἀλεκτρύων γενναῖος ἐν ἑτέρᾳ τροφῇ
ἐστιν, ὁ δ᾽ ἀγεννὴς καὶ δέδιε τὸν κρείττονα.
ἄνθρωπος ἂν δ᾽ ᾖ χρηστός, εὐγενής, σφόδρα
15 γενναῖος, οὐδὲν ὄφελος ἐν τῷ νῦν γένει.

70

THEOPHOROUMENE

*Eight fragments of Theophoroumene, quoted
by ancient authors*

1

Stobaeus ('On those prospering undeservedly') cites the
whole fragment with the heading 'from Menander's *Theo-
phoroumene*'. Several parts of it are quoted independently
by a variety of authors, who fail to identify the source pre-
cisely (see the facing page); among these Plutarch identifies
the speaker as 'the old man of comedy'.

KRATON

Suppose a god walked up to me and said,
"Kraton, you'll come back after death once more,
And be just what you want—a dog, sheep, goat,
Man, horse. You've got to live two lives, it's all
A law of destiny. Pick what you want."   5
I think I'd give a speedy answer: "Make
Me anything—but *not* a man! This creature's
The only one to thrive or fail unfairly.
A champion horse is groomed more tenderly
Than others. If you're born a pedigree   10
Dog, then your status is much higher than
A mongrel's. Pure-bred cocks get special food,
And there the riff-raff also fear their betters!
With men, though, great distinction, honour and
Good birth are useless in our present age.   15

---

1 Κράτων Gesner: κρατῶν mss. (SMA) of Stobaeus.   4 δὶς
βιῶναι MA: διαβιῶναι S.   5 ἑλοῦ SM: αἱροῦ καὶ ἑλοῦ A.
13 ὁ δ' S: οὐδ' MA.   14 ἂν δ' Meineke: ἐὰν SMA (ἐὰν ᾖ
ἄνθρ. χρ. A).   15 ὄφελος ἐν SA: ὠφέλησεν M.

71

πράττει δ' ὁ κόλαξ ἄριστα πάντων, δεύτερα
ὁ συκοφάντης, ὁ κακοήθης τρίτα λέγει.
ὄνον γενέσθαι κρεῖττον ἢ τοὺς χείρονας
ὁρᾶν ἑαυτοῦ ζῶντας ἐπιφανέστερον."

19

16 πράττει γὰρ πάντων ὁ κόλαξ ἄριστα ms. A of Athenaeus.
16–17 δεύτερος mss. NAB of Euripides scholiast (for δεύτερα ὁ,
correct in Stobaeus).   17 τρίτα λέγει mss. of Stobaeus: τρία
λέγει ms. N and τρίτατος λέγεται ms. A of Euripides scholiast.

2 (2 Kö, 225 K)

Stobaeus, Eclogae 3. 3. 6 (περὶ φρονήσεως), with the head-
ing Μενάνδρου Θεοφορουμένῃ·

ὁ πλεῖστον νοῦν ἔχων
μάντις τ' ἄριστός ἐστι σύμβουλός θ' ἅμα.

Yes-men do best of all, blackmailers win
The second prize, and spitefulness comes third.
Better be born an ass than see the dregs
Live in a brighter limelight than oneself!"

*In this play the role of the speaker Kraton, identified by
Plutarch (see above) as an old man, is now obscure, although
he is likely to have been the father of one of the three known
young people (Lysias, Kleinias, the demoniac girl) in the plot.
Equally obscure is the incident which gave rise to Kraton's
splenetic outburst about the undeserved success of social infe-
riors.*

2

Stobaeus ('On prudence'): from Menander's *Theophorou-
mene*,

          The man with most discernment
  Makes the best prophet and adviser too.

*These words paraphrase a line of Euripides (Helen 757) spo-
ken by a long-winded old retainer of Menelaos. Context and
speaker in Menander's play are hard to divine, but some help
appears to be given here by Alciphron, who composed a
series of fictitious letters much influenced by the situations of
New Comedy. In one of these (4. 19. 21) Alciphron pretends
that 'Glykera' is writing to 'Menander', and the writer refers
obliquely to prophecies made by 'your demoniac girl'. Thus
the speaker of the present fragment may be speaking disdain-
fully of a prophecy made by the play's heroine in her demo-
niac state.*

MENANDER

3 (3 Kö, 224 K)

Athenaeus 11. 504a (ὁ Πλούταρχος) ἔδωκε ⟨τὴν φιάλην⟩ τῷ παιδὶ περισοβεῖν ἐν κύκλῳ κελεύσας, τὸ κύκλῳ πίνειν τοῦτ᾽ εἶναι λέγων, παρατιθέμενος Μενάνδρου ἐκ Περινθίας (fr. 4) . . . καὶ πάλιν ἐκ Θεοφορουμένης·

καὶ ταχὺ τὸ πρῶτον περισοβεῖ ποτήριον
αὐτοῖς ἀκράτου.

1 Corr. Cobet: ταχὺ πάλι τὸ ms. A.

4 (4 Kö, 226 K)

Athenaeus 11. 472b: θηλυκῶς δὲ τὴν θηρίκλειον εἶπε Μένανδρος ἐν Θεοφορουμένῃ·

μέσως μεθύων ⟨τὴν⟩ θηρίκλειον ἔσπασεν.

τὴν om. ms. A, suppl. Schweighaeuser.

5 (5 Kö, 227 K)

A scholiast on Plato, *Clitopho* 407a(2) (p. 187 Greene): παροιμία·

ἀπὸ μηχανῆς θεὸς ἐπεφάνης.

ἐπὶ τῶν ἀπροσδοκήτως ἐπ᾽ ὠφελείᾳ ἢ σωτηρίᾳ φαινομένων· ἐν γὰρ ταῖς τραγῳδίαις ἐξ ἀφανοῦς θεοὶ ἐπὶ τῆς

---

[a] On this character (Plutarch of Alexandria, not the essayist from Chaeronea) see Barry Baldwin, *Acta Classica* 20 (1977), 47.

[b] Thericles was a celebrated Corinthian potter around 400 B.C. who produced black high-lustre ware which became very popular in Athens during the following century. Not long after

3

Athenaeus: Plutarch[a] gave (the cup) to the slave with an order 'to whizz it around', explaining that this meant 'drinking (from one beaker passed) around the whole circle', producing as evidence a passage from Menander's *Perinthia* (fr. 4) . . . and further from *Theophoroumene*,

> He whisks around them quickly the first cup
> Of undiluted wine.

A description of a drinking party which may perhaps have taken place in the inn mentioned at line 29 of the papyrus fragments. Undiluted wine was normally drunk only in toasts.

4

Athenaeus: Menander in *Theophoroumene* used the word θηρίκλειος (Thericlean cup[b]) as a feminine,

> Half drunk, he drained the Thericlean dry!

This may, but does not necessarily, come from the same context as fr. 3.

5

A scholiast on Plato's *Clitopho*: a saying,

> You've turned up like a god upon a crane!

Applied to those turning up unexpectedly to help or rescue, since in tragedies gods would appear on stage from some-

the potter's death the term 'Thericlean cup' was also applied to cups of a distinctive shape, with concave sides and small handles, not necessarily made by Thericles himself. See my *Alexis: The Fragments. A Commentary* (Cambridge 1996/1997), on fr. 5.

σκηνῆς ἐφαίνοντο. Μένανδρος Θεοφορουμένῃ.

6 (6 Kö, 228 K)

A scholiast on Plato, *Phaedo* 99c (p. 14 Greene):
παροιμία·

δεύτερος πλοῦς.

ἐπὶ τῶν ἀσφαλῶς τι πραττόντων, παρ' ὅσον οἱ διαμαρτόν-
τες κατὰ τὸν πρότερον πλοῦν ἀσφαλῶς παρασκευάζονται
τὸν δεύτερον. ἐμνήσθη δὲ ταύτης ... Μένανδρος ...
Θεοφορουμένῃ.

7 (7 Kö)

Photius (α 1592 Theodoridis) s.v. ἀναπετῶ· ἀναπετάσω.
Μένανδρος Θεοφορουμένῃ.

8 (8 Kö)

The *Etymologicum Magnum* (388.36): εὐάντητος· ἡ 'Ρέα.
ἀνταίαν γὰρ αὐτὴν ἐκάλουν διὰ τὸ δυσάντητον εἶναι καὶ
τοῖς ἀναντῶσιν ἐν τοῖς ὄρεσι δυσχεραίνειν· τὸ Νικαδίου
ὑπόνημα Θεοφορουμένης, κατ' εὐφημισμόν· δυσάντης γάρ
ἐστι καὶ ὀργίλη τοῖς ἀντάζουσιν ἐν τοῖς ὄρεσι· τὸ 'Αρτίου.

'Αρτίου ms.: < 'Αμ>αρτίου conj. Sylburg.

---

[a] In several Greek tragedies, especially those of Euripides, a
final resolution of a dramatic impasse is provided by the sudden
intervention of a deity making his or her appearance suspended
from a crane: the *deus ex machina.*

where out of sight.[a] Menander in *Theophoroumene*.

6

A scholiast on Plato's *Phaedo*: a saying,

Next best way.[b]

Applied to people accomplishing an object securely, insofar as those who have come a cropper in an earlier voyage achieve the second one without fail. This saying was mentioned by . . . Menander in . . . *Theophoroumene*.

7

Photius has an entry stating that Menander in *Theophoroumene* used ἀναπετῶ in place of the regular Attic form ἀναπετάσω as the future tense of ἀναπετάννυμι (I open/unfold/spread out).

8

The *Etymologicum Magnum* has the following curious and probably garbled entry: εὐάντητος (well met), sc. the goddess Rhea. They called her 'meetable' because she was a bad person to meet, and made trouble for those who encountered her on the mountains. So Nicadius' *Commentary on Theophoroumene*. A palliative use, for she is bad to meet and angry with those who come upon her on the mountains. So Artius' *Commentary*. It also means 'responsive to supplica-

----

[b] Literally 'second voyage'. Menander elsewhere (fr. 205 KT) explains this saying much more imaginatively than the scholiast: 'The next best way—this saying clearly means / That if you've lost fair winds, you use your oars.'

σημαίνει δὲ τὸν εὐϊκέτευτον· ἄντεσθαι γὰρ τὸ ἱκετεῦσαι.

One further fragment, whose attribution to
Θεοφορουμένη *is very uncertain*

9 (9 Sandbach in second edition of Oxford Text)

The *Etymologicum Magnum* (782.8): ὑπογράφω· καταβάλ-
λομαι, σκιαγραφῶ, βεβαιῶ· τὸ Ἁμαρτίου ὑπόμνημα.

Sandbach's attribution of this fragment to *Theophoroumene* is
extremely speculative. It rests on two assumptions: (1) that the
references to Ἀρτίου in fr. 8 and Ἁμαρτίου here are in one of
the two places a corruption of the other (hence Sylburg conjec-
tured <Ἁμ>αρτίου in fr. 8); and (2) that the other author,
whether called Artius or Hamartius, wrote no other commentary
than that on the *Theophoroumene*.

tion', for 'to supplicate' is the same as ἄντεσθαι (to meet/to supplicate).[a]

One further fragment, whose attribution to Theophoroumene is very uncertain

9

The *Etymologicum Magnum* defining the verb ὑπογράφω: I commit to writing, I draw in perspective, I confirm/pledge. Hamartius' commentary.[b]

[a] Nothing is known about Artius (if this name is correctly transmitted: see opposite on fr. 9) or Nicadius, but the latter apparently wrote a commentary on *Theophoroumene*, presumably Menander's play. If the entry in the *Etymologicum Magnum* derives ultimately from Nicadius, it seems legitimate to infer that Menander applied the adjective εὐάντητος to Rhea, the great mother goddess of Crete, who was often identified with Cybele (see my note on line 54 of the papyrus fragments of *Theophoroumene*), probably in a lost part of the hymn sung by the demoniac girl to Cybele and the Corybantes.

[b] If this entry ultimately derives from a commentary on Menander's *Theophoroumene* (but see opposite), it implies that the word ὑπογράφω was used in this play in one of the three listed meanings. The second is perhaps the most likely, for the verb appears to be used in the sense 'I make an outline sketch' first in the fourth century B.C.

KARCHEDONIOS
(THE MAN FROM CARTHAGE)

INTRODUCTION

Manuscripts

O᾿ = *P. Oxyrhynchus* 2654, six fragments which come
from three successive columns of a papyrus roll written in
the first century A.D., with extremely mutilated remains of
60 or so lines of text. First edition: E. G. Turner, *The
Oxyrhynchus Papyri*, 33 (1968), 1–8, with a photograph
(pl. I).

Three other papyrus fragments have been tentatively
assigned to the *Karchedonios*. Two of them are:

(i) *P. Oxyrhynchus* 866, here also designated as O, a
tiny scrap of papyrus from the first century A.D., written in
a hand which shows some (but not perhaps very close)
similarity to one of the major hands deciphered in *P. Oxy-
rhynchus* 2654. It contains the middle portions of seven
lines of text, in which the word Κ]αρχηδονιο[('Cartha-
ginian', v. 5) appears. First edition: B. P. Grenfell and
A. S. Hunt, *The Oxyrhynchus Papyri*, 6 (1908), 173–175,
where the scrap was assumed to be a fragment of prose.
Its attribution to *Karchedonios* was suggested by E. G.
Turner, *The Oxyrhynchus Papyri*, 33 (1968), 7 f., repub-
lishing it with a photograph (pl. I).

(ii) *P. Cologne* 4 (often referred to by its inventory
number 5031), a small fragment written in the same two

hands as the textual portions of *P. Oxyrhynchus* 2654 and therefore very probably deriving from the same roll of papyrus, possibly from the same play; identification of the author as Menander is to some extent supported by the presence of Ἰκόνιον in 129, attested for this playwright by the *Etymologicum Magnum* 470.45. *P. Cologne* 4 contains the ends of the last nine lines in one column and the beginnings of the last eight lines in the next. First edition: Ludwig Koenen, *Zeitschrift für Papyrologie und Epigraphik* 4 (1969), 171 f., with a photograph (pl. IX) but no identification; its attribution to *Karchedonios* was made by the same scholar in *Zeitschrift für Papyrologie und Epigraphik*, 5 (1970), 60. It was re-edited by Bärbel Kramer, *Kölner Papyri* 1 (1976), 21–23.

Both of these fragments are published here. The third, *P. Oxyrhynchus* 3966, is not. In publishing this scrap of papyrus from the first century A.D. containing 15 partly damaged lines of New Comedy, E. W. Handley (*Relire Ménandre*, Geneva 1990, 138–143, cf. 162–166, and *The Oxyrhynchus Papyri*, 59, 1992, 51–59) noted the close similarity of its handwriting to that of *P. Oxyrhynchus* 2654 and *P. Cologne* 5031, and consequently suggested that *P. Oxyrhynchus* 3966 might also come from Menander's *Karchedonios*. At the same time he noted that the subject-matter of 3966—the ritual of bringing water for a nuptial bath from a spring, in a procession involving water-carrier, piper and singer—had no known links with what little is known of the plot of Menander's *Karchedonios*, but did agree at several points with that of the same dramatist's *Phasma*, where a wedding was a prominent motif, a girl was locked up in the house just like a girl mentioned in 3966 v. 13 (or 12, if one discounts any line-numbering for the sign X]OP[OΥ after v. 4 indicating a choral entr'acte), and the lyrics that allegedly occurred in *Phasma* could have included the resolved anapaests or proceleusmatics of 3966 v. 12 (11). Hence *P. Oxyrhynchus* 3966 is better not connected with Menander's *Karchedonios*, but assigned rather to *Phasma* or to some other play with which links can be discerned (Thomas Gelzer, *Relire Ménandre*, 165 f., makes a case for *Georgos*).

Fragments 1 to 7 are quotations from a variety of sources; 1 to 6 are certainly, but 7 only tentatively, assigned to this play. See the introduction to vol. I, pp. xxiv–xxv.

The fragments preserved in *P.Oxy.* 2654 are severely mutilated, and only one passage of continuously coherent text, a mere nine lines in length (31–39), emerges amid the medley of line-endings, line-beginnings, and line-middles that constitute the remainder of this papyrus. Nevertheless, these remains are important for several reasons. Firstly, they are positively identified as part of Menander's *Karchedonios* because lines 7–8 coincide with an ancient quotation from this play (fr. 228 Körte-Thierfelder) made by Stobaeus. Secondly, they afford substantial support to the argument that Plautus' *Poenulus* was not adapted from Menander's *Karchedonios*, as many had believed, but from another Greek comedy, almost certainly the *Karchedonios* written by Menander's older contemporary, Alexis. Even before the publication of the new Oxyrhynchus fragments, the ties between two fragments of Alexis (105 and 265 Kassel–Austin, the former definitely assigned to Alexis'

Karchedonios) and two passages in Plautus' play (1318, 522–525), where Alexis' words appear in Roman translation, made the theory that here Plautus was adapting Alexis and not Menander plausible enough, especially since no similar ties could convincingly be shown to exist between the ancient quotations from Menander's *Karchedonios* and the Plautine text. In the new papyrus fragments from Menander's play the scene seems to be Athens, the Carthaginian is in pursuit of a girl who claims to be a free Athenian (38 f.), and the Carthaginian himself talks about being registered as a member of an Attic deme (39). Plautus' *Poenulus*, on the other hand, is set in the Aetolian city of Calydon, and the Carthaginian of the title is an old man searching for his lost Carthaginian daughters now living in the house of a pimp who had bought them from their kidnapper. The situations in the two plays seem to be quite different.[1]

Two further points of interest emerge from the dramatic situation which the fragments reveal. Three[2] characters can be identified. One is a slave (lines 10, 35), the second possibly a young and free Athenian, and the third apparently Menander's man from Carthage. The Carthaginian appears to be on stage when the text of *P.Oxy.* 2654 begins, and he retires into the background

[1] For a fuller discussion of the problems relating to the determination of Plautus' Greek model (or models), see now the introduction to *Karchedonios* in my commentary on Alexis (Cambridge 1996/1997), with full bibliography.

[2] The interpretation suggested here differs in several particulars from that advanced by E. G. Turner (*The Oxyrhynchus Papyri*, 36, 1968, 2–3 and 8) and F. H. Sandbach (both the Oxford Text and the 1973 *Commentary*). See Dario Del Corno, *Gnomon*, 42 (1970), 252.

on hearing a door open (4). The slave and the young man now enter, discussing the difficulties caused by an unspecified person's folly (6–8). After unintelligible references to a brother, a father and guardians (16–18), the slave questions the Carthaginian about his identity in a way designed to recall or parody the identification procedures followed when an Athenian citizen was being registered in his deme (30 ff.: see (?) Aristotle, *Ath. Pol.* 42. 1). The third point of interest is a legal one. The Carthaginian seemingly hopes to be registered in an Attic deme and intends to 'take' (in marriage?) a free Athenian girl (37–39). Only men of free Athenian parentage on both sides, however, were legally permitted in Menander's day to be registered in an Attic deme[1] or to marry a free Athenian girl. Yet Menander's Carthaginian evidently believed himself to be of non-Athenian ancestry, at least on his mother's side (35–37). Unfortunately the papyrus breaks off before we can learn how this difficulty was resolved.[2]

The fourth and final point of interest also relates to the Carthaginian's description of his ancestry. He names his maternal grandfather as 'Hamilcar the general' (35). Fiction is not real life, but it appears likely that Menander chose this impressive ancestry for his hero in order to add a touch of verisimilitude to his plot. In real life a Hamil-

---

[1] Cf. A. R. W. Harrison, *The Law of Athens: Procedure* (Oxford 1971), 205 ff.

[2] The young man from Carthage could, for example, have really been a free-born Athenian kidnapped as an infant, transported to Carthage, and brought up there by an aristocratic Carthaginian family in the belief that he was a native Carthaginian.

car had been a Carthaginian general at the battle of the River Crimisus in Sicily, where either in 343 B.C. or (more probably) 339 he was defeated by Timoleon, the Corinthian liberator of Greek Sicily. A second Hamilcar led an army in Sicily in 319 and acted as mediator in the strife between Agathocles, the tyrant of Syracuse, and some other Greek cities in 313, dying shortly afterwards in Carthage. A third Hamilcar was his successor as general in Sicily, landing there in 311 but being captured and executed by the Syracusans in 309. No didascalic notice survives for Menander's *Karchedonios*, and the play cannot be firmly dated, but it seems plausible enough that when Menander's hero, probably a young man, claimed to be Hamilcar's grandson, the playwright intended his audience to link this name with that of one of the Carthaginian generals (the second or third in the above list, most probably) whose successes and failures in Sicily had doubtless become topics of conversation in Athenian barbers' shops in the last twenty years of the fourth century.

Two other papyrus scraps are tentatively attributed to the *Karchedonios*, as noted above. One, a previously published shred from Oxyrhynchus (*P.Oxy.* 866), is too tiny, mutilated and uninformative for the validity of the attribution to be a matter of much moment. The other scrap (*P. Cologne* 4) is equally mutilated but far more interesting. Written apparently in the same two hands as the text on *P.Oxy.* 2654, its source as a fragment from the same roll is hardly open to question; but did *P.Oxy.* 2654 originally comprise one or more plays? If *P. Cologne* 4 does derive from Menander's *Karchedonios*, it probably adds to the cast-list a soldier whose equipment is itemised at line 109. At line 130 a slave Daos is addressed; was this perhaps the name of the slave who has a part in the fragments of *P.Oxy.* 2654?

The line-numbering in this edition coincides with that of Turner's original publication and of Sandbach's Oxford Text (*Menandri Reliquiae Selectae*, Oxford 1972[1], 1990[2]) for the text of *P.Oxy.* 2654; the few lines of *P.Oxy.* 866 are numbered here for convenience 81–87, and those of *P. Cologne* 4 (inv. 5031) 101–109 and 122–130.

No hypothesis or cast-list is preserved for this play.

Dramatis personae, so far as they are known:

The Carthaginian, a young man believing himself to be of
    Carthaginian ancestry but perhaps of Athenian birth
A slave
A man who enters with this slave, probably free and Athe-
    nian, possibly young
Possibly a soldier
Possibly a parasite or slave, attendant on the soldier
Possibly Daos, a third slave, unless this character is to be
    identified with one (or even both) of the other slaves
    listed above

In the lost part of the play other characters may have had speaking parts, including perhaps the brother and the father of the man who enters with the slave. One of the free characters in the play may have had a name beginning Ap- or At- (Apollodoros?). A chorus, perhaps of tipsy revellers, would have performed the entr'actes.

ΚΑΡΧΗΔΟΝΙΟΣ

(We cannot tell to which act of the play the mutilated fragments of *P.Oxy.* 2654 belong. From the first of its three columns, containing lines 1–23, only the right-hand side is preserved. Nothing remains from 1–3 apart from]πατρὸς 2,]ν πάλιν 3. Then come seven lines of more coherent text, which apparently start with the Carthaginian in mid-speech.)

ΚΑΡΧΗΔΟΝΙΟΣ (?)

]. . ἐψόφηκεν· ἐπανάγω

4

In the apparatus to lines 1–61 of this play, those supplements whose author is not named were made by the ed. pr., E. G. Turner, *The Oxyrhynchus Papyri*, 36 (1968), 1–8.   4–6 Part-division and identification of speakers suggested by Del Corno (4) and Arnott (5–6).

KARCHEDONIOS

(The Man from Carthage)

(*SCENE: Probably a street in Athens, with two or three houses visible to the audience. Their inhabitants, however, are now unknown to us.*)

(*P.Oxy. 2654 contains badly mutilated fragments of 60 lines or so from a single act of the play. From the opening three lines only two words survive:* father's (2) *and* again (3). *Lines 4 to 10 yield a more coherent text, although the identity of the speakers is disputed. If the Carthaginian of Menander's title was on stage alone at the beginning of our fragments, he could have been delivering a monologue which ended with him hearing a door open and deciding thereupon to withdraw into the background, lines 4 f.*)

CARTHAGINIAN (?)

(*in mid-speech ?*)
           that door']s [just] rattled. I'll withdraw   4
[Back here.]

(*As the Carthaginian retires into the background, two men enter from one of the houses on stage. One is certainly a slave, the other not so readily identifiable, but references later in their conversation to 'your brother' (16), a 'father'*)

ΝΕΑΝΙΑΣ (?: beginning his speech after
the line-opening?)

5].ην θῆτε· μηδὲν μηδέπω
  ].ον.

ΟΙΚΕΤΗΣ

οὐ κεχείμασται σφόδρα
]ος; ἔργον ἐκ πολλοῦ χρόνου
ἄνοιαν ἡμέρᾳ μεταστῆσαι μιᾷ.

ΚΑΡΧΗΔΟΝΙΟΣ (?)

τουτὶ τὸ κακὸν τί] ἐστι; περὶ τίνος λαλεῖ
10 ὁ τρισκακοδαί]μων; οὗτός ἐστιν οἰκέτης

(Lines 11–23 contain no connected passage of text:
]ην[. . . . . . .] τοίνυν λαλεῖ 11,]τι προ[. . . . .]ω ποει 12,
]ος ἂν ἐγὼ λα[λ]ῶ 13,] ἔπαθες; ὅ τι λέγεις λέγε· 14,
].τερα θει.[. .]οι 15,].το τἀδελφῷ νέμεις 16,]. . .θεις
γὰρ πατὴρ 17, -ων]ύμων ἢ κυρίων. (Change of
speaker) πάντας τρόπους 18,]ων βου[σὶ]ν ο[ὗτ]οσὶ
κακὸν 19,]ις βοῦς ε[. . . . .].ωδ[20,]α[21,] εὐθὺς
ηνθ.[22,]ης τύχης 23. A sliver of papyrus attached to
the foot of the column has on it]κλ[; this probably

7–8 KT fr. 228

8 ἄνοιαν ἡμέρᾳ μεταστῆσαι mss. of Stobaeus, *Ecl.* 2. 31. 19:
]μεταστῆναι O. 9 Speaker identified by Del Corno.
9–10 Suppl. Handley. 13 Suppl. Austin.

(17), and 'guardians' (18), together with the conventional patterns of double entries from one house in Menander, make it more probable that the second character was free than a slave, and young perhaps rather than old.)

YOUNG MAN

(to the slave)

      [Don't] make [him]. Nothing ever must   5

[   ]

SLAVE

      Been badly buffeted,

[This   ]? Surely not! It's hard to cure

Longstanding folly in a single day!

CARTHAGINIAN

(overhearing the slave, and aside)

[Now what the devil']s [this]? What can [the wretch]

Be yammering about? He is a slave . . .   10

(The identity of the 'badly buffeted' figure is obscure, but clearly the slave's words here have made the Carthaginian prick up his ears. Lines 11–29 yield only contextless words and phrases, rarely assignable to their speakers and often puzzling: 11 so he's yammering, 12 what (?) . . . he's doing or (with a new speaker intervening here) do it, 13 (the slave?) I yammer, 14 you've suffered? Do say what you mean!, 16 (the slave?) you're (or are you?) assigning to your brother, 17 father, you see, 18 or of guardians, followed by a different speaker saying In every way (?), 19 this fellow here . . . bad for cows (!), 20 cow or cows, 22 at once, 23 fortune, 24 nor (?), 26 trays or tray[-carrier(s)], 27 I . . . well, 29 go away. The slave and his companion here doubtless continued their conversation, possibly with occasional asides from the Carthaginian. The subject of

belongs to 21, 22, or 23, at a distance of several letters after the preserved portions of text. Line 23 appears to have been the final line of the column.

Of the first six lines in column ii (24–29) only a few letters from near the line-ends survive:].τα μητεγ[24,]επηι.ιδημ[25,]... σκαφη[26,] ἐγὼ καλῶς (possibly the end of the line ?) 27,].ομειπ[28,] ἀπελθ[29. A stretch of virtually continuous text then follows, opening with a remark in answer to something said in the previous line.)

ΝΕΑΝΙΑΣ (?)

30   ἥ]κιστα· .[...] πρόσεισιν [οὗ]το[ς].

ΟΙΚΕΤΗΣ

[οὐκ] ἴσω[ς,

βέλτιστ[ε, σ]αυτὸν ἀγνοῶν ἐλήλυθας.

ΚΑΡΧΗΔΟΝΙΟΣ

οὐκ οἴομαί γε.

ΟΙΚΕΤΗΣ
καὶ τίς ἐστί σοι, φράσον,

μήτ]ηρ;

ΚΑΡΧΗΔΟΝΙΟΣ

ἐμοί;

30 Supplementation and part-division in the second half of the line suggested by Handley.

their conversation cannot now be detected, but it appears to have included references to family business, to judge from the allusions to the young man's (?) brother, a father, and legal guardians in lines 16–18, and possibly also to questions of citizenship, to judge from the mention of 'trays' or 'tray-carrier(s)' in line 26. Resident aliens in Athens (the 'metics') carried trays in the Panathenaic procession, and were in consequence given the nickname of 'tray-carriers'. The 'cows' of 19–20 were presumably proverbial, but the proverb in which they featured has not yet been identified. At line 30 we come again to a passage well enough preserved for Menander's dialogue to speak for itself.)

YOUNG MAN

(*to the slave*)[a]
No, no — [you see,] this man's approaching.

(*The Carthaginian has now come forward, and is accosted by the slave.*)

SLAVE

Sir,　　30
You've surely come here knowing who you are?

CARTHAGINIAN

(*drily*)
I think so.

SLAVE
Tell me then your mother's name.

CARTHAGINIAN
My mother's name?

[a] Could this be in answer to the slave's suggestion in line 29 that the speaker should 'go away', sc. leave the stage?

ΟΙΚΕΤΗΣ

νή· καὶ τίνος πατρὸς λέγε.
τ]οὺς δημό[τ]ας νόμιζε ποιεῖν ἐγγραφάς.

ΚΑΡΧΗΔΟΝΙΟΣ

35 θυγατὴρ Ἀμ[ί]λκου τοῦ στρατηγοῦ, δραπέτα,
Καρχηδονίων ἐμή 'στι μήτηρ. τί βλέπεις;

ΟΙΚΕΤΗΣ

ἔπειτ' Ἀμί[λκου] θυγατριδοῦς ὢν πράγματα
ἡμῖν παρ[έ]χε[ις], οἴει τε λήψεσθαι κόρην
ἀστήν;

ΚΑΡΧΗΔΟΝΙΟΣ

ἐπειδ[άν γ' ἐγ]γραφῶ κατὰ τοὺς νόμους.

ΟΙΚΕΤΗΣ

40 ἀλλ' ἁγνὰ γὰ[ρ   ] ὁ κῆρυξ αὐτόθι
41 του[   ]πις.

ΚΑΡΧΗΔΟΝΙΟΣ (?)

εἶτα τί;

(Of the remaining four lines of the column only a few
letters at the beginnings and ends can be deciphered:
(change of speaker: to οἰκέτης ?) ελ.[   ]αι βαρὺς 42,
κα..[.]ηγ[   ]. ἐκεῖ 43, .ν[   ]ν τινος 44, .λ.[   ]
τήμερον 45.

From column iii a few letters are preserved opening
each line: a paragraphus below 47, ⁊ εν.[48, χ τη[
49, ειρ[50, χ επε[51, ⸓ τοσ.[52, ευγ.[53, αξι.[54,

SLAVE

Yes, and your father's. Just
Imagine it's a registration by
The deme.[a]

CARTHAGINIAN

You scamp, my mother is a daughter 35
Of Hamilcar, the general of Carthage.[b]
What does that look mean?

SLAVE

So you plague us, you
Intend to have[c] a city girl—you, Hamilcar's
Grandson?

CARTHAGINIAN

Yes—when I'm duly registered.

SLAVE

But here the crier [   ] pure 40

*(The rest of P.Oxy. 2654 is too mutilated for coherent
translation. The conversation between the slave and the
Carthaginian obviously continued for some time, and the
slave may have pointed out that only free-born Athenians
could be registered in the deme and marry Athenian girls.
A convincing supplement for the missing middle of line 40*

[a] When a free male Athenian reached the age of eighteen, he
became a full citizen, but before his citizenship was registered he
had to submit to an examination about his age, parentage and
status in his deme. Cf. A. R. W. Harrison, *The Law of Athens:
Procedure* (Oxford 1971), 205–207.

[b] See the introduction to this play.

[c] 'To have as wife' probably, but the Greek word is ambigu-
ous.

_τί_ φ[ής; 55, απολ[56, ἐναν[τί- 57, _ουσπ_[58, _ηπω_[59, οψε[60, εν.[61. At this point these papyrus fragments break off. The marginal signs at lines 48, 49, 51 and 52 are puzzling; the 'anchor' sign at 48 possibly indicated that a verse had been omitted here by mistake and was supplied at the foot of the column, the 'chi' marks at 49 and 51 may have been intended to refer the reader to notes in the commentary, and the long, forked paragraphus at 52 perhaps stigmatised that verse as of suspect authenticity: cf. E. G. Turner, *Greek Papyri*, Oxford 1968, 112 ff.)

Two further papyrus fragments which are
tentatively assigned to Καρχηδόνιος

(a) *P. Oxyrhynchus* 866, a small scrap attributed to this play because (i) the word Κ]αρχηδονιο[occurs in its fifth line (85), and (ii) its handwriting is not dissimilar to one of the hands in *P.Oxy.* 2654. Its text runs: 81]πολισμου[, 82]αι πυθομε[, 83 ἀπ]οβαλούσῃ[, 84]ε καθόλου [, 85 Κ]αρχηδονιο[, 86]ρενεισπι.[, 87]ρεν[.

56 Either Ἄπολ[λον (ed. pr.) or just possibly Ἀπολ[λοδωρ- (Arnott: cf. 125).

Other remains in column ii and on two dissevered scraps (frs. 5 and 6 Turner), written in hands different from those of the play text, seem to contain mutilated portions of a commentary, but the damage is too great for any sense to be made out of them:]ιτεθισ.[/]κα /].μνρωβ.[/].ιη[under line 46;]εουσ...[/].κρν.[/].ασησω [fr. 5;].ον[.]δεη[/]..λ.λη.ουχ.[/]εργα fr. 6.

has not yet been devised, but the 'crier' was presumably the officer of the deme whose job it was to make public announcements about matters such as registration. After line 40 only a few words are intelligible, all uninformative. At the end of 41 the Carthaginian asks What then?, *to which in 42 the slave makes a reply including the word* severe. *43 yields only* there, *44 of* some, *45* today, *55* What do you say?, *56* Apol[lo] (?), *57* Opposite. *Changes of speaker are marked in the papyrus at lines 47, 53, 54, 58 and 59.*

P.Oxy. 2654 originally contained, in addition to the text of the Karchedonios, a commentary or at least a series of notes on difficult or disputed passages of the play. A few fragments of these notes survive, but in so damaged a state that hardly a single word from them can be safely understood or translated.)

Two further papyrus fragments which are tentatively assigned to Karchedonios

(a) *P. Oxyrhynchus 866 contains bits of seven lines only:*
81 my city (?), *82* learn[ing] (?), *83 some woman* throwing away *or* losing, *84* as a whole, *85* Carthaginian; *86 and 87 are too mutilated to yield any sense. Does this fragment come from a conversation about the Carthaginian's origins?*

(a) *P. Oxyrhynchus* 866   81 μον or ην.   83 Suppl. Turner.
85 Suppl. Grenfell, Hunt.

(b) *P. Cologne* 4 (inv. 5031), mutilated portions of two columns of text written in the same two hands as the text of *P.Oxy.* 2654, and so almost certainly deriving from the same papyrus roll, possibly even from the same play. *P.Oxy.* 2654 was written with 23 lines in each column of text; it is likely therefore that there was a gap of 13 lines between the bottom of column i of *P. Cologne* 4 and the top surviving line of its column ii. Its text runs as follows:

	column i		*column ii*
101	]ματ[	123	[...]σδιδ[
	ἀνθ]ρωπι[ν		[..]σδιδομ[ε
	]ει γαμεῖν	ΑΠ. (?)	[...]έχω γ[
	]α ῥαιδίως	126	[..].μευντ[
105	]ου φθόρου		ἀλλοτριοι[
	-τυ]χέστερος		XXXX
	]ικην ἐμοῦ	128	ἐξεληλυθε[
	ἀ]κολουθήσω φέρ[ω]ν		
109	θ]ύλακον, πήραν, κράνος	129	Ἰκόνιον α[
		130	Δᾶ', ἑλοῦ[

(b) *P. Cologne* 4   102, 106, 108, 109 Suppl. Koenen.
107 εστιμου Col., with στι deleted.   109 Above θ]υλακον Col. has κ]ωδι(ον) as a variant reading.   123 ff. Trochaic tetrameters.   125 The marginal sign (ΑΠ or alternatively ΑΤ) is probably an abbreviation of the speaker's name: Ἀπολλόδωρος?   127–128 The interlinear sign is puzzling; it could indicate the omission of a line or passage, an act-ending, or some other feature considered notable; cf. the single χ before lines 49 and 51 of *P.Oxy.* 2654.   128–129 A vacant space seems to have been left between these two lines.   129–130 These lines are indented three letters.   129 The *Etymologicum Magnum*, 470.45 cites Menander (fr. 852 Körte-Thierfelder = here ?) for scanning Ἰκόνιον with its first syllable short.

100

(b) P. Cologne 4 (inv. 5031) is considerably more informative. It contains the ends of nine lines at the bottom of one column and then, after a lacuna of 13 lines, the beginnings of eight more lines at the bottom of the adjacent column. A few words can be deciphered: human (?) *102,* to marry *103,* easily *104,* bane *105,* more fortunate *or* more [un]fortunate *106,* me (genitive case) *107,* I'll follow, carrying / [ ] bag, pouch, helmet *108–109,* give *123,* give again *124,* I have (?) *125,* alien (as adjective) *127,* He *or* She's come out *128,* Iconium *129,* Daos, pick (?) *130. The earlier words (101–107) cannot be related to an identifiable context, but 108–109 are most likely to have been spoken by a soldier's attendant—slave or parasite—with reference to that soldier's equipment (cf. Kolax, 29 f.). Lines 123 ff. appear to be trochaic tetrameters—evidence perhaps of a new scene beginning in the gap after line 109 (unless, that is, 101–109 were also written in trochaic tetrameters!). Nothing can be made of the situation in 123–127, but there are paragraphi above and below 128, and the speaker of 125 is identified by a blurred and abbreviated name in the margin which may be read as 'Ap.' or 'At.'. No known character in Menander's plays has a name beginning with either pair of letters, but Apollodoros would be a conceivable name for a free Athenian. Between 127 and 128 the scribe may have omitted a line or a passage, or indicated an act-break.*[a] *Between 128 and 129 the scribe has left a blank space, of uncertain significance; an act-break is the least plausible hypothesis here, however, since in the previous line the speaker seems to have announced someone's arrival on stage from one of the stage houses, and characters do not thus enter at the last line of an act. The 'Iconium' mentioned in 129 is*

---

[a] See the critical apparatus, *ad loc.*

* * *

Six fragments of Καρχηδόνιος,
quoted by ancient authors

1 (226 Körte-Thierfelder, 260 Kock)

Athenaeus 9. 385de: ὀψάριον δὲ τῶν μὲν ζώντων ἡμεῖς
λέγομεν, ἀτὰρ καὶ ... ἐπὶ τοῦ ἰχθύος ... Μένανδρος
Καρχηδονίῳ·

   ἐπιθυμιάσας τῷ Βορέᾳ <λιβαν>ίδιον
   ὀψάριον οὐδὲν ἔλαβον· ἑψήσω φακῆν.

1 ἐπιθυμιάσας and <λιβαν>ίδιον Bentley: ἐπιθυμίσας and
ἴδιον ms. A.

probably the city in Lycaonia about 100 miles from the south coast of Asia Minor. Could this have been the area where the soldier whose equipment is listed in 109 had been a mercenary? 130 indicates that a slave Daos was a character in the scene; even if P. Cologne 4 is rightly assigned to the Karchedonios, we still dare not assume that Daos was the name of the slave in the fragments of P.Oxy. 2654, for the comedies of Menander sometimes include as many as three slaves in a single cast (for example, Dyskolos, Heros).

*   *   *

*Six fragments of Karchedonios,
quoted by ancient authors*

1

Athenaeus: Along with our contemporaries we use the word ὀψάριον, but ... it was applied to fish also ... by Menander in *Karchedonios,*

To Boreas[a] I offered incense, but
I got no fish. I'll boil some lentil soup.

One possibility is that these were the first words on entry of a parasite or slave who had gone fishing the previous night and now reports his lack of success (contrast Gripus in Plautus, Rudens 906 ff.). How such a remark and entry would fit into the plot of Karchedonios, however, remains obscure. Lentil soup was typically a poor man's substitute for fish.

[a] The god of the North Wind.

MENANDER

2 (227 KT, 261 K)

Stobaeus, *Eclogae* 4. 24b. 27 (ὅτι ἀσύμφορον τὸ ἔχειν τέκνα) cites line 1 with the heading Μένανδρος Καρχηδονίῳ. A scholiast in mss. E and M of Homer, *Odyssey* 1. 215 (1 p. 40 Dindorf) and Eustathius' commentary on the same passage (1412.15) cite both lines with the name of the playwright but not the play.

αὐτὸν γὰρ οὐθεὶς οἶδε τοῦ ποτ' ἐγένετο,
ἀλλ' ὑπονοοῦμεν πάντες ἢ πιστεύομεν.

1 αὐτὸν Eustathius and the scholiast: αὐτὸς mss. of Stobaeus. οὐθεὶς mss. of Stobaeus: οὐδεὶς Eustathius, scholiast. τοῦ ποτ' Eustathius: πῶς ποτ' scholiast, πῶς mss. of Stobaeus.

3 (230 KT, 261 K)

Photius (1. 392 Naber) and the *Suda* (λ 626 Adler) s.v. Λιτυέρσης· εἶδος ᾠδῆς. Μένανδρος Καρχηδονίῳ·

ᾄδοντα Λιτυέρσην ἀπ' ἀρίστου τέως

Lemma Καρχηδονίῳ Hemsterhuys: Χαλκηδονίῳ Gale ms. of Photius, Χαλκηδονίων mss. of *Suda*.

4 (231 KT, 265 K)

Stobaeus, *Eclogae* 3. 9. 16 (περὶ δικαιοσύνης), with the heading Μενάνδρου Καρχηδονίου, and 4. 1. 21 (περὶ πολιτείας), with the heading Μενάνδρου,

τὸ καλῶς ἔχον που κρεῖττόν ἐστι καὶ νόμου.

5 (232 KT, 266 K)

Pollux 10. 73: ἀσκοπυτίνη· . . . καὶ Μένανδρος δ' ἐν Καρχηδονίῳ κέχρηται τῷ ὀνόματι.

2

Stobaeus ('That having children is inconvenient', citing v. 1 as 'Menander in *Karchedonios*'); a scholiast on Homer's *Odyssey* and Eustathius (citing both lines as 'Menander'):

> For no one knows who his own father is —
> We all assume it, or take it on trust.

3

Photius and the *Suda* illustrating the use of λιτνέρσης (harvest song): Menander in *Karchedonios*,

> Singing a harvest song from lunch the while

Context and speaker are unknown. A legend seems to have been invented to account for the word λιτνέρσης. In it 'Lityerses' became a son of King Midas of Phrygia, challenging travellers to a reaping contest, flogging the losers, and eventually being himself killed by Heracles. See Gow's edition of Theocritus, commentary on 10. 41.

4

Cited twice by Stobaeus: in 'On justice' with author and title, in 'On government' with author's name only.

> Virtue outranks, I fancy, even law.

Context and speaker are unknown.

5

Pollux: ἀσκοπυτίνη (leather flask); ... Menander has used the noun in *Karchedonios*.

The flask may have been mentioned as one of the soldier's accoutrements (see lines 108–109).

6 (233 KT, 265 K)

A scholiast on Aristophanes, *Vespae* 1502 (c: p. 232 Koster): ὁ
μέσατος· . . . ἀντὶ τοῦ μέσος· καὶ Μένανδρος Καρχη-
δονίῳ.

*One further fragment, tentatively
assigned to* Καρχηδόνιος

7 (229 KT, 263 K)

The *Suda* (χ 465 Adler) s.v. χρεία· . . . καὶ παροιμία·

χρεία διδάσκει, κἂν ἄμουσος ᾖ, σοφόν
Καρχηδόνιον.

τούτεστιν, ἐνδεχομένην ἐκ τοῦ καιροῦ ποιησάμενοι τὴν
ἐπίνοιαν.

2 Καρχηδονίῳ conjectured by Meineke (as indication of the
cited fragment's source). Lemma, ποιησάμενος or -ησασθαι
conj. Badham.

6

A scholiast on Aristophanes' *Wasps* notes that 'Menander too
(sc. as well as Aristophanes) in *Karchedonios*' used the
unusual superlative form μέσατος (midmost) in place of the
normal positive form μέσος (middle).

*One further fragment, tentatively
assigned to Karchedonios*

7

The *Suda* s.v. χρεία (need/necessity) includes the following
note: . . . and a proverb,

Need teaches wisdom even to a clod
From Carthage (?).

This means: making his intelligence receptive as a result of
the opportunity.

*Here the Greek word (Καρχηδόνιον) translated as 'from
Carthage' has sometimes been interpreted not as part of the
verse quotation but as a garbled indication that the source of
the words 'Need teaches wisdom even to a clod' was '(Menan-
der) in Karchedonios'. We cannot be certain whether the
attribution to this comedy is correct or not, but the quoted
words cleverly fuse together two famous Euripidean conceits:
'Love teaches one to be a poet, even if / A clod before' (fr. 663
Nauck[2]), and 'Need teaches wisdom even to a dolt' (fr. 715
Nauck[2]); compare also Euripides, Electra 375 f.*

KITHARISTES

(THE LYRE PLAYER)

INTRODUCTION

Manuscripts

Berl. = *P. Berlin* 9767, a fragment containing three successive columns (= 97 or 98 lines of text) from a papyrus roll written at the end of the first century B.C. Its provenance has not been stated. The first and third columns are badly mutilated, and all three have patches of abrasion. First edition: W. Schubart and U. von Wilamowitz-Moellendorff, *Berliner Klassikertexte, V: Griechische Dichterfragmente, II: Lyrische und Dramatische Fragmente* (Berlin 1907), 115–122, with a photograph of lines 35 to 101 (pl. VI); lines 44–68 are reproduced also in W. Schubart, *Papyri Graecae Berolinenses* (Bonn 1911), plate 11a. No photograph of lines 1–34 has been published.

O = *P. Oxyrhynchus* 3968, a fragment containing the ends of 30 lines in one column and the beginnings of 21 in the next, written in the third century A.D. Although it is printed here (after fragment 13), its attribution to *Kitharistes* is very uncertain: see the introduction to frs. 10–13. First edition: E. W. Handley, *The Oxyrhynchus Papyri*, 59 (1992), 70–74, with a photograph (plate V).

Turn. = *P. Turner* 5, from Oxyrhynchus; an extract written in the second or third century A.D., and containing 12 or so lines which partially agree with fragment 1 as cited from the play by Stobaeus, *Eclogae* 4. 33. 13 and Plutarch, *Moralia* 466a. Its readings are cited here under fragment 1. First edition: E. W. Handley, *Papyri Greek & Egyptian . . . in Honour of Eric Gardner Turner* (London 1981), with a photograph (plate III).

Fragments 1–13 are quotations from a variety of ancient sources; 1–9 are certainly, but 10–13 only tentatively, assigned to this play. See the introduction to volume I, pp. xxiv f.

The identification of *P. Berlin* 9767 as part of Menander's *Kitharistes* is practically certain, although the papyrus text nowhere coincides with an ancient quotation from the play. Stobaeus (*Eclogae* 4. 33. 13) and Plutarch (*De tranq. anim.* 3 = *Moralia* 466a), however, cite from the *Kitharistes* a passage (fragment 1) in which a man named Phanias is addressed, and the Berlin papyrus mentions a Phanias who is a κιθαριστής ('lyre player', 96 ff.).

The papyrus is very informative about the antecedents to the plot, but some of its hints are difficult to interpret. Three successive scenes can be identified. Of the first only the mutilated ending survives. In it a woman (cf. line 2) and a man (note the gender of the participle in line 17) are having a discussion in which marriage (7), perhaps desertion (10), and a rape (19–20) are mentioned. If the male speaker is identical with the raper and has promised to marry but possibly since deserted his victim, he is most probably the Moschion who appears in the third scene of the papyrus fragments, as we shall see. The woman to whom he is perhaps confessing his guilt is addressed by him as 'dearest' (2); she is accordingly more likely to be his mother than a connection of the raped girl.[1]

At the end of this scene there may be a three-line space in the papyrus (28–30) indicating an act-break. Although only the extreme ends of lines are preserved at this point, it is clear that none of the lines immediately preceding 28 closed with any of the formulaic phrases habitually used by Menander to introduce the chorus directly before its first appearance at the end of Act I.[2] There are three possible explanations for this combination of circumstances. The assumption of an act-break may be mistaken. Or Menander may have chosen to end a first act without resorting to the known formulas which identify the chorus' approach. Or thirdly, despite their expository function these papyrus scenes may straddle not the first and second acts, but rather the second and third. The last explanation seems to me the most likely; the presence of explanatory material at this stage of the play is not a compelling objection to it, since Menander often delays apparently expository narrative to a later

---

[1] So first T. B. L. Webster, *Studies in Menander* (1st edition, Manchester 1950), 53. Would Moschion have used the same endearment to the nurse (so Del Corno's edition of Menander, 450) or the mother of the girl he had raped and then apparently abandoned, leaving Ephesus (the scene of his adventure) for Athens? There are dramatic reasons also for believing that the girl's immediate entourage was not seen on stage thus early in the play: see below. This and other problems connected with the plot of the *Kitharistes* are dealt with at greater length in some notes on the play which I have published in *Zeitschrift für Papyrologie und Epigraphik*, 31 (1978), 26–32.

[2] See the introduction to *Georgos*.

stage in the play (see for instance *Dysk.* 407 ff., *Epit.* 451 ff., *Samia* 219 ff.).

The second of the papyrus scenes, which opens the new act if the above argument is correct, is still largely an unsolved puzzle. Two men enter, discussing the misfortunes of one of them. This sufferer has apparently just returned from abroad, where he was in contact with a wealthy 'daughter' (35–37) who seems later to be described as his 'wife' (43). The text is badly abraded in several vital places, and we cannot follow all the details of the story. For some reason or other, however, this woman has not arrived in Athens and an accident such as shipwreck is suspected. The most plausible identification of this sufferer is Phanias, the lyre player of the title. He was rich (see frs. 1 and possibly also 11), and had in Ephesus a daughter with whom, as the next scene shows, Moschion had fallen in love. Ephesus then was presumably the city abroad that Phanias had visited, but how do the wealthy 'daughter' (who was his wife) and his own daughter (whom Moschion loved) fit into the story as we know it? The most economical combination of the facts and hints that occur in the various fragments seems to me to be as follows: Phanias had met in Ephesus many years before a woman who had borne him a daughter there. Phanias had deserted her, returning to Athens. He had recently revisited Ephesus, met again the woman (who was now rich), and married her. She had set out for Athens, probably with her daughter, ahead of him, but had not found her way to his house. This fact can easily be understood if her daughter, raped previously by Moschion in Ephesus, had a pregnancy to conceal; mother and daughter could perhaps have found accommodation

clandestinely in Athens (with Moschion's help?: see
22–26; in this case Moschion's desertion of the daughter
would only have been temporary), but this is just one
possibility.

At the end of their scene Phanias and his companion,
whose identity remains a mystery (could he have been an
Athenian connection of Phanias' wife?), leave the stage,
and Moschion's father appears. He has been summoned
by his son, who enters shortly afterwards and explains that
while in Ephesus he fell in love with Phanias' daughter.
The papyrus breaks off before we hear the father's reac-
tion to Moschion's news, but it is informative in one other
important respect. We learn from it that Moschion's
father lived in one of the stage houses (63), and that Pha-
nias occupied the house next door (100 f.).

Speculation about the missing portions of Menander's
plots is rarely profitable; but Phanias' wife and daughter
doubtless turned up safely in the end, and Moschion
would have been allowed to marry Phanias' daughter
after her mother turned out to be not an Ephesian but a
free Athenian woman by birth.[1] A fragment cited by Sto-
baeus (fr. 4 here) names one of the characters in the play
as Laches. This name is normally given by Menander and
his colleagues to older men (*Heros, Fab. Inc.*, probably
Perinthia; cf. C. Austin, *C.G.F.P.* frs. 250, 255; Terence,
Hecyra); in this play Moschion's father and Phanias' com-
panion are the known candidates.

Phanias is one of the less common character names of

---

[1] It can hardly have been a coincidence that the Athenian
deme which Menander chose for Phanias (Euonymon: see on
lines 97 f.) had close links with one of the civic tribes in Ephesus.

later Greek comedy; outside *Kitharistes*, it appears in two Menandrean fragments (once by conjecture) from unknown plays, in two anonymous monostichs and in one badly mutilated papyrus (O) with no other links to *Kitharistes* than this name. Since there is at least a possibility that all five derive from one and the same source, they are printed here without much confidence as fragments 12–13, 10–11 and papyrus fragment O. The last of these five would add two names to the cast-list: a slave Sosias (O.i.1, O.i.20) and a *hetaira* Thais (O.ii.5), presumably a minor character totally different from the title-figure of Menander's *Thais*. The uncertainty, however, of the attribution of this papyrus to *Kitharistes* prevents me from including their names in the cast-list below; see also the introduction to fragments 10–13.

The line-numbering of Berl. coincides with that of Sandbach's Oxford Text and Körte's third Teubner edition. No hypothesis, didascalic notice, or cast-list survives for this play. Its production date is unknown.

Dramatis personae, so far as they are known:

Moschion, a young Athenian in love with Phanias' daughter
A woman, most probably Moschion's mother
Phanias, a now wealthy lyre player
An unidentified companion of Phanias (? some connection of Phanias' wife)
Moschion's father

Either Phanias' companion or Moschion's father or a now unknown third character in this play was named Laches.

116

In the missing portions of the play several other charac-
ters doubtless had speaking roles, including Phanias' wife,
if my reading of the plot is correct. If Phanias' daughter
appeared on stage, her part was probably of minor im-
portance, and may have been played by a mute. One or
more slaves, played by a mute or mutes, carried Phanias'
baggage inside at line 52. There was certainly a chorus,
possibly of tipsy revellers, to perform the entr'actes.

ΚΙΘΑΡΙΣΤΗΣ

(The Berlin papyrus begins in mid-scene, with Moschion probably in conversation with his mother. Only the ends of the last 27 lines of the scene are preserved, and assignment of individual lines to either of the two speakers is in most cases impossible:]νον πολύν τινα 1, (Μοσχ.)]ω φιλτάτη 2,]η δεδυκέ[ν]αι 3,]ει κ[α]ρδίαν 4,]ος δ' ἦν τῷ κακῷ 5,]νν γάμου 7,]μια 8,]εν...ς 9,] κατέλιπες 10,]ω 11,]τε δὴ 12,]ων 13, σ]υναπήρκει δέ μοι 14,]λθης τῆς ἐμῆς 15,]νως πως ἄφνω 16, (Μήτηρ)]ν λέγων τρέχεις 17,]εται 18,] ὕβρει τὸ γεγονὸς 19,] βίᾳ 20,]ων αὐτὴν σύ μοι 21,]ν μητέρα 22,].αι τί σοι 23, ο]ὐθένος 24,]ουν ἔδει 25,] λάθρᾳ 26,]ερων 27.

After line 27 there is a blank space three lines in extent (= 28–30 in the traditional line-numbering followed

In the apparatus to this play, those supplements whose author is not named were made in the first edition of the Berlin papyrus by U. von Wilamowitz, *Berliner Klassikertexte*, V. ii (Berlin 1907), 115–122.   6 Abrasion has removed all traces of letters in this line.   9, 15]ενο[..]ο and]λοπε respectively read by Schubart, Wilamowitz;]ενα τις tentatively and]λθης by Arnott.

---

[a] The arguments for postulating an act-break at lines 28–30 and for identifying the acts are given on pages 118 and 120 and in the introduction to *Kitharistes*.

[b] Cf. the introduction to *Kitharistes*.

KITHARISTES

(The Lyre Player)

(SCENE: A street somewhere in Athens, probably with two houses visible to the audience. One belongs to Phanias the lyre player, the other to Moschion's father.)

(The Berlin papyrus preserves mutilated portions of 101 lines probably from the end of the second act and the beginning of the third.[a] *When the papyrus begins, Moschion appears to be on stage in conversation with his mother, according to the hypothesis which seems to me most reasonable.*[b] *Of this scene, however, only the final 27 line-ends are preserved, yielding a series of disconnected words and phrases which can scarcely ever be attributed to a definite speaker:* a lot of [time (?)] *1*, dearest *as an address to a woman (and so spoken by Moschion) 2*, to have entered/sunk *3*, heart *4*, was ... in (?) trouble *5*, of marriage *7*, you deserted *as a statement or a question 10*, was enough for me *14*, of (?) my *15*, somehow suddenly *16*, saying ... you *(masculine)* run *(spoken by Moschion's mother) 17*, by (?) violence ... what's happened *or* what's been born *19*, by force *20*, you ... her (?) to me *21*, mother *22*, something for you *23*, of (?) nothing *24*, had to *or* ought to have *25*, furtively *26*, in love (?) *27*. *It is tempting but probably reckless to suggest that Mos-*

here) with no sign of abrasion. The most probable explanation is that the scribe originally wrote here the note
<u>XO P Oϒ</u> as an indication of an act-break.)

ΜΕΡΟΣ Γ΄ (?)

(Line 31 will in that case begin a new act. The opening scene appears to be a dialogue between Phanias, the lyre player of the title, and an unnamed but probably free male companion. Of the scene's first three lines only the endings are preserved: πά]νθ' ὅσα 31,]ας 32,]ονον 33. After line 33 there may just possibly have been, at the bottom of column i of the papyrus, a further line of text from which no letters now survive, and then we reach column ii, where the text is much more complete although still badly abraded in places. Phanias' companion (here designated simply as ΑΝΗΡ) seems to be in mid-speech when line 35 begins.)

ΑΝΗΡ

35   ζηλοῖς, λαβών τε τὴ[ν . . . . . ἐλ]ήλυθ[ας
θυγατέρα δεῦρο, πλουσίαν θ' [ἤγ]ῃ μόνη[ν
ταύτην, σεαυτὸν δ' οὐχί;

35–101 Berl. uses dicola to indicate changes of speaker, but only when the changes occur in mid-line.   36–38 Deciphered (not perhaps always convincingly) and suppl. Schubart.

---

  [a] The events which appear to form the background to this conversation are discussed in the introduction to this play.

chion may have been confessing his sins here to his mother. Had he raped a girl (19–20) whom he had then promised to marry (7 ?) but now, by his mother's accusation (if she spoke line 10), had abandoned? If he had committed these offences, the girl in question was presumably Phanias' daughter, whom he had admired in Ephesus (cf. 94 ff.) and perhaps deserted there on his departure for Athens.

With line 27 this scene and perhaps also the second act may have come to an end, Moschion leaving by the side-entrance to the right which was imagined to lead towards the city centre, and his mother going off into her house. After their departure, the chorus enter to give their second entr'acte performance.)

ACT III (?)

(After the departure of the chorus, Phanias and a companion enter from the left, the direction of the harbour. They are probably attended by one or more slaves carrying a lot of luggage. From the first four lines of the new scene only one intelligible phrase survives: everything that in 31. At line 35, however, we come for the first time in the papyrus fragment to a coherent passage, although the text is still severely abraded in places. Phanias' companion is in mid-speech.)

PHANIAS' COMPANION[a]
                    [Of her position]
You're envious? You've married ['s] daughter,   35
[You]'ve come here, and you [think] that *she* alone
Has money, while *you* haven't?

ΦΑΝΙΑΣ

πάντ᾽ ἐγ[ὼ μό]νης
ταύτης λογίζομαί τε .[.]υ[.....]νεμην.
ἐλευθέρα τ᾽ ἦν καὶ πόλεως Ἑλλη[νί]δος,
40   καὶ πάντα ταῦτ᾽ ἐκτησά[μην].

ΑΝΗΡ

ἀ[γαθ]ῇ τύχῃ.

ΦΑΝΙΑΣ

οὐ δεῖ λαβεῖν με πορνο[βοσκοῦ] θρέμ[ματα.

ΑΝΗΡ

τί δὴ τὸ λυποῦν σ᾽ ἐστί; [τί ποτ᾽ οὐ]κ ἤγαγες
ἐνταῦθα τὴν γυναῖκα κα[ὶ τὴν οὐσία]ν;

ΦΑΝΙΑΣ

οὐκ οἶδ᾽ ὅπου γῆς ἐστιν.

ΑΝΗΡ

οὐ[κ ἐλήλ]υθεν;

ΦΑΝΙΑΣ

45   οὔπω γε· νυνί, τῶν χρόν[ω]ν ὄντων μακρῶν,
λογίζομαι πᾶν, μή τι κατὰ θάλατταν ᾖ
ἀτύχημα γεγονὸς ἢ περὶ [λῃσ]τάς.

40 ἀ[γαθ]ῇ τύχῃ assigned to Phanias' companion by Arnott (a dicolon could have been lost in the mid-line abrasion).
41 θρέμ[ματα suppl. Sandbach   42 [τί ποτ᾽] suppl. Arnott.
43 Suppl. Körte.   44 οὐ[κ ἐλήλ]υθεν assigned to Phanias' companion by Sandbach (εστινου[Berl., apparently).
46 τοπαν Berl.: corr. Wilamowitz.   47 [λῃσ]τάς suppl. van Herwerden.

PHANIAS

All the wealth

Is hers alone, I reckon, [and
Free-born she was, belonged to a Greek city —
[I]'ve gained all *this*, as well!
(*Phanias here points to the extensive baggage sur-
rounding him.*)

PHANIAS' COMPANION

Good luck to you!   40

PHANIAS

No need for me to take tarts (?) from a pimp!

PHANIAS' COMPANION

So what's upsetting you? [Why ever] didn't
You bring your wife here with [the property]?

PHANIAS

I don't know where on earth she is!

PHANIAS' COMPANION

She's not

Arrived?

PHANIAS

Not yet. And with the length of time   45
I picture all the hazards now—at sea
Perhaps some mishap, or with [pirates].[a]

[a] Piracy was especially prevalent throughout the Aegean Sea
in the period after the death of Alexander the Great, when
Menander was writing his plays. See H. A. Ormerod, *Piracy in
the Ancient World* (Liverpool 1924), especially 122–130, and
W. K. Pritchett, *The Greek State at War* 5 (Berkeley, Los Ange-
les, Oxford 1991), 312–324, 339–341.

MENANDER

ΑΝΗΡ

μηθαμῶς.

ΦΑΝΙΑΣ

οὐκ οἶδ᾽· ἀθυμῶ καὶ δέδοιχ᾽ ὑπερβολῇ.

ΑΝΗΡ

εἰκός τι πάσχειν.

ΦΑΝΙΑΣ

πρὸς ἀγορὰν δ᾽ οὕτως ἅμα
50   προάγων ἀκούσῃ καὶ τὰ λοίφ᾽, ὧν μοι γενοῦ
σύμβουλος.

ΑΝΗΡ

οὐθὲν κωλύει με.

ΦΑΝΙΑΣ

ταῦτα δὲ
εἴσω τις ἀ[γέτ]ω τὴν ταχίστην ἐκποδών.

ΜΟΣΧΙΩΝΟΣ ΠΑΤΗΡ

καὶ τί ποτ᾽ ἂν εἴη; πάνυ γὰρ οὐχ αὑτοῦ ποεῖ
ἔργον. μεταπέμπετ᾽ ἐξ ἀγροῦ με Μοσχίων,
55   ὃς ἄλλοτ᾽, εἰ μὲν ἐνθάδ᾽ ὢν τύχοιμ᾽ ἐγώ,
εἰς ἀγρὸν ἔφευγεν· εἰ δ᾽ ἐκεῖσ᾽ ἔλθοιμ᾽ ἐγώ,
ἐνταῦθ᾽ ἀναστρέψας ἔπινε. καὶ μάλα

47 μημαθως Berl.: corr. Maas.
48 αθυμωι Berl.   52 Suppl. Körte.

PHANIAS' COMPANION

(*horrified*)

No!

PHANIAS

I can't be sure. I'm wretched, and extremely
Frightened.

PHANIAS' COMPANION
It's natural to worry.

PHANIAS
Come
To town with me and then you'll hear the rest.   50
I need your guidance here.

PHANIAS' COMPANION
There's nothing to prevent
Me.

PHANIAS
(*to the slave or slaves with the luggage*)
Hurry and get this away inside!

(*While the luggage is conveyed by the slave or slaves
into Phanias' house, Phanias and his companion walk
off by the side-entrance on the right in the direction of
the town-centre. Shortly afterwards Moschion's father
hurries on to the stage by the opposite side-entrance,
having come from his farm in the country.*)

FATHER
Now what the devil's up? It's not like him
At all, this! Moschion has called me from
The farm. Before, when chance has brought me here,   55
He's run off to the farm. When I've gone there,
He's charged back here—and boozed! Quite sensible

125

κατὰ λόγον· οὐ παρῆν ὁ νουθετῶν πατήρ.
οὐκ [εἶχον ὀρ]γήν· καὶ γὰρ αὐτὸς ἐγενόμην
60 εἷς [τῶν δυνα]μένων οὐσίαν μικρὰν ποεῖν.
οὐκ [ἠδίκηκε]ν ἡ γυνὴ κατὰ τοῦτό γε,
ἀλλ' ἐξ ἐμο[ῦ] 'στιν· οὐθὲν ἀγαθὸν γοῦν ποεῖ.
εἰσιτέον εἴ[σω] δ' ἐστίν. ἂν δὲ μὴ τύχῃ
ὧν ἔνδο[ν, ἄρτ]ι πρὸς ἀγορὰν πορεύσομαι·
65 ἐκεῖ γὰρ αὐ[τό]ν που πρὸς Ἑρμαῖς ὄψομαι.

ΜΟΣΧΙΩΝ

ἆρ' οὖν ὁ π[ατὴρ] ἐλήλυθ', ἢ πορευτέον
ἐμοὶ πρ[ὸς ἐκεῖ]νόν ἐστιν; οὐ γὰρ δεῖ χρόνον
τὸ πρᾶ[γμα λαμ]βάνειν [ὅ]λως οὐδ' ὁντινοῦν.
ἤδη δο[κεῖ μοι πρ]οσ[μένειν

ΜΟΣΧΙΩΝΟΣ ΠΑΤΗΡ (?)

70 αἰτεῖν [. . .]αι.ε[
οἶμαι μένειν δεῖ[
προσμεινάτω τὸν ε[

ΜΟΣΧΙΩΝ (?)

[

ΜΟΣΧΙΩΝΟΣ ΠΑΤΗΡ

ἐγὼ δὲ περὶ σοῦ.

ΜΟΣΧΙΩΝ

χαῖρ[ε,

ΜΟΣΧΙΩΝΟΣ ΠΑΤΗΡ

καὶ σύ γε . . . . λε[

58 Corr. Arnott: γαρην Berl.   59 Suppl. Sandbach.
60 [δυνα]μένων suppl. Körte.   62 Suppl. Schubart.

Of him—no father there to criticise!
[I've] not [felt] cross, for I myself was one
Of those who [knew the art] of squandering   60
Their assets. *Here* my wife [is innocent]!
From me he gets it—good-for-nothing that
He is! I'd better go inside. If he's
Not in the house, I'll go [straight] into town.
I'll find him by the Herms[a] there, probably.   65

(*As Moschion's father turns to go off into his house,
Moschion himself enters by the side-entrance to the
right. He does not at first see his father, who pauses in
the background by his door.*)

MOSCHION

Well, has my [father] come, or do I have
To go and find him? This affair can't be
Delayed at all—no, not one second! [I]
Think [I'll wait] now [69

(*At this point we come to the third column of text on the
papyrus, where for some of the lines only the first half is
preserved and for the others less even than that. Because
of this mutilation we cannot be certain about all the*

---

[a] A large group of statues of Hermes at the north-western
entrance to the Athenian agora. This place was particularly asso-
ciated with the young men of the cavalry, and was doubtless a
regular rendezvous of the idler sons of rich men. See H.A.
Thompson and R.E. Wycherley, *The Agora of Athens* (Princeton
1972), 94–96.

---

63 Suppl. Sudhaus.   65, 67, 68 Suppl. Schubart.
69 δο[κεῖ suppl. Wilamowitz, the rest van Herwerden.
70–101 In the mutilated state of this column of text the part-
division at several points is highly uncertain.

MOΣXIΩN

75 οὐκ ἔλεγον εὐθὺς [
    ἀλλ᾽ ἀνδρεϊστέον .. [

MOΣXIΩNOΣ ΠATHP (?)

τίνα λογον; ἀεὶ προσ[
πολλὰ περὶ πολλῶν [

MOΣXIΩN

γῆμαί με βούλει κα[ὶ
80 φρονήσεως γὰρ τοῦτ[ο

*changes of speaker in the next 32 lines, but the general
drift of the dialogue can be followed. After line 69 Mos-
chion moves towards his own door, while his father speaks
two lines and a bit apparently (70–72a), aside from Mos-
chion. This speech includes the phrases* To ask *(70),* I
think [I] ought to stay *(71), and* Let him wait for the *(72).
We may perhaps infer that although the father has
observed the son's arrival, he makes no immediate move
forward, expecting rather that his son should make the
first approach. By line 72 Moschion has evidently seen
his father, and he may possibly have made some remark
now lost (directly to his father, or more probably aside) in
the second part of line 72, to which his father responds
(almost certainly in an aside) with* I too, concerning you!
*at the beginning of 73. Moschion now politely greets his
father,* Hello, *(with the rest of 73), to which his father
responds with the conventional* Hello to you, too *(74).
Moschion then probably makes his first attempt to intro-
duce the subject for which he has sought this interview
with his father, with* I didn't say at first [   ] / But now I
must be brave—[I'll broach a subject] *(75–76). but
before Moschion can explain what his subject is, his father
appears to interrupt him:* What subject? Always [   ] /
A lot about a lot of things [   ] *(77–78). Moschion now
comes to the point:* You'd like me married. [I've held back
before,] / For this [needs] careful thought [and   ]
*(79–80). Before Moschion can explain that he now wishes
to get married (to Phanias' daughter), his father once
again intervenes, launching into a delightfully smug
lecture on how to choose a wife. Even though the text is
infuriatingly mutilated hereabouts, the irony of the
speech comes clearly through.)*

129

ΜΟΣΧΙΩΝΟΣ ΠΑΤΗΡ

ὦ Μοσχίων, ἄλλην μ[
ἕτοιμος, εἰ μὴ προστιθ[
ἦν δεῖ λαβεῖν· αὐτ[..] δὲ [
ἐλευθέραν· τοῦτο πολὺ [

85 μόνον κατὰ λόγον· εἰ δ' α[
πρὸς τὸ γένος ἐστίν· ἀλλ[
εἰ παρθένον δὴ π[ρ]ότε[ρον
σύμβουλον ἂν καλῆς [
αὐτὸς κεκρικὼς [

90 ἃ δὴ δέδωκας [...].[
μηθεὶς ματην.π[.]ω.[

ΜΟΣΧΙΩΝ

τὰ δ' ἄλλ' ἄκουσον. σπ..[

90–91 The speaker here could perhaps be Moschion.
91 μάτην or μὰ τὴν (but none of the conventional male oaths,
e.g. Δήμητρα or Γῆν, fits the traces).

FATHER

Well, Moschion, [I'm] ready [to accept   81
Another, if [you] don't agree to take
[The girl] you ought. [You must be sure to pick
A free-born girl. That's easily [the first
[And] only sound criterion. [Make sure   85
Her pedigree is [spotless. Verify
[That she's] a virgin first! [Words, though, are vain,
If you're consulting [me on marriage, when
[You]'ve chosen [first the bride you want yourself!
So what you've given [90
Let nobody in vain [

*(The bracketed supplements here, it must be emphasised,
are simply speculative attempts at linking the preserved
fragments of text. They assume (perhaps mistakenly) that
Moschion's father had previously chosen for him a bride
whom the son did not want. What emerges most clearly
from the speech, however, is the irony of Moschion's situa-
tion as he listens to his father's description of an accept-
able bride. Moschion wishes to marry Phanias' daughter,
who at this stage of the play appears not to be a free-born
Athenian, but a native of Ephesus; she is no virgin, but
probably pregnant by Moschion; her pedigree would not
be spotless, if her mother was not married to Phanias at
the time of her conception or for years afterwards. Lines
90–91 are of uncertain import; they could alternatively be
the opening lines of Moschion's reply to his father, as the
son describes his own adventures in Ephesus (92 ff.).
Here rather more of Menander's Greek has survived the
mutilation of the column.)*

MOSCHION

But listen to the rest. [I sailed   92

εἰς τὴν Ἔφεσον· ἔπεσον [
τῆς Ἀρτέμιδος ἦν τῆς Ἐ[φεσίας
95 δειπνοφορία τις παρθένω[ν
εἶδον κόρην ἐνταῦθα Φανίου [τινὸς
Εὐωνυμέως.

ΜΟΣΧΙΩΝΟΣ ΠΑΤΗΡ
Εὐωνυμεῖς κἀ[κεῖ τινές
εἰσ' ἐν Ἐφέσῳ;

ΜΟΣΧΙΩΝ
χρέα μὲν οὖν [
ἐντεῦθεν.

ΜΟΣΧΙΩΝΟΣ ΠΑΤΗΡ
ἆρα τοῦ κ[ι]θαριστο[ῦ Φανίου
100 ταύτην λαβεῖν ἐσπούδακ[ας τὴν θυγατέρα
101 τοῦ γείτονος νῦν ὄντος; ου.ο[

(After line 101 the papyrus breaks off.)

*   *   *

93 E.g. ἔπεσον [τότ' (Arnott) εἰς ἔρωτ' ἐγώ (Sandbach).
99 εντανθεν Berl.   100 θυγατέρα suppl. Sudhaus.

---

^a The title of this 'feast-parade', at which young men and maidens of Ephesus annually celebrated the goddess Artemis with a dinner, was the Daitis, according to the late Byzantine *Etymologicum Magnum* (s.v. Δαιτίς). See now C. Calamé, *Les choeurs de jeunes filles en Grèce archaïque*, I (Rome 1977), 178–183.

^b Euonymon was an Attic deme which appears to have been situated about four miles south of the city of Athens and just to

To Ephesus. I fell [in love. You see,
There was for Artemis [of] E[phesus
A girls' parade and feast.[a] [95
I saw there Phanias's girl—[he's] from
Euonymon.[b]

> MOSCHION'S FATHER
>   Euonymeans there
> In Ephesus too?

> MOSCHION
>   No, [he'd gone] from here,
> [Collecting] debts.

> MOSCHION'S FATHER
>   And so [you're] keen to marry
> This [daughter] of the lyrist [Phanias],   100
> Who's now our neighbour? [101

*(At this point the papyrus breaks off, leaving the rest of
this conversation a matter merely for speculation. Mos-
chion may have confessed that he had made this girl preg-
nant and promised to marry her; his father may have
pointed out that the laws of Athens forbade its citizens to
marry non-Athenian girls. It would be folly to take specu-
lation further.)*

*   *   *

the west of the southern slopes of Mount Hymettus (cf. Bölte in
RE vii (1912), s.v. *Halai*, 2226.63 ff.; and J. S. Traill, *The Political
Organization of Attica* (*Hesperia*, Supp. Vol. 14, 1975), 38). By a
curious coincidence, which may well have been exploited by
Menander in a lost part of the play, one of the five civic tribes in
Ephesus was also named Euonymean, according to legend hav-
ing been originally founded by settlers from the Attic deme.

133

MENANDER

Nine fragments quoted from Κιθαριστής
by ancient authors

1 (1 Körte, 281 Kock)

This fragment is a composite, assembled from several
sources. Lines 1–7 (omitting 5A) are cited by Stobaeus, *Eclo-
gae* 4. 33. 13 (σύγκρισις πενίας καὶ πλούτου) with the head-
ing Μενάνδρου. Lines 1–5 (to καθεύδειν) are introduced by
Plutarch, *Moralia* 466a (*De tranquillitate animi* 3) with the
words ἱκανῶς ὁ Μένανδρος ὑπομιμνήσκει (sc. that some
people are believed to pass lives free from pain) λέγων·
ᾤμην—καθεύδειν; he then paraphrases lines 6–7 and finally
quotes lines 8–10. Line 8 on its own became a celebrated
quotation; those who cite it include Stobaeus, *Eclogae* 4. 34.
54 (περὶ τοῦ βίου, ὅτι βραχὺς καὶ εὐτελὴς καὶ φροντίδων
ἀνάμεστος), introducing it as Μενάνδρου Κιθαριστῇ (the
one identification of the play from which this fragment
derives). The fragment also overlaps a papyrus from Oxy-
rhynchus (*P. Turner* 5) which writes its text as if it were prose,
coinciding exactly with Stobaeus' and Plutarch's version of vv.
1–5, adding a new line between 5 and 6, condensing the pre-
viously known version of vv. 6–9 into two lines, and finally
adding three further but now badly mutilated lines.

> ᾤμην ἐγὼ τοὺς πλουσίους, ὦ Φανία,
> οἷς μὴ τὸ δανείζεσθαι πρόσεστιν, οὐ στένειν
> τὰς νύκτας οὐδὲ στρεφομένους ἄνω κάτω
> "οἴμοι" λέγειν, ἡδὺν δὲ καὶ πρᾷόν τινα
> 5 ὕπνον καθεύδειν, ἀλλὰ τῶν πτωχῶν τινα
> 5A κακοπαθίαν ταύτην ἰδίαν [ἐ]λογιζό[μ]ην.
> 6 νυνὶ δὲ καὶ τοὺς μακαρίους καλουμένους
> ὑμᾶς ὁρῶ πονοῦντας ἡμῖν ἐμφερῆ.

134

KITHARISTES

Nine fragments quoted from Kitharistes
by ancient authors

1

The various authors who quote different parts of this frag-
ment are listed on the facing page; most important are Sto-
baeus (who alone identifies the play source, in 'On life, that it
is brief, cheap and full of care') and Plutarch. A papyrus (*P.
Turner* 5) contains a version of these lines possibly prepared
for school use; in some places it abbreviates, in others it sup-
plements the other surviving texts.

Rich people, Phanias, who never need
To raise a loan—I used to think their nights
Weren't fraught with sighs, with tossing up and down
And cries of deep distress. I thought their sleep
Was sweet and gentle—this, though, I believed   5
To be a private misery of the poor.   5A
But now I see that even so-called nobs   6
As rich as you have troubles just like us.

---

2 μήτε Γ group of mss. (Plutarch).   3 ονουδε *P.Turner.* ἀνύκτω
mss. SMA (Stobaeus), ἄνω καὶ κάτω CVJ (Plut.).   4 Above
οιμο[ι] λεγειν (*P.Turner*) traces of (?)]ηξεσθ[as comment or
correction. λέγων A (Stob.). δέ τινα καὶ GZab (Plut.). Above
πραυν (sic) [τ]ινα (*P.Turner*) is written ωμην, repeating the gov-
erning verb from v. 1.   5A τασηδιαν originally *P.Turner* with
correcting υτηνι written above; line omitted by Stobaeus.
6–9 *P.Turner* reduces these four lines to νυνει δε κ[α]ι του[ς]
μακαριους υμα[ς ο]ρω ποιουντας ημειν [......]ν εδοξω β[ι]ω.
7 πονοῦντας Geel: ποιοῦντας SMA (Stobaeus), cf. *P.Turner.*

MENANDER

ἆρ' ἐστὶ συγγενές τι λύπη καὶ βίος;
τρυφερῷ βίῳ σύνεστιν, ἐνδόξῳ βίῳ
10 πάρεστιν, ἀπόρῳ συγκαταγηράσκει βίῳ.
οὐδεὶς [ἀλύπως γὰρ] βεβίωκ' ἄν[θρωπος ὤν·
    ] κατε. .ηπτ.[   ]ρων
13 καταν[

8 Cited also by Diogenes Laertius 7. 68 (naming neither author
nor play), by a schoolboy making a list of Menandrean mono-
stichs (*P.Berlin* 16136 line 5, second century A.D.: first published
by G. Manteuffel, *Journal of Juristic Papyrology* (New York,
Warsaw), 2 (1948) 87 ff. = *Pap.* VI. 5 Jäkel), and in the Byzantine
collections of these monostichs (line 54 Jäkel); it is parodied also
by John of Gaza at the beginning of his *Ecphrasis, Proem* 1.
9 σύνεστιν to βίῳ omitted in G[1] (Plutarch).   10 Line omit-
ted by Y (Plutarch).   11 Suppl. Handley.

2 (2 Kö, 282 and 735 K)

Stobaeus, *Eclogae* 4. 32a. 2 (πενίας ἔπαινος) cites the whole
fragment with the heading Μενάνδρου Κιθαριστῇ. Plu-
tarch, *Moralia* 524e (*De cupiditate diuitiarum* 4) may be
paraphrasing lines 2–3 when he writes τήν γε χρηματικὴν
(sc. πενίαν), ὥς φησιν ὁ Μένανδρος, εἶς ἂν φίλος ἀπαλ-
λάξειεν εὐεργετήσας.

ΦΑΝΙΑΣ (?)

τὸ κουφότατόν σε τῶν κακῶν πάντων δάκνει,
πενία. τί γὰρ τοῦτ' ἐστίν; ἧς γένοιτ' ἂν εἶς
φίλος βοηθήσας ἰατρὸς ῥᾳδίως.

Given to Phanias first apparently by van Leeuwen.

Can pain and life be brothers? Pain may haunt
A life of luxury, sit by a life
Of fame, grow old inside a life of need.   10
No man [on earth] has lived [without some pain].   11

*The papyrus continues with remains of one and a bit more
lines, which are too mutilated to yield up their sense. The
speaker here, obviously a poor man, could be the compan-
ion who entered with Phanias in the second scene of the
Berlin papyrus (31 ff.), here commiserating with him
after Phanias had received some bad news which we can
no longer identify. One possibility would be Phanias' dis-
covery that his daughter was pregnant.*

2

Stobaeus ('Praise of poverty'), identifying the source as
Menander's *Kitharistes*. Plutarch may be paraphrasing lines
2–3 when he writes: Lack of money at least, as Menander
says, can be eliminated by the beneficial service of one
friend.

PHANIAS (?)
The lightest of all ills is bothering
You—poverty! And what is that? One friend
Who helps can medicate it easily.

*Speaker and context cannot be identified with any degree of
confidence, but here we could perhaps have part of Phanias'
reply to what a companion said in fr. 1. In that case Phanias'
point would have been that while poverty could easily be
remedied, his own sufferings were less susceptible to
medicine.*

3 (3 Kö, 382 K)

Stobaeus, *Eclogae* 3. 9. 17 (περὶ δικαιοσύνης), with the heading Μενάνδρου Κιθαριστῇ·

ΜΟΣΧΙΩΝ (?)

εἰ τοὺς ἀδικηθέντας, πάτερ, φευξούμεθα,
τίσιν ἂν βοηθήσαιμεν ἄλλοις ῥᾳδίως;

Given to Moschion first apparently by van Leeuwen. Lemma, Μενάνδρου mss. MA, τοῦ αὐτοῦ ms. S (the previous citation was Menander, *Karchedonios* fr. 4). Κιθαρισταῖς SMA (but Κιθρ- M): corr. Meineke. Line 1 εἰ S: ἐπὶ M (ἐπὶ corrected to εἰ A). φευξόμεθα M.

4 (4 Kö, 284 K)

Stobaeus, *Eclogae* 3. 9. 18 (περὶ δικαιοσύνης), with the heading ἐν ταὐτῷ (sc. as fr. 3, which directly precedes),

τὸ μηθὲν ἀδικεῖν ἐκμαθεῖν γάρ, ὦ Λάχης,
ἀστεῖον ἐπιτήδευμα κρίνω τῷ βίῳ.

5 (5 Kö, 285 K)

Athenaeus 12. 511a: καὶ Μένανδρος δ᾽ ἐν Κιθαριστῇ περί τινος μουσικευομένου λέγων φησί·

φιλόμουσον εἶναι < – ⏑ – > αὐτὸν πάνυ
ἀκούσματ᾽, εἰς τρυφήν τε παιδεύεσθ᾽ ἀεί.

1 Lacuna posited by Sandbach.

3

Stobaeus ('On justice'): in Menander's *Kitharistes*:

MOSCHION (?)

Father, if we avoid the victims of
A wrong, who else can we help easily?

Moschion presumably attempted to persuade his father to let him marry Phanias' daughter, either in the scene whose beginning is preserved in the Berlin papyrus (53 ff.), or later in the play. Fragment 3 could be one of his arguments; Moschion had clearly wronged Phanias by raping his daughter.

4

Stobaeus ('On justice', directly after fr. 3): in the same play,

Laches, I deem that learning never to
Do wrong's a civilised design for life.

In later Greek comedy the name Laches is normally given to older men (see the introduction to Kitharistes); Moschion's father and Phanias' companion are the two known candidates in this play. If Laches was Moschion's father, the speaker here is unlikely to have been the son, for sons in Menander do not address their fathers by name.

5

Athenaeus: Menander too in *Kitharistes* mentions a man playing a musical instrument, and says,

He's fond of music, quite [adores] good tunes,
And studies every day the primrose path!

Phanias seems to be the subject of this fragment, and clearly its speaker is biased against him. Could this have been Moschion's father, opposing his son's projected marriage?

MENANDER

6 (6 Kö, 286 K)

Athenaeus 6. 247ef: μνημονεύει δὲ τοῦ μὲν οἰκοσίτου . . .
Μένανδρος . . . ἐν Κιθαριστῇ·

οὐκ οἰκοσίτους τοὺς ἀκροατὰς λαμβάνεις.

7 (7 Kö, 287 K)

Stobaeus, *Eclogae* 4. 46. 9 (περὶ ἐλπίδος), with the heading
Μενάνδρου Κιθαριστοῦ·

οὕτω τι πρᾶγμ' ἐστ' ἐπίπονον τὸ προσδοκᾶν.

lemma Κιθαριστοῦ ms. M: Κιθαριστῇ ms. A.

8 (8 Kö, 288 K)

Stobaeus, *Eclogae* 1. 7. 1 (ὅτι ἀλόγιστος ἡ φορὰ τῆς
τύχης), with the heading Μενάνδρου Κιθαριστοῦ. The line
appears also in the Byzantine collections of monostichs
ascribed to Menander (874 Jäkel).

ὡς ποικίλον πρᾶγμ' ἐστὶ καὶ πλάνον τύχη.

9 (9 Kö, 289 K)

Photius (2. 164 Naber) s.v. σκοῖδος· ταμίας τις καὶ διοικη-
τής· Μακεδονικὸν δὲ τοὔνομα, διόπερ Μένανδρος ἐν Κιθα-
ριστῇ σκοῖδον Διόνυσον λέγει.

6

Athenaeus: the word οἰκόσιτος (living at one's own expense / paying for oneself) is mentioned by ... Menander ... in *Kitharistes*:

Your audiences aren't paying for themselves!

Phanias presumably is here addressed by somebody who claims that the lyre-player needed to bribe his audiences to listen to him.

7

Stobaeus ('On hope'): from Menander's *Kitharistes*,

So wearisome a thing is expectation!

Phanias, waiting for his wife? Moschion, hoping to marry Phanias' daughter? Or somebody trying to commiserate with one of these?

8

Stobaeus ('That the swing of fortune is irrational'): from Menander's *Kitharistes*,

How checkered and two-faced a thing is chance!

See also the facing page. Speaker and context are unknown.

9

Photius defining σκοῖδος: a governor, steward; the noun is Macedonian, and so in *Kitharistes* Menander calls Dionysus a σκοῖδος.

In Sophocles' Antigone 1152 the chorus call Iacchus, with whom Dionysus is often identified, 'the steward', but it would be unwise without further information to speculate about Menander's intentions here in using an unusual word.

Four further citations and a papyrus fragment,
whose attribution to Κιθαρίστης *is highly uncertain*

Fragments 10 to 13 inclusive are quotations from Menander with no title specified, but they have all been tentatively assigned to *Kitharistes* (10 and 11 by A. Borgogno, *Hermes* 99 (1971), 274 f.; 12 and 13 by F. H. Sandbach, *Commentary* 418) solely because a character named Phanias is addressed certainly in three of them and conceivably in the fourth (13), if a doubtful conjecture is there accepted. *P. Oxyrhynchus* 3968 (O), a mutilated fragment of later Greek comedy, also mentions a Phanias; for this reason its first editor suggested its assignment to *Kitharistes*. All five attributions are possible, but they vary in probability. Although Phanias appears as a character only in *Kitharistes* among extant papyrus texts of Menander, it is unlikely that the name was used only in

10

P. Vienna 19999A (first published by Hans Oellacher, *Mitteilungen aus der Papyrussammlung der Nationalbibliothek in Wien*, 3rd series (1939), 36 ff. = *Pap.* IV in Jäkel's edition of the monostichs) is a schoolboy's collection, written in the first century A.D., of 24 monostichs each beginning with a different letter of the Greek alphabet. The first runs

ὦ Φανία, μὴ πρόσεχε διαβολαῖς μά[την.

μά[την suppl. Oellacher.

11

The eighth monostich in *P. Vienna* 19999A runs

ῥᾴθυμος ἂν ᾖς, Φανία, πένης ἔσει.

*Four further citations and a papyrus fragment,
whose attribution to Kitharistes is highly uncertain*

this one play. A man named Phania is mentioned in three
plays by Terence (*Andria* 928 ff., *H.T.* 169, *Hecyra* 458:
the first two adapted from Menandrean originals) as a
person implicated in the plot but not appearing on stage.
When Cicero, *Ad fam.* 2. 13. 2 refers to a Phania as a 'wit-
ness from comedy', and Lucian, *Dial. Meretr.* 4 gives a
lover named Phanias to a courtesan named Bacchis, the
impression gained by the reader is that this name was not
uncommonly given to old men in comedy. On the other
hand, Alciphron's allusion (3. 11) to 'the wealthy Phanias'
may well be a memory of Menander's *Kitharistes*, where
Phanias was portrayed as rich (see fr. 1 and possibly also
11).

10

A schoolboy's exercise on a papyrus now in Vienna contains
24 disconnected lines of Menander, including

> Don't waste your time on scandal, Phanias.

*If this line does come from Kitharistes, its speaker and con-
text are unknown. Aspersions are made about and to Phanias
in fragments 5 and 6, however, and there seems to have been
at least one skeleton in Phanias' cupboard, if his own daugh-
ter was conceived as a result of a rape (see the introduction to
Kitharistes).*

11

Fragment 10's papyrus also contains the following line, which
is cited also in another papyrus and in Byzantine collections
of monostichs (see opposite):

> Be lazy, Phanias, and you'll be poor!

This line occurs in other collections of monostichs (*P. Bouriant* 1, first published by P. Jouguet and P. Perdrizet, *Studien zur Palaeographie und Papyruskunde* (Leipzig), 6 (1906), 148 ff., line 17 = *Pap.* II. 17 Jäkel; line 698 of the Byzantine collections in Jäkel).

Fragment 11 ἂν or ἐὰν Byzantine collections: εαν the two papyri. ἧς *P. Vienna*, Byzantine collections: εση *P. Bouriant*. φανια *P. Vienna*: πλούσιος a trivialising variant in *P. Bouriant* and Byzantine collections.

12 (797 KT)

Strabo 10. 5. 6 (p. 486 Casaubon): παρὰ τούτοις (sc. the inhabitants of Ceos) δὲ δοκεῖ τεθῆναί ποτε νόμος, οὗ μέμνηται καὶ Μένανδρος·

καλὸν τὸ Κείων νόμιμόν ἐστι, Φανία·
ὁ μὴ δυνάμενος ζῆν καλῶς οὐ ζῇ κακῶς.

προσέταττε γάρ, ὡς ἔοικεν, ὁ νόμος τοὺς ὑπὲρ ἑξήκοντα ἔτη γεγονότας κωνειάζεσθαι τοῦ διαρκεῖν τοῖς ἄλλοις τὴν τροφήν.

This note (with its quotation) is substantially copied by Stephen of Byzantium s.v. Ἰουλίς (Iulis was the chief town of Ceos). Parts of the fragment appear, garbled and without any attribution (καλὸν τὸ Κεῖον νόμιμον and ὁ μὴ καλῶς ζῶν οὐ ζῇ κακῶς), in Byzantine collections of proverbs (L. Cohn, *Philologus*, suppl. 6 (1882), 256 f., 263; O. Crusius, *ibid.* 267 f.).

---

[a] The only plausible occasion for such an Athenian siege was directly after the battle of Marathon, when Miltiades raided Paros and some of the neighbouring islands. See A. M. Pridik, *De Cei insulae rebus* (Berlin 1892), 24 ff., and F. Lasserre's Budé edition of Strabo, book 10 (Paris 1971).

Context and speaker are unknown. It is curious, however, that other citers of this line corruptly substitute the word 'affluent' for the name 'Phanias' (sc. 'If you're lazy as well as affluent, you'll be poor'). In Kitharistes Phanias was certainly portrayed as a wealthy man (see the introduction to frs. 10–13), and this fact might help to explain the corruption in these other versions of the line, as well as giving indirect support to its attribution to this play.

12

Strabo: These people (sc. the inhabitants of Ceos) apparently once had a law enacted, which Menander in fact recalls:

> That Cean custom's splendid, Phanias —
> The man who can't live nobly won't live ill!

The law apparently ordered men over sixty to take hemlock, in order that there might be food enough left for the remainder.

Strabo identified the occasion of this enactment as an Athenian siege which was raised before the new provisions were carried out.[a] Ceos (today called Kea or Tziá) is a small island in the Cyclades 13 miles east of Cape Sunium. In Menander's time this law was presumably no more than a folk memory, providing a source for pleasantries like that of the unidentified speaker here, who plays on the ambiguity in 'won't live ill' (is the negative attached to 'live' or 'ill'?). The reason for the pleasantry is now difficult to grasp. Admittedly the Phanias of Kitharistes suffered hard blows during the course of the play, such as his wife's apparent disappearance and the disgrace of his daughter's pregnancy. He could easily have expressed a feeling that life was no longer worth living, and so invited this riposte.

13 (544 KT)

Stobaeus, *Eclogae* 4. 1. 31 (περὶ πολιτείας), with the heading Μένανδρου (ms. M) or τοῦ αὐτοῦ (ms. A: the previous extract being Menander fr. 543 KT),

> ἔργον ἐστί, Φανία,
> μακρὰν συνήθειάν <τιν’> ἐν βραχεῖ χρόνῳ
> λῦσαι.

Lemma omitted in ms. Br.   1 Φανία Gataker: πανία mss. MA, παπία (which could be right) Br.   2–3 συνήθειαν ἐν βραχεῖ λῦσαι χρόνῳ mss.: corr. Arnott.

P. Oxyrhynchus 3968 (O)

column i: line ends

1	]ει, Σωσία		] ὦ θ[ε]οί,
	ὥ]σπερ τυφλῷ		ἀ]κήκοα
	]ντω[.]· τί γάρ		κε]κτημένης
	] Παρθενί		].
5	] ἐνθάδε	20	] Σωσία
	] λανθάνειν		] πάνυ
	λανθά]νειν, τάλαν		].[ ]α·
	] δυστυχῆ		]..α·
	μ]έσου		]νθανε
10	]της τρέφειν	25	ἐλ]αβεν
	τ]ρέφεις		].εσ.ν
	] Φανίας		]..[
	]λο. λαβεῖν		]ι.ν[
	].. λέγων		]λα[
15	προ]κόλπιον	30	].[

All the decipherments and supplementation here were made by the ed. pr., E. W. Handley, except in line 9 (Turner). Raised

13

Stobaeus ('On government'): with the heading 'from Menander' or 'from the same author' (sc. as the previous extract),

> Phanias,[a] it's hard
> To end long years of comradeship in a
> Few moments.

Context and speaker are unknown, and hardly worthy of speculation since attribution of this fragment to Kitharistes is so questionable.

[a] Or 'Daddy', if one accepts here an equally plausible conjecture.

P. Oxyrhynchus 3968 (O)

This papyrus scrap contains the ends of the top 30 lines from one column (i) and the beginnings of the top twenty from the next (ii); the interval between i.30 and ii.1 could be anything up to 25 lines, since columns of 55 lines are not unknown. Only individual words survive from each line.

Column i: 1 O Sosias, 2 just as to one blind, 3 what?, 4 (?) O Parthenis, 5 here, 6 to conceal, 7 [con]ceal? Dear me!, 8 unfortunate, 9 (?) middle, 10 to rear, 11 you rear, 12 Phanias, 13 to take, 14 *(a man)* saying, 15 breast-fold, 16 O gods!, 17 I've heard, 18 mistress, 20 O Sosias, 21 quite, 24 (?) conceal, 25 he took.

Two speakers can be identified in column i: a slave named Sosias (addressed at 1, 20) and a woman ('Dear me!' in 7

---

points have been identified at the ends of i.22 and i.23, and dicola suspected at the ends of i.1 and i.12.

column ii: line beginnings

1   πρὶν [
    ἐλευ.[
    τί προ[
    ἀλλ' ἐτε[
5   καὶ Θαῒς [
    κάλλισ[τ
    τουτ.[
    μόνος [
    το]ὺς παῖδ[ας
10 ἰχθῦς ἀπ[
    αὐτοὺς πε.[
    λιβανωτ[ὸ
    ἄπ[α]ν ὑπο[
    ε. .[   ].ο.[
15 ηγ.[
    τηρ[
    ε.θη.[
    παρα.[
    παρι.[
20 .[

*is confined to, and the oath in 16 is common with, women)
perhaps called Parthenis, if the decipherment in 4 is cor-
rect. The woman seems to be listening to a tale or scheme,
presumably outlined by Sosias, that affects her emotion-
ally; it may involve concealment (6 f.) and a new-born
baby that is being reared (10 f.; the breast-fold of a
woman's dress was used for concealing recognition-tokens
in Epitrepontes 382: see vol. I p. 430 n. 1).*

*Column ii: 1 Before, 2 Free or Will come, 3 What, 4 But,
5 And Thais, 6 Finest or No, thank you, 7 This, 8 Alone,
9 The slaves or The boys, 10 Fish, 11 Them, 12 Incense,
13 All.*

*Whether the same two speakers are involved in column ii
is uncertain. The mentions there of 'fish' (10) and
'incense' (12) are puzzling.*

*The reference to a Phanias in i.12 inspired the
papyrus' first editor tentatively to identify the source of
this fragment as Kitharistes; this attribution can be sup-
ported by its possible references to a new-born baby, if
Moschion's rape of Phanias' daughter in that play had
resulted in a pregnancy.[a] Yet other characters named
Phanias may have existed in lost plays of Menander,[b] and
the mention of a Thais in ii.5 of the papyrus must provide
a stumbling block to the attribution, since there appears
to be no place for a hetaira with this name in what is so far
known of this play's plot.*

[a] See the introduction to *Kitharistes*.
[b] See the introduction to fragments 10–13 above.

KOLAX
(THE FAWNER)

INTRODUCTION

Manuscripts

O.1 = *P. Oxyrhynchus* 409 + 2655, the broken remains of four columns of a single papyrus of the second century A.D., which originally contained a selection of excerpts from the play (see below). Preserved in whole or part are lines A1–13, B14–53, C190–199, D200–224 and E225–255. First editions: of *P.Oxy.* 409, B. P. Grenfell and A. S. Hunt, *The Oxyrhynchus Papyri*, 3 (1903), 17–26, with two photographs (pls. II, III, containing the ends of A2, A6, the scholion on B28, B34–53, C190–D203, D215–224, E225–237); of *P.Oxy.* 2655, E. G. Turner, *The Oxyrhynchus Papyri*, 33 (1968), 9–14, with two photographs (pls. II, III, containing D204–224 with D204–220 also at double size, E225–232, E238–255 and line ends of B33–53).

O.5 = *P. Oxyrhynchus* 1237, scraps from presumably a complete text of the play, written probably in the third century A.D. It contains the ends of B52–69, the beginnings of B90–98 and five other unplaced scraps (here fr. 13a–e). First edition: A. S. Hunt, *The Oxyrhynchus Papyri*, 10 (1914), 93–95; no photograh is published.

O.25 = *P. Oxyrhynchus* 3534, a further tiny and unplaced (here = fr. 12) scrap of papyrus from the third century

153

A.D. First edition: E. W. Handley, *The Oxyrhynchus Papyri*, 50 (1983), 49 f. with a photograph (pl. I).

Fragments 1 to 11 are quotations in later authors (see Introduction to Volume I, pp. xxiv f.), 1 to 6 being firmly, but 7 to 11 only conjecturally, assigned to the play. Fragments 12 (= O.25) and 13 (a–e; from O.5) are unplaced scraps of papyrus. These fragments are printed after the end of the continuous play text, together with three testimonia to the play.

Of Menander's *Kolax* only about 50 lines can be printed entire, and another 90 or so with gaps, but their interpretation and relation to the plot are complicated by three unusual features.

  (i) O.1, the main source of what survives, never contained a complete text of the play, but was simply a collection of excerpts. Some of the evidence for this is clearly visible on the papyrus: a one-line gap between A13 and B14 most probably marking the end of one excerpt and the beginning of the next,[1] the use of a $\delta\iota\pi\lambda\hat{\eta}\ \dot{\omega}\beta\epsilon\lambda\iota\sigma$-$\mu\acute{\epsilon}\nu\eta$ (a critical sign in the shape of >—) under line B53 and above C190 to signify the end of an excerpt, and the fact that one excerpt begins in the middle of a verse (C190), although the scribe aligned its opening word with the normal left margin. O.5, which must originally have held a text of the whole play, provides further proof, because it contains fragments of lines (B54–69, B90–98) that followed the end of one (B) of O.1's excerpts. There are several possible explanations for such an excerption of

  [1] For a less probable alternative explanation see the text *ad loc.*

Kolax. In the third century B.C. a new form of performance became popular all over the Greek-speaking world, in which small groups of professional entertainers performed extracts from earlier Greek dramas, often setting them to music.[1] Secondly, Plutarch (*Mor.* 673a–b, 712b–d, 854a–b) notes that informal recitations of excerpts from Menander's plays became a stylish feature in symposia. Thirdly, Plato (*Laws* 7. 811a, cf. *Protagoras* 325e–326a) mentions the practice of memorising selected passages from drama as an important element in a boy's education at school. O.1 could have been designed for any of these three activities.

(ii) A second complication arises from the fact that Plautus appears to have adapted Menander's play for the Roman stage in his *Colax.* Only three short fragments (and a disputed fourth) survive from the Plautine comedy; although none of them exactly translates anything remaining from Menander's Κόλαξ, their subject-matter is closely related to that of the Greek original. Fr. I of *Colax* appears to be a personal or reported claim of the soldier to have possessed a golden goblet, matching at least the ambience of Κόλαξ fr. 2; the Plautine fr. II, like Κόλαξ C195 ff., introduces flatterers and kings together into one context, but the point is different; and the request for an invitation in *Colax* fr. III could be addressed by Gnathon's counterpart to Pheidias' with reference to the meal with whose organisation the latter

[1] Surviving examples are listed by B. Gentili, *Theatrical Performances in the Ancient World* (Amsterdam and Uithoorn 1979), 19 f. See now also Menander, *Perikeiromene* 796, and my introduction to that play.

155

seems in Menander to have been involved (Κόλαξ A10 ff., fr. 1).[1]

(iii) A final and much more difficult complication is provided by the Latin poet Terence's admission in the prologue to his *Eunuchus* (30–33 = testimonium II) that when adapting Menander's Εὐνοῦχος for his play, he introduced into it two characters from Menander's Κόλαξ, the fawning parasite (*parasitus colax*) and the braggart soldier (*miles gloriosus*). Although too little survives from either Menander's Εὐνοῦχος or his Κόλαξ for us to establish with certainty just what material Terence took from the latter play, those sections of Terence's *Eunuchus* in which the soldier Thraso and his parasite Gnatho are involved contain a great amount of material designed to amuse the audience without advancing the plot (232–253, 255–264, 395–433), as well as providing scenes which require four speaking actors (454–506, 785–811, 1025–1094). It is plausible to assume from these facts alone that Terence was largely telling the truth at *Eunuchus* 30–32, and that his replacement of a single character in Menander's Εὐνοῦχος by the *Kolax's* duo of soldier and parasite forced him to stage several scenes where they were present with more than Menander's maximum of three speaking characters. Fortunately this assumption is supported by a little adventitious evidence: Κόλαξ frs. 3 certainly and 5 probably were adapted by Terence at *Eunuchus* 498 (cf. also 425 f.) and 238, while Donatus (on v. 228 = testimonium III) implies that parts

---

[1] See also V. Jarcho's discussion in M. Capasso (ed.), *Papiri letterari greci e latini: Papyrologica lupiensia*, I (Galatina Congedo 1992), 325–330.

at least of *Eunuchus* 232–291 were taken from Menander's Κόλαξ.

The Terentian connection implies that Menander's Κόλαξ is likely to have been a play in which a soldier, accompanied by a self-interested fawner, was the rival of a free young man for the favours of an expensive *hetaira*. Such a scenario does not conflict with most of the information that can be gleaned from the surviving fragments of Κόλαξ. These provide some relevant characters: for instance a soldier named Bias (B32, lemma of fr. 2, name of speaker in fr. 12 v. 6) and a free young man named Pheidias (B19); but they point also to some differences from Terence's *Eunuchus*. In the Roman play Thais is a *meretrix* operating independently but in search of a patron; in Κόλαξ her counterpart seems to have been owned by a pimp (πορνοβοσκός B19, the speaker of E225–237). If the final scene of Terence's *Eunuchus* was adapted from that of Κόλαξ, as now seems generally agreed,[1] Menander's play would have had a surprising but characteristically unsentimental ending in which the fawner persuaded the free young man and the soldier to share the *hetaira* and thereby secured his own future prosperity (cf. Terence, *Eunuchus* 1058–1060, 1084–1088).

In the Roman play there is only one fawner or parasite, named Gnatho; the fragments of Menander's Κόλαξ, however, appear to provide evidence of two: one called Gnathon ('Jawman': B67, B68), the other Strouthias ('Sparrow': frs. 2 with its lemma, 3 and 10). The

---

[1] See now J. Barsby's edition of the play, commentary on Act V scene viii (forthcoming, Cambridge).

references to Strouthias clearly show that he was the soldier's companion and so the counterpart of Terence's Gnatho, but who then was Menander's Gnathon? There are two possibilities. Gnathon and Strouthias could have been different names borne by a single character, who adopted Strouthias as an alias when associating with the soldier, but used his real name Gnathon when talking to other characters such as Pheidias and Daos. In three plays of Plautus parasites exploited two names: Curculio in the play named after him adopts the name Summanus for a trick (413), while Ergasilus in *Captiui* has the nickname Scortum (69), and Gelasimus in *Stichus* refers to himself once (242) as Miccotrogus. Yet if Gnathon was the real name of the title figure in Menander's Κόλαξ and Strouthias only an assumed name, why then does one papyrus (O.10) identify the speaker of its line 5 as Strouthias rather than Gnathon? Accordingly it seems wiser to accept the alternative possibility and simply assume that in this play Bias and Gnathon were different characters, the latter being a parasite who had perhaps attached himself to Pheidias during the absence abroad of the latter's father.[1] A plot in which the two rival lovers were encouraged by their more imaginative lackeys into schemes aimed at winning the *hetaira* from the pimp by force or trickery would have offered plenty of scope for a New-Comedy poet, and made an ending in which she was shared between them piquantly apposite.

[1] Admittedly Menander's title is Κόλαξ in the singular, but that could be accounted for by the fact that Strouthias may have been the dominant character in the play (like the title figure of Terence's *Phormio*), and Gnathon by comparison only a subordinate figure.

KOLAX

The scanty remains of Κόλαξ yield a little further information about its characters and plot. Bias' career as a mercenary appears to have made him a successful and wealthy man (B15, B29, B37 f., B42–44, B50, E231). A dinner in celebration of the goddess Aphrodite (fr. 1) provided an appropriate highlight in a play focussing on purchased sex; if Pheidias was the speaker of A1–13, he may have been one of the celebrants. Several other characters with roles in the play are named—slaves named Daos (speaker at B67 and B92), Doris (see on B18) and perhaps Trachelion (see on fr. 12).

No hypothesis, didascalic notice, or cast-list is preserved for *Kolax*.[1] Although its date of production is nowhere recorded, the surviving fragments of text include three references to external events and people which place it between the late 320s and 300. At D205 the speaker mentions Astyanax, a celebrated athlete who won his event three times running at the Olympic games, and one of these successes was in 316 B.C. From fr. 2 we learn that Bias had served in Cappadocia, a large province of the old Persian Empire that stretched from the Taurus mountains in the south to the Black Sea in the north and the River Euphrates in the east; it was fought over by

---

[1] Identification of Menander's Κόλαξ as the source of the papyrus fragments listed above (O.5, O.25, excerpt B at least of O.1) rests on three facts: (i) B42–44 were already attributed to the play by Stobaeus (*Eclogae* 3. 10. 21), (ii) O.5 overlaps with O.1, (iii) O.25 has two character names (Bias, Strouthias) which are known from quotations of the play in Athenaeus 10. 434c (fr. 2) and Plutarch, *Moralia* 57a (frs. 3 and 2. 3–4). It is reasonable to assume that the other excerpts in O.1 also come from Κόλαξ, but the evidence for this is entirely circumstantial.

Alexander's successors, and Diodorus Siculus describes campaigns there with Greek soldiers in 322 (31. 19), 320 (18. 40), 315 (19. 57. 4, 60. 2) and 302/1 (19. 113. 4). Fr. 4 alleges that Bias had been the lover of some notorious *hetairai* in Athens, including two (Chrysis, Anticyra) who co-operated with Demetrius Poliorcetes in turning the Parthenon into a brothel in 304/3.

Previous editions of Κόλαξ number the surviving lines continuously and thus fail to indicate that its main papyrus source contains only excerpts. In this Loeb edition each of the certainly separate extracts (there may in fact be more of them than have yet been identified) is distinguished by a prefixed letter (A–E). The line numbers that then follow agree most closely with those in C. Austin's edition (*Comicorum Graecorum Fragmenta in Papyris Reperta*, Berlin 1973, pp. 171–179), but in order to avoid any duplication of numbers that might result from the discovery of O.5, I have added 100 arbitrarily to all line numbers from C190 (= 90 Austin) onwards. The numberings found in Körte's third edition (Kö), in Sandbach (S), and (where differing) in Austin (Au) are appended in brackets.

Dramatis personae, so far as they are known:

Pheidias, a free young man in love with a *hetaira*
Bias, a wealthy soldier in love with the same *hetaira*
Strouthias, Bias' lackey, the fawner of the title
Daos, a male slave, perhaps Pheidias' attendant
A pimp, owner of the *hetaira*
A cook

Gnathon, lackey to another character, possibly Pheidias
(unless Gnathon is another name used by Strouthias)
? Trachelion, another male slave, if this name is correctly
identified

In the missing sections of the play other characters will
have had speaking parts: including certainly the *hetaira*
who was loved by both Pheidias and Bias, and possibly
Doris, a female slave, and Sosias, the cook's slave, unless
these were mutes. There was presumably also a chorus to
perform the entr'actes.

ΚΟΛΑΞ

Excerpt A

(*This extract looks like an expository entrance monologue from early in the play, in which the speaker first describes past events of his life succinctly but, because of gaps in the text, puzzlingly. It seems that his father, like several others in Greco-Roman comedy—Demeas in Menander's Samia, Theopropides and Charmides in Plautus' Mostellaria and Trinummus, Demipho in Terence's Phormio—had gone abroad on business, leaving the speaker in an*

(The identity of the male speaker is uncertain, but the substance of his remarks suggests a free young man, probably Pheidias.)

ΦΕΙΔΙΑΣ (?)

ἄπι]στον ἐν τῷ νῦν βίῳ

]ων τῶν πατέρων γεγενημένος·

]ς υἱόν, ὡς πᾶσιν δοκε[ῖ.

(1 Kö, S)

In the apparatus to this play, those conjectures and supplements whose author is not named were made by the edd. prr. of O.1 (*P.Oxy.* 409) and O.5 (*P.Oxy.* 1237), B. P. Grenfell and A. S. Hunt. A1–A13 O.1. A1 Suppl. Turner.

KOLAX

(The Fawner)

Excerpt A

*otherwise empty house (4–5). A young child of unspeci-
fied sex is then described as being under the control of
guardians (6); this child may have been a girl with a role
in a sub-plot. In line 8 the speaker succumbs to his
present misery, perhaps a result of some success by the
wealthier Bias in attracting the services of the hetaira that
they both love. At line 10 he mentions an urgent duty,
connected with a social occasion. This is most likely to
have been the dinner in honour of Aphrodite Pandemos
for which the cook of fr. 1 was hired; we do not know who
was in charge of the arrangements (line 12), but the
speaker seems to have been asked to receive (13) the par-
ticipants in his own house.)*

PHEIDIAS (?)

suspicious] in my present life.

a child of [   ] fathers.

] son, as all agree.

] ἐπὶ πράξεις τινά[ς

A5 τὴν ο]ἰκίαν ἐμοὶ κενήν

τ]ὸ παιδάριον· [α]ὐτὸς τροφήν,

(7)]ν διοικηταῖς τισιν·

ὦ κακό]δαιμον, τυχὸν ἴσως

]ων ἀθλίως οὔ[τ]ω σφόδρα·

A10 τοῦ]τό μοι π[ο]ητέον

σ]ύνοδος ἡμῶν γ[ί]νεται

(12)] ἑστιάτωρ δεσ[π]ότης

A13] δέχεσθαι <δ᾽> εἶ[πέ] μοι

(In the papyrus between excerpts A and B there appears to be a vacant line dividing the two, unless—a less likely alternative—excerpt A continued with the beginning of a further line, now torn off.)

Excerpt B

(The second extract is a dialogue at first apparently between two characters. One is Pheidias, addressed by name at B19, and his remarks, at least in the earlier part of this excerpt, are easily picked out, since he seems to be presented as a self-pitying wimp. The person conversing with him in the earlier exchanges is harder to identify. He is certainly male (addressed as ἄθλιε B25), and this rules out Doris, mentioned in the corruptly unmetrical B18. This leaves most plausibly either a slave such as Daos,

A5 Suppl. Sudhaus.   A6, A8 Suppl. Leo.   A11 γε[.]νεται O.1 (γ[ί]γνεται Grenfell and Hunt).   A13 <δ᾽> suppl. Arnott.

>] on some business ventures.
>
>] the house to me unoccupied   A5
>
>] the young child, whose upbringing he
>
> Himself [entrusted   ] to some guardians
>
> Oh! un]happy me, perhaps
>
>] in such depths of misery.
>
> this] is what I must do —   A10
>
>] we have a gathering
>
>] host and M.C.
>
>] and told (?) me to receive.   A13

Excerpt B

(It is impossible to know where in the play comes the scene from which this excerpt derives, but if papyrus O.1 arranges its excerpts in their dramatic order, B will form part of an early scene subsequent to A. The extract begins with a conversation between Pheidias and probably Gnathon, but its first eleven lines (B14–24) are too badly damaged to allow translation line by line. Pheidias is the

who could have been Pheidias' personal attendant, or one
of the two parasites, if we assume that there were two. As
Gnathon's name is twice mentioned later in the scene, the
second time in an address to him (B67, B68), it is perhaps
safer to guess that it was he who was present with Phei-
dias at the beginning of this excerpt.)

ΦΕΙΔΙΑΣ

B14 (15)   ].α δεῖ το. .εντ[.].[. .]
B15   λα]μπρὸν ἢ δόξῃ μέγαν.
   ]ν· εἰ δὲ μή, τρίτον
   ]αινιαν· ἀγρίαν ἄγε
   ]αρα.

ΓΝΑΘΩΝ (?)

   νῦν ἐγὼ †Δωρὶς†
(20)   θαρρεῖ]ν, Φειδία.

ΦΕΙΔΙΑΣ

   θαρρεῖν; ἐμοὶ
B20   τῆ]ς ἐμ[ῆ]ς ταύτης μέλει
   ] εἴπῃ φλήναφον·
   ὦ δέσποι]ν' Ἀθηνᾶ, σῷζέ με.

ΓΝΑΘΩΝ (?)

   ἀ]κριβῶς τὰ πάτρια
(25)   το]ὺς αὐτο[ύ]ς, πόλεις
B25   ]ουσι.

B17 εγωδωρις unmetrically at line-end; δωρις perhaps added
here by the scribe because it had been omitted earlier in this line
or somewhere in the next.   B19 Suppl. Leo, Sudhaus.

*first speaker (B14–18). He describes somebody (? the sol-
dier Bias) as* glorious or mighty by repute *(B15); this is
followed by puzzling references to* if not, a third *(B16) and*
bring a wild *(B17). The other man appears to respond
with something like* I [advise you] now to [cheer up],
Pheidias *(B18–19), but plausible supplementation of the
lacuna there and interpretation of the surviving text are
further bedevilled by the scribal error of a non-metrical
insertion of the female slave name* Doris *after the word* I.
*Pheidias' retort (B19–22) seems pathetic, but lacunae in
our text also make it puzzling:* Cheer up? This [/   ] of
mine is my concern! / [   ] talk *(or talks)* utter rot! /
[Lady] Athena, rescue me! *The depression which
inspires Pheidias' prayer will presumably have sprung
from his jealousy at Bias' success with the hetaira. The
other speaker apparently now attempts a high-faluting
explanation of the present situation, with references to*
exactly our ancestral customs *(B23) and* the same [   ],
cities *(B24), although the textual gaps blur the point of his
remarks. The passage that follows allows line-by-line
translation, despite the presence of some infuriating gaps.
Bias' present wealth is contrasted with his past tribula-
tions, and ascribed to some villainy or other.)*

B20 Suppl. Leo.   B22 ὦ suppl. Sudhaus.   B23]κρειβως
O.1: suppl. Grenfell and Hunt, corr. Körte.   B24 ποιλεις O.1
before correction.   B25 μάτην γὰρ εὐσεβ]οῦσι suppl. Sud-
haus.

ΦΕΙΔΙΑΣ

τί λέγεις, ἄθλιε;

ΓΝΑΘΩΝ (?)

τοῖς] πονηροῖς τοὺς θεοὺς
οὐδὲ]ν ἀγαθὸν πράττομεν·
ἀλλ' ὅδ' ὁ διμοιρίτης] φέρων αὐτός ποτε
(30)   θύλακ]ον, πήραν, κράνος,
B30   ]ον, διβολίαν, κώδιον,
           τ]ύχης ὄνος φέρει
           ἐξ]αίφνης Βίας
           ]νεμον.

ΦΕΙΔΙΑΣ

τὸν ἐνθαδὶ
(35)   ... κακοδαι]μ[ο]νοῦντα πέρυσι[...].ει.[
B35   .... τ]ὴν διατριβὴν παρέ[χον]τα σ.[
      απ[......]ον· σκωπ[τ]ομένου[...].σπ[
      ευπ[.... πεν]τήκοντα πα[ῖ]δες ἐχόμε[νοι
      οπο[....]..[.]ης ὄ[π]ισθεν. οἴχομαι.

ΓΝΑΘΩΝ (?)

(40)   ..κ[........] κατέπτηκέν ποθε[ν
B40   πόλ[ιν προδούς τι]ν' ἢ σατράπην ἢ στ[ρατόπεδον
      π.[.........]νεστι δῆλός ἐστι.

B26 μᾶλλον βοηθεῖν τοῖς] suppl. Sudhaus.   B27 Suppl.
Leo.   B28 ἀλλ' ὅδ' ὁ suppl. Körte, διμοιρίτης Grenfell and
Hunt from the marginal scholion in O.1: διμοιρίτ(ης)· ὁ
διπλοῦν λαμβάνων τῶν στρατιωτ(ῶν) μισθόν.   B29 Suppl.
Austin (cf. Men. *Karchedonios* 109).   B30 διαβολιαν O.1
before correction.   B34 Suppl. Leo.   B35 τ]ὴν suppl.

PHEIDIAS

       Rascal, what do you mean?   B25

GNATHON (?)

The gods [are more inclined to help (?) the] villains.
[By being good,] we don't do any good! [Yet this
[Chap here on double pay[a]] himself will carry
[His   ] bag, lunch-pack, helmet,
               ] lance, sheepskin rug —   B30
      this wretched] donkey hauls around —
        ] suddenly [flush] — Bias,
             ]

PHEIDIAS

             This fellow here,
down on] his luck a year ago, [
     ] providing [you] amusement [B35
     ] when he was jeered [
     ] fifty servants, stick[ing] close
       ] behind him. I'm washed up!

GNATHON (?)

[Why worry?] He has skulked away from something —
[Betrayed some] city, governor[b] or army —   B40
[   ] is, quite clearly!

   [a] Literally 'two-share man'. A marginal note on the papyrus,
which enables us to supplement this word here, provides also its
explanation: 'any soldier who receives double pay'.

   [b] Literally 'satrap', originally a governor of a province in the
Persian Empire, but the title was retained by Alexander and
some of his successors after that empire was overthrown.

Sudhaus, παρέ[χον]τα Turner.   B37 πεν]τήκοντα and ἐχό-
με[νοι suppl. Sudhaus.   B40 πόλ[ιν προδούς τι]ν' suppl.
Wilamowitz, στ[ρατόπεδον Sudhaus.

MENANDER

ΦΕΙΔΙΑΣ

πῶς;

ΓΝΑΘΩΝ (?)

οὐθεὶς ἐπλούτησεν ταχέως δίκαιος ὤν·
ὁ μὲν γὰρ αὐτῷ συλλέγει καὶ φείδεται,
(45) ὁ δὲ τὸν πάλαι τηροῦντ' ἐνεδρεύσας πάντ' ἔχει.

ΦΕΙΔΙΑΣ

B45 ὡς ἄδι[κον εἶπας].

ΓΝΑΘΩΝ (?)

ὀμνύω τὸν Ἥλιον,
εἰ μὴ φέ[ρων ὁ παῖ]ς ὄπισθ' ἐβάδιζ[έ] μου
τὰ Θάσ[ι]α, [καί τις] ἦν ὑπόνοια κραιπάλης,
ἐβόω[ν ἂν αὐτῷ π]αρακολουθῶν ἐν ἀγορᾷ·
(50) "ἄνθρωπε, πέρυσι πτωχὸς ἦσθα καὶ νεκρός,
B50 νυνὶ δὲ πλουτεῖς. λέγε, τίν' εἰργάζου τέχνην;
τοῦτό γ' ἀπόκρ[ιν]αι. πόθεν ἔχεις τοῦτ'; οὐκ ἄπει
ἐκ τῆς [ὁδοῦ 'τέ]ρωσε; τί διδάσκεις κακά;

B42–44 Kock fr. 294   B49–50 Kock fr. 731

B42 ταχέως O.1 (without accent), mss. of Stobaeus, *Eclogae* 3. 10. 21: ταχὺ monostich 688 Meineke (*Fragmenta Comicorum Graecorum* 4, Berlin 1841, 360).   B45 εἶπας suppl. Wilamowitz (εἶπες Grenfell and Hunt).   B48 αὐτῷ suppl. Körte. B50 νυνὶ O.1: νῦν mss. of Symeon's lexicon (R. Reitzenstein, *Index Lectionum* (Rostock 1892/3), p. 8 s.v. ἦσθα) and of Eustathius's commentary on Homer, 1833.58.
B52–53 O.1, O.5.   B52 ὁδοῦ suppl. Sudhaus.

PHEIDIAS

How?

GNATHON (?)

No one made money fast by honest means.
One man is thrifty and stocks up, another
Waylaying someone vigilant for years
Keeps all his loot.

PHEIDIAS

How [wrong]!

GNATHON

On oath I swear   B45
That if [this lad][a] weren't walking at my heels
With these from Thasos,[b] [and] no hint of booze,
I'd follow [him][c] and shout in our town centre[d]
"Last year, sir, you were destitute, all bones —
And now you're wealthy. Say, what was your calling?   B50
Answer that! Where's it come from? Move aside,
Out of my [way]! Why do you teach what's evil?

[a] When Gnathon entered for this scene, he must have been closely followed by a slave carrying two or more containers of wine, perhaps for the forthcoming celebration in Pheidias' house (see A10–13 and fr. 1), to which doubtless Gnathon had been invited. In that case the slave could have belonged to Pheidias; could he have been Daos, a silent onlooker in this scene until B67?

[b] Sc. containers of wine from the island of Thasos, some 30 miles north east of Mount Athos. This wine was highly praised in antiquity: deep red in colour (Aristophanes fr. 364 Kassel-Austin), with a bouquet suggesting apples (Hermippus fr. 77 Kassel-Austin).

[c] Bias.

[d] Literally, the (Athenian ?) agora.

171

B53   τί λυσιτελεῖν ἡμῖν ἀποφαίνεις τἀδικεῖν;"
                                    ]με;

ΦΕΙΔΙΑΣ
                                    ναί.

(In O.1 excerpt B closes with B53; O.5 has lines B52–53
and preserves scraps of B54–69; then, after a gap of about
20 lines, it preserves the beginnings of some (B90–93,
B96–97) of a further 9 lines; five unplaced scraps of O.5
are printed at the end of this play as fr. 13a–e).

ΓΝΑΘΩΝ (?)

B55 (56)   ] καὶ πέπρακ' ἄρα
                ]α ἐλπίδων
                ]εκεινουμενω
                ]νην δήπου . . . . .
(60)   ]εχω· τὸ δ' ἐγκα[λεῖν
B60   ].μ'· ὡς οὐ δέον
                ]ω τὸν χρώμενον.

ΦΕΙΔΙΑΣ
            ἐ]μβεβρόντησαι πάλαι
                ]κλινων μάτην
(65)   τ]αῖς χερ[σὶν
B65   ] τουτονὶ
                ]ς λαμβάνειν.

ΓΝΑΘΩΝ (?)

[   ]

ΔΑΟΣ
                    οὐκουν Γνάθω[ν
                ]οιγε.

Why prove to us that profit comes from crime?"   B53
] me (?) ?

PHEIDIAS

Yes.

*(At B53 O.1's second excerpt closes, probably with
Gnathon in mid-speech; O.5's fractured text of the lines
that immediately follow seems to indicate that Gnathon
may have followed up his imaginary public attack on Bias
with a direct question to Pheidias: perhaps something like
'[Do you understand] me?', to which Pheidias simply
answers 'Yes' (B54). The following lines are too broken to
reveal more than a few contextless phrases: from Gnathon
possibly and he's sold after all B55, hopes B56, presum-
ably B58, I have (?), and to make this accusation (?) B59,
it being needful B60, the man using B61; from Pheidias
an apparently irritated you've long been a crackpot B62,
turning (?) in vain B63, the hands (?) B64, this here B65,
to take (B66). The main subject-matter of these exchanges
cannot be identified, although B55 may perhaps be a ref-
erence to the pimp's having sold his hetaira to Bias.*

*O.5 brings Daos into the conversation at this point (cf.
the note on B46); he mentions Gnathon (B67), and this is*

B53 λυσιτελει O.1.   αποφαινες O.1:]οβαινεις O.5.
B54–98 O.5.   B54 Dicola before and after ναι in O.5.
B61, B66 Dicola after χρωμενον and λαμβανειν in O.5.
B65 Suppl. Sudhaus.   B67 δαοσ written above ουκουν in
O.5 to identify speaker.

ΦΕΙΔΙΑΣ (?)

$$\hat{\omega} \ \Gamma\nu\acute{\alpha}\theta\omega\nu, \ [$$

B69 (70)
$$]\mu\beta[$$

(After B69 there is a gap of perhaps between 16 and 22 lines, the figure depending on the number of lines in each column of the papyrus. Then O.5 preserves the openings of a few more lines.)

(?)

B90 (71) $\pi\epsilon\rho\alpha\nuο\hat{\upsilon}\mu\epsilon\nu.$

(?)

$\omega[$

(?)

(71 Au) $\tau\grave{ο}\nu \ \pi\ο\rho\nu\ο\beta\ο\sigma\kappa\acuteο[\nu$

(?)

B92 $\pi\acute{\alpha}\nu\tau\omega\nu.$

ΔΑΟΣ

$\pi\ο\lambda\upsilon.[$

B93 (74 Kö, 73Au) $\alpha[$, B94 [, B95 (75 Au) [, B96 (75Kö, 76Au) __ευ, B97 (76Kö, 77Au) $\mu\alpha[$, B98 (77Kö, 78Au) [with traces of a marginal name in the left margin ($\theta.[$ or $\beta.[$).

B90, B91, B92 and B96 have paragraphi under the lines in O.5.   B90 Dicolon after $\pi\epsilon\rho\alpha\nuου\mu\epsilon\nu$ in O.5.   B92 Dicolon before $\pi\ο\lambda\upsilon.$ and $\delta\alphaο\sigma$ written above it to identify speaker in O.5. Five other unplaceable scraps from O.5 are printed below as fragment 13.

followed by an address to Gnathon by Pheidias (B68). A lacuna of between about 16 and 22 verses now intervenes, before O.5 supplies the opening letters of some further lines (B90–98); four words or phrases can be made out, we'll carry it through (B90), the pimp (B91), and all answered by Daos with much (B92). One possibility is that a plan against the pimp—perhaps to kidnap the het- aira—is being devised. Five other tiny scraps from O.5, perhaps originally deriving from this scene, have been identified but remain unplaced; they are printed below as fragment 13.)

MENANDER

Excerpt C

(Do the next 35 lines in O.1 form two excerpts (here numbered C190–199, D200– 224) or just one? No clearly decipherable mark or space in the papyrus under C199 registers a break between extracts (but see the critical apparatus), and the characters involved could be the same throughout: a slave addressing his young master in C (cf. C191), the young master and either his slave or (more probably) another adviser such as Gnathon in D. Yet the shift of focus between C190–199 (the damage caused by κόλακες) and D200–214 (the need to be on guard against plots and attacks) seems both too abrupt and too irrational for a single continuous extract, and so the 35 lines are here separated. It seems reasonable to guess from the subject-matter of C190–199 that Daos is addressing Pheidias, but we cannot exclude the possibility that there are two free young men in this play (cf. e.g. *Dyskolos*), or two slaves serving Pheidias. The excerpt begins in mid-line.)

ΔΑΟΣ (?)

C190	εἷς ἐστ[ι]ν, εἷς
	δι᾽ οὗ τὰ πάν[τ]᾽ ἀ[π]όλωλε, τρόφιμε, πράγματα
(87)	ἄρδην, [λ]έγω σ[οι .].…ν· ὅσας ἀναστάτους
	πόλεις ἑ[όρ]ακα[ς, τ]οῦτ᾽ ἀπολώλεκεν μόνον
	ταύτας, ὃ νῦν δι[ὰ] τοῦτον ἐξεύρηκ᾽ ἐγώ.
C195	ὅσοι τύραννοι πώποτ᾽, ὅστις ἡγεμὼν
	μέγας, σατράπ[ης], φρούραρχ[ο]ς, οἰκιστὴς τόπ[ο]υ,
(92)	στρατηγός—οὐ [γὰρ] ἀλλὰ τοὺς τελέως λέγω
	ἀπολωλότας—[νῦν τ]οῦτ᾽ ἀνῄρηκεν μόνον,
C199	οἱ κόλακες. οὗτοι δ᾽ εἰσὶν αὐτοῖς ἄθλιοι.

Excerpt C

(If Daos is the speaker, he must be commenting here on some disaster that the fawner—Strouthias presumably—has produced for Pheidias. Its precise nature and timing are uncertain, although it probably had something to do with an intervention by Strouthias aimed at securing the contested hetaira for Bias.)

DAOS (?)

(addressing Pheidias)

Master, there's one man, just one   C190
Who's caused this total holocaust in our
Affairs, I tell [you bluntly]. All the towns
You've seen laid waste have been destroyed by this
One thing, and it's through him[a] I've now discovered
This. All dictators, every mighty leader,   C195
State governor, commander, colonist[b]
Or general—I mean precisely those
Completely ruined—this one thing's destroyed
Them now: the fawners—they have caused their misery!   C199

[a] Presumably Strouthias.

[b] The three officials named are literally 'satrap' (see on B40), 'commander of a garrison' and 'founder of a city', in that order.

C190–199 O.1.   C190 O.1 aligns its text with the beginnings of the preceding and following lines. Second εἷς suppl. Sudhaus but deciphered in an abraded text by Petersen.   C194 δι[ὰ] τοῦτον deciphered by Leo.   C198 Punctuation before [νῦν by Sandbach.   C199 οὗτοι deciphered by Leo, δ' by Rea. Under the beginning of C199 a paragraphus is inserted (but without the addition of a dicolon at its end); this may possibly be either a scribal error for, or the abraded remains of (cf. E. G. Turner, *Oxy. Pap.* 50 (1968), 13), a διπλῆ ὠβελισμένη.

Excerpt D

(See above, introduction to excerpt C. The first speaker is probably Pheidias, but the second cannot be identified with certainty; it could be Pheidias' slave Daos, but the imaginative suggestion of an attack that took the pimp off his guard might come better from Gnathon.)

ΦΕΙΔΙΑΣ (?)

D200   σοβαρὸς μὲν ὁ λόγος· ὅ τι δὲ τοῦτ' ἐστίν ποτε

(96)   οὐκ οἶδ' ἔγωγε.

ΓΝΑΘΩΝ (?)

π[ᾶ]ς τις ἂν κρίνας κακῶς

εὔνουν ὑπολάβο[ι] τὸν ἐπιβουλεύοντά σοι.

ΦΕΙΔΙΑΣ (?)

(98 Kö, S)   κἂν μὴ δύνητα[ι];

ΓΝΑΘΩΝ (?)

πᾶς δύναται κακῶς ποεῖν,

(99 S)   ἂν μὴ φυλάττῃ. τὸν σφόδρ' ἰσχυρὸν [

D205   .[.]..θεν .ιον 'Αστυάνακ[το]ς ὑ[πτίου

D204 Punctuation by Arnott.   D205–213 Suppl. Turner, apart from D205 ὑ[πτίου Handley, D211 ἀντιβλέπ[ει Arnott (αντιβλεπ[decipered by Arnott, Austin).   D205 At the bottom of the column (under E237) O.1 has a scholion on Astyanax:] 'Αστυάνακτος· τοῦ Μιλησίου ['Ασ]τυάν[ακτ]ος πολλοὶ σφόδρα [τ]ῶν κωμῳδιογρ(άφων) μέμν[ην]τ(αι). ἐγένετο γ(ὰρ) παγκρατιαστ(ὴς) κρά[τ(ιστος) τῷ]ν καθ' αὑτόν, ἠγω[νί]σατο δ(ὲ) κ(αὶ) πυγμῇ. Ἐρατοσθένης (FGrH 241 F 8) δ' ἐ[ν τῷ] ¯ τῶν Ὀλυμπιονικ(ῶν) προσθεὶς (corr. C. Wendel, _Überlieferung und Entstehung der Theokritscholien_, Berlin 1920, 107 and n. 1: προσθεις O.1) ρ̄ῑσ̄ 'Ολυμπι(άδα or άδι)

KOLAX

Excerpt D

(Excerpt C provided a slave advising his master about the iniquity of lackeys; excerpt D runs on parallel lines, but now we have a more flamboyant character, most plausibly identified as Gnathon, instructing his man how to overcome an enemy. If Pheidias here too is the pupil, the enemy must be (i) the title figure, (ii) the pimp, or most probably (iii) the soldier Bias himself. Holes and abrasion in the papyrus, together with our ignorance of the preceding context, make the sequence of ideas at times incoherent, but Gnathon's main suggestion seems to be that Pheidias' best chance of 'wiping out' his opponent (hyperbole doubtless for defeating him in a fight) will come if he can catch him off his guard.)

PHEIDIAS (?)

Your discourse was imposing, but I don't   D200
See what its point was.

GNATHON (?)

All bad judges would
Assume the schemer's[a] well-disposed to you.

PHEIDIAS (?)

Though he lacks power?

GNATHON (?)

Anyone can harm you, if
You're off your guard. The very strong [

---

[a] If Pheidias and Gnathon are the two speakers, the schemer must be Strouthias, Bias' attendant and the fawner of the title.

φ(ησίν)· Ἀ[στ]υάναξ ὁ Μιλήσιος ϛ (so O.1: ? an error for Γ: so Jacoby) τὴν περίοδον ἀκονιτεί.

κ[α]τακειμένου, δοίδυ[κι .]....τα[.].[....]καις
(102 S) τ]ὴν ῥῖνα συντρίψαιμ..[.]μ[..]..[....]αν,
ἀλλ' οὐχ ὁ πέντε μνα[ῖ]ς κατεσ[κ]ευα[σμένος
ἐπ' αὐτὸ τοῦθ' ἥκων, ἵν' ἐκειν[.....]κυ[
D210 οὐ[κ ε]ὑπόρως ἂν τοῦ[τ' ἐ]πόησε τ....αμ..[
φυ[λ]άττεται [γὰρ .]εξε.[.].λεινε· ἀντιβλέπ[ει
(107 S) ...τεαλ[.].ς οἶδεν ὄντα· κα[ὶ] νε..υσ...[
......] φυλ[ά]ξεταί σ' ὁμοίως [...]..α[
                    ]ει[ ]πι. θυρα[ ] [
D215 .].[....]..[.] σαυτοῦ [το]ὺς φίλου[ς
(100 Kö) ..[ ] πρὸς βίαν με.[....]πησ.[.]αν[
(112 S) τ..[.]πεις τι χωρήσει γὰρ αὐτ[ό]θ[εν
μ[ε]ταπέμψεθ' [ἑ]τέρους [..] στρατ[ιώτας, ἀλλ' ἴσως
οὔ σ' ἄρα φυλάξει. παῖδες. ἐκτριβή[σεται
D220 ἤτοι ποθ' οὗτος ἢ σύ· πιστευθεὶς δ[ὲ σὺ
(105 Kö) ὑπεναν[τί]ον τε μηθὲν ὧν ποεῖ[ς ποεῖν

D210 του[...]ποησα O.1: tentatively corr. Arnott.
D215 Suppl. Turner.   D217 τι χωρήσει deciphered by
Turner, αὐτ[ό]θ[εν Arnott.   D218, D220 ἀλλ' ἴσως and δὲ
σὺ suppl. *exempli gratia* Arnott (δὲ already Sudhaus).
D219 Suppl. Jensen (ἐκτριβο[ίμεθ' ἂν Grenfell and Hunt also
possible).

---

[a] See the introduction. The papyrus here has a useful scho-
lion: 'Very many comic poets mention Astyanax of Miletus. He
proved himself the leading pancratiast of his day. He competed
also at boxing. Eratosthenes, adding the date 316 B.C. in the [(?)]
book of his *Olympic Victors*, says "Astyanax of Miletus: six (so the

        ] When Astyanax[a] lies on   D205
His back, [you could   ] smash his nose [   ] with
A pestle [
But not the man who's paid five hundred drachmas
And shows up just for this,[b] to [   ] that [
He'd not have done it easily [D210
He's on his guard [   ] looks eye to eye
      ] knows that he (?) is [
    ] he'll guard against you just like [
         ] door [
           ] his (?) friends [D215
    ] with violence [
              ] will come at once (?) [
He'll send for other soldiers, but perhaps
He'll not repel you. Servants![c] Either he
Or you will be wiped out. But if you're trusted,   D220
And don't behave at all abnormally,

---

papyrus: perhaps an error for 'three') times (sc. victor) in the four-year cycle without having to fight.'" Athenaeus (1. 413ab) says that Astyanax won three times in successive Olympics. Pancratiasts competed in a brutal form of physical combat, combining features of wrestling and boxing which brought it closer to Oriental martial arts than to traditional European types of prizefighting: see my commentary on Alexis, introduction to *Pankratiastes* (Cambridge 1996/1997).

  [b] A man hired presumably to rough somebody up or even kill him.

  [c] At this point presumably the speaker knocks on somebody's door and calls for the slaves inside to open it. Cf. for example *Dyskolos* 461–464, 911 f., 916, *Epitrepontes* 1076 f., *Misoumenos* 607, *Perikeiromene* 188, 261.

(117 S) δόξας, ἔχεις τὸν ἄνδρ' ἀφύλακτον, ἔ[κτοθεν
         τῶν πραττομένων, τῆς οἰκίας· ὃν [δ' ἂν τρόπον
D224   β[ο]ύλῃ, διοικηθήσεται τὰ λοιπά σοι.

Excerpt E

(The subject-matter here clearly identifies the speaker as
the pimp who owns the hetaira loved by both Pheidias
and Bias.)

ΠΟΡΝΟΒΟΣΚΟΣ

E225   χ]οῦτ[ος .].χ. .τ.ς φανερός; οὐ λιμοὶ [
(110 Kö) ἔχον[τ]ες ἐν τ[αῖ]ς χερσίν, ἀλλο δ' οὐδὲ ἕν,
(122 S)   ὧν ἔσθ' ὁ γείτων. ἀλλ' ἐὰν αἴσθηθ' ὅμ[ως,
          πρόσεισιν ἐξήκ[ο]νθ' ἑταίρους παραλαβ[ών,
          ὅσ]ου[ς] Ὀδυσσεὺς ἦλθεν εἰς Τροίαν ἔχω[ν,
E230   βο]ῶν, ἀπειλῶν "ἄν σε μή, μαστιγία,
(115 Kö) . . . . . π]έπρακας πλέον ἔχοντι χρυσίο[ν."
(127 S)   . . . .]. .τι[.]αρα πωλῶ· μὰ τοὺς δώδεκα [θε]ούς,
          . . . .]όμ[ε]ν[ο]ς διὰ τοῦτον. ἡ μία λαμβάνει
          ὅσον οὐχ]ὶ δέκα, τρεῖς μνᾶς ἑκάστης ἡμέρας
E235   παρὰ τοῦ] ξένου. δέδοικα δ' οὕτω λαμβάνειν.
(120 Kö) ἐκ τῆς ὁ]δοῦ γὰρ ἁρπάσονθ', ὅταν τύχῃ,
(132 S)   αὐτήν.] δικάσομαι, πράγμαθ' ἕξω, μάρτ[υρας

D223 Suppl. Sudhaus (ὃν deciphered by Petersen).
D224 Traces of a διπλῆ ὠβελισμένη under the beginning of the
line in O.1.   E225 χ]οῦτ[ος suppl. Turner.   E233 Corr.
Leo: ηνιαλαμβανεν apparently O.1.   E234 Suppl. Leo.
E236 Suppl. Sudhaus.   E237 αὐτήν suppl. Robert, μάρτ[υ-
ρας Leo (μάρτ[υρες Grenfell and Hunt).

You'll have the fellow[a] off his guard, [away
[From] his activities, his house! And you'll arrange
The other matters in whatever way you wish!   D224

Excerpt E

*(The speaker contrasts poor clients (like Pheidias) who
might come with friends and break into his establishment
(compare Aeschinus in Terence's Adelphoe) and wealthy
ones (presumably like Bias) who pay very high prices.)*

PIMP

And he—a clear [   ]. They're the hungry poor,   E225
Aren't they, with [cudgels] in their hands, that's all!
He's[b] close to them! But still, if he gets wind,
He'll come with sixty mates that he's enrolled —
The number that Odysseus took to Troy[c] —
With yells and threats: "Blackguard, if I don't get you,   E230
Who've sold her to a man who has more money!"
              ] why trade her? By the twelve great gods[d]
              ] it's not through him! The one girl earns
Almost as much as ten — three minas every
Day from the soldier. I'm afraid of so   E235
Much income. They[e]'ll abduct her, given the chance.
I'll be in court, have bother, witnesses   E237

---

[a] Bias presumably.   [b] Pheidias presumably.
[c] *Iliad* 2. 637 says that Odysseus came to Troy with twelve
ships and presumably several hundred soldiers, but Menander
here may be confusing this with the one ship that on the way
home from Troy survived the Laestrygonian debacle (*Odyssey*
10. 130–132).   [d] The twelve gods of Olympus. In the Attic
canon they were paired: Zeus, Hera; Posidon, Demeter; Apollo,
Artemis; Ares, Aphrodite; Hermes, Athena; Hephaestus, Hestia.
[e] Pheidias and his friends presumably.

```
        ..[
        η βουλε......[
E240    ε.υ..τε κειμεν[
        ᾧ βούλεταί τις τ[
        τὰς τετταράκον[τα
        ξέ[ν]ου [
        ου[.]αν.[.].[
E245    ἐμοῦ δὲ το..ενε[
        ουτ..οινειστε[
        καὶ τὰς θεραπαιν.[
        ἦν γὰρ ε[.] ἔλαττον [
        εἴσω παρελθὼν τ[
E250    .]...ον οὗτος ὁ στρ[ατιώτης
        ἀλαζονευησθ[
        επ..ου.μεν σοιτ.
        .δον[.]αοσεστιο
        .].[.].ον[ ].α..εσουν.[
E255      ].[ ]...εν[
```

*   *   *

Six fragments of Κόλαξ,
quoted by ancient authors

1 (1 Körte and Sandbach)

Athenaeus 14. 659d: Μένανδρος ἐν Κόλακι τὸν τοῖς τετρα-
δισταῖς διακονούμενον μάγειρον ἐν τῇ τῆς πανδήμου
Ἀφροδίτης ἑορτῇ ποιεῖ ταυτὶ λέγοντα·

KOLAX

(*After E237 this papyrus of extracts contains the openings of the next eighteen lines; in the first fifteen are neither words nor marks that would prevent our interpreting them as a continuation of the pimp's speech. Yet too little of each line remains for any continuous or coherent sense:* or *or than wish E239,* lying (?) *E240,* for whom *or what one wishes E241, the (feminine) forty E242, soldier or stranger or guest E243,* but me *or of me E245,* and the slave girls *E247,* for . . . was . . . less *E248,* having gone (*masculine*) by *or to or in E249, this soldier (?) E250,* you (*plural*) are humbugs *E251,* to you *E252,* is *E253.*)

*   *   *

Six fragments of Kolax,
quoted by ancient authors

1

Athenaeus: Menander in *Kolax* makes the cook who is serving the fourth-day celebrants in the festival of Aphrodite Pandemos (= Of All the People) utter these words:

E242 Corr. and suppl. Turner: τεττερακον[O.1.
E243 Suppl. Turner.   E249 Corr. Arnott: εσω O.1.

MENANDER

ΜΑΓΕΙΡΟΣ

σπονδή. δίδου σὺ σπλάγχν' ἀκολουθῶν. ποῖ βλέπεις;
σπονδή. φέρ', ὦ παῖ Σωσία. σπονδή· καλῶς.
εὔχου. θεοῖς Ὀλυμπίοις εὐχώμεθα
Ὀλυμπίασι, πᾶσι πάσαις—λάμβανε
5 τὴν γλῶτταν ἐν τούτῳ—διδόναι σωτηρίαν,
ὑγίειαν, ἀγαθὰ πολλά, τῶν ὄντων τε νῦν
ἀγαθῶν ὄνησιν πᾶσι. ταῦτ' εὐχώμεθα.

2 φερεωπλειωωσια ms. A: corr. Heringa.   καλω A: corr. Mus-
grave.   7 ὀνησιαν A: corr. Casaubon.

2 (2 Kö and S)

Athenaeus 10. 434bc (citing the whole fragment): ἔπινε δὲ
Ἀλέξανδρος πλεῖστον … Μένανδρος ἐν Κόλακί φησι,
and 11. 477e (citing lines 1–2): κόνδυ· ποτήριον Ἀσιατικόν.
Μένανδρος Κόλακι,

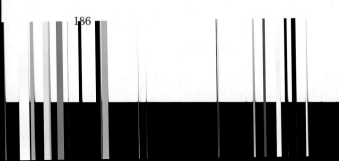

COOK

Pour! Follow, and give me the heart and lungs. Where
    are
You looking? Pour! Come, Sosias boy, pour! That's fine.
Pray! Let us pray to all the Olympian gods,
And goddesses—meanwhile, you take the tongue—
That they vouchsafe to everyone protection,   5
Health, all that's good, and profit from the good
Things now before them. Let us pray for that.

If we combine the hints provided by Pheidias' remarks at
A10–13 and the pimp's at E227–237 with the information
given by this fragment and Athenaeus' introduction to it, we
can deduce that a major (? and final) feature of the plot was a
feast for young men who met on the fourth day of the month
in order to celebrate Aphrodite and enjoy the favours with
which she was associated. Doubtless Pheidias was one of the
young men involved, and some of the diners were the 'mates'
that the pimp feared he might enrol.

    The fragment itself is a speech by the man hired to kill and
cook the sacrificial animal for the occasion. He informs a
slave named Sosias, who could have been owned by himself
or by one of the other characters, about the conventional
order of procedure on these occasions. Three libations of
wine were poured initially, and the heart and lungs of the
animal that had been sacrificed, along with the liver and kid-
neys, were eaten as a ritual preliminary to the meal. The
tongue, on the other hand, was a delicacy that the cook
wished to appropriate for himself.

2

Athenaeus 10: Alexander the Great used to drink a very great
deal, . . . Menander says in *Kolax*,

ΒΙΑΣ

κοτύλας χωροῦν δέκα
ἐν Καππαδοκίᾳ κόνδυ χρυσοῦν, Στρουθία,
τρὶς ἐπέπιον μεστόν γ'.

ΣΤΡΟΤΘΙΑΣ

Ἀλεξάνδρου πλέον
τοῦ βασιλέως πέπωκας.

ΒΙΑΣ

οὐκ ἔλαττον, οὐ
5 μὰ τὴν Ἀθηνᾶν.

ΣΤΡΟΤΘΙΑΣ

μέγα γε.

See also Plutarch, *loc. cit.* at fr. 3 below (citing part of lines
3–4).   1–2 δέκα ἐν and στρουθία ms. A at Ath. 10: δέκα καὶ
ἐν and στρουθίον A at Ath. 11.   3 ἔπιον A and Epitome at
Ath. 10: corr. Meineke: 3–4 Corr. Bentley: πέπωκας τοῦ
βασιλέως A and Epitome at Ath. 10, τοῦ βασιλέως πλέον mss.
of Plutarch. The correct part-divisions were first established in
Daléchamp's Latin translation of Athenaeus.

3 (3 Kö and S)

Plutarch, *Moralia* 57a (*Quomodo adulator ab amico
internoscatur* 13): καθάπερ ὁ Στρουθίας συμπεριπατῶν
(corr. Körte: ἐμπεριπατῶν mss.) τῷ Βίαντι καὶ κατορχούμε-
νος τῆς ἀναισθησίας αὐτοῦ τοῖς ἐπαίνοις· Ἀλεξάνδρου
τοῦ βασιλέως πλέον πέπωκας (an inaccurate citation of
fr. 2, lines 3–4: see above), καὶ

ΣΤΡΟΤΘΙΑΣ

γελῶ τὸ πρὸς τὸν Κύπριον ἐννοούμενος.

Corr. Cobet: γέλωτι and ἐνηθούμενος mss.

BIAS
Strouthias, in Cappadocia
Three times I drained a beaker made of gold,
Brimful. It held five pints.

STROUTHIAS
You've drunk more than
King Alexander!

BIAS
On my oath, it was
No less!

STROUTHIAS
Yes, that's a lot! 5

Athenaeus 11, defining the κόνδυ (beaker) as 'an Asiatic cup',
again cites (with the heading 'Menander in *Kolax*') the first
two lines of this fragment, while Plutarch (see fr. 3 below)
quotes Strouthias' remark in lines 3–4.

*A conversation between the boasting soldier and his fawning
lackey probably from the scene adapted by Terence in
Eunuchus 391–453. On the allusion to Cappadocia, see the
introduction to this play. 'Five pints' translates Menander's
'ten κοτύλας'; in Athens a κοτύλη was about nine twentieths
of a pint. It must, however, be remembered that ancient
Greeks did not drink their wine neat, but mixed it with vary-
ing proportions of water.*

3

Plutarch: just like Strouthias when walking around with Bias
and taking advantage of the latter's stupidity by his plaudits:
'More than King Alexander have you drunk,' and

STROUTHIAS
I'm laughing, thinking of that joke against
The Cypriot.

189

4 (4 Kö and S)

Athenaeus 13. 587d: Μένανδρος δ' ἐν Κόλακι τάσδε κατα-
λέγει ἑταίρας·

ΣΤΡΟΤΘΙΑΣ (?)
Χρυσίδα, Κορώνην, Ἀντικύραν, Ἰσχάδα
καὶ Ναννάριον ἔσχηκας ὡραίαν σφόδρα.

5 (7 Kö and S)

Athenaeus 7. 301d: ἡλακατῆνες· . . . εἰσὶ δὲ κητώδεις, ἐπι-
τήδειοι εἰς ταριχείαν. Μένανδρος Κόλακι (corr. Clericus:
κολωσι A) φησι:

κωβιός, ἡλακατῆνες,
κυνὸς οὐραῖον

ἡλακατῆνες καὶ κυνὸς ms. A here, but in citing the same words
from Mnesimachus (fr. 4. 35–36 Kassel-Austin) immediately
before and at 9. 403b the same ms. correctly omits the unmetri-
cal καί.

---

[a] See S. M. Goldberg, *Understanding Terence* (Princeton
1986), 110 and n. 22.

[b] It is just possible, however, that 'Nannarion' here was a pet-
name for the mother Nannion herself; in that event we must
assume that Bias was presented in this play either as middle-aged
or as capable of falling for a much older woman.

Plutarch first cites part of fr. 2 inaccurately, then quotes another remark by Strouthias referring back to something said earlier in the play, probably about the 'Cypriot bullock' of fr. 6. It is likely that Terence found these Cypriot allusions impossible to translate for a Roman audience when he adapted the relevant sections of Menander's Kolax in his Eunuchus, and so he replaced them with a joke about a Rhodian (419–426) and a later comment (497 f.: Gnatho: Ha ha ha! Thraso: Why're you laughing? Gnatho: It's what you just said — / And when the joke about the Rhodian comes to mind).[a]

4

Athenaeus: Menander in *Kolax* lists these *hetairai*,

STROUTHIAS (?)

Chrysis, Corone, Anticyra, Ischas and
Most beautiful Nannarion—you've had them all.

This is likely to be Strouthias again, buttering up the soldier by alleging that Bias had made love to the leading hetairai of his day. Chrysis and Anticyra were mistresses of Demetrius Poliorcetes (see p. 160); Corone was, and Nannarion may[b] *have been, daughters of Nannion, a celebrated hetaira of the preceding generation.*

5

Athenaeus: ἠλακατῆνες (an unidentified kind of tuna): ... they are enormous, and suitable for pickling. Menander says in *Kolax*,

Goby and tunnies,

And a slice from a dogfish's tail.

This fragment is couched in anapaestic dimeters, a metre found elsewhere in Menander (for instance Leukadia, fr. 1),

191

6 (8 Kö and S)

A compilation of Greek proverbs based on Zenobius (2. 82:
E. Miller, *Mélanges de littérature grecque* (Paris 1868),
p. 366):

βοῦς Κύπριος,

ἴσον τῷ "σκατοφάγος εἶ". λέγονται γὰρ οἱ βόες ἐν
Κύπρῳ σκατοφαγεῖν. μέμνηται ταύτης (sc. τῆς παροιμίας)
Μένανδρος ἐν Κόλακι. Cf. Diogenian 3. 49 Leutsch-
Schneidewin.

*Five quotations in ancient authors assigned to
Κόλαξ with varying degrees of probability*

7 (745 Körte-Thierfelder)

Plutarch, *Moralia* 547c (*De se ipsum citra inuidiam laudando*
21): ἔνιοι μὲν οὖν κολακεύοντες αὐτοὺς ὥσπερ γαργαλί-
ζουσι καὶ φυσῶσιν, ἔνιοι δὲ κακοήθως οἷόν τι δέλεαρ
μικρὸν εὐλογίας ὑποβάλλοντες ἐκκαλοῦνται τὴν περιαυτο-
λογίαν, οἱ δὲ προσπυνθάνονται καὶ διερωτῶσιν, ὡς παρὰ
τῷ Μενάνδρῳ τὸν στρατιώτην, ἵνα γελάσωσιν·

---

[a] See especially H. G. Nesselrath, *Die attische Mittlere
Komödie* (Berlin and New York 1990), 267–280.

*but much more popular in early fourth-century comedy,
where long speeches in it, often about food, seem to have been
delivered as recitatives.*[a] *This brief fr. of Menander in fact
appears to plagiarise a section of one such recitative (fr. 4.
35–36 Kassel-Austin) by Mnesimachus, a mid-fourth-century
comic poet, and it is possible that Menander was here deliber-
ately reviving an obsolete mode in order to give variety to a
long speech by either the cook or one of the two parasites (cf.
Gnatho's remarks in Terence's Eunuchus 255–264).*

6

[Zenobius]:

Cypriot bullock,

Equivalent to 'You eat shit'. Bullocks in Cyprus are said to
eat dung. Menander mentions this proverb in *Kolax*.

*See my comment on fr. 3 above. The soldier Bias was here
probably telling a story about how he had insulted a Cypriot
with this remark; the anecdote seems to have been adapted by
Terence in Eunuchus 419–427, where a Rhodian is substi-
tuted for the Cypriot, and a Roman proverb in which the sol-
dier's victim is called a hare replaces the Greek vulgarism.*

*Five quotations in ancient authors assigned to
Kolax with varying degrees of probability*

7

Plutarch: Some fawners as it were titillate their patrons by
flattery and puff them up, others elicit self-praise by mali-
ciously scattering a crumb of commendation as a sort of bait,
while others cross-question them and ask for additional
detail in order to raise a laugh, as with the soldier in Menan-
der:

MENANDER

ΣΤΡΟΤΘΙΑΣ (?)

"πῶς τὸ τραῦμα τοῦτ' ἔχεις;"
"μεσαγκύλῳ." "πῶς, πρὸς θεῶν;" "ἐπὶ κλίμακα
πρὸς τεῖχος ἀναβαίνων." ἐγὼ μὲν δεικνύω
ἐσπουδακώς, οἱ δὲ πάλιν ἐπεμυκτήρισαν.

1 πῶς δὴ τὸ ms. D. This fragment was assigned to Κόλαξ first by Cobet; see also P. G. McC. Brown, *Zeitschrift für Papyrologie und Epigraphik*, 92 (1992), 96 f., suggesting a parasite as its speaker.

8 (746 KT)

Plutarch, *Moralia* 547de (*De se ipsum citra inuidiam laudando* 22): . . . ὅπου καὶ (so ms. D: καὶ omitted by most mss.) κόλακι καὶ παρασίτῳ καὶ δεομένῳ δύσοιστον ἐν χρείᾳ καὶ δυσεγκαρτέρητον (so Γ group of mss.: the rest δυσκαρτέρητον) ἑαυτὸν ἐγκωμιάζων πλούσιός τις ἢ σατράπης ἢ βασιλεύς, καὶ συμβολὰς ταύτας ἀποτίνειν (so C¹DZ: ἀποτείνειν the rest) μεγίστας λέγουσιν, ὡς ὁ παρὰ Μενάνδρῳ·

σφάττει με, λεπτὸς γίνομ' εὐωχούμενος.
τὰ σκώμμαθ' οἷα τὰ σοφὰ καὶ στρατηγικά,
οἷος δ' ἀλαζών ἐστιν ἀλιτήριος.

ταῦτα γὰρ οὐ πρὸς στρατιώτας μόνον οὐδὲ νεοπλούτους εὐπάρυφα καὶ σοβαρὰ διηγήματα περαίνοντας (παραινοῦντας ms. G), ἀλλὰ καὶ πρὸς σοφιστὰς καὶ φιλοσόφους καὶ στρατηγοὺς ὀγκουμένους ἐφ' ἑαυτοῖς καὶ μεγαληγο-

2 σκώμαθ' mss. G¹X¹YSC². τὰ στρατιωτικὰ καὶ σοφὰ G, σοφά τε καὶ J before correction, ΠΖ. 3 οἷς NRhSi. ἀλιτήριος W (ὁ ἀλι- N): ἀλιτήριος the rest. This fragment was tentatively assigned to Κόλαξ first by Kock; see also Brown, *op. cit.* in apparatus to fr. 7, 94 f., suggesting Strouthias as the speaker.

KOLAX

STROUTHIAS (?)
"What gave you this wound?"
"A javelin." "How on earth?" "While climbing up
A ladder on a wall." I demonstrate —
No joking — but they sneered at it again!

*Plutarch elsewhere cites passages from Menander's Kolax (see
frs. 2 and 3), and although he does not identify the play here
or at fr. 8, both fragments fit in well with what we know of
Kolax and its portrayal of the relationship between the
soldier Bias and his acolyte Strouthias, who sometimes com-
bines ridicule with a pretence of commendation. This ani-
mated little speech would well suit a Strouthias describing a
past incident when some unidentified person asked a vain-
glorious Bias about a war wound, and Strouthias ridiculed
the soldier by a presumably comic mime of what had hap-
pened on the scaling ladder.*

8

Shortly after his citation of fr. 7 above, Plutarch writes: In
these cases even a fawner, a parasite, a down-and-out in his
extremity finds it hard to tolerate and endure a wealthy man
or governor or ruler glorifying himself, and they call this the
most exorbitant bill they have to pay, like the man in Menan-
der,

He slaughters me, high-living makes me thin!
What clever, military jokes! What a
Pretentious charlatan that devil is!

That's what (we are) accustomed to feel and say when faced
not only with soldiers or the nouveaux-riches as they tell their
flamboyant, egocentric tales, but also with professors and
pundits and generals who pontificate and swell up with self-
conceit.

ροῦντας εἰωθότες πάσχειν (corr. Wyttenbach: φάσκειν
mss.) καὶ λέγειν . . .

9 (5 Kö and S)

Erotian, *Glossary on Hippocratic Terms* (p. 116 fr. 60
E. Nachmanson, Göteborg 1918): γενέτησιν· οἱ μὲν "τοῖς
γονεῦσιν", οἱ δὲ "συγγενέσιν", οὕτως Ἀττικῶν (corr.
Schneidewin: ἀττικῶς mss.) λεγόντων, ὡς καὶ Φιλήμων (so
the mss., but Meineke conjectured Μένανδρος because the
fr. seems to have been translated by Terence in *Eunuchus*
237 f., *em / quo redactus sum. omnes noti me atque amici
deserunt*, spoken by the parasite Gnatho) ἐν Κόλακί φησιν·

ἀλλ' οὐδὲ γεννήτην δύναμ' εὑρεῖν οὐδένα,
ὄντων τοσούτων, ἀλλ' ἀπείλημμαι μονος.

10 (6 Kö and S)

Plutarch, *Moralia* 57a (*Quomodo adulator ab amico
internoscatur* 13): οὐκ ἀπ' εὐθείας ἐπάγει (mss. FDZab:
ἐπανάγει other mss.) τὸν ἔπαινον, ἀλλ' ἀπαγαγὼν πόρρω
κυκλοῦται καὶ

πρόσεισιν, οἷον ἀψοφητὶ θρέμματος,

ἐπιψαύων καὶ ἀποπειρώμενος.

Fragment 10 was assigned to Menander's Κόλαξ by Meineke,
partly because Hesychius, the lexicographer of the 5th century
A.D., has the entry ἀψοφητί· ἠρεμά, ἡσύχως· <Μένανδρος>
Κόλακι (so Meineke: the ms. has ἡσύχως, κολακεια).

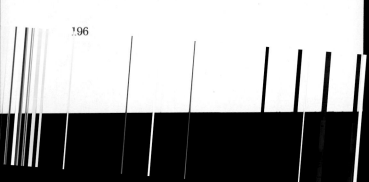

See above on fr. 7. If this fragment comes from Kolax, the speaker can hardly be any other than a jaundiced Strouthias.

9

Erotian: γενέτῃσιν (dative plural of γενέτης). Some use this word to mean "fathers", others "relatives"; the latter is the Attic usage, just as Philemon (*sic*) says in his *Kolax*:

> But I can't find a single relative—
> There are so many—I'm caught all alone!

Nowhere else is a play with the title Kolax attributed to Philemon, and it is likely that here Erotian or a copyist wrote Philemon in error for Menander, especially since Terence apparently adapted these two lines in his Eunuchus when he made his parasite say "See what / I'm reduced to — all acquaintances and friends abandon me!"

10

Plutarch follows up his two quotations from Menander's *Kolax* in fr. 3 (above) by saying that the fawner, when dealing with cleverer people, 'does not introduce his praise directly in a frontal attack but goes off in a wide circuit and

> Comes up in silence, as with a wild beast,

whose temper one tries by touching it lightly.'

It is likely that this iambic trimeter, cited without name of author or title of play, also comes from Menander's Kolax, partly because of the context in which it is embedded, but partly also because it contains the comparatively rare word ἀψοφητί, translated here as 'in silence', and this word seems to be attested for Kolax in an admittedly corrupt entry (s.v.) in Hesychius' lexicon, which is most satisfactorily corrected to 'quietly, gently, as in <Menander's> Kolax'.

11 (907 KT, 9 S)

Pollux 7. 86: τὸ δὲ σανδάλιον οὐ μόνον Μένανδρος εἴρηκε.

Thierfelder noted that Terence, *Eunuchus* 1028 (also spoken by Gnatho), which runs *utinam tibi commitigari uideam sandalio caput*, might indicate that the word σανδάλιον occurred in the Κόλαξ.

Some small papyrus fragments which do not overlap any otherwise known part of the play

12

O.25, an unplaced scrap

```
                    ] εὐφυῶς κ[
                  ΤΡΑΧ[
        : κα]κος κακῶς ἀ[πόλοι-
                      ΣΤΡΟΥ(ΘΙΑΣ)
              ]δη: νὴ Δι' .[
              ἄ]νθρωπος .[
                  ] Στρουθία, ...
                          ΒΙΑΣ
              ].ιο.[  ].: χαῖρε
```

2 Suppl. Handley (with ἀπόλοιο or ἀπόλοιτο). Tentatively ΤΡΑΧ[(ΗΛΙΩΝ) Arnott.

11

Pollux: Menander is not the only person to have used the word σανδάλιον (sandal).

Menander could have introduced the word into one or more plays other than Kolax, but in a scene in the Eunuchus likely to have been adapted by Terence from this play, the parasite is made to say 'Oh, if only I could see her sandal softening his skull!'

Some small papyrus fragments which do not overlap any otherwise known part of the play

12

This tiny scrap of papyrus (O.25) is perhaps more remarkable for its identification of the three speakers present as Strou(thias) (3), Bias (6) and (?) an otherwise unknown slave Trach(elion) (2), than for the isolated words of text that can be deciphered ([be damned to you or him] damnably (2) spoken by (?) Trachelion, by Zeus (3) spoken by Strouthias, hello (6) spoken by Bias; it is uncertain who said cleverly (1) and man (4) or who addressed Strouthias by name in 5. It is possible, however, that this scrap comes from the passage adapted by Terence at Eunuchus 416 ff.; there the three speakers are Thraso the soldier, Gnatho the parasite, and a slave Parmeno, and their conversation includes a curse on the other two by Parmeno (418 f., cf. 431), and the words 'cleverly' (sapienter 416, cf. 427: spoken by the parasite) and 'man' (hominem 417, homini 425).

13

Five tiny unplaced scraps of O.5

(a)   (b)   (d)

       ].μενα[   ]εμε[   ].λοτο[
       ]ω : χαλ[
         ]μ ὀβολου   (c)   (e)
      ]εστιν αρπα[
5   ].σε δ' ὁρᾷς [   ]σει[   ]ποτω[
       ]. γὰρ σειτ.[
         ]θελε[

Three testimonia about Κόλαξ

I (Test. 52 Körte–Thierfelder)

An anonymous lexicon related to the *Etymologicum Gudianum* published by J. A. Cramer (*Anecdota Graeca e codicibus manuscriptis Bibliothecae Regiae Parisiensis* 4 (Oxford 1841), 25.17) under the heading καραδοκεῖν refers to Τιμαχίδης . . . ἐν τῷ τοῦ Κόλακος (corr. Meineke: κόλεικος ms.) ὑπομνήματι.

II

Terence, *Eunuchus* 30–33:

     Colax Menandrist. in east parasitus Colax
     et miles gloriosus. eas se non negat
     personas transtulisse in Eunuchum suam
     ex Graeca.

32 suum *A before correction.*

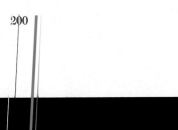

13

These five small scraps of O.5 may come from its passages
B52–69 and B90–98, or from elsewhere in the play. Few
words can be deciphered: is and (?) snatch a4, you see a5,
for a6, (?) wish a7, (?) drink e.

Three testimonia about Kolax

I

An anonymous lexicon s.v. καραδοκεῖν (to wait for) refers to
'Timachides in his commentary on the *Kolax*.'

Timachidas (the correct spelling of his name) of Lindos flour-
ished at the turn of the second and first centuries B.C., and is
known as a glossarian, parodist, commentator and co-author
of a list of dedications to Athena at her temple in Lindos. It is
likely but not certain that the Kolax on which he wrote a com-
mentary was Menander's play.

II

From the prologue to Terence's *Eunuchus*:

   Kolax is by Menander. In it there's Kolax
   A fawner, and a braggart soldier. He[a] admits
   He took these characters into his *Eunuch*
   From the Greek play.

The relevance of this admisison is discussed at length in the
introduction to Kolax.

   [a] Terence.

III

Donatus (1. 314 Wessner) commenting on Terence, *Eunuchus* 228 HIC QUIDEM EST PARASITUS GNATHO: haec apud Menandrum in Eunucho non sunt, ut ipse professus est, 'parasiti personam et militis' (v. 26), sed de Colace translata sunt.

III

Donatus' commentary on Terence's *Eunuchus* 228: IN-
DEED IT'S GNATHO THE PARASITE: these words are
not in Menander's *Eunouchos*, as he[a] himself confessed, 'the
character of parasite and soldier' (*Eunuchus* 25), but are
taken from *Kolax*.

See the introduction to Kolax.

[a] Terence.

KONEIAZOMENAI
(WOMEN DRINKING HEMLOCK)

INTRODUCTION

Manuscripts

Z = *P. Ross.-Georg.* I.10, a fragment of papyrus of the second century A.D., containing the ends of the last 20 lines of one column and the opening letters of the first 17 lines in the next. It is reported now to be in the Kekelidze Institute for Manuscripts, Library of the Georgian Academy of Sciences, Tbilisi, Georgia. First edition: Gregor Zereteli (the name is now normally transliterated Tsereteli), *Zhurnal Ministerstva narodnago prosvescheniya* (St Petersburg), 19 n.s. (January-February 1909), part V, pp. 89–96; it was republished by Zereteli and O. Krueger, *Papyri Russischer und Georgischer Sammlungen*, I (Tbilisi 1925), 64–69. No photograph has been published.

B/S = *P. Berlin* inv. 21312 + *P. Schubart* 27, a fragment of papyrus of the second or third century A.D. from Philadelphia. It originally contained an anthology of quotations, including fr. 1 of *Koneiazomenai*. First edition: O. Bouquitaux-Simon, *Proceedings of the XIXth International Congress of Papyrology*, I (Cairo 1992), 468 and 479.

Fragments 1 and 2 are ancient quotations from the play (see my introduction to volume I of the Loeb Menander, pp. xxiv f.).

The title of this play implies that two or more women (either just before its opening or more probably in the course of its plot) drank poison hemlock (*Conium maculatum*).[1] A very toxic yellowish resin in the plant's roots (cf. Theophrastus, *HP* 9. 8. 3) makes even a small dose rapidly fatal, as any Athenian in Menander's audience would have known, in view of its employment in Athens as an accepted method of execution. Juices extracted from other parts of the plant, however, were used beneficially as a solvent for healing drugs (cf. Pliny, *HN* 25. 152–153). We have no means of knowing why the women in Menander's play decided to drink hemlock. One possibility is a real attempt at suicide, in order to avoid an even worse fate (cf. Antheia in the novel by Xenophon of Ephesus, 3. 5. 11); another would be a bogus drink producing a feigned death, as part presumably of a confidence trick (cf. Chairestratos in Menander's *Aspis* 329 ff.).

The fractured remains of vv. 18–20 in the Tbilisi papyrus exactly match two and a half lines cited from Menander's *Koneiazomenai* by Stobaeus, *Eclogae* 4. 44. 45 (fr. 306 Kock). This identifies the dramatic source of the papyrus, but the latter's text yields no clues as to why any hemlock was imbibed. The papyrus text seems to come from late in the play—perhaps the very beginning

---

[1] The Greek title Κωνειαζόμεναι could be passive (Women Forced to Drink Hemlock) or middle (Women Drinking Hemlock: voluntarily?); the latter is perhaps more probable, especially if a note in the lexicon of Photius s.v. κωνειαζομέναις· θανάσιμον φάρμακον πινούσαις ('women taking hemlock: women drinking a lethal drug') was originally composed in order to explain Menander's title.

of the fifth and final act, if its first editor was right to think that before v. 1 the mark XOPOY, indicating a choral interlude, originally stood. In the surviving lines a man (v. 12) who is probably young converses with somebody else—perhaps a slave from his household—about an unexpectedly happy turn of events, leading to a wedding (v. 5) that is possibly being arranged for him by his father. Another character named Chaireas appears also to be involved (v. 9); elsewhere in New Comedy this name is regularly given to young men (Menander, *Aspis, Dyskolos*; anon. fr. 251. 3 Austin; Terence, *Eunuchus*). Tyche, the goddess of fortune, is praised for her intervention (vv. 13–20), leaving us to wonder whether Menander had used her here as a divine prologue just as he did in *Aspis*.

No hypothesis, didascalic notice, or cast list is preserved for this play. Its production date is unknown.

Dramatis personae, so far as they are known:

Young man
A slave from the young man's household (?)

Other characters might have included the young man's father, the Chaireas mentioned in v. 9, Tyche as a divine prologue. The rest of the cast is unknown. The women who drank hemlock may have played a major or only incidental role. There was presumably also a chorus to perform the entr'actes.

ΚΩΝΕΙΑΖΟΜΕΝΑΙ

(The major papyrus fragment may come from the begin-
ning of Act V: see the introduction above. A young man is
conversing, possibly with a slave.)

ΝΕΑΝΙΣΚΟΣ

? 15 letters]η[..]εμ[..]ο[....].
ἐνύπν]ιον.

ΟΙΚΕΤΗΣ (?)

εἰ καθεῦδομεν
] τάλαντα πένθ' ἅμα
] κόσμον.

ΝΕΑΝΙΣΚΟΣ

οὐκ ἐγρήγορα

ΟΙΚΕΤΗΣ (?)
τοὺς γ]άμους γ' ἤδη ποεῖ.

5

Those corrections and supplements whose author is not named
here were made by the ed. pr., G. Zereteli.   1 At a distance of
1.1 cm above the opening lines in Z is written [τει[/]να[/
]ο[.   5]αμουσηδη with γ added above ση Z.   τοὺς suppl.
Wilamowitz.

KONEIAZOMENAI

(Women Drinking Hemlock)

(SCENE: unknown. Events of the first four acts: unknown, apart presumably from the drinking of the hemlock.)

(In the main part of the papyrus fragment a young man is conversing with another person, most plausibly identified as his slave.)

YOUNG MAN
    ] dream.

SLAVE (?)
                If we're asleep.   2
        two] talents, and an extra five
        ] finery.[a]

YOUNG MAN
             I'm not awake.

SLAVE (?)
    ] he's preparing now [the] wedding.   5

[a] In the broken text here the speaker seems to be reporting first the size of a dowry, and secondly a smaller figure (? five minas = one twelfth of a talent) for the provision of a trousseau and incidentals for the bride. Cf. my notes on *Aspis* 35, *Dyskolos* 740, 843.

211

MENANDER

κροτ]ών.

ΝΕΑΝΙΣΚΟΣ

τί λέγεις;

ΟΙΚΕΤΗΣ (?)

κροτών· ἐγὼ
] δειλινὸν παρῆν.

ΝΕΑΝΙΣΚΟΣ

τί οὖν;

ΟΙΚΕΤΗΣ (?)

κ]αθήμενος λαλεῖ

ΝΕΑΝΙΣΚΟΣ

τίν]ι;

ΟΙΚΕΤΗΣ (?)

Χαιρέᾳ.

ΝΕΑΝΙΣΚΟΣ

ποῦ; βούλομαι

10

]

ΟΙΚΕΤΗΣ (?)

ἐγγ]ύς τις ἔστιν ἐξέδρα
οἶσθ]α δήπου· δεξιᾶς.
]σιν.

6 κροτ]ών . . . κροτών suppl. and interpreted by Wilamowitz. Z
provides a scholion to this line: τι λεγ[εις] / υγι[αι]ν[ει] (suppl.
tentatively Zereteli).   9 τίν]ι suppl. Sudhaus.   11 Suppl.
Körte.

fit as] a flea.[a]

> YOUNG MAN
>> What's that you say?

> SLAVE (?)
>>> Flea! There I was
> last] evening.

> YOUNG MAN
>> What then?

> SLAVE (?)
>] he sits and chats

> YOUNG MAN
> [Who with?]

> SLAVE (?)
> Chaireas.[b]

> YOUNG MAN
>> Where? I should like
>]

> SLAVE (?)
>] There's a bench [near here]   10
>] on the right—[you know] of course!

---

[a] κροτών is literally a tick (*Ixodes ricinus*: see I. C. Beavis, *Insects and other Invertebrates in Classical Antiquity*, Exeter 1988, 56–60), and there was a Greek proverb ὑγιέστερος κροτῶνος, 'healthier than a tick' (cf. Zenobius 6. 23, citing it in Menander fr. 263 KT). In the translation I have adopted the closest English parallel known to me.
[b] See the introduction to this play.

ΝΕΑΝΙΣΚΟΣ

ὄψομ' εἰσιών.

ο]ὺ δικαίως τῇ τύχῃ
κ]ακῶς εἴρηκά που·
15   ἔ]οιχ' ὁρῶσά τι
      ]ς τοῖς πόνοις δ' εἰργαζόμην
      ]ων γὰρ οὐκ ἂν ἐπέτυχον
      ] ὥστε μηδεὶς πρὸς θεῶν
πράττων κακῶς λίαν ἀθυμήσῃ ποτέ·
20   ἴσως γὰρ ἀγαθοῦ τοῦτο πρόφασις γίνεται.

column ii of Z

_ἀγορ[21, ...[22, παν[23, [ἀ]πε[24, τον[25, [.]εμ[
26, _συμ[27, _α.μ[28, . . .[29, προη[30, ανθο[31,
. . .ε[32, πολλ[33, κατα[34, μηπ[35, ὀγκου[36,
ἀποδ[37.

18–20 Kock fr. 306

12 It is uncertain whether Z has εισιων· (so Körte, who con-
tinues the following lines to the young man) or εισιων:
(Zereteli).   15 Suppl. Körte.   18 (ὥστε)—20 (γίνεται)
Stobaeus, *Eclogae* 4. 44. 45 citing Μένανδρος Κωνειαζομέ-
ναις.   18 μηθεὶς mss. of Stob. and originally Z: μηδεισ after
correction Z.   20 γεινεται: Z.

*   *   *

KONEIAZOMENAI

YOUNG MAN

        ] I'll go in and see.
[I've] not [done] right [to rail at] Lady Luck.
I have perhaps abused [her, called her blind,]
[But now she's saved me] — clearly she can see!   15
[I really toiled], but by my toils achieved
[Nothing worthwhile]. I'd not have gained success
[Without her help]. And so let no one, please,
Ever be too despondent if he fails.
That *may* become an agent of good fortune!   20

(A dicolon at the end of v. 20 marks the end of the speech. After v. 20 the papyrus preserves just the opening letters of a further 17 lines. There are paragraphi under 21, 27 and 28, indicating either continuation of the conversation between the young man and (?) his slave, or a new scene with new characters. Little sense can be made out of 21–37: market or buy (?) 21, the 25, many 33, weight or dignified (?) 36.)

*   *   *

MENANDER

Two fragments of Κωνειαζόμεναι,
quoted by ancient authors

1 (1 Körte and Sandbach)

This fragment is cited in three anthologies. (i) Stobaeus,
Eclogae 3. 21. 2 (περὶ τοῦ "γνῶθι σεαυτόν"): Μενάνδρου
Κωνειαζόμεναις (corr. Hense: κοταβιζούσαις ms. S (with
compendium), κωταζομέναις mss. M (with compendium)
and A). (ii) Orion 1. 18 (F. G. Schneidewin, *Conjectanea
Critica: Insunt Orionis Thebani Antholognomici tituli VIII*,
Göttingen 1839, 43): ἐκ τῶν Κωνειαζομένων (corr. Schnei-
dewin: Κωνεαζομένων ms.; the author's name is omitted
because the previous extract was ἐκ τῶν Στρατιωτῶν
Μενάνδρου, fr. 380 KT). (iii) An anonymous anthology whose
mutilated remains survive on papyrus (B/S: see introduction
to Κωνειαζόμεναι).

> τὸ "γνῶθι σαυτόν" ἐστιν, ἂν τὰ πράγματα
> εἰδῇς τὰ σαυτοῦ καὶ τί σοι ποιητέον.

1 σαυτόν B/S, ms. A of Stobaeus: σεαυτόν mss. SM of Stob.
2 εἰδῇς B/S: ἴδης (or ἴδης) mss. of Stob., Orion.   σαυτοῦ
MA of Stob., ms. of Orion (σαυ[B/S): ἑαυτοῦ S of Stob.

2 (2 Kö and S)

The scholia of mss. P and M of Clemens, *Paedagogus* 2. 26
(p. 305. 3 ff. Stählin[3]): Ἐπιμενίδης· οὗτος ἐκάθηρε τὰς Ἀθή-
νας. ἦν δὲ Κρὴς τῷ γένει καὶ σοφώτατος· οὗ καὶ Μέναν-
δρος μέμνηται ἐν ταῖς Κωνειαζομέναις.

---

[a] A well-known Greek maxim, meaning basically 'Know that
you are a human being, not a god', with an influence probably
equal to that of one of the Ten Commandments in Christian soci-
ety. In the sixth century B.C. it was inscribed on the Temple of

KONEIAZOMENAI

*Two fragments of Koneiazomenai,
quoted by ancient authors*

1

Stobaeus ('On the saying "Know thyself"') with the heading 'Menander in *Koneiazomenai*'; Orion with the heading 'from *Koneiazomenai*'; and an anonymous anthology of quotations on papyrus.

> This "Know thyself"[a] means if you understand
> Your own affairs and what you ought to do.

Context and speaker unknown.

2

A scholiast on Clement of Alexandria's *Paedagogus*: Epimenides. This man purified Athens. He was a Cretan by birth and most wise. Menander in fact mentions him in *Koneiazomenai*.

Epimenides was a religious teacher and worker of miracles whose achievements belong more to the world of legend than to historical reality; he was assumed to have lived 157 or 299 years, to have once slept for 57 years, and to have possessed a shaman's ability to travel outside his own body. The date when he purified Athens was disputed: around either 600 B.C. (after the massacre of Cylon's associates) or 500 B.C. The context in which Menander mentioned him is now unknown, but it may be worth noting that he was sometimes identified as one of the Seven Wise Men. See E. R. Dodds, The Greeks and the Irrational (Berkeley and Los Angeles 1951), 141–143.

Apollo at Delphi, and later its formulation was attributed to the Seven Wise Men. See Walter Burkert, *Greek Religion* (English translation by J. Raffan, Oxford 1985), 148.

LEUKADIA

(THE GIRL FROM LEUCAS)

INTRODUCTION

Manuscripts

O.i = *P. Oxyrhynchus* 4024, a scrap of papyrus written in the first century A.D. It contains fragments of ten iambic trimeters that probably began the play. Proof of its authorship is given by line 5, which coincides with Menander fr. 686 KT (cited without play-title); its attribution to *Leukadia* is supported by two circumstances. References in it to a rock (2, 8) apparently described as high (10) in the vicinity of a temple of Apollo (1, 4) point to Leucas as the scene of the play (see below); and Turpilius, *Leucadia* fr. XI[1] appears to be an adaptation of lines 2–3 of the papyrus. First edition: P. J. Parsons, *The Oxyrhynchus Papyri*, 60 (1994), 42–46, with a photograph (pl. III).

O.ii = *P. Oxyrhynchus* inv. 50 4B 30H (5), still not assigned a definitive number. This consists of a number of fragments from a papyrus roll of the first century A.D. or perhaps slightly later. Only one fragment (A) has been published; its attribution to *Leukadia* is less than certain,

---

[1] The Turpilius fragments are cited here and below in the numbering of O. Ribbeck, *Comicorum Romanorum Fragmenta*[3] (Leipzig 1898) 113–118. Fr. XI runs *miseram terrent me omnia / maris scopuli, sonitus, solitudo, sanctitudo Apollinis*, 'All this frightens me, poor me — / Sea rocks, sound, desolation and Apollo's overwhelming awe!'

but its references to travel (38), local customs (43) and particularly the 'big rock' (42) are persuasive. First (provisional) edition: E. W. Handley, *Bulletin of the Institute of Classical Studies*, 26 (1979), 84–87; no photograph is yet available.

Fragments 1 to 8 are quotations in later authors (see the introduction to volume I, pp. xxiv f.). Fr. 1 seems to fit on to the end of O.i, and fr. 2 to follow shortly after. The other fragments are printed after O.ii. Three testimonia, which provide ancient information about the play, are also printed: I after fr. 2, II and III after fragment 8.

Pictorial Evidence

A mosaic of the third century A.D. from the 'House of Menander' at Mytilene in Lesbos. This mosaic is inscribed just ΛΕΥΚΑΔΙΑΣ (with no indication of the act from which its scene is taken), and is difficult to interpret. The person standing in the centre has a garland of leaves on the head and seems to be holding a palm branch in the right hand. If this is a woman, she may well be the temple servant who appears in O.i and is addressed in fr. 5. An old man who faces her on her left has his right hand extended in a gesture of astonishment or concern; an old man is mentioned in O.ii (v. 36). On the right is a woman, also garlanded, with her hands to her face; she may be the young heroine. On the extreme right stands a tiny figure holding an unidentified object; one possibility is that a statue of the god Apollo is portrayed carrying a model of his temple, another is that some other character is represented, drawn to a smaller scale because in this scene he was a mute (like Syros' wife in the *Epitrepontes* mosaic:

see volume I p. 382). Standard edition of the mosaic: S. Charitonidis, L. Kahil, R. Ginouvès, *Les Mosaïques de la Maison du Ménandre à Mytilène* (*Antike Kunst*, Beiheft 6, Berne 1970), 55–57, colour plate 7 and black-and-white plate 23.

Leukadia was chosen as a title by several comic playwrights in the fourth century B.C. and perhaps later—Alexis, Amphis and Diphilus—as well as by Menander, while Antiphanes wrote a *Leukadios* (Man of Leucas). Leucas (now usually called Levkadha) is one of the Ionian Islands, north of Cephalonia and Ithaca, its northern part approaching close to the coast of Acarnania south of the Gulf of Ambracia. It takes its name (= 'White Place') from the precipitous chalk cliff of Cape Leucatas (now Dukato) at its south-western tip, from which criminals were thrown, daredevils tested their nerve, and unhappy lovers such as Sappho (see v. 12 of O.i/fr. 1 and the note there) were said to have made suicide leaps. The cape was crowned by a Temple of Apollo reduced now—like Menander's *Leukadia*—to a few small fragments.[1]

Plays of later Greek Comedy with ethnic titles normally feature the adventures of a character who comes from one city or area to another (often Athens), the latter then being the scene of the play (cf. e.g. Menander's *Karchedonios, Perinthia*), but the scene of Menander's *Leukadia* is clearly (cf. vv. 1 f.) the Temple of Apollo on Cape Leucatas.

If we possessed only the papyrus fragments, the ancient quotations and the mosaic scene from Menan-

---

[1] Bürchner's excellent account of the island in *RE* s.v. *Leukas* is accompanied by an excellent map (2217–2218).

der's *Leukadia*, it would be difficult even to hazard guesses about its plot. These remains suggest only that the play began with a conversation in iambic trimeters between a young girl (? the titular heroine) and the temple servant (O.i, perhaps O.ii), during which the latter sang or chanted a passage in anapaestic dimeters (O.i/fr. 1 vv. 11–16 and fr. 2, see also testimonium I). The girl has just arrived by sea, like Palaestra and Ampelisca in Plautus' *Rudens*. The two girls in the Roman play were trainee *hetairai* in the possession of a pimp, and had been shipwrecked on the coast near Cyrene; we are totally ignorant of the girl's status in *Leukadia*, but it seems more likely that the boat in which she had been travelling had merely been blown off course, if she was travelling in company with the father and son mentioned in O.ii.

This would be all that could safely be said about Menander's plot, if nineteen generally informative fragments from a Latin adaptation of the play by Turpilius had not survived (see above, s.v. O.i). The Roman fragments[1] yield several clues to the structure of Turpilius' plot, which is unlikely to have differed very much from that of the Menandrean original, but these clues sometimes produce puzzles rather than solutions. We hear about a boat being ordered to accelerate (XIV: ? the boat that in O.ii v. 41 of Menander was blown along), a man pursuing a girl after previously snubbing her (I, III),

---

[1] These are most satisfactorily edited in the Teubner edition of Ludowica Rychlewska (Leipzig 1971), 29–37, which adheres to Ribbeck's numbering, although the editor's interpretation of the hints that these fragments provide for the plot is not always convincing (see my review of her earlier edition in *Gnomon* 40, 1968, 32).

a girl rejecting a young man's advances (VI), a girl kissing an old man (IV), a girl named Dorcium who is heartbroken (XV, cf. IX), an unhappy man calling on the gods for help (XII), a lover's confession of his or her passion (VIII), someone acting insanely (XIII), and a (? final) dinner. Too many pieces of the plot's jigsaw are lost for any attempt at reconstruction to be successful, but clearly one or two girls were involved with one or two men in a love tangle perhaps more complicated than usual in New Comedy, doubtless with a happy resolution at the end. Further than that it is unsafe to go; we can ask questions but not produce answers. Was the girl in O.i the counterpart of Turpilius' Dorcium? Was she enslaved and a trainee *hetaira*, or free? Where did she come from, and if she travelled in the boat with the father and son of O.ii, what (if any) was her connection with them? How was the temple servant involved? Was she a lost relative of the girl?

One thing can be stated with confidence: both the Menandrean original and the Turpilian adaptation dealt with the experiences of ordinary people of the time. Ribbeck's theory (see p. 220, n. 1) that these two comedies burlesqued the fable of Sappho and Phaon (see fr. 1) was shown to be untenable by Wilamowitz[1] many years ago; Menander is not known to have written a form of comedy that was already obsolescent thirty years before he came on to the scene, although the adventures of his

[1] *Sappho und Simonides* (Berlin 1913), 26. Konrad Gaiser, *Menanders 'Hydria'* (*Abhandlungen der Heidelberger Akademie der Wissenschaften, Philologisch-Historische Klasse*, 1977/1, 440–482), has an ingenious but overspeculative discussion of the previously known fragments of Menander's play.

everyday characters may have been designed to resemble in some ways the legendary ones of Sappho and Phaon, just as the adventures of other contemporary Greeks in Menander's *Sikyonios* and *Epitrepontes* may have been intended partly to recall the momentous experiences of mythological heroes and heroines.[1] No hypothesis, didascalic notice, or cast-list is preserved for this play. Its production date is consequently unknown.

Dramatis personae, so far as known:

A girl, recently arrived on Leucas, perhaps identical with the title figure and/or the Dorcium of Turpilius' adaptation

The female servant in the Temple of Apollo on the island of Leucas

Probably an old man and his son, one of them perhaps called Kleinias

In the lost portions of the play other characters would have had speaking roles, and presumably there was a chorus to perform the entr'actes.

[1] See my paper in J. H. Betts and others (edd.), *Studies in Honour of T. B. L. Webster*, 1 (Bristol 1986), 1–9.

ΛΕΥΚΑΔΙΑ

Papyrus fragment O.i + book fragment 1 (258 Körte-Thierfelder)

O.i may be the opening of the play. E. W. Handley (in an unpublished hand-out for a lecture on 'Menander and the Art of Popular Entertainment') noted that book fragment 1 (258 KT) fits neatly on to the end of v. 10 of O.i, with the temple servant switching from iambic trimeters to anapaestic dimeters in mid-speech; in Euripides' *Ion* (1440–1442) Kreousa similarly in mid-speech switches from iambic trimeters to lyrics.

Strabo 10. 2. 9 (p. 452 Casaubon) introduces lines 1 to 5 (ἄναξ) of book fr. 1 as follows: ἔχει δὲ (sc. ὁ Λευκάτας) τὸ τοῦ Λευκάτα Ἀπόλλωνος ἱερὸν καὶ τὸ ἅλμα τὸ τοὺς ἔρωτας παύειν πεπιστευμένον, "οὗ δὴ— Σαπφώ", ὥς φησιν ὁ Μένανδρος, "τὸν ὑπέρκομ-πον—δέσποτ' ἄναξ" (v. 5), and continues ὁ μὲν οὖν Μένανδρος πρώτην ἀλέσθαι (so most mss.: ἅλασθαι mss. enx) λέγει τὴν Σαπφώ, οἱ δ' ἔτι ἀρχαιολογικώ-τεροι Κέφαλόν φασιν ἐρασθέντα Πτερέλα (corr. Tzschucke: Πτερόλα C, Περόλα D, Πταρόλα all the other mss. of Strabo) τὸν Δηιονέως. Hesychius quotes from line 5 (from εὐφημείσθω) to the end of the fragment (Λευκάδος ἀκτῆς), s.v. (λ 719) Λευκάδος· Μένανδρος Λευκαδίᾳ (corr. Bentley: λευκαδεσι ms. H). Bentley was the first to see that the Hesychius citation fol-lowed that of Strabo without a break.

LEUKADIA

(The Girl from Leucas)

(*SCENE: The Temple of Apollo perched on Cape Leucatas in the island of Leucas, with a statue of the god by the entrance-doors. At least one other building is likely to have been visible to the audience, but its occupant or occupants cannot be identified.*)

(*Papyrus O.i appears to contain the play's opening lines. The woman who acts as the temple servant is on stage, probably at the temple doors. A girl enters, carrying an empty jar. She has just arrived at the Temple of Apollo on Cape Leucatas.*)

MENANDER

ΠΑΙΔΙΟΝ

Ἄ]πολλον, εἰς [οἷο]ν κατῳκίσθης τό[πον.
ἅ]παντα πέτρα καὶ θάλαττ᾽ ἐστὶν κ[άτω
ἰ]δεῖν φοβερά τ[ι]ς.

ΖΑΚΟΡΟΣ
χαῖρε πολλά, παιδίον.

ΠΑΙΔΙΟΝ

νὴ καὶ σύ γ᾽, ἥτις εἶ ποθ᾽.

ΖΑΚΟΡΟΣ
ἥτις εἰμ᾽ ἐγ[ώ;

5   ἡ ζάκορος ἡ κοσμοῦσα τὸν νεώ, τέκνον.
ἐφ᾽ ὕδωρ βαδίζεις;

ΠΑΙΔΙΟΝ

ναιχί.

ΖΑΚΟΡΟΣ
τουτὶ πλ[ησίον;

ἱερ[ὸν θεοῦ ᾽στι ν]ᾶμα.

ΠΑΙΔΙΟΝ

μῆτερ φιλτάτ[η,

ἄκουσον· οἶσθ᾽ ε]ἴ που πέτρα ᾽στιν, εἰπέ μοι,
ἀφ᾽ ἧς ὁ κλισμὸς] ἰθύς, ἵνα τοὺς —

5 KT fr. 686

In this apparatus those supplements whose author is not named
were made by the ed. pr. of O.i, P. J. Parsons.   2 Or κ[ύκλῳ,
suppl. Holwerda.   3 τ[ι]ς suppl. Handley.   πολλα origi-
nally omitted in O.i and then added above επαιδιον.   7 ν]ᾶμα
suppl. Parsons, the rest Handley.   8, 9 Suppl. Handley.

LEUKADIA

Papyrus O.i and book fragment 1

GIRL
(addressing the statue by the temple doors)
Apollo, [what a] spot you're lodged in here!
Nothing but rocks, and sea [below]. It looks
Frightful![a]

TEMPLE SERVANT
My hearty greetings, child.

GIRL
Yes, and the same
To you, whoever you may be!

TEMPLE SERVANT
Whoever I
May be? Child, I'm the servant who looks after   5
The temple. Going for water?

GIRL
Yes.

TEMPLE SERVANT
This here,
[Near-by, Apollo's] holy spring?

GIRL
Dear mother,
[Please] tell me, [do you know] if there's a cliff
[That drops] straight down, so that the—

[a] These lines are clearly the Greek original of fr. XI of Turpil-
ius' *Leucadia*: see p. 220, n. 1.

MENANDER

ΖΑΚΟΡΟΣ

ἐνθαδί,

10   ὁρᾷς, μεγάλη τις. τὴ]ν [γὰ]ρ ὑψηλὴν λέγεις,
       οὗ δὴ λέγεται πρώτη Σαπφὼ
       τὸν ὑπέρκομπον θηρῶσα Φάων'
       οἰστρῶντι πόθῳ ῥῖψαι πέτρας
       ἀπὸ τηλεφανοῦς. ἀλλὰ κατ' εὐχὴν
15   σήν, δέσποτ' ἄναξ, εὐφημείσθω
16   τέμενος πέρι Λευκάδος ἀκτῆς.

11–16 KT fr. 258, Arnott fr. 1.

10 [γὰ]ρ suppl. Austin. O.i ends at 10; 11–16 = book fr. 1,
placed here by Handley.   12 Φάων' Casaubon: Πφάων most
mss. of Strabo, Πφάον x.   15 ἄναξ omitted in mss. enx of
Strabo.   16 πέρι Bernhardy, ἀκτῆς Musurus: περὶ and ακτις
ms. H of Hesychius.

---

[a] In Menander's day the sixth-century Lesbian poetess Sap-
pho was believed to have fallen in love with Phaon, a mythologi-
cal Lesbian ferryman who once conveyed the goddess Aphrodite
free of charge from his island to the mainland of Asia Minor, and
was rewarded by her with an oil that transformed him into the
most handsome man in the world. When Sappho was spurned by
him, legend made her commit suicide by leaping into the sea
from the cliff of Cape Leucatas. There is no known historical
basis for the story, which in all probability was the brainchild of
some Athenian playwright of Old or Middle Comedy (? Plato the
comic poet in his *Phaon*).

[b] Apollo.

[c] Cephalus was an old Attic hero, and Pterelaus a king of the
Teleboans; this appears to be the only reference to the unhappy
love affair.

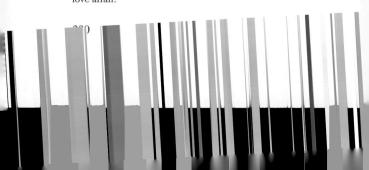

LEUKADIA

TEMPLE SERVANT

(pointing)

Here, [you see],
  [A big one.] You must mean [that] towering crag —   10

(The temple servant here begins to sing (or chant) a long monody in anapaestic dimeters, of which book fr. 1 preserves the first six verses.)

> Where 'tis said Sappho first, when pursuing her
>   proud
> High and mighty Phaon,[a] in her frenzied desire
> Threw herself from the cliff that an eye can discern
> From afar. Even so, by your wish and command,
> O my master and lord,[b] let due silence enshroud   15
> Your demesne on the headland of Leucas!   16

(Papyrus O.1 ends at v. 10. Book fr. 1 (here vv. 11–16) fits neatly on the end of v. 10. Vv. 11–15 (up to 'lord') are quoted by the geographer Strabo with the comment (10.2.8) 'It (sc. Cape Leucatas on Leucas) has the temple of Apollo Leucatas and the Leap which was believed to end sexual passion: "Where—first," as Menander says, "when pursuing—master and lord." So Menander says that Sappho made the leap first, but those who are far better antiquarians claim that Cephalus the son of Deioneus, when in love with Pterelaus, jumped first.'[c] Vv. 15 (from 'let due silence') to the end of the fragment are quoted by Hesychius in his lexicographical entry for '(Of) Leucas'; by prefixing to his citation 'Menander in the Leukadia' he (unlike Strabo) identifies the play.)

231

MENANDER

Fragment 2 (259 Körte-Thierfelder)

From Choeroboscus' commentary on the grammarian Theo-
dosius (1. 330. 32 Hilgard): ἰστέον ὅτι τὰ εἰς ΥΣ λήγοντα
θηλυκά, εἰ μέν εἰσι βαρύτονα, διὰ καθαροῦ τοῦ ΟΣ κλί-
νονται, οἷον πίτυς πίτυος, χέλυς χέλυος—σημαίνει δὲ
τὴν κιθάραν, ὡς τὸ (ὡς τὸ omitted by mss. NC)

ΖΑΚΟΡΟΣ

πάμφων᾽ οὐρεία χέλυς

οὕτω (omitted by NC) Μένανδρος ἐν Λευκαδίᾳ (so NC:
ἐλκαδίᾳ ms. V).

Testimonium I

A scholion in ms. A of Hephaestion's περὶ ποιημάτων com-
ments on the expression κατὰ περιορισμοὺς δὲ ἀνίσους at
6.3 as follows (p. 173. 12 f. Consbruch): οἷά ἐστιν ἡ εἰσβολὴ
τῆς Λευκαδίας Μενάνδρου.

LEUKADIA

Fragment 2

Choeroboscus: It must be realised that if feminine (nouns) ending in ΥΣ are accented barytone, they decline with a pure ΟΣ (in the genitive singular), like πίτυς πίτυος (pine-tree), χέλυς χέλυος—this means 'lyre', as in

> (TEMPLE SERVANT)
> O my lyre of the hills, many-toned

So Menander in *Leukadia*.

A further anapaestic dimeter from the temple servant's monody.

Testimonium I

A scholiast's comment on Hephaestion's use of the phrase 'with regard to unequal divisions' (sc. of strophes in Greek lyric): 'just like the beginning of Menander's *Leukadia*.'

Normally in Greek lyric the metrical structure of an individual strophe was exactly matched by a counterpart, and the implication of the scholiast's comment here is that something similar might be expected in a song written in anapaestic dimeters: i.e. that a sequence of complete dimeters that closed with a catalectic dimeter (a paroemiac like v. 16 of O.i/fr. 1) would be matched by an exactly corresponding sequence, but this apparently did not happen in the anapaestic song of the temple servant in Menander's Leukadia. The attestation that this 'unequal division' came at the beginning of Menander's play is the only evidence from antiquity about its position in the play.

MENANDER

Papyrus fragment O.ii

ΠΑΙΔΙΟΝ (?)

```
31      ]απολλ.....[ ]θ.[
        ]...εα.πο...ριγε.[
        ]θέζειν ω...ετερ[
        ἐ]πεισέπλει μὲν ἡ [..].[..].[
35      ] ἀκόλουθος καταπλυν[ε]ῖ[ν] με.[..]..[
        ] νεανίσκῳ πατήρ ἐστιν γέρων
           ]..τὴν γυναῖκα βούλεται
           ] συγγενὴς ἐφόδια πλούσια
        ]ήκουσεν, ἐπέμεν' οὐκέτι
40      (?)]
```

ΖΑΚΟΡΟΣ (?)

```
        ]ως ἐρωτικόν, τάλαν,
        ]χθη μὲν ὑπ' ἀνέμου τινὸς
        ]αυτην δὲ τὴν μεγάλην πέτραν
        ]υτο τοὐπιχώριον
        ].ν' αὐτοὺς παθεῖν
45      ]τί ποτ' ἂν ποήσῃ. τοῦθ' ὅσαν
```

In the apparatus here any supplement or correction whose author is not named was made by the ed. pr. of O.ii, E. W. Handley. Speech-division at v. 40 and part-assignments generally suggested *exempli gratia* by Arnott.   34 Suppl. Arnott.
35 -πλυν[ε]ῖ[ν] Arnott.   40 ερωτικον O.ii.
44].ναιαυτους O.ii.   45 ποιηση O.ii.

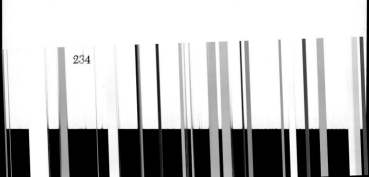

LEUKADIA

Papyrus fragment O.ii

*(The lines of this morsel are here numbered 31–51. It is
only tentatively attributed to Leukadia, and its speakers,
speech-divisions and position in its play cannot be identi-
fied with any certainty. Much of its material, however, is
expository, and this points to an early scene. One possi-
bility is that we have here a later part of the opening con-
versation between the young girl and the temple servant,
after the metre had returned to iambic trimeters; the word
τάλαν (poor thing) in v. 40 indicates a female speaker,
and if φ[ι]λτ[άτη (dearest) is correctly supplied at v. 49,
we have again a form used by the young girl at v. 7 in
addressing the servant. The papyrus is badly mutilated,
but vv. 34–50 can perhaps usefully be set out in full.
Before this section v. 31 yields either Apollo or many (?
things), and 33 other.)*

GIRL (?)

(giving an account of her arrival in Leucas?)

] after that the [ship] sailed in [	34
] following to drench me (?) [	35
] youth has an old father	
] wants her (?) [to be his] wife	
] relative [ ] extensive means for travel	
] heard, no longer waited	
]	

TEMPLE SERVANT (?)

Poor thing, how passionate!	40
] was [driven] by a wind off course	
] this mighty cliff	
] the local custom	
] them (?) to suffer	
] what he is to do. Whoever	45

235

]ιναι τὰ [. .].[.]. θεῶν
]σ᾽.

ΠΑΙΔΙΟΝ (?)

εὔξατ᾽, ἂν ὁ Κλεινίας
]. διὰ κενῆ<ς> καὶ λαβε[
] μὴ θελήσῃ, φ[ι]λτ[άτη,
τ]ὴν ἀρετὴν .[
]του[

48 κενηκαι O.ii.   49 Suppl. Arnott.

Fragment 3 (261 KT)

Olympiodorus' commentary (p. 30 Busse) on Aristotle, *Categories* 1 (1ᵃ1, ὧν ὄνομα μόνον κοινόν): πρὸς τοῦτό φαμεν διττὸν τὸ ὄνομα· τὸ μὲν πτωτικόν, ὃ καὶ τοῖς γραμματικοῖς ἔθος καλεῖν οὕτω, τὸ δὲ φερόμενον κατὰ πάσης λέξεως σημαινούσης τι. οὕτω γὰρ καὶ ὁ Μένανδρος ἐν προοιμίοις τῆς Λευκαδίας ὀνόματα ἐκάλεσεν πᾶσαν λέξιν, ὡς σὺν θεῷ μαθησόμεθα.

---

[a] Or 'He'.

] this [   ] the [   ] of [the] gods
                    ]

       GIRL (?)
            She[a] prayed, if Kleinias
          ] in vain, and to take (?)
          ] may not wish, my dear
          ] excellence [50

(The gaps in the papyrus here make the clues that this passage provides to the plot of its play tantalisingly difficult to interpret. Presumably the girl was travelling in a ship that was blown off its course to Cape Leucatas. How were the young man and his father involved with her? Was Kleinias the young man's name? Did he wish to marry the girl? Was the girl travelling in order to avoid him, or for some other purpose?)

Fragment 3

Olympiodorus, commenting on a phrase in the opening line of Aristotle's *Categories* ('things whose "name" only is shared'): With regard to this, we say that 'name' is an ambiguous term. One meaning is a declinable noun, and that in fact is how grammarians customarily use the word. The other meaning covers every expression that means anything. In the introduction to his *Leukadia* Menander too used the word 'names' in this way, to mean every kind of expression, as we shall find out, god willing.

Presumably when an expression of the second type occurred in the play, the speaker or somebody else applied to it the term 'names', a word that ancient Greek grammarians commonly used in the sense of 'nouns'. Since ὀνόματα, the Greek word for 'names', would not fit metrically in a normal ana-

MENANDER

Fr. 4 (255 KT)

Stobaeus, *Eclogae* 3. 10. 20 (περὶ ἀδικίας), with the heading
Μενάνδρου Λευκαδίᾳ (so mss. SM: λευκαδεία A). The frag-
ment is cited also in the Paris gnomological corpus (*codex
Parisinus* 1168) directly after another Menander quotation
without play or author being named.

> ὅστις ὑπέχει χρυσίῳ
> τὴν χεῖρα, κἂν μὴ φῇ, πονηρὰ βούλεται.

2 βούλεται Paris ms. 1985 (according to Gaisford) and Grotius:
βουλεύεται mss. SMA of Stobaeus and the Paris corpus.

Fr. 5 (256 KT)

Stobaeus, *Eclogae* 4. 32. 6 (περὶ πενίας, 1: πενίας ἔπαινος),
with the heading Μενάνδρου (so ms. M: μ^ε S, τοῦ αὐτοῦ
(after Menander fr. 618 KT) A) Λευκαδίᾳ (MA: title omitted
in S).

> ἀεὶ νομίζονθ᾽ οἱ πένητες τῶν θεῶν.

νομίζονθ᾽ ms. A and Trincavelli edition: νομίζοντ᾽ mss. SM.

Fr. 6 (257 KT)

The *Etymologicum Genuinum* (R. Reitzenstein, *Geschichte
der griechischen Etymologika* (Leipzig 1897), 194), Photius
(p. 1.244 Naber) and the *Suda* (ζ 9 Adler) cite the fragment
s.v. ζάκορος· νεωκόρος· ἤγουν ἡ διακονοῦσα περὶ τὸ ἱερόν.
Μένανδρος Δὶς ἐξαπατῶντι (fr. 5 Arnott and Sandbach, 112
KT) . . . καὶ ὁ ὑπηρέτης. Λευκαδίᾳ·

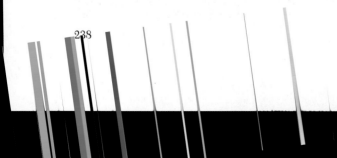

*paestic dimeter sequence, the words 'introduction to his
Leukadia' must refer to a lost part of the opening scene when
the anapaests had been succeeded by iambic trimeters.*

Fr. 4

Stobaeus ('On injustice'), with the heading 'Menander in
Leukadia'; an anonymous anthology in a Paris ms. also cites
the fragment without naming either author or play.

> A man who holds his hand outstretched for cash
> Plans villainy, though he may yet deny it!

Speaker and situation are unknown.

Fr. 5

Stobaeus ('On poverty, I: praise of poverty'), with the head-
ing 'in Menander's *Leukadia'*:

> The poor are always held to be gods' creatures.

Speaker and situation are unknown.

Fr. 6

Three Lexica, all defining ζάκορος as follows: temple atten-
dant, or the woman who works in and around the shrine—so
Menander in *Dis Exapaton* (= fr. 5 Arnott) . . . — and the
male (*sic*) servant—so in *Leukadia,*

(?)

ἐπίθες τὸ πῦρ, ἡ ζάκορος.

ΖΑΚΟΡΟΣ

οὑτωσί;

(?)

καλῶς.

Part-division Arnott.   ἡ ζάκορος *Et. Gen.*, Photius: ἡ ζάκορος ἱερέως *Suda* (? misplaced here by a scribe from an original position before ὑπηρέτης). οὑτωσὶ καλῶς *Suda*: οὑτοσὶ καλός Photius, both words omitted in *Et. Gen.*

Fr. 7 (262 KT)

A scholion on Aristophanes' *Acharnians* 284 (Σᵛᵉᵗ·, c Wilson) τῷ δὲ συντρίβειν καὶ Μένανδρος κέχρηται ἐν Λευκαδίᾳ καὶ ἐν Ἀσπίδι (sc. συντετριμμένην, v. 73).

Fr. 8 (260 KT)

Zenobius 6. 13 (vulgate recension, Leutsch–Schneidewin 1 p. 165) s.v. τὰς ἐν τῇ φαρέτρᾳ ψηφῖδας· Φύλαρχός (mss. PHB: φιλ- mss. vulg.) φησι (*FGrH* 81 F 83, 2A p. 188 Jacoby) τοὺς Σκύθας μέλλοντας καθεύδειν ἄγειν τὴν φαρέτραν, καὶ εἰ μὲν ἀλύπως τύχοιεν τὴν ἡμέραν ἐκείνην διαγαγόντες (mss. BV and *Suda*, see below: διάγοντες vulg.), καθιέναι εἰς τὴν φαρέτραν ψηφῖδα λευκήν· εἰ δὲ ὀχληρῶς, μέλαιναν. ἐπὶ τοίνυν τῶν ἀποθνησκόντων ἐκφέρειν τὰς φαρέτρας καὶ ἀριθμεῖν τὰς ψήφους· καὶ εἰ εὑρεθείησαν πλείους αἱ λευκαί, εὐδαιμονίζειν τὸν ἀπογενόμενον. . . . καὶ Μένανδρος δέ φησιν (BV: φασι other mss.) ἐν Λευκαδίᾳ (corr. Meineke: Λευκάδι BV, Λευκαδίῳ other mss.) τὴν ἀγαθὴν ἡμέραν λευκὴν καλεῖσθαι (corr. Meineke: καλεῖν

240

(?)

Attendant, put the fire on!

TEMPLE SERVANT

Like this?

(?)

Fine!

This line seems to be part of a dialogue in which the temple servant is being requested by an unidentified character to place burning wood or charcoal (presumably from a brazier) on the altar outside her temple. It seems odd that the lexica define such temple servants as male, when the Greek word for 'attendant' in the fragment itself is accompanied by a feminine form of the definite article.

Fr. 7

A scholion on Aristophanes' *Acharnians*: and Menander has used the word συντρίβειν (to shatter/buckle/beat) in *Leukadia* and in *Aspis* ('buckled' v. 73).

Fr. 8

The collection of proverbs attributed to Zenobius: 'The pebbles in the quiver'. Phylarchus[a] says that when Scythians were going to bed, they brought their quiver, and if they had spent that day free from pain or grief, they dropped into the quiver a white pebble, but if the day had been troublesome, a black one. So at the time of their deaths the quivers were brought out and the pebbles counted. If the white ones were found to be more numerous, they called the man who had

---

[a] A Greek historian living in the third century B.C.

mss.). See also *Suda* s.v. λευκὴ ἡμέρα (λ 323 Adler) with substantially the same information but omitting any reference to Menander.

Two further testimonia about Λευκαδία

II (p. 96 KT)

The expanded version of Servius' commentary ('Servius auctus', 'Servius Danielis') on Virgil, *Aeneid* 3. 279 s.vv. VOTISQUE INCENDIMUS ARAS: ... Varro enim templum Veneri ab Aenea conditum, ubi nunc Leucas est, dicit, *(corr. Ribbeck:* nunc leucasem dicit *ms. F,* ubi et leucata mons est *T,* ubi nunc leucate *codex Ambrosianus,* ubi nunc Leucatem dicit *vulgate mss. of Daniel)* quamuis Menander (menarder *F*) et Turpilius (torpi- *F*) comici *(Ambros.:* commici *F,* comicus *T)* a Phaone *(Commelinus:* facione *F,* fauone *T, Ambros.)* Lesbio id templum conditum dicunt.

III (p. 96 KT)

Harpocration (λ 10, p. 163 Keaney): Λευκας· ... νῆσός ἐστι πρὸ τῆς Ἠπείρου κειμένη ... ἐν μέσῳ δὲ καὶ τὸ Μενάνδρου ἡ Λευκαδία.

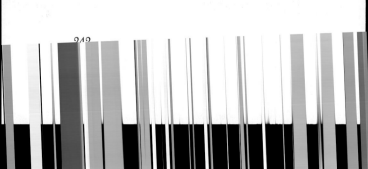

departed happy ... Menander too says in *Leukadia* that a good day is described as 'white'.

Two further testimonia about Leukadia

II

The expanded version[a] of Servius' commentary on Virgil: For Varro says that Aeneas founded the temple to Venus where Leucas now is, although Menander and Turpilius say that this temple was founded by Phaon of Lesbos.

The juxtaposition of the names of Menander and Turpilius here make it highly probable that this allegation about Phaon and the temple occurred in Menander's Leukadia. Did the allegation follow the reference to Sappho's suicide in the anapaestic dimeters of O.i/fr. 1 vv. 11–16? Did the commentary confuse temples of Apollo and Aphrodite? We have no means of knowing.

III

Harpocration s.v. Λευκάς ('Leucas'): ...It is an island lying opposite the Epirus ... Menander's play the *Leukadia* also (is set) inside (the island).

This statement confirms what can be inferred from O.i/fr. 1 and O.ii about the scene of the play.

[a] Sometimes called the Daniel version, because it was first printed in P. Daniel's edition of 1600. Cf. especially J. J. H. Savage, *Harvard Studies in Classical Philology*, 43 (1932), 77–121.

MISOUMENOS or THRASONIDES
(THE HATED MAN or THRASONIDES)

INTRODUCTION

Manuscripts

I = *P.IFAO* (an acronym for the *Institut Française de l'Archéologie Orientale* in Cairo) 89, a fragment from the top of a column of a papyrus roll, written in the third century A.D., perhaps as a school exercise. It contains lines 1–18[1] of the play. First edition: B. Boyaval, *Zeitschrift für Papyrologie und Epigraphik*, 6 (1970), 1–5 with a photograph (pl. I); re-edited by L. Koenen, *ZPE* 6 (1970), 99–104, and 8 (1971), 141–142 with a new photograph (pl. III); cf. E. G. Turner, *The Oxyrhynchus Papyri*, 48 (1981), 9–10.

C = *P. Cologne* 282, a further fragment from the same roll as *P.IFAO* 89, now in Cologne, containing portions of lines 18–30. First edition: M. Gronewald, *Kölner Papyri*, 7 (1991), 1–4 with a photograph (pl. Ia).

O.19 = *P. Oxyrhynchus* 3368, seven fragments (plus further scraps) of a papyrus of the third century A.D., containing (complete or in part) lines 1–18, 33–45, 51–68, 85–100 and eight insecurely placed lines (here provisionally numbered 241–248).

[1] On the new line-numbering, see later in the introduction to this play.

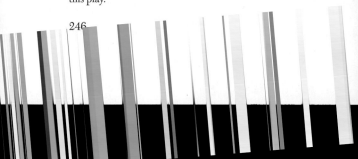

O.20 = *P. Oxyrhynchus* 3369, two papyrus sheets from the third century A.D., pasted together and containing portions of lines 12–54 and 78–94.

O.21 = *P. Oxyrhynchus* 3370, three fragments of a papyrus roll from the third century A.D., containing portions of lines 29–43.

O.22 = *P. Oxyrhynchus* 3371, a tiny scrap of papyrus from the second century A.D., containing the play title Μισού[μενος] Μενά[νδρου].

Definitive editions of O.19–22 by E. G. Turner, *The Oxyrhynchus Papyri*, 48 (1981), 1–21 with photographs (pls. I, II); see also his *The Papyrologist at Work = Greek, Roman and Byzantine Studies* monograph 6, (1972), 48–50 (O.19 vv. 1–18), and "The Lost Beginning of Menander Misoumenos", *Proceedings of the British Academy*, 63 (1978), 315–331 (O.19, 20).

O.11 = *P. Oxyrhynchus* 2657, three fragments of papyrus from the third century A.D., containing portions of lines 301–392 and a few letters from a further 17 lines (here fr. 2). First edition: E. G. Turner, *The Oxyrhynchus Papyri*, 33 (1968), 55–65 with photographs (pls. IV, V).

O.10 = *P. Oxyrhynchus* 2656, nine fragments from four leaves (two of them conjugate) of a papyrus codex written probably in the fourth century A.D., containing lines 501–806 and 959–996, mostly very mutilated (but 532–540, 560–578, 611–623, 631–638, 646–650, 659–688, 695–725 complete or less severely damaged); the title Μενάνδ[ρου] Θρασων[ίδης] is preserved at the end. First edition: E. G. Turner, *New Fragments of the*

Misoumenos of Menander = *Bulletin of the Institute of Classical Studies*, suppl. 17 (1965), with complete photographs (pls. I–IX); re-edited by him in *The Oxyrhynchus Papyri*, 33 (1968), 15–55. Lines 786–806 are re-edited by Margaret Maehler, *The Oxyrhynchus Papyri*, 59 (1992), 67–69.

B.3 = *P. Berlin* 13932, a fragment from a papyrus codex of the fifth century A.D., discovered at Hermupolis and containing portions of lines 532–544 and 560–572. First edition: W. Schubart, *Griechische literarische Papyri = Berichte der Sächsischen Akademie der Wissenschaften zu Leipzig, Philologisch-historische Klasse*, 97/5 (1950), 47–50; cf. H. Maehler in *Lustrum*, 10 (1965), 154–156, C. Austin in *The Oxyrhynchus Papyri*, 33 (1968), 17–19. No photographs are yet published, but this edition has benefited from unpublished ones kindly supplied by Dr C. Austin.

B.2 = *P. Berlin* 13281, the lower part of one leaf of a papyrus codex of the third century A.D., containing most of lines 567–578 and 611–622. First edition: U. von Wilamowitz-Moellendorff, *Dichterfragmente aus der Papyrussammlung der Königlichen Museen 6: Neue Komödie = Sitzungsberichte der Preussischen Akademie der Wissenschaften* (Berlin 1918), 747–749; cf. W. Schubart, H. Maehler and C. Austin, *locc. citt.* under B.3 above. No photographs are yet published, but this edition has benefited from unpublished ones kindly supplied by Dr C. Austin.

O.3 = *P. Oxyrhynchus* 1013, fragments of the lower part of one leaf of a papyrus codex from the fifth or sixth

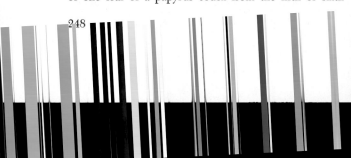

century A.D., containing portions of lines 642 (or 643) to 646 (or 647), 649–665, 677–680, 683–700. First edition: A. S. Hunt, *The Oxyrhynchus Papyri*, 7 (1910), 103–110, without a photograph; cf. E. G. Turner, *New Fragments of the Misoumenos of Menander = Bulletin of the Institute of Classical Studies*, suppl. 17, (1965), 42–45 and 48–51 with a photograph (pl. IX) of 642 (or 643) to 645 (or 646) and 649–656, and *The Oxyrhynchus Papyri*, 33 (1968), 32–40.

O.23 = *P. Oxyrhynchus* 3967, a scrap from a papyrus roll of the third century A.D., containing the middle portions of lines 784–821. First edition: M. Maehler, *The Oxyrhynchus Papyri*, 59 (1992), 59–70, with photograph (pl. V).

O.7 = *P. Oxyrhynchus* 1605, a narrow strip from a papyrus roll of the third century A.D., containing small portions of lines 919–932 and 948–974. First edition: B. P. Grenfell and A. S. Hunt, *The Oxyrhynchus Papyri*, 13 (1919), 45–47. No photograph is published.

O.26 = *P. Oxyrhynchus* 4025, a tiny scrap of the first century A.D. containing bits of six successive lines which have been plausibly assigned to the play. It is printed here as fragment 1, where the reason for its attribution to *Misoumenos* is given, and the attempt to match it with lines 752–756 rejected. First edition: P. J. Parsons, *The Oxyrhynchus Papyri*, 80 (1994), 46–47, with photograph (pl. III).

Fragments 1 (= O.11 fr. 3), 2 (= O.23 fr. 3) and 3 (= O.26) are unplaced scraps of papyrus, fragments 4 to 11 are attested quotations from the play by later authors (see introduction to Volume I, pp. xxiv f.), and fragment

249

12 a possible quotation. These fragments are printed after the end of the continuous play text, together with five testimonia to the play which seem informed and informative.

Pictorial Evidence

A mosaic of the third century A.D. from the 'House of Menander' at Mytilene on Lesbos. This mosaic is inscribed Μ{Ε}ΙΣΟΥΜΕΝΟΥ ΜΕ(ΡΟΣ) Ε (*Misoumenos*, Act V), but since the three characters portrayed are not identified by name (as they are e.g. on the *Encheiridion* and *Epitrepontes* mosaics in the same house: see vol. I of this edition, pp. 358 f. and 381 f.), while the fragments of text preserved from the fifth act are scanty and mutilated, it is difficult to identify two of the figures or to explain what they are doing. On the right stands a woman (presumably Krateia, the slave girl owned and loved by Thrasonides) wearing a blue cloak and tunic, both edged with black, and an elaborate frontal. Her right arm is raised well above her shoulder. In the middle there is a man dressed in a white tunic and cloak, whose gesture is uncertain. On the left stands a man in a white tunic; his head is turned towards the other two, and he appears to be tightening around his neck a scarf whose ends are held firmly, one in each hand. One possibility is that the character on the left is Getas, Thrasonides' slave, using his gesture with the scarf to mime a recent threat or attempt by his master to strangle himself, while Krateia and her newly discovered father Demeas react with horror. Alternatively, the central figure could be Krateia's brother, whose arrival proved that previous reports of his death at the hands of Thrasonides were false; in that case Getas on his left would now be reacting with pleasure, since Krateia's hatred of Thrasonides, arising from her belief that he had killed her brother, might now be replaced by affection. Standard edition of the mosaic: S. Charitonidis, L. Kahil and R. Ginouvès, *Les mosaïques de la Maison du Ménandre à Mytilène* = *Antike Kunst*, Beiheft 6 (Berne 1970), 57 ff. and colour plate 8; the authors draw attention to a cake-mould of the third century A.D. from Ostia which may possibly portray the same scene (p. 60 and plate 26; see also T. B. L. Webster, *Monuments Illustrating New Comedy*[2] = *BICS* Supplement 24 (1969), p. 222 IT 80 and M. Maehler, *The Oxyrhynchus Papyri*, 59 (1992), 62 n. 6, but contrast M. Bieber, *The History of the Greek and Roman Theater*[2] (Princeton 1961), 241 and pl. 793, interpreting the mould design as a scene from tragedy).

This play is virtually always in our sources given the title Μισούμενος, but the colophon in one papyrus (O.10: see above) names it Θρασων[ίδης. The existence of alternative titles was not unusual in ancient Greek drama, and a common reason for this was the popular tendency to refer to a play by the name of its leading character rather than by its official title.[1] In *Misoumenos* the role of the soldier Thrasonides appears to have so impressed audiences and readers that a mention of his name alone was often deemed enough to identify a reference to the play (see e.g. testimonia I, II, III). It was one of Menander's most popular plays; more papyri derive from it than from any other play, and ancient quotations from its opening scene in particular are remarkably

[1] See especially R. H. Hunter's edition of Eubulus (Cambridge 1983), 146 ff.

numerous (11, of which 6 come from the first fifteen verses).

Although portions of over 590 of its lines survive, most of these are mangled and lacunose, and only about 160 are anywhere near complete, with a relatively small proportion yielding sections of continuous and so fully intelligible text (1–17, 88–97, 611–622, 659–688, 696–720 in my numbering). There are inevitably several passages of text whose interpretation is now uncertain, at times because it is linked to incidents in lost portions of the plot. In these places the translation cannot fail to be controversial.

Mainly as a result of this, it is difficult now to decide how far *Misoumenos* deserved its ancient celebrity, even though there are signs enough of imaginative writing, individualised characterisation (at least for Thrasonides and Getas) and entertaining situations to make us lament the existing state of the play's text. Certainly it would have needed capable actors, for Menander has incorporated in the preserved portions of text a number of passages which require their speakers to imitate voices other than their own (55 f., 85–87, 87 f., 532–534, 693–695, 698–700, 706–711, 797–798, 968–969). There is additionally a long monologue by Thrasonides (757–816) in which he not only imitates Krateia's voice but also is involved in an argument with himself.

No hypothesis, didascalic notice, or cast-list is preserved for *Misoumenos*. Although its date of production is nowhere recorded, it contains references to events in Cyprus which were probably intended to provide a plausible historical background to the staged action. At 632 ff. Demeas complains that in Cyprus war had scattered families, and Getas goes on to explain that this was how Krateia came to be a slave of Thrasonides.[1] Fragment 5 appears to identify Thrasonides as having served with distinction under one of the kings of Cyprus. These references may imply that Thrasonides was presented as a mercenary who had fought in support of one of the ten Cypriot kings when Ptolemy I was campaigning between 321 and 309 B.C. to bring the island under his control, and it seems likely that the play was written at some time during or shortly after that period.[2]

With considerable hesitation I have decided on a complete renumbering of the lines of the play. Editors of the papyri discovered before the Second World War numbered their lines sequentially, without allowing for lacunae, and so when further texts came to light in the last thirty years or so they could be accommodated to the pre-existing schemes at times only by the addition of letters and stars (thus A1–A100, 194a, 194b, 375a, 375b, 380a, 380b, 404*–418*), which are clumsy and confusing. Accordingly I have introduced a new scheme which may be more straightforward and still serviceable in the future if further portions of text surface from the Egyptian sands. It does not aim to be accurate after line 100, and does not imply any theories about the length of gaps in

[1] The context here leaves it unclear whether Krateia was enslaved in Cyprus or elsewhere. If she and her family were Athenians, she could have been seized by pirates during a raid on the coast of Attica (compare Men. *Sik.* 354 ff.), and then shipped off and sold as a slave in Cyprus.

[2] So E. G. Turner, *BICS*, suppl. 17 (1965), 17, and see especially G. F. Hill, *A History of Cyprus*, 1 (Cambridge 1940), 113–115, 156–178.

our text or the original length of the play, about which no information has survived. An attempt has been made to keep the last one or two digits, wherever possible, identical with those in the recent editions of E. G. Turner (*The Oxyrhynchus Papyri*, 33, 1968, 15 ff.), F. H. Sandbach (Oxford 1972[1], 1990[2]) and F. Sisti (Genoa 1986). As a further aid I add these scholars' line-numberings in brackets.

	Arnott	Sandbach, Sisti and (in Acts IV, V) Maehler
Act I	1–100	A1–A100
Act 1	241–248	p. 364 Sandbach[2] (unnumbered) = fr. 1 Sisti
?Act II	401–493	1–93
Act III	501–676	101–275 (including 194a, 194b)
Act IV	677–816	276–403 (including 375a, 375b, 380a, 380b) Sandbach, Sisti along with 404*–413* Maehler
Act V	817–821	414*–418* Maehler
Act V	919–932	404–417 Sisti
Act V	948–996	418–466 Sandbach, Sisti

Dramatis personae, so far as they are known:

Thrasonides, a mercenary soldier just returned from a
    campaign in Cyprus
Getas, male slave of Thrasonides
Krateia, a young slave girl owned and loved by
    Thrasonides

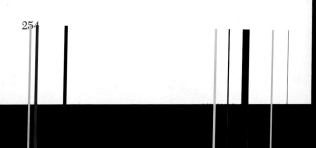

Krateia's nurse, apparently named Chrysis[1]
Demeas, Krateia's father, newly (?) arrived from Cyprus
Kleinias, a young (?) man
An old woman, slave of Kleinias, apparently named Syra[1]

In the missing sections of the play other characters will
have had speaking parts: almost certainly a god or god-
dess as prologue, probably Krateia's brother, possibly the
unidentified fat-faced man of 560 f. Simiche, an elderly
(?) female slave probably owned by Thrasonides, and a
cook appear as mutes in preserved sections of the text;
they may have had speaking roles in one or more lost
scenes. There was also a chorus to perform the
entr'actes.

[1] See the note on line 555.

ΜΙΣΟΥΜΕΝΟΣ

ΘΡΑΣΩΝΙΔΗΣ

(A 1) ὦ Νύξ, σὺ γὰρ δὴ πλεῖστον Ἀφροδίτης μέρος
μετέχεις θεῶν, ἐν σοί τε περὶ τούτων λόγοι
πλεῖστοι λέγονται φροντίδες τ' ἐρωτικαί,
ἆρ' ἄλλον ἄνθρωπόν τιν' ἀθλιώτερον
5 ἑόρακας; ἆρ' ἐρῶντα δυσποτμώτερον;
πρὸς ταῖς ἐμαυτοῦ νῦν θύραις ἕστηκ' ἐγὼ
(A 7) ἐν τῷ στενωπῷ, περιπατῶ τ' ἄνω κάτω—
ἀμφοτερά<κι>ς—μεχρὶ νῦν, μεσούσης σού σχεδόν,

1–2 KT fr. 789; 4–5 *Mis.* fr. 6 Kö.; 6 KT fr. 664.

1–11 I, O.19   4 αρααλλον O.19: τίνα ἄλλον ΣC² and
Ἄπολλον other mss. of Plutarch *Mor.* 525a citing lines 4–5.
ἀθλιώτερον Σθn of Plut.,]θλιωτερον O.19: ἀθλιώτατον other
mss. of Plut., αθλιωτατο[I.   5 εορακας O.19: ἑώρακας mss.
of Plut. ἆρα Σθn of Plut., αρα O.19: ἢ other mss. of Plut.
δυσποτμώτερον mss. of Plut.,]ποτμω[.]ερον O.19: δυσποτμω-
τατο[I.   6 νῦν omitted by Apollonius *Synt.* 2. 107 (II. 2
p. 209. 5 Uhlig) citing this line.   7 περιπατω I: -πατων O.19.
8 ἀμφοτερά<κι>ς Arnott: αμφοτερας O.19 (]εχ[..]ννν I).

MISOUMENOS

(The Hated Man)

(SCENE: A street in a city which is not identified in the preserved portions of the play; it is perhaps more likely to have been Athens than a city on an island in the east Mediterranean such as Rhodes. This street is backed by at least two houses, one belonging to Thrasonides, the other to Kleinias; a third house, belonging to the otherwise unidentified fat-faced man of 620 f., might be either visible on stage or more probably imagined as just beyond a side entrance. The play's opening is preserved. In the middle of a cold and wet night Thrasonides is seen, sometimes pacing to and fro before his house, sometimes standing miserably in his doorway.)

THRASONIDES

O Night—for you've the largest share in sex
Of all the gods, and in your shades are spoken
Most words of love and thoughts charged with desire—
Have you seen any other man more racked
With misery? A lover more ill-starred?   5
Now either at my own front door I stand,
Here in the alley, or I saunter up
And down, both ways (?), when I could lie asleep

ἐξὸν καθεύδειν τήν τ' ἐρωμένην ἔχειν.

10 παρ' ἐμοὶ γάρ ἐστιν ἔνδον, ἔξεστίν τέ μοι
καὶ βούλομαι τοῦθ' ὡς ἂν ἐμμανέστατα

(A 12) ἐρῶν τις, οὐ ποιῶ δ'. ὑπαιθρίῳ δέ μοι
χειμ[ῶνος ὄ]ντος ἐστὶν αἱρετώτερον
ἐστη[κέναι] τρέμοντι καὶ λαλοῦντί σοι.

ΓΕΤΑΣ

15 τὸ δ[ὴ λεγόμ]ενον, οὐδὲ κυνί, μὰ τοὺς θε[ούς,
νῦν [ἐξι]τητόν ἐστιν, ὁ δ' ἐμὸς δεσπότης

(A 17) ὥσπερ θέρους μέσου περιπατεῖ φιλοσο[φῶν
τοσαῦτ'. [ἀ]πολεῖ μ'. οὐ δρυινός; [.]. .εα. .π[
δ]ιατριβων γ' ενκα. . .πεσ[

20]. .ει τὴν θύραν. ὦ δυστυχής,
τί οὐ καθεύδεις; σύ μ' ἀποκναίεις περιπατῶν.

9 Adesp. fr. 282 Kock; 10–12 *Mis.* fr. 5 Kö.; 15 Alciphron 2. 27. 1;
20–21 KT fr. 124 + *Mis.* fr. 9 Kö.

9 ἐξὸν Chariton 4. 4. 7, scholia to Eur. *Phoen.* 478, Ar. *Ach.*
1164b and Eustathius 232.32 citing the line: εξω O.19. τε O.19, τ
I: τε omitted by mss. of scholia and Eustath. ἔχειν Chariton,
εχει[I: εχει O.19, ἔχων scholia and Eustath.   10 τεμοι O.19,
τε[I: τε omitted by mss. of Plut. *Mor.* 525a citing the line, some
of them giving ἔνδον ἔνδον.   11 τουτοως O.19, τουτ'θως
I.   12–17 I, O.19, O.20   12 οὐ ποιῶ δέ mss. of Plut.,
]ιωδε· I: ουτωωδε O.19.   13 Suppl. Turner:]τοσεστ[.]ν I,
]ντοσε[O.20, χειμ[. . . . . .]εστιν O.20 with insufficient space for
what is clearly the correct text.   14 Suppl. Rea. λαλουντι
O.20, λα[. . .]ντι I: καλουντι O.19.   15 δ[ὴ λεγόμ]ενον
suppl. Austin, Turner, θε[ούς Turner (τουσθ[I, το[O.20: τωθεω
O.19).   16 [ἐξι]τητόν West: [. . .].ητεον O.19.   17 Suppl.
Handley.   18 C, O.19, O.20. τοσαῦτ' Barigazzi: τοσουτ

258

Till now, when you, O Night, have nearly run
Half course, and clasp my love. She's in there—in   10
My house, I've got the chance, I want it just
As much as the most ardent lover—yet
I don't . . . I'd rather stand here shivering
Beneath a wintry sky—chatting to you!

(*Getas now emerges from Thrasonides' house, but at first keeps his distance from his master, who is at this point walking up and down.*)

GETAS

Dear gods! It isn't fit even to allow   15
A dog [outside] now, as [they say]![a] My master,
Though, tramps round like a professor,[b] just as if
It were midsummer!—he'll . . .   18

(*The following line and a half are too fractured for coherent translation. Getas goes on to say '[Is]n't he like an oak' (i.e. (?) 'stupid'), presumably referring to Thrasonides, and then there is a reference to 'wasting time' or 'pastimes/discourses'.*)

[He . . .] the door. Poor fellow, why   20
Aren't you asleep? Your tramping worries me.

[a] An adage of the time.
[b] Literally 'doing all this philosophising'. In Menander's time the comic poets of Athens ridiculed philosophers and other teachers for a habit of pacing up and down as they lectured. See my commentary on Alexis (Cambridge 1996/1997), fr. 151 (147K) lines 1–3.

---

apparently O.19.   19–28 C, O.20.   19 Either δ]ιατρίβων (participle) or -τριβῶν (noun).

(A 22) ἢ καὶ καθε]ύδεις; περίμεν' εἰ μ' ἐγρη[γ]ορὼς
ὁρᾷς.]

ΘΡΑΣΩΝΙΔΗΣ

[Γέτα, σ]ὺ δ' αὐτὸς ἐξελήλυθας;
τί βουλό]μενος; πότερα κελευσθε[ί]ς; <ο>ὔποτε
25 ὑπ' ἐμοῦ γάρ,] ἢ τὸ τοιοῦτον ἀπὸ σαυτοῦ π[ο]ῶν;

ΓΕΤΑΣ

μὰ Δί', οὐκ ἐ]κέλευον οἱ καθεύδ[ο]ντες.

ΘΡΑΣΩΝΙΔΗΣ

Γέτα,
(A 27) παρῆσθας, ὡς] ἔοικε, κηδεμὼν ἐμός.

ΓΕΤΑΣ

εἴσελθε κἂν νῦν, ὦ μακάρι'· ἐν πα[ντ]ὶ γὰρ
ἦσθας μακ]άριος.

ΘΡΑΣΩΝΙΔΗΣ

τίς; [ἀ]τυχῶ δεινῶς, π[αθών
30 ἤδη κάκ', ὦ Γέ]τα, <τὰ> μέγιστ'· ἀλλ' οὐδέπω
καιρὸς καθο]ρᾶν σ'· ἐχθὲς γὰρ εἰς τὴν οἰκ[ί]αν

28 *Mis.* fr. 11 Kö.

22 ἢ καὶ καθε]ύδεις; suppl. Sandbach, ἐγρη[γ]ορὼς Turner.
23 ὁρᾷς; (Thr.) Γέτα suppl. Sandbach *exempli gratia.* σ]ὺ δ'
αὐτὸς Handley:]νδιαυτος O.20.   24 τί βουλό]μενος; suppl.
Sandbach, Barrett, πότ[ε]ρα Sandbach, κελευσθε[ί]ς and
<ο>ὔποτε Austin (υποτε O.20).   25 ὑπ' ἐμοῦ γάρ suppl.
Sandbach, π[ο]ῶν Turner π[οι]ων probably O.20).   26 μὰ
Δί' οὐκ suppl. Sandbach (μὰ Δί' already Handley), καθεύδ[ο]ν-
τες Turner.   27 παρῆσθας suppl. Sandbach, ὡς Cockle.

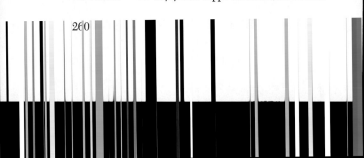

260

[Or] are you [really] sleeping?
> (*Getas now intercepts Thrasonides.*)
>> Wait, if you're awake
[And see me.]

THRASONIDES

[Getas,] is that *you* out here? [What do]
[You want?] Were you given orders? Not [by me]!
Or is such action all your own idea?   25

GETAS

[Good heavens! no] orders came from men asleep!

THRASONIDES

Getas, it seems [you came here] as my nurse!

GETAS

Good sir, do go in now—[you've] always [had]
Good luck.[a]

THRASONIDES

Who? Me? My luck's been terrible,
[Getas! I'm in the] greatest [trouble], but   30
You've not had [time to notice] yet, you only

---

[a] Getas' pun on ὦ μακάρι' ('good sir!') and the following μακ]άριος (literally 'lucky') is difficult to convey effectively in English.

---

28 κἂν νῦν scholion on Dem. 2. 14 citing Getas' words:]αινυν O.20. πα[ντ]ὶ suppl. Handley.   29–30 C, O.20, O.21.   29 ἦσθας suppl. Sandbach, μακ]άριος Lloyd-Jones, [ἀ]τυχῶ Gronewald (]τυχω[C,]υτω O.20), π[αθών Arnott.   30 [ὦ Γέ]τα suppl. Gronewald, the rest (with <τὰ> before μέγιστ') Arnott. Change of speaker before τίς suggested by Gronewald: dicolon after, not before τις in O.20 (O.21 here illegible).
31–32 O.20, O.21.   31 καιρὸς suppl. Arnott, the rest Turner.

(A 32) ἐλήλυθας τὴν ἡμετέ[ρα]ν σὺ διὰ χρό[νο]ν.

ΓΕΤΑΣ
τὸ στρατό]πεδον γὰρ [ὡς] ἀπῆρα καταλιπὼν
ἦσθ' εἰκό]τως εὔψυχος· [ὅτ]ι δὲ τάττομαι
35   ἐπὶ τῆς π]αραπομπῆς τ[ῶ]ν λαφύρων, ἔ[σχ]ατος
ἥκω. τί δὲ τὸ λ]υποῦν σ';

ΘΡΑΣΩΝΙΔΗΣ
ἐλείν' ὑβρίζομαι.

ΓΕΤΑΣ
(A 37) ὑπὸ τίνος;]

ΘΡΑΣΩΝΙΔΗΣ
ὑπὸ τῆς αἰχμαλώτου· πριάμενος
αὐτήν, πε]ριθεὶς ἐλευθερίαν, τῆς οἰκίας
δέσποιν]αν ἀποδείξας, θεραπαίνας χρυσία
40   ἱμάτια δο]ύς, γυναῖκα νομίσας.

ΓΕΤΑΣ
εἶτα τί;
γυνή σ' ὑβ]ρίζει;

ΘΡΑΣΩΝΙΔΗΣ
καὶ λέγειν αἰσχύνομαι·

32 Suppl. Turner:]τηνημετε[..]νσυδιαχρο[..]ν Ο.20,]νεληλυ-
θασσνδ.α...ν.. Ο.21 (with the first word in the line presumably
misplaced after ἡμετέραν).   33–43 Ο.19, Ο.20, Ο.21.   33 τὸ
στρατό]πεδον Sisti (after τοῦ στρατο]πέδον deciph. and suppl.
Cockle):]πεδον Ο.20,]ωι Ο.21.   [ὡς] suppl. Handley.
34 ἦσθ' suppl. Gronewald, εἰκό]τως and [ὅτ]ι Turner. ευψυχοσ
Ο.19, ε.ψυ[.][.] Ο.20: ευ.[.]..δηχ.ρ[..]τομα. Ο.21.   35 Suppl.
Turner.   36 ἥκω suppl. Belardinelli and Gronewald, the rest

Returned home yesterday—it's been so long!

GETAS

[When] I set out, leaving [the] camp behind,
[You were quite] cheerful. I was put in charge
[Of] bringing back the spoils,[a] and [that's why I'm]   35
Last [home. But what's] distressing you?

THRASONIDES

                    I'm sadly being
Abused.

GETAS

    [By whom?]

THRASONIDES

            That captive girl. I bought
[Her], promised her her freedom, made her my
House[keeper], gave her servants, jewellery
[And clothes], considered her my wife.

GETAS

                  What then?   40
[A wife] abuses [you]?

THRASONIDES

            I'm even ashamed to say —

[a] Like Daos at the beginning of Menander's *Aspis*. We must
assume that Thrasonides and Krateia had arrived home from the
campaign in Cyprus a good while before.

Turner.   37 Suppl. Turner.   38 αὐτήν suppl. Austin, πε]ρι-
θεὶς Handley.   39 Suppl. Turner.   40 ἱμάτια suppl. Austin
and Sandbach, δο]ὺς Turner.   41 Suppl. Turner from Apollo-
nius *Synt.* 1. 41 (II. 2 p. 37. 6 f. Uhlig) ἐκκείσθω δὲ ὑποδείγ-
ματα, τοῦ μὲν προτέρου 'πῶς ἡ γυνή σ' ὕβρισε;'

(A 42) ὄφιν, λέ]αιναν —

ΓΕΤΑΣ
ἀλλ' ἔμοιγ' ὅμως φράσον.

ΘΡΑΣΩΝΙΔΗΣ
μισεῖ νέον] με μῖσος.

ΓΕΤΑΣ
ὦ Μ[α]γνῆτι· σὲ
μισεῖν; ἄτοπ]α γὰρ ὑπονοεῖς.

ΘΡΑΣΩΝΙΔΗΣ
ἢ 'νθρώπινον

45   οἴει τὸ τυχό]ν τ' εἶναι τόδ';

ΓΕΤΑΣ
οὐδὲ κ[υ]ρία

(Speakers and part-divisions in the next four lines are uncertain.)

]...[.].αν.[.].[   ].αι σφόδρ[α
(A 47)   ..[   ].στειναιγα[
                 ]πειρ...[
                 ].[.]....[

42 ὄφιν suppl. *exempli gratia* Arnott, λέ]αιναν Turner. ἔμοιγ'
West: either εμοισ' (Turner) or εμοιγ' (Rea) O.20.   43 νέον
suppl. Austin, the rest deciph., suppl. and corr. Turner (μεισος
O.20,]μει[O.21).   44–45 O.19, O.20.   44 Suppl. Turner.
]ηνθρωπιν.[O.20: ανθρωπινον O.19   45]ντ'εινα..οδεστιν
followed by dicolon O.20 (]τιν[   ]ουδ[O.19): εστιν del. Turner,
who also suppl. κ[υ]ρία.   46–50 O.20.

[Snake, savage monster!]

GETAS
Tell me, even so!

THRASONIDES
[She hates] me with a [strange new] hatred.

GETAS
Oh,
Opposite poles![a] [Hate] you? [A weird] idea!

THRASONIDES
So
You think it's [normal, natural]?

GETAS (?)
She's not in charge   45

(*Of the next four lines only a few, mainly incomprehensible, letters are preserved, but* very much *can be deciphered at the end of 46. Continuous text returns towards the end of 50.*)

---

[a] This implied comparison of Krateia's present loathing (of Thrasonides) to the repulsion of (unlike) magnetic poles shows that the phenomenon was familiar already in Menander's time; later references to it can be found in Plutarch, *Moralia* 376b, and Marcellus Empiricus, *De medicamentis* 1. 63. A magnet's power of attracting iron, however, was known in Greece to the philosopher Thales as early as the sixth century B.C. See G. S. Kirk, J. E. Raven, M. Schofield, *The Presocratic Philosophers* (Cambridge 1983[2]), 93 ff.

MENANDER

ΘΡΑΣΩΝΙΔΗΣ

50   τηρῶ τὸν Δία

ὕοντα πολλῷ νυκτὸς [οὔσ]ης, ἀστραπάς,

(A 52) βροντάς, ἔχων αὐτὴν δὲ κατάκειμ'.

ΓΕΤΑΣ

εἶτα τί;

ΘΡΑΣΩΝΙΔΗΣ

κέκραγα "παιδίσκη· βαδίσαι γάρ", φημί, "δεῖ

ἤδη με πρὸς τὸν δεῖν'," <ὑπ>είπας ὄνομά τι.

55   πᾶσ' ἂν γυνὴ δὴ τ[ο]ῦ[τό γ'] εἴποι "τοῦ Διὸς

ὕοντος, ὦ τάλαν; [πρὸς ἄνθρ]ωπόν τινα;

(A 57) __σκεπτ[__   ]αστα[

58   __ηδ[__

(Lines 59–64 are torn off in O.19, apart from illegible
traces of the opening letter of 59 and the opening three
letters of 64.)

65   του[

        ε. .[

(A 67) ο. .[

68   εκ.[

(Lines 69–84 are torn off in O.18, but O.20 provides the
opening letters of 78–84.)

50–51 KT fr. 721

50 τὸν Δία Turnebus: τοναια mss. of Nonius Marcellus, *De
compendiosa doctrina* IV p. 387 Mercier = II p. 620 Lindsay,
citing this passage (O.20 here illegible).   51–54 O.19, O.20.
51 υονταπολλω O.19 (O.20 here defective): υοντατιοχω

THRASONIDES

(*in mid-speech?*)

I'm waiting for   50
A heavy downpour after dark, with lightning and
Thunder—then I'm in bed with her!

GETAS

What then?

THRASONIDES

I call out "Girl," I say "I've got to go
To see a man now," filling in some name.
Then any woman would respond [like this]:   55
"In this rain! You poor thing! [To see a man]

*(The next 28 lines (57–84) in the papyri are either totally
lost or so badly damaged that only occasional words can
be deciphered in the continuing dialogue between Thra-
sonides and Getas, which appears now primarily to have
the function of describing the soldier's relationship with
Krateia. Thrasonides may begin line 57 with* one must
consider, *but whether Thrasonides here refers to himself*

---

mss. LB^A, τοντατιοχω other mss. of Nonius. [οὔσ]ης Handley
from]ησ O.20: O.19 ends line with νυκτοσαστ..πασβροντας
(βροντάς transposed to beginning of 52 by Handley).
52 αὐτὴν δὲ Handley: δεαυτην O.19. κατάκειμ' Handley
(]ατακειμ[O.20): κατακειμαι O.19 followed by one-letter space.
53 Corr. Turner: βιδισαι O.19 (]δισαι O.20).   54 δεῖν','"
<ὑπ>είπας Arnott: δεινα ειπας O.19 (with space between να
and ει filled by prolonged tail of α).   55–68 O.19.   55 Suppl.
Handley. It is uncertain where the quotation beginning τοῦ
Διὸς ends.   56 Suppl. Austin and West.   57 σκεπτ[έον
suppl. *exempli gratia* Turner.

MENANDER

ΘΡΑΣΩΝΙΔΗΣ (?)

78   φησωνμο[

(A 79)   ὁ τοῖχος ουτ[

80   ερεισεαυτ[

 οὐκ εἰκότ[

ΓΕΤΑΣ

(A 82)   ὦ τᾶν, ταπ[

τρόπον τε.[

ὑπερεντρ[υφ

ΘΡΑΣΩΝΙΔΗΣ (?)

85   αὕτη 'στί· [πρ]όσεχ', ὦ φιλ[τάτη, τὸν νοῦν ἐμοί·

παρορωμένῳ δὲ πε[ριβαλεῖς παραχρῆμά μοι

(A 87)   φιλονικίαν, πόνον, μανί[αν

ΓΕΤΑΣ

τί, ὦ κακόδαιμον;

ΘΡΑΣΩΝΙΔΗΣ

ἀλλ' ἔγωγ' ἄν, φι[λοφρόνως

κλη[θ]εὶς μόνον, θύσαιμι πᾶσι τοῖς θε[ο]ῖ[ς.

ΓΕΤΑΣ

90   τί [νε]ὸν ἂν εἴη τὸ κακόν; οὐδὲ γὰρ σφόδρ' εἶ

78–84 O.20.   78–81 assigned to Thrasonides by Turner.
80 ἐρεῖ σεαυτ[or ἐρεῖς ἑαυτ[.   84 Suppl. Turner.
85–94 O.19, O.20.   85, 87 Suppl. Turner.   85 αυτηεστ[
O.20.   86 Suppl. *exempli gratia* Turner.   88 Suppl. Lloyd-
Jones. Change of speaker indicated by Turner: no paragraphus
in O.19, O.20.   89 Suppl. Turner.   90 [νέ]ον Sisti: π[οι]ο-
ναν O.19, τι[O.20.   σφοδραει O.19.

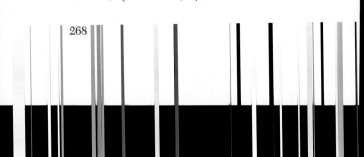

or whether he is still quoting Krateia's words is uncertain.
Between 78 and 81 Thrasonides appears to be speaking,
but the surviving words (78 tell = perhaps to tell me, 79
the wall, 80 you or he or she will say, 81 not seemly/likely)
do not illuminate their context. At 82 Getas intervenes
and possibly goes on to the end of 84; his identifiable
words (82 Oh sir, 83 a way, 84 too haughty or too extra-
vagant) may belong to a context in which Thrasonides'
troubles are being explained at least partly as a result of
his low pay and Krateia's more extravagant expectations.)

THRASONIDES

[That's what] she is. "Darling, give [me your heart].   85
If you ignore me, [you'll fill me at once]
With jealousy, distress and frenzy [

GETAS

Poor man, why so?

THRASONIDES

          "And yet, if greeted [with kind words],
I'd sacrifice to all the gods."[a]

GETAS

          But what
The hell's gone wrong [now]? You're not too repulsive,   90

[a] Presumably here Thrasonides is apostrophising Krateia.

ἄκ[ρ]ως ἀηδὴς ὥστε γ᾽ εἰπεῖν· ἀλλά σο[ι

(A 92) τὸ μικρὸν ἀμέλε[ι] τοῦ στρατιωτικοῦ [βλάβη·
ἀλ[λ]᾽ ὄψιν ὑπεράστειος· ἀλλὰ μὴν ἄγ[εις
ἐφ᾽] ἡλικίας ..ναα.ε...ποθεν.[

ΘΡΑΣΩΝΙΔΗΣ

95 κακῶς ἀ[π]όλοιο· δεῖ τὸ πρᾶγμ᾽ εὑρεῖν [ὅ τι
ἐστίν ποτ᾽, αἰτίαν ἀναγκ[α]ίαν τινὰ

(A 97) δεῖ]ξαι.

ΓΕΤΑΣ
μιαρὸν τὸ φῦλόν [ἐσ]τι, δέσ[π]οτ[α.

ΘΡΑΣΩΝΙΔΗΣ
ἂν μ]ὴ παρῇ[ς]—

ΓΕΤΑΣ
σὺ δέ γ᾽ ἃ διηγεῖ, δέσπ[οτα,
....]ομο..... πρός [τι] συκάζει τέ [σε

100 αὐτό]νομο[ς· ο]ὐκ ἀεὶ γ[ὰρ ε]ὔλογός τε [τις

(The rest of Act I is lost, apart from one scrap of eight
mutilated verses in O.19 (fr. C) which is difficult to place.
In it Getas is conversing with another character (probably

91–93 Suppl. Turner.   91 Continued to Thrasonides by
Turner: paragraphus and deleted speaker's name in left-hand
margin of O.20.   γεειπεν O.19.   92 μεικρον O.19.   93 Suppl.
Turner, who rightly ignores paragraphus under the line in O.20.
αλλαμμην O.19 with second μ deleted and another ην written
above it.   94 ἐφ᾽ suppl. Arnott.   95–100 O.19.   95–97 Suppl.
Turner.   97 Change of speaker suggested by Handley (?
παρη[ς:]συ O.19).   98–100 Deciph. and suppl. Turner (the
beginning of 100 very hesitantly).

Not unduly so, to speak of. But of course
The meagreness of army pay [won't help]!
Your features, though, have charm. And yet [you]
       bring
[A girl in] her prime [

THRASONIDES
(*angered by Getas' reference to Krateia*)
Be damned to you! We must discover [what]'s   95
The matter, and [show] some compelling cause.[a]

GETAS
But master, women are a filthy crowd!

THRASONIDES
[If you] don't stop—

GETAS
(*interrupting*)
                    What you're describing, master,
] for [some] reason, she's enticing [you]
On purpose. There's not always [any] logical   100

(*A further scrap, printed on p. 272 but too badly damaged
for continuous translation, is plausibly assigned to the
first act. It appears to derive from a later conversation
between Thrasonides and Getas. From Thrasonides' ini-
tial speech only 241* come down, *242* her not . . .ing, *Getas
and 243* she going away *can be deciphered; Thrasonides is
clearly still harping on the rift between himself and
Krateia. Getas responds with 244* [Ap]ollo, *and very mili-
tary . . . , 245* now you see; I'm going in . . . , *246* muggers
on me . . . walking around . . . , *247* and avoiding them,
laid back. Thrasonides then makes a further speech, from*

    [a] Sc. for Krateia's coolness to Thrasonides.

Thrasonides) about a woman (probably Krateia), and he
announces that he is going inside in order apparently to
avoid some approaching muggers. The latter remark is
very similar to an attested variation (in Alexis fr. 112 Kassel-Austin) of the formula for introducing the chorus at
the end of the first act, and it may have had that function
here; for this reason I provisionally number the lines of
this fragment 241–248.)

ΘΡΑΣΩΝΙΔΗΣ (?)

241	].π[..]...[.]δ.[ ].ωκαταβη.[
	ἐκ]είνης οὐκ ...οὔσης, Γέτα [
(fr. C 3)	]νης· ....[...] ἀπιοῦσα δ[

ΓΕΤΑΣ (?)

	Ἄπ]ολλον, καὶ μάλα στρατιωτ[ικ
245	]ασαι νῦν ὁρᾷς· εἰσέρχομα[ι
	]. λωποδύτας μοι περιπ[ατῶν
(7)	τ]ούτους τε φ[ε]ύγων ἐκλύτ[ως

ΘΡΑΣΩΝΙΔΗΣ (?)

248	]τερος, ὦ τάλαιπ[ωρ'

(ΜΕΡΟΣ Β΄)

401	]ν
	]ς
(3 Si)	]

241–248 Supplements and assignments to speakers suggested by
Turner.   401–494 O.11.

which only 248 poor [fellow] can be made out. If the muggers mentioned by Getas are the approaching chorus, this scrap would have come right at the end of the first act.

In that case probably 100 lines or more have been lost between the scrap and line 100. It is hazardous to speculate in detail about what this gap would have contained, but most probably a delayed prologue speech by a now unidentified divine figure would have given an accurate account of the events that preceded the stage action, and so would have dispelled for the audience some of the mysteries and misunderstandings that continue to plague the human characters for most of the play. Doubtless this prologue would have explained how Demeas, his daughter Krateia and a grown-up son had been separated by warfare in Cyprus. The daughter had been enslaved as a prisoner of war and purchased by Thrasonides, who had fallen desperately in love with her. The son had been involved in the fighting, and was now believed by Krateia to have been killed by Thrasonides, because the latter now possessed her brother's sword and probably had boasted of slaying the man who had wielded it. Hence Krateia's aversion to Thrasonides. It is conceivable that Thrasonides' victim had been another man who snatched up the wrong sword in an emergency (compare Aspis 106 ff.), and Krateia's brother had escaped unscathed.)

(ACT II)

(A further papyrus (O.11) contains 94 badly mutilated lines which do not overlap with any of the other papyri or with quoted fragments of the play, but clearly belong to the Misoumenos, as its first editor E. G. Turner pointed

```
                              ]εκ. .[. . .]τομου
405      (ΓΕΤΑΣ ?)           ]ετους λογίζεται
                             γ]εγενημένον
(7 Sa, Si)                   ].π ὑπονοεῖς
                             ] δέσποτα
         (ΘΡΑΣΩΝΙΔΗΣ)        εἰ]σιών, Γέτα
410                          ]ικεκ.[ ]..[ ] πόνους
                             ].φεισ. . .ις
(12)                         ]. ἀνεῳγμένον
                             ]οἶκτον π. .εμοι
                             ].ζυ[
415                          ].ας εἶδέ (?) τις
                             ]α. .ηχεν γέ μοι
```

406 Suppl. and corr. Turner:]εγεννημενον O.11.

407 ὑπονοεῖς deciphered by Sisti.

408 δέσποτα implies that Getas speaks here, but it is uncertain where his speech begins.

409 Suppl. Turner. The address to Getas implies that Thrasonides now speaks.

415 εἴδε O.11.

416–417 Demeas may enter hereabouts and begin speaking.

---

[a] See especially E. W. Handley, *Entretiens Hardt* 16 (1970) 11 f.

*out. O.11 names a Getas (402), a Krateia (442, probably
459), and a ξένος ('stranger' or 'guest-friend' 424, 427,
431) who is old (437, 453) and comes from another city
(431), though apparently he was not ransoming slaves
(432 f.); all these details (except perhaps the last) tie in
perfectly with the plot of Misoumenos. The old ξένος
must be Krateia's father Demeas, appearing here for the
first time in the play, at some point before the events of
Act III in which he takes a leading part. O.11 can hardly
derive from Act I, where the existing papyrus fragments
and the postulated divine prologue would occupy too
many lines for the insertion of O.11 into that act to be fea-
sible; these 94 lines must then belong to Act II, most prob-
ably its second half, because it is characteristic of
Menander[a] to introduce surprising new developments
such as the unexpected arrival of a new character like
Demeas towards the end of an act. Hence I provisionally
number these lines 401–494.*

*The mutilation of O.11 makes continuous translation
and confident assignment of parts often impossible. Its
opening section (401 to somewhere about 414–415)
involves two characters, Getas (409) and his master (408)
Thrasonides. The subject of their conversation can no
longer be identified (405 yields* he *or more probably* she
considers: the person being discussed by Getas and his
master is most likely to have been Krateia; *406 having
become* or happened, *407 you suspect,* 408 O master, *409
going in, Getas, where the person going is male,* 410 dis-
tress *or toils,* 412 having been opened, *413 pity for me),
but these lines suggest that for some unknown purpose
one of the two characters goes off into Thrasonides' house
shortly after 409; this is more likely to have been Getas,*

275

(17)	(ΔΗΜΕΑΣ)	περὶ ἐκεί]νης γράμμα[τ]α
		δε]ῦρ' ἄγω
		] τί βούλεται;
420		ἐ]κ[εί]νην τὴν θύραν
		τὴ]ν οἰκίαν
(22)		].ος γὰρ ἂν κόψαντί σοι
		]ηγ' ἔστηκ' ἐγὼ
		]α:
		(?)
		οὑτοσί (?), ξένε
425		ἐκεί]νου γράμματα
		]δο.τι. . .λαβε
(27)		]ρανω, ξένε
		]. . .η. . ἡμέρας
		]. .αινονσα.ας

417 περὶ suppl. Arnott, the rest Turner.
418 Suppl. Handley.
420 Suppl. Austin.
423 εστηκαεσω with correcting γ written over σ of εσω.
424 Corr. Turner: οντοσει O.11.
425 Suppl. Turner.
429 σαβασ or σαθασ O.11: σ<π>άθας conj. Turner.

*leaving Thrasonides alone to deliver a short monologue
about his woes (410, 413) before he makes his exit, proba-
bly into an unidentified house either on or just off stage
where he has an invitation to dine and drink (see 571 f.
below).*

*When Demeas comes on to an empty stage, he is possi-
bly alone, possibly accompanied by two or more slaves
(see below on 449–474). He has probably just arrived at
the scene of the play after a voyage from Cyprus, and is
making for Kleinias' house. Kleinias appears to have been
a friend of Demeas, and may have induced Demeas to
visit him by sending him a letter (cf. 417, 425) with news
about one or both of Demeas' children. It is impossible to
say at what line precisely Demeas enters (415 either*
someone saw *or but if someone could be Thrasonides or
Demeas), but by 417 Demeas is delivering an entrance
monologue (417* letter, *418* here (?) I bring, *419* what does
it mean?), *which, with its closing references to* that door
(420) and the house *(421), suggests that he has now
reached Kleinias' door and is preparing to knock on it.*

*The person who opens the door repeatedly addresses
Demeas not by name but as* ξένε, *here probably* stranger
*(424, 427, 431), and does not know where he has come
from (431). This rules out his or her identification as
Demeas' friend Kleinias; more probably it was Kleinias'
old female slave who appears again later in the play,
where she is addressed by name as Syra (see 555 below)
and comments on Demeas' odd behaviour (576 ff.); cf. also
the discussion of 501–531 below. The first part of their
conversation, after the old woman has said* to you having
knocked, you see *(422) and Demeas has responded* I'm
standing *(423), is too badly damaged to be comprehen-*

430   ] οὐκ ἔχω λέγειν

ΓΡΑΤΣ
]μεθα· ποδαπὸς εἶ, ξένε;

ΔΗΜΕΑΣ
(32)   ἐγώ; πα[ρά Κύπρου.]

ΓΡΑΤΣ
[σώμα]τ' οὖν λυτρούμενος
ἥκεις σὺ [δεῦρο;]

ΔΗΜΕΑΣ
[μὰ τὸν Ἀ]πόλλω, 'γὼ μὲν οὔ,
ἀλλ' ἕνεκα [   ].τος γενομένης
435   ζητοῦσι μ[   ]..νύεται
αὕτη δὲ π[οῦ 'στὶ

ΓΡΑΤΣ
τί] φής;

ΔΗΜΕΑΣ
τοῦτό μοι
(37)   συμπρᾶξ[ον

432 πα[ρὰ Κύπρου] (with dicolon after it) suppl. Turner,
[σώμα]τ' Handley, who suggested punctuation after ἐγώ.
433 ἥκεις σὺ Austin: ηκεισσσυ O.11. δεῦρο suppl. Austin, μὰ
τὸν Ἀ]πόλλω Handley. 'γὼ μὲν Handley: γεμεν O.11.
434 O.11 has αλ with second λ written above. 436 π[οῦ suppl.
Austin, 'στὶ Arnott, τί Sisti. 437 συνπραξ[O.11: corr. and
suppl. Turner, who suggested change of speaker after it (no para-
graphus below the line in O.11).

*sible; a mention of his (?) letter (425) perhaps comes from
Demeas' explanation of his presence at Kleinias' door (see
above), but other phrases hereabouts (the slave's words
this [person/thing] here, stranger (424), take or took 426,
day or days 428) are just isolated pieces of a lost jigsaw.
At 430 the text is less mutilated for a few lines.)*

DEMEAS

                    ] I can't say   430

OLD WOMAN
] we [   ]. Stranger, where's your home?

DEMEAS
My home? It's [Cyprus].

OLD WOMAN
                    Is that why you've come
[Here], ransoming [slaves]?

DEMEAS
                    Heavens, no! Not I!
I came for [a girl] who's become [
Men seek (*or* seeking) [435
But w[here is] she herself?

OLD WOMAN
                    [What do] you mean?

DEMEAS
Join me in this [   ].

279

ΓΡΑΤΣ

]μαι τόδε, γέρον,

ἄλλοις πα[

ΔΗΜΕΑΣ

ἰ]χνεύων πάλιν

ἐὰν δαμ[

ΓΡΑΤΣ

[   ]

ΔΗΜΕΑΣ

]νη

440   σωτὴρ κ[εκλήσει

ΓΡΑΤΣ

τί τοὔνομ' [

ΔΗΜΕΑΣ

(42)   <u>Κράτειαν</u> [

ΓΡΑΤΣ

<u>ἔστιν πα[</u>
<u>οὗτος γὰρ .[</u>

ΔΗΜΕΑΣ

445   ὦ Ζεῦ τρ[ο]π[αῖε
ἀπροσδοκ[ητ

(47)   .μινα.[
<u>.μονηα[</u>

α]γόρευετ' ον[

450   ].αντωναρκ.[

]ιδίῳ παρεστ[

280

OLD WOMAN
Old man, that's [best left],
I think (?), to others.

DEMEAS
[   ] tracking again.   438

(The text now reverts to isolated phrases in uncertain contexts. At 440 Demeas says [You will be called] my saviour; at 441 the old woman asks What's the name [of your daughter], to which Demeas replies Krateia (442). Here the two are clearly discussing the fate of Demeas' missing daughter, and when Demeas in 445 goes on to call out O Zeus, god of defeats (using an invocation voiced also by Deianeira in fear that her own children might be enslaved as captives: Sophocles, Trachiniae 303), following this with the word unexpected in 446, it seems likely that he has just learnt that a girl called Krateia lives next door as Thrasonides' slave (could οὗτος, this [man or thing] in 444 be a reference to Thrasonides?).

From 449 to 464 only occasional words can be deciphered: you (plural) are speaking 449 (? Demeas, referring to the old woman and others in Kleinias' house; or the old woman, meaning either Demeas and his family or Demeas and his present entourage, if he did not enter

---

437 τοδ'ε O.11.   438 Paragraphus under the line in O.11.
ἄλλοις or ἀλλ' οἷς. ἰ]χνεύων suppl. Turner.   440 Suppl.
Turner.   442–484 O.11's paragraphi are here printed below
the text, because speakers and speech-divisions are often diffi-
cult to identify.   442 Corr. Turner: κρατιαν O.11.   445 Suppl.
Turner.   449 Suppl. Arnott (]γορευετ' Sisti).

(52)   ..[   ]ει[.]..αρπ[

        λε[...ε]ύξασθαι, γέρο[ν

        ἔμελλ[....].[.]ε...[.].σι[

455   .πλο.[...].λ..μοι.[ ].. [

        ἐπει[..]. θεῶν αδ[

(57)   .π...[..]. δος μοι.[

        πῶς [..].ρα...σ[

        Κρά[τεια....]μφ[

460   τ[......]...τ' ὀψ.[

        πη[.....]σ.[.].εν.[..]νγ.[

(62)   α...[.]δ.κ[..]ν.[..]συμ[

        παι......λιν.[..].ου

        κ.[..].ξε[.]...λλ.[ ]ντου.[

465   μὰ Δ[ία τ]ὰ τουπ.α.μοναλ[

        τρο.[...] δύ' ἑκατέρωθε[

(67)   καὶ τοῦτο φοβερ[ὸ]ν ἐκπ[

        φέρ' εἰς τὸ πρόσθε μοι, γερ[

        εἰς τὴν [ὁ]δόν. γελοῖον ε[

470   εἴσω λαβοῦσα· τουτονὶ δ.[

                      ΓΡΑΤΣ

        ἀλλ' εὐθὺς αὐτῷ τὴν α.[

(72)   ὅπου 'στὶ μηδὲ τόνδ' ἐα[

        πόει τὸ σαυτοῦ πρῶτον [

        καλῶς· ἐγὼ δὲ συνβρα[

                    ΔΗΜΕΑΣ

475   πῶς οὖν;

alone: see above on 415–417), to pray (*or* vaunt), old man
453, gods 456, give (?) me 457, Kra[teia (?)] 479; *but up
to this point there is no need to assume the presence of any
new speaker. There follows a less chaotic group of lines
(465–478) whose opening halves are reasonably well pre-
served.*)

OLD WOMAN (?)

By Zeus, no [465

DEMEAS (?)

] two on either side [

OLD WOMAN (?)

And that [is] frightening[

DEMEAS (?)

[Old woman (?)], please bring forward [
Into the street. [It's] funny [
Taking inside. But the [man] here [470

OLD WOMAN (?)

But [   ] to him (?) at once the [
Where he (*or* she *or* it) is, and don't let (?) him (?) [
Do your own job first [
Well. I [

DEMEAS

How then?

---

453 Suppl. Turner.   459 Suppl. Austin.   464 Three other
letters written above .ξϵ.   465, 467, 469 Suppl. Turner.
466 δυοϵκατϵρωθϵ[O.11.   470 λαβουσα or λαβοντα O.11.
471, 475 Speech assignments uncertain.

ΓΡΑΥΣ

[ἐρ]ώτα τὴν [
εὕροιμεν ἀ[ν]απαύσαντ[
(77) ἀλλ᾽ εὖ παθὼν .. χάριν [
αὐτὴν γυναῖκα π[ροσ]δρ[αμ
καν[ ]αι..σαι.ει[..]..[
480 ὑμ.[ ].[.].ενειμεσ[...].
____μὰ τ[οὺ]ς θεοὺς κτ[
(82) ____τρε.[..].μενος γε[
ορα.[..].νε.κ᾽υ.[
____δαν.[..]αναιτων[
485 κάκ[ι]σ[το]ς ἀνδρῶ[ν
.[......]τοπραξ[
(87)   ]μι παντ.[
           ]ονευρων[
           ] γυναικ.[
490   ]αι χάριν [
           ]ν λέγω μ[
492   ].[

475, 476, 478, 481 Suppl. Turner.   485 Suppl. Coles.

OLD WOMAN

Ask the [475
We find him hindering [
But faring well [   ] favour [
Her as a wife (?). Running to (?) [478

(*These lines pose several problems, apart from the assign-
ment of the words to the proper speakers. Who or what
are 'two on either side' in 466? Has Demeas brought two
slaves with him as a ransom for his missing son and
daughter? Who or what is to be brought 'forward . . . into
the street' at 468–469? Presumably not Krateia, for at
least two reasons: there is no evidence that she was inside
Kleinias' house, and the Greek for 'bring (a person)' is
normally* ἄγε *not* φέρε. *And probably not the sword of
Demeas' son, either; although this has an important func-
tion in the plot, there is no evidence that at this point it
was in Kleinias' house, or that its relevance was known to
Demeas. And who is to take what inside at 470? It is
probable, but not certain, that the taker is female, and so
likely to be Kleinias' old servant herself, but further spec-
ulation here is hazardous. Next, who is the man referred
to in 470, 471, 476 and possibly 472? The remarks involv-
ing him point most convincingly to Thrasonides, who
would be likely to hinder any attempt by an unknown
man to see the woman whom Thrasonides had already
said he considered as his wife (40). And finally, what is
the job mentioned in 473?*

*From 479 onwards the papyrus yields only isolated
words and phrases (no, by the gods 481, worst of men 485
(? a description of Thrasonides), act 486, having found
488, woman or wife 489, favour 490, I say 491), and we
have no means of identifying the action. It is unlikely that*

(There is a gap of uncertain length between the end of papyrus O.11 at 492 and the beginning of O.10 at a line provisionally numbered here as 501. In that gap Act II ended and III began; since the remains of Act III cover 176 lines, it is unlikely that much of that act before line 501 is missing. O.10's desperately mutilated text also contains probably more than half of Act IV before it breaks off at line 806; several other papyri overlap with it and each other, providing often less damaged texts of a number of passages: B.3 532–544, 560–572; B.2 567–578, 611–622; O.3 642–665, 677–700.)

(ΜΕΡΟΣ Γ´)

501	]οποι
	ὀ]λίγον
(103)	]α...ον
	]νπ...μ.ι.
505	]αλιν προσδ[
	]ρω.
(107)	ἐγέ]νετ᾽ ἄρα
	].[ ].[..].ν
	]α

501–1066 Those supplements and corrections whose author is not named were made by the ed. pr. of O.10, E. G. Turner, *New Fragments of the Misoumenos of Menander, Bulletin of the Institute of Classical Studies*, Supplement 17 (London 1965) and *The Oxyrhynchus Papyri*, 33 (London 1968), 15–155.
501–531 O.10.   505 προσδ[έχου or προσδ[όκα Turner.

---

[a] Olive branches were carried by suppliants, who would often seek sanctuary at an altar, and it is likely that such was the inten-

at this point Demeas went on to knock on Thrasonides'
door. The only person who could have opened the door in
Thrasonides' absence (see on 414–417 above) would have
been Getas, but at 617 ff. (note especially 625) Getas and
Demeas were apparently still total strangers to each
other.)

(ACT III)

(Act II ended and III began in the gap between 492 and
the line provisionally numbered as 501. Only occasional
words can be made out in the mutilated remains of
501–531: little 502, ? accept or expect 505, ? happened
507, ? sword 509, ? I have come 514, and some or whom?
517, who (feminine) you are 519, couldn't 520, to be 521,
a suppliant's olive-branch[a] 522, 532, ? the stranger 525.
These allow us neither to establish the subject matter nor
to name the speakers, of whom at times (e.g. 532–541)
there may be three, one certainly (cf. 519) female. It is
possible that Getas entered early in Act III (did he utter
514?), intending to speak with Kleinias' old female slave,
but retired into the background as an eavesdropper when
he found her conversing with somebody else whose name
appears to have contained the letters ry *(see n. on 555),*
perhaps Krateia's nurse. The questioning 'who you are' in
519 may imply that at this point the two women did not

tion here, bringing the stage altar into play. In Athens such a
branch could also be deposited by any citizen as a token that he
wished a complaint to be heard in the assembly, but there is no
evidence that the scene of *Misoumenos* is Athens or that this pro-
cedure was referred to here. See especially John Gould, *Journal
of Hellenic Studies*, 93 (1973), 74–103, and P. J. Rhodes' com-
mentary on [Arist.] *Ath. Pol.* 43. vi (Oxford 1981), pp. 527 f.

Γ]ΡΑ[ΤΣ

ξί[φ

510   ].χα[

].ρω[.......]π[

(112)   ]..[....].ιμ[

].. μενα

(ΓΕΤΑΣ ?)

ἐλήλ]υθα

515   π.....[   ]α·

.ι[...]..[....].ι[...]ο.[..]α.[.].[

(117)   .] καί τιν' α.α[....].[...]..[..]μ[

].ωσ.ο.ιμεν[..].ιων.οκ.[...]ει.[.]εμο[

σὺ δ' ἥτις εἶ πα..[...........]χρον[

520   οὐκ ἂν δυναι[   ].νον[

εἶναι με.[

(122)   ἱ]κετηρίαν [

..].ρ[...]λα[....]...[   ].[

...[....].τ[   ]...[

525   το]ῦ ξέν[ου

.]αυ[.....].αν.[   ].... εωμ[

(127)   .]..[....].ρενθ[....]..[   ]...[

ο..[....]πεπαικ[

.].[........].ωνως:

509 Above]ξι[is written]ρα[, presumably to identify a new
speaker (γ]ρα[ῦς or even Συ]ρα perhaps rather than Κ]ρά[τεια
or Θ]ρα[σωνίδης): see below on 555.   513 γεγε]νημένα
Austin.   514 ἐλήλ]υθα suppl. Austin.   521 εἶναι deciph.
Austin, Handley.   528 Or]πεπεικ[.   529 Dicolon after
ωνωσ deciphered by Austin.

know each other. If the word 'sword' is correctly read in
509, it might perhaps be linked with an incident in the
play described by Arrian, Discourses of Epictetus 4. 1. 19,
who claims when quoting fr. 4 of Misoumenos (see below,
on that fragment) that at one point Thrasonides asked for
a sword and was denied it by Getas. The character here
who mentions the sword may be the old woman, if a muti-
lated interlinear identification of speaker here is correctly
filled out as either Σύ]ρα, Syra or γ]ρα[ῦς, old woman[a]*;*
in that case could she be referring to that incident or to a
consequential request by Getas for permission to deposit
in Kleinias' house all the weapons that Getas could find in
Thrasonides' house, including Krateia's brother's sword,
in order to forestall any attempt by Thrasonides to com-
mit suicide? The reference to the stranger in 525 suggests
that the two (? female) speakers had gone on to talk about
the arrival of Demeas.

At 532 the accession of a second papyrus helps to pro-
vide a more comprehensible text for seven of the next ten
lines. Even so, identification of speakers, division of parts
and interpretation of the subject matter all remain haz-
ardous, and the translation given below can be nothing
more than a guess. Most probably three characters are on
stage. It seems most likely that the main conversation
continues between Krateia's nurse (was she the person
carrying the olive-branch mentioned at 522, 532, 553, and
perhaps also 642, and protesting as Krateia's proxy about
either the latter's position in Thrasonides' household or
the disappearance of Krateia's brother's sword which
Getas had transferred next door along with all the other

---

[a] Unfortunately, this identification is not certain; the inter-
linear remains can be filled out also as Θ]ρα[σωνίδης (Thra-
sonides) or Κ]ρά[τεια (Krateia). See also 555 below.

ΤΡΟΦΟΣ (?)

φε[

530   τ[.].[. . . .].νπερι. .[.].[. .].[

a[. .]. . . .[. .]γησ[

ΓΡΑΤΣ (?)

(132)   ἱκετηρίαν· τί λέγουσ';

ΤΡΟΦΟΣ (?)

                "ἐμοὶ μαχεῖ, τάλαν·"

"[μ]ὰ Δί', ἀλλ' ἐκεί[νῳ]," φ[ησ]ί, "δεινὸν γὰρ βίον

ζῇ κ[α]ὶ ταλαίπωρόν τ[ι]ν' —

ΓΕΤΑΣ (?)

              οὐ γάρ;

ΤΡΟΦΟΣ (?)

                  μακάριον

535   αὕτη δὲ καὶ ζηλωτὸν ὄντ'."

ΓΕΤΑΣ (?)

             οὕτω [τ]ι[ς] ἦν

Γύ]γης.

ΤΡΟΦΟΣ (?)

[ἄ]μεινον <δ'> οἶδε τά γ' ἑαυτῆ[ς] τινός.

532–544 B.2, O.10.   532 Punctuation after ἱκετηρίαν uncertain. B.3 has a dicolon after ταλαν, apparently marking the end of a reported speech.   533 ἐκεί[νῳ] suppl. Webster.   534 ονγαρ (with dicola before and after) B.3; assigned to Getas as an aside by Arnott.   535–536 οὕτω—Γύ]γης assigned to Getas by Arnott (in B.3 no dicolon after ὄντ', possibly one after ἦν; in O.10 possibly lower dot decipherable after]γησ).   535 δὲ deciphered by Austin.   536 Γύ]γης and <δ'> tentatively suppl.

weapons belonging to the soldier?) and Kleinias' old slave
woman. In the background a third character seems to
lurk, most probably Getas. He utters occasional asides
that are eventually overheard by the women, one of whom
orders him off at 541.)

OLD WOMAN (?)

A branch? What did you say?

NURSE (?)

        "Oh dear, will you   532
Oppose *me*?" "Heavens, no! *Him*," he says, "he's living
A dreadful and unhappy life —"

GETAS (?)

(*aside*)

         That's right!

NURSE (?)

"—While hers is flush and envied!"

GETAS (?)

(*aside*)

        That's just how he was — 535
A Gyges[a] (?)!

NURSE (?)

Still, she knows her business best[b]! 536

[a] A king of Lydia in the early seventh century B.C., who
became a legend for wealth and success in his battles against
enemies and rivals, and in the present context would be an
appropriate object of comparison for a victorious mercenary like
Thrasonides. [b] Literally 'better than anyone'.

Arnott, $[\check{\alpha}]\mu\epsilon\iota\nu o\nu$ and $\tau\acute{\alpha}\ \gamma'\ \acute{\epsilon}\alpha\upsilon\tau\hat{\eta}[\varsigma]\ \tau\iota\nu\acute{o}\varsigma$ suppl. and deci-
phered by Handley.

(137) τοῦτ᾿ ε[..]κ[ ]εμον τον...αυ.. τουτονὶ
..].εμ᾿ α[ ]ε..εıναı[.....].το καθήμενον.

ΓΕΤΑΣ (?)

τί] τοῦτο;

ΓΡΑΥΣ (?)
τοῦτο; τίς πότ᾿ ἐστιν;

ΤΡΟΦΟΣ (?)
ἔστι γὰρ

540 παρά τινος ὁ ψιθυρισμός· οἶδ᾿ ἐγώ.
ἀπαλλάγηθ᾿ ἐν[θένδ᾿]· ἐγὼ τ...γ..νημ[...]ναι:

ΤΡΟΦΟΣ (?)

(142) ἐσθ᾿ [.]δεμε..[.] παρ᾿ ἐμοῦ[γε τὸ τρο]φεῖον δ᾿ ἔχεις,
ὦ θυ[γα]τρίδιο[ν, ο]ὐ δῆλα; ...[....]ν πᾶν λέγει
.....]σθ[ ]μα[..........]..[...]υτωμο[

545 ....]..τακ.[
.[.]δε[ῖ]ξον [... δακ]τύλιον [

ΓΡΑΥΣ (?)

(147) φιλων γε.[.......]παρ[

ΤΡΟΦΟΣ (?)

ὁ τοιοῦτο[ς ...]..

539 Parts assigned by Arnott (the only dicolon visible is after
εστιν in B.3). 541 ἐν[θένδ᾿] Kraus: γηθ᾿ε[O.10 with a letter
from an interlinear *nota personae* or less probably a badly-
written rough breathing above it,]ηθεν..... B.3.
542 .σθ[.]τεμε O.10 with αλ written above .σ and δ above τ.
ἐμοῦ[γε τὸ τρο]φεῖον suppl. Arnott. 543 ὦ deciphered by
Austin. 545–549 O.10. 546 δε[ῖ]ξον suppl. Austin.

*(If my interpretation is correct, at the beginning of 532
Kleinias' old slave is asking Krateia's nurse to tell her
about a recent conversation that the nurse has had with
another character, most probably Getas, who now in
asides proceeds to confirm the accuracy of the nurse's
report; that conversation might have occurred as the
nurse was preparing to leave Thrasonides' house on her
mission of supplication, with Getas attempting to stop her
(532 f.). It appears that the nurse did not yet know why
Krateia had turned against Thrasonides. Lines 537–538
are badly mutilated, yielding only* this *and* this man (?)
here *(537) and* sitting (?) down *(538); the last remark for
some reason arouses Getas into a comment clearly audible
to the two women.)*

GETAS (?)

What's that?

OLD WOMAN (?)
(now noticing Getas' presence)
    That? Who is he?

NURSE (?)
(approaching Getas)

      These whispers come 539
From a specific source, I know! Away 540
[From here] with you!

*(After the request at 541 that the character here identified
as Getas should depart, the text once more becomes so
mutilated for a dozen lines that only disconnected words
and phrases can be made out. It is probable but not
certain that Getas departed into either a stage house
(Kleinas'? but see below on 576 ff.) or one off-stage
nearby, where he observed the events described at*

293

ΓΡΑΥΣ (?)

.[

θαιμάτ[ι]α ..[..]δετα[

550   ἔπειτα προσ[..]τυ...[

τὴν γῆν κροτοῦσαν· κα[.].[

(152)   σ]πείσονθ' ἐ[πι]τρέπω.[..]ι.[....]ε̣ραν.ι[.].τ[

ἔσ]τιν [το]ιαῦθ' [· ἱκε]τηρίων ...[...]...[

..]ωτι[..] μανθ[άν]ειν [τό]δ' οὐκέτι

555   ὃ] καὶ θεοὶ θέλ[οιεν].

ΤΡΟΦΟΣ (here named [.]ΡΥ[in the papyrus)

ἀπίω[μεν], Σύρα.

ΓΕΤΑΣ (?)

ἐγὼ [......] ἄχθομαι δέ, νὴ τὴν ...[

(157)   ..]με[.].[......].ν..ον.τα..ειπ[

]ιουφ[

]μελ[...]έρχεται πά[λιν,

548 O.10 identifies the second speaker in this line with a supra-
lineal].Σ, more probably [ΓΡΑ]ΥΣ than [ΓΕΤ]ΑΣ.   549
θαιμάτ[ι]α suppl. several.   552 ἐ[πι]τρέπω suppl. Austin (or
-τρέπων ?).   555 O.10's identification of speaker could be
[Τ]ΡΥ[ΦΗ, Φ]ΡΥ[ΓΙΑ or Χ]ΡΥ[ΣΙΣ. Σύρα tentatively de-
ciphered by Arnott.[1]   556]γωμεν[O.10 with μεν crossed
out.   559 Suppl. Austin.

[1] After this was in proof, Dr Colin Austin informed me that
the conjecture Σύρα here and the identification of the nurse's
name as Chrysis are now confirmed by a fragmentary papyrus
from Oxyrhynchus identified and edited by Dr N. Gonis, who
will publish it in *The Oxyrhynchus Papyri*, vol. 64. The papyrus
is referred to in advance of publication by courtesy of the Egypt
Exploration Society, London.

556–575. After his departure the dialogue between the two women continues; we can decipher from the nurse's words you've been fed (?) by me, dear daughter, isn't that clear (?), . . . he (*or* she) says every (*or* everything) *542 f. and* show . . . ring *546; Kleinias' slave responds with of* friends *or* kissing (?) *547, the nurse then has* such a (*548*), *before Kleinias' old slave says* the garments *549 and then 550, and refers to some woman (?)* beating the ground *551 and to some man* about to make a libation, I entrust *552. From 553 to 555 the remains are less disconnected but still mysterious.*)

OLD WOMAN (?)

It's something like that. Branches [553
           ] this no longer to be hidden [
And may the gods desire it!

NURSE

Let's depart, Syra.   555

(*It is difficult to make head or tail of what is going on. The nurse presumably apostrophises Krateia as her surrogate daughter, and the talk of a finger ring (546) and of garments (549) may imply their use as recognition tokens. 551–553 is puzzling; the mention of 'branches' (553) must take us back to the ritual of supplication mentioned at 522 and 532, and may imply here a failed attempt to conceal it (554) from somebody's (? Thrasonides') notice. The two women participating in the scene presumably depart to their separate houses at 555; this line may help in establishing the name of Kleinias' slave as Syra, if the last word in 555 is correctly so deciphered, and that of the nurse as containing the letters -ry- (Chrysis, Phrygia, Tryphe ?), since the papyrus so identifies the speaker of the final*

560   κατέλειπον· ἦσ' ἄν[θ]ρω[πος ...].[...] παχ[ὺς
       τὴν ὄψιν· ὗς ἄνθρωπ[ος

(162)   τὰ γύναι' ἵν' ἔξωθ' ἐπιθεωρε[ῖν
       ἆρ' οὗτός ἐστι δοῦλος †καὶ λύω[
       ἦσεν ποτ' αὐτῶν θάτερος σα[φέ]στε[ρον,

565   τὸν ἄνδρα .... ὦ πολυτίμητ[οι θεοί,
       ἐπὶ πᾶσιν ἀ[γαθ]οῖς, τοῦτο δὴ τὸ τοῦ λόγου,

(167)   πίνων δικαίως ἦσεν ἀνθρώπων [χορός.
       ἀγαθὸν ἄκουσμ' ἥκεις πρὸς ἡμᾶς· ἀλλὰ τί
       ἐνθά]δ' ἔ[τι] κάμπτεις καὶ πάλιν στέλλει, διδοὺς

570   τὰς συμβολὰς εἰ μή τι κακὸν ἡμᾶς ποεῖς;
       λῆρος· κελεύσω τοῦτον ἐπὶ δεῖπνον πάλιν

(172)   τὸν δεσ[πό]την καλέσαντα; φανερῶς ἐστι γὰρ
       μιαρός. β]αδιοῦμ' εἴσω δὲ καὶ πειράσομαι
       κρύπτω]ν ἐμαυτὸν ἐπιθεωρῆσαί τι τῶν

575   ποιουμέ]νων ἔνδον λαλουμένων θ' ἅμα.

560–566 B.3, O.10; where only one of the two is cited, the other
may be assumed to be lacunose.   560 ἦσ' (and supplements)
Austin: ησ B.3.   561 ἄνθρωπ[B.3.   562 Corr. Merkel-
bach: εξωθενεπιθεωρε[B.3.   563 So B.3, unmetrically after
the hephemimeral caesura ([...]..οσεστ[O.10).   564 ἦσεν
Turner: ησεν B.3.   ποτ' B.3 after correction, ποτε O.10: ποθ
B.3 originally.   θατερος B.3 after correction,]τερος O.10:
θατερον B.3 originally.   565 Text uncertain: ?]..ισγαρω
O.10, ? κα.. or μι.. before ὁρᾶνῶ B.3.   566 Variant readings
in B.3 and O.10, supplemented by Handley with πᾶσιν ἀγα-
θοῖς] and πᾶσιν ὄν]τως respectively.   567–572 B.2, B.3,
O.10; see above on 560–566.   567 δικαίως B.3:]οισ O.10.
Suppl. Arnott.   569 Suppl. Sisti (ἔτι also Sandbach).   570 ποεις
B.2: ποιεις O.10.   571 κελευσω B.3,]λευσω B.2 after

words of 555.)

(Getas now re-enters from the unidentified house and delivers a vivid but puzzling monologue about the events he has witnessed. Its opening four lines are too mangled for continuous translation, but I'm vexed *seems to be Getas' opening remark at line 556.)*

GETAS

(in mid-speech)

] comes [back] —	559
I left them (?) there. A fat-faced man sang [	560
The fellow [was] a pig [	
The women, to watch them from outside [	
Is he a slave? [	
One of the pair sang more distinctly (?). Him	
] O most honoured [gods]! There in	565
The lap of luxury—that's the accepted	
Phrase—[a chorus] of men did rightly drink and sing!	
Your coming to us *is* good news, but why	
Turn round again and come back here and pay	
Your shot,[a] unless you're doing us some injury?	570
That's nonsense! He invited master—shall I urge	
Him to come back to dinner? Clearly he's	
[A scoundrel]. I'll go in, [conceal] myself,	
And try to keep an eye on anything	
That's being [done] and said too in the house.	575

[a] Dinners and drinking parties in which each guest paid his own share of the costs were a common feature in the social life of wealthier bachelors in Menander's Athens; see my commentary on Alexis (Cambridge 1996/1997), introduction to fr. 15.

---

correction:]λενω B.2 before correction.   573–577 B.2, O.10: see above on 560–567.   573 μιαρός suppl. Arnott. 574–575 Suppl. Wilamowitz.

ΓΡΑΤΣ

ἀτοπώ]τερον τούτου, μὰ τὼ θεώ, ξένον

(177) οὐπώπο]τ' εἶδον· αἲ τάλας, τί βούλεται;

ἐν τῷ γὰ]ρ οἴκῳ τὰς σπάθας τῶν γειτόνων

]τ[... α]ὐτὰς εἰς μέσον

580]νο[..]. [πο]λὺν [χ]ρόνον

]...η.[..]εν ταύτας [φ]ράσαι

(182) τῶν σπ]α[θ]ῶν εἰ βούλεται

ΓΡΑΤΣ (?) or ΔΗΜΕΑΣ

]αλλα[..].....

ΔΗΜΕΑΣ

]δεῖξον αὐτάς.

ΓΡΑΤΣ

θήσ[ο]μ[αι

585].μι. .ις.

ΔΗΜΕΑΣ

καλῶς.

μὴ κατα]φρονήσῃς.

ΓΡΑΤΣ

ἐγὼ

(187)].εἶδον.

576 ff. assigned to Kleinias' old slave by Turner.   577 Suppl.
Wilamowitz. 578 Suppl. Edmonds. 579–610 O.10. 581 ταυ-
την O.10 with correcting ασ above ην.   582 Suppl. Mette.
584 Dicolon misplaced before αυτασ in O.10, with γ[ρ]αυ(ς)
above identifying the speaker.   585 : καλωσ· O.10 with δ[η]⁻
above identifying the speaker as Δ[η](μεας).

*(The relevance to the plot of the events described here is
now uncertain. Who is the 'fat-faced' man that has
invited Thrasonides to dine and drink in his house? It is
unlikely to be either Demeas or Kleinias. The former is
hardly yet in a position to act as host, and the description
of the fat-faced man here hardly matches that of Demeas
at 620 f.; in Kleinias' dining-room, on the other hand, no
party is mentioned as going on while Demeas was examin-
ing a collection of swords there (578 ff.). We are obliged
to assume that the host is a character in the play so far
unidentified, perhaps for instance a brothel-keeper, with a
house on or more probably just off-stage; in that case
Getas' vituperations and ideas about keeping an eye on
things would be more readily comprehensible. At the end
of his monologue Getas exits again, presumably to the
scene of the party (cf. the comments above on 409 ff.).
After his departure Kleinias' female slave enters from her
master's house, to report on a strange incident. The open-
ing part of her speech is slightly damaged but in places
easily supplemented.)*

OLD WOMAN

I swear I've [never] seen a more [eccentric] guest   576
Than this one! Oh, poor chap, what can he want?
[He's   ] in the dining-room
His neighbours' swords, [he pulls] them out   579

*(It seems clear that Demeas has—or is about to—come
across his son's sword among those transferred by Getas
from Thrasonides' to Kleinias' house. After 579 we have
only disjointed words and phrases from a scene in which
the old woman is soon joined (at 582 or 583) by Demeas,
who follows her out of Kleinias' house. The last three or*

ΔΗΜΕΑΣ

ἂν [γὰ]ρ [ε]ὗ
] τὴν θύραν κόψασά μοι.

ΓΡΑΤΣ

αὐτὸ]ς μ[ὲν οὖν σὺ] κόπτε· [τί] μ' ἐνοχλεῖς, τάλαν;

ΔΗΜΕΑΣ

590   ].. [.].. .[. .]

ΓΡΑΤΣ

λά]β'. ἀποτρέχω· δέδειχά σοι.
].. .[ἐ]κκάλει κα[ὶ δι]αλέγου
(192)   ].. ..[   ].[.]a.a.[.].

ΔΗΜΕΑΣ

ὦν [τυγ]χάνω
].[   ]ενα[. .]υ τὴν ἐμὴν ταύτην ὁρῶ.

ΓΡΑΤΣ

(194a)   κ]όψει τ[ὴν θύραν· [κό]ψ[α]ς δ' ἔτι
595(194b)   ].[. . . . . .]σα.ην ἔγωγέ φη[μι .].. .ονθ' ὅλως
(195)   ..σ[. .]τοπασαν[. .]..[. . . . . .]ς· καλοῦ

587 Above αν is written δη(μεας) to identify the speaker. [γὰ]ρ
[ε]ὗ suppl. Kassel.   590 λά]β'. ἀποτρέχω suppl. and deci-
phered by Sandbach. δεδιχα O.10.   591 [ἐ]κκάλει suppl.
and deciphered by Handley.   592 Above the ω of ων a diago-
nal stroke (identifying the speaker as δ[η](μεας) ?).]θανω O.10
corrected to]χανω: suppl. Austin.   593 αρω. in O.10 cor-
rected to ορω: apparently.   594 originally omitted in O.10
and added by a second hand.   ]σδετι or]σαετι O.10.
595 φη[μι] suppl. Austin.

*four lines of the old woman's entrance monologue yield
only* a long time *(580), to point them (the swords?) out
(581). Demeas bids the old woman* Show them *(? again
the swords, 584), to which she responds* I'll put *(584). In
585 f. Demeas may say* Thank you *or* No, thank you. / . . .
Don't despise (?) [me]. *The woman's reply contains the
word* I *(586).*

*The text remains badly fractured until 607, but
between 588 and 595 it is possible to decipher enough
meaningful phrases for the drift of the conversation
between Demeas and Kleinias' female slave to be partially
discerned.)*

DEMEAS

. . . you] knocking at the door for me.   588

OLD WOMAN

[No,] knock [yourself]! Why bother me? Oh dear!

DEMEAS

[   ]

OLD WOMAN

Take   ]. I'm running off, I've shown to you   590
] *You* call them out and talk to them.

DEMEAS

] Just now I'm (?)
] I see this [   ] of mine

OLD WOMAN

he']ll knock on the door. After knocking [he'll]
Still [   ] I say [   ] at all (?)   595

*(Clearly Demeas, in pursuit either of his daughter or of an
explanation about how Thrasonides came to possess
Demeas' son's sword ('this . . . of mine' in 593 could refer*

ΔΗΜΕΑΣ (?)

.ρυ[. . .].ομ[   ]ησάμην
. . .].[   ].[   ]ποτε
. . . . .]σ[   ]

ΓΡΑΤΣ (?)

.θει[. . . . . .]νπρο.[
600   ]ερ[. . . .].π[. .[. .]σω
                   ]τισε
(201)   ].[ἐλευ]θέρα:
                ]τ[   ]ωθ.[
.υ[   ].. [.].[   ].. [   ]θετο
605   ἐνθύμιόν μοι τοῦτο γέγονεν ἀρτίως
.[.]..[. . . .]εθ[. .]τοσωστ[   ].. [ ]ου.ε.[
(206)   π]ροσ[. . .]. . .

ΔΗΜΕΑΣ

παῖ, παῖδε[ς]· ἐ[π]ανάξω· ψ[οφεῖ
αὐτῶν προϊὼν τις εἰς τὸ πρ[όσθ]ε[ν τὴν θύραν.

605 Lexicon Symeonis

597 O.10 may have a paragraphus under the line.   599 Possibly *nota personae* in O.10 over θει.   605]τουτογεγον[O.10 suppl. by Bühler from quotation of the whole line in the *Lexicon Symeonis* s.v. ἐνθύμημα· οὐχ οὕτω (sc. προστρόπαιον) Μένανδρος, ἀλλ' ἐπὶ διαλογισμοῦ τινος καὶ ἐνθυμήματος· καὶ ἐν Μισουμένῳ· ἐνθύμιόν μοι (μ corrected from σ) τοιοῦτον (sic) γέγονεν ἀρτίως.   607–608 Suppl. Sandbach (but Menander also uses the orthography πρόσθε).

---

[a] On the staging of this entry by the nurse (here played by a mute, because of the convention in Menander's plays that a maximum of three speaking characters could be on stage at any one

to either), wants Kleinias' old slave to knock on Thra-
sonides' door for him, but she refuses, insisting that
Demeas should do his own knocking and questioning.
What she claims to have shown Demeas (590) remains
uncertain.

From 596–607 the text is far too tattered generally to
reveal more than an occasional word (fine 596, ever 598),
apart from one whole line which was quoted from the play
by a Byzantine lexicographer and fits the scanty traces of
line 605 in the papyrus.)

This has just started to weigh on my mind.   605

(It must have been spoken by Demeas, and most probably
refers to the worrying implications of his son's sword
being now in Thrasonides' possession.

At or slightly before 607 Kleinias' old slave must have
carried out her threat and made her exit into Kleinias'
house, leaving Demeas alone to knock on Thrasonides'
door. Just as he begins to knock, however, he hears some-
body inside the house approaching the door and causing
it to creak and rattle as it is unlocked or unbolted. This
causes Demeas to panic and step aside. The door is
opened by Krateia. She enters, absorbed in conversation
with her nurse,[a] who may come out before Krateia and so
perhaps block Krateia's view of her father. The text here
for a few lines is much better preserved.)

DEMEAS
(banging on Thrasonides' door)
              Servant, servants! I'll step back. One of   607
Them's coming forward, he's [unlocked the door.

time) and Krateia, see especially the Gomme–Sandbach *Com-*
mentary on line 208 (their numbering) and K. B. Frost, *Exits and*
Entrances in Menander (Oxford 1988), 83 f.

ΚΡΑΤΕΙΑ

οὐκ ἂν [δυ]ναίμην κ[α]ρτερ[εῖ]ν [

610   τ[ό]τ᾽ ἐ[. . .]νον. τί ταῦτ.[

ΔΗΜΕΑΣ

ὦ Ζεῦ, τίν᾽ ὄψιν οὐδὲ προσδ[οκωμένην

(211)   ὁρῶ;

ΚΡΑΤΕΙΑ

τί βούλει, τηθία; τί μοι λαλεῖς;

πατὴρ ἐμός; ποῦ;

ΔΗΜΕΑΣ

παιδίον, Κράτεια.

ΚΡΑΤΕΙΑ

[τίς

καλεῖ με; πάππα, χαῖρε πολλά, φίλτατ[ε.

ΔΗΜΕΑΣ

615   ἔ]χω σε, τέκνον.

ΚΡΑΤΕΙΑ

ὦ ποθούμενος φαν[είς,

ὁρῶ σ᾽, ὃν οὐκ ἂν ᾠόμην ἰδεῖν ἔτι.

609 In left margin of O.10 γυ(νη) κρατεια identifies the
speaker. κ[α]ρτε[ρε]ῖν suppl. Handley.   611–622 B.2, O.10.
611 Left margin of O.10 has δη⁻, of B.2]ασ, identifying the
speaker. προσδ[οκωμένην suppl. Wilamowitz.   612 τηθια
B.2: τηθεια O.10.   613 Suppl. Jensen.   614 B.2 wrongly
inserts dicolon after καλειμε and in the left margin wrongly
identifies the speaker here as .ε (= γε(τασ ?). πάππα Wilamo-
witz: παπ[O.10, παπα B.2, but see D. M. MacDowell, comm.
on Ar. *Wasps* 297 (Oxford 1971). φίλτατ[ε suppl. Wilamo-
witz.   615 Paragraphus under the line in B.2, not in O.10.
φαν[είς suppl. Wilamowitz.

KRATEIA

(*to her nurse*)
I couldn't endure [
                    ] why these [610

DEMEAS

(*recognising Krateia*)
O Zeus, what vision so [surprising] do
I see?

KRATEIA

(*still to her nurse*)
     What do you mean, nurse? What do you say?
My father? Where?

DEMEAS

(*approaching Krateia*)
               Krateia, child!

KRATEIA

(*turning from her nurse to Demeas*)
                         [Who]'s calling
Me? Daddy, dearest, O god bless you!

DEMEAS

(*embracing her*)
                    Child,
You're in my arms.

KRATEIA
             You'[ve] come, I missed you, let   615
Me look at you, I didn't think I'd ever
See you again!

(*Getas now enters from the scene of Thrasonides' party
(see above on 409 ff.), and is taken aback by the scene
which meets his eyes.*)

ΓΕΤΑΣ

(216) ἐξῆλθεν ἔξω. παῖ, τί τοῦθ'; αὕτη τί σ[οί,
ἄνθρωπε; τί ποεῖς οὗτος; οὐκ ἐγὼ 'λε[γον;
ἐπ' αὐτοφώρῳ τόνδε τὸν ζητούμε[νον
620   ἔχω. γέρων οὗτός γε πολιὸς φαίνε[ται,
ἐτῶν τις ἑξήκονθ', ὅμως δὲ κλαύ[σεται.
(221) τίνα περιβάλλειν καὶ φιλεῖν οὗτος [δοκεῖς];

ΚΡΑΤΕΙΑ

ο]ὑμὸς πατήρ, Γέτα, π[ά]ρ[εστιν.]

ΓΕΤΑΣ

[τίς λόγος

οὕτω γελοῖος; ου.....[
625   τίς εἶ· πόθεν θ' [ἥκεις;

ΔΗΜΕΑΣ

αὑτὸς πορε[υθεὶς
(226) ταύτης.

ΓΕΤΑΣ

ἀληθῶς γ[άρ, Κράτειά, σοι πατὴρ
ὅδ' ἐστὶν ὁ γέρων;

ΚΡΑΤΕΙΑ

λάμ[βαν' αὐτὴν μάρτυρα.

617 Left margin on O.10 has γετας, of B.2 γε^τ(ας), identifying
the speaker. Suppl. Handley.   618–622 Suppl. Wilamowitz.
619 αυτοφωρω B.2: αυ.[.]φορω O.10.   622 No paragraphus
under the line in B.2 (line-opening lacunose in O.10). περι-
βαλλειν O.10 after correction: περιβαλειν O.10 originally,
B.2.   623 to 641 or 642 O.10 alone.   623 κρ[O.10 in left
margin. Supplements (τίς λόγος exempli gratia) by Sand-

GETAS

She's come outside! Oh, heavens! What's this?
What's she [to you], sir—you there, what's your game?
[Did]n't [I] say so? I've caught the object of
My search red-handed! Looks grey-haired and old,   620
He must be sixty—yet he'[ll] pay for this!
You—who [do you think] you're kissing and embrac-
      ing?

KRATEIA

Getas, my father['s here].

GETAS

                    [What story could]
[Be] so absurd? Not (?) [
                    (*He turns to question Demeas.*)
Who are you? Where['ve you come from?]   625

DEMEAS

Travelling alone (?) [
This girl.

GETAS

            [Krateia,] can this old man be
Truly [your father]?

KRATEIA

(*pointing to her nurse*)
                    Use [her as a witness.] (?)

---

bach.   625 Suppl. Kumaniecki.   626 δη O.10 in left margin.
πορε[υθεὶς suppl. Mette, πορε[ύομαι Kumaniecki.
627 Suppl. tentatively Sandbach.   628 Suppl. *exempli gratia*
Arnott.

ΓΕΤΑΣ

τί τοῦτο; καὶ σύ, γρᾴδ[ι]ο[ν,

630 καλεῖς; πόθεν, βέλτιστε, [. . . .].[.]ολ[
οἴκοθεν;

ΔΗΜΕΑΣ

ἐ[βο]υλόμην ἄν.

ΓΕΤΑΣ

ἀλλ’ [ἐτ]ύγχαν[ες

(231) ἀπόδημος ὢν ἐκεῖθεν;

ΔΗΜΕΑΣ

ἐκ Κύπρου παρὼ[ν
ἐνταῦθα πρῶτον τῶν ἐμῶν ταύτην ὁρ[ῶ.
καὶ δῆλον ὡς ἔσπαρκε τῶν οἴκοι τινὰς
635 ὁ κοινὸς ἐχθρὸς πόλεμος ἄλλον ἀλλαχῇ.

ΓΕΤΑΣ

ἔχει γὰρ οὕτως· αἰχμάλωτος γενομένη
(236) αὕτη πρ[ὸ]ς ἡμᾶς ἦλθε τοῦτον τ[ὸ]ν τ[ρ]όπον.
δ]ραμὼν δέ σοι τὸν δεσπότην ἤδη καλῶ.
.[. . . . . .]. . . . . . .[.].[. .]. .[.]α.

ΔΗΜΕΑΣ

οὕτω πόει.

(Holes and abrasion in the following six lines of O.10
make it impossible to identify speech divisions and speak-
ers (whether Demeas or Krateia). O.3 here supplies a
few extra letters, but they do not match anything pre-
served in O.10.)

631 δη above ε[and γε above αλλ[O.10 indicating speakers.
ἀλλ’ deciphered by Handley, ἐτ]ύγχαν[ες suppl. Kassel.

GETAS

What's that? Old woman, do you really call
[Him master]?

(*The nurse mutely nods her assent. Getas then addresses
Demeas again.*)

          Sir, where [have you come] from now?   630
From home?

DEMEAS

I wish I could have!

GETAS

                But were you
In fact away from home?

DEMEAS

             I'm here from Cyprus. She's
The first part of my family I've seen.
War is man's common enemy. It's scattered
Asunder members of my household, that's   635
Apparent.

GETAS

      It's the way things go. She came
To us like that, a prisoner of war.
I'll run and call my master now to you.
[   ]

DEMEAS

           Do that.   639

---

632 δη above εκ O.10.   636 γε⁻ O.10 in left margin.
636, 639 γενομένη and οὕτω πόει deciphered by Handley.
638 Suppl. Handley.

O.10

640　　. . .]. .[. .]ˑ[.].[.].πο. . . .υμ[. . . .]. . .
　　　.[10 letters]. . .ιτ.κα.[. . . . . .].ων.[
(241)　　. . . . ἱ]κετη[ρ]ίαν . . .[. .]φο.[. . . .].αρη.[.
　　　.[10 letters]. . . ι[　7　]ιτ.[.].αι.[
　　　ε[13 ? letters]. . [
645　　12 letters]φ. . .νου[. . .].[. . .]. .[
　　　. .]ει[. .].[. . .].μεν : οτετηλ[ο]υ. .[

O.3

642 or 643　　　　　　]. .[
　　　　　　　　　]πα[
(243 or 244)　　　].πάτρ[
645 or 646　　　　]κέτι[
646 or 647　　　　]μο. .κλ.[

ΔΗΜΕΑΣ

647　　ὁ] δ’ οὐκέτ’ [ἔ]στι; τίς λέγει σοι τὸν λόγο[ν;

ΚΡΑΤΕΙΑ

　　εὖ οἶδ’.]

642–647 Scraps preserved in O.3 here may come from near the
beginning of either 642–646 or 643–647.　　642 ἱ]κετη[ρ]ίαν
(O.10) deciphered and tentatively supplied by Turner.　　644 or
645]θυγατρ[(O.3) is also possible.　　646 τηλ[ο]υρό[ς or
τηλ[ο]ῦ. .[(O.10) Handley.　　646 Either μεν: or μενσ with
the σ badly abraded (O.10).　　647 ὁ] suppl. Austin and Mette,
the rest Turner.　　648 (O.10) εὖ οἶδ’ suppl. Sandbach,
assigned to Krateia by Sisti.

(*Getas now dashes off to fetch Thrasonides. The papyri
containing the text from 639 to 646 are so mutilated that
only a few words of the conversation between Krateia and
Demeas in these lines can be made out:* olive-branch *pos-
sibly in 642 (if rightly deciphered, presumably a reference
to the situation described in 522, 532 and 553),* father *or*
daughter *perhaps in 644 or 645,* [no] longer *in 645 or 646,
and* faraway *646. When a coherent but still damaged text
resurfaces at 647, the talk is focused on Krateia's brother,
now believed dead. The distribution and assignment of
parts in the following verses cannot always be inferred
with confidence from what is preserved and decipherable
in the papyri, and scholars have differed radically about
these matters (cf. the Gomme and Sandbach Commen-
tary, Oxford 1973, 452 f.). The arrangement presented
here, which concurs with all but one (see the critical
apparatus in 650) of the assignments and divisions identi-
fiable in the papyri, assumes that at the beginning of this
scene only Krateia had been induced by Thrasonides' pos-
session of her brother's sword to believe her lover's boasts
that he had slain its owner, while Demeas had not been
led into any suspicion of his son's death by sight of that
sword in Kleinias' house. At 647 Demeas has just been
told by Krateia that his son is dead.*)

DEMEAS

And [he]'s alive no more? Who's told you this?   647

KRATEIA

[I know for sure.]

311

ΔΗΜΕΑΣ

ἀπ[ό]λωλ'.

ΚΡΑΤΕΙΑ

οἴμοι τάλαινα τῆς ἐμ[ῆς
ἐγὼ τύ]χης. ὡς οἰκτρά, πάππα φίλτατε,
650   π]επόνθαμεν.

ΔΗΜΕΑΣ

τέθ[ν]ηχ';

ΚΡΑΤΕΙΑ

ὑφ' οὗ γ' ἥκιστ' ἐχ[ρῆν.

ΔΗΜΕΑΣ

οἶσ]θας σὺ τοῦτον;

ΚΡΑΤΕΙΑ

οἶδα καὶ συν[
(251)   ἁλοῦσα . . . . .[.]ουσα του[. . . .]λι[. . .]. .[

648 ἀπ[ό]λωλ' and ἐμ[ῆς suppl. Turner: απ[.]λωλα O.10
followed by dicolon (this line not preserved in O.3).
649–665 O.3, O.10.   649 ἐγὼ suppl. Webster, τύ]χης Hunt.
ὡς deciphered by Handley. πάππα Turner: παπα O.10 (torn off
in O.3), but see apparatus on 614.   650 π]επόνθαμεν suppl.
Hunt, τέθ[ν]ηκ' and ἐχ[ρῆν Handley. Dicola after both]επον-
θαμεν O.3 (omitted by O.10) and τεθ[ν]ηκε O.10 (also O.3).
υφουτηκιστ'ε[(with δη as indication of speaker written above
υφ) O.10, ὑφου[O.3: ὑφ' οὗ deciphered by Turner, τ corrected
to γ' by Austin; ὑφ' οὗ γ' ἥκιστ' ἐχ[ρῆν attributed against the
papyrus to Krateia by Merkelbach, Mette.   651]θασυτουτον
O.3 (torn off in O.10): suppl. and corr. Turner.   652 αλουσα-
μιλλα[O.3 (so Turner and Webster), but ἁλοῦσ' ἄμιλλά (or

312

DEMEAS
That's finished me!

KRATEIA

Oh, [I]'m
Crushed by my fate! How grievous, dearest father,
Are our afflictions!

DEMEAS
He's been killed?

KRATEIA

By one he least   650

Deserved to be[a]!

DEMEAS
You know the man?

KRATEIA

I do, and [

Taken prisoner [

(*From 651 to 658 only the opening words of each line are
preserved, but they reveal that the conversation between
Krateia and Demeas moves from the death of Krateia's
brother to the subject of what Krateia and Demeas should
do now.*)

---

[a] At this point she avoids naming Thrasonides.

-ίλλᾳ) [τ'] οὖσα does not provide acceptable sense.   652,
653 Paragraphi under the line in O.3.

ΔΗΜΕΑΣ

διὰ τί, Κράτεια, φ[.]ρ[

ΚΡΑΤΕΙΑ

ὁ τοῦτο πράξας ε.[

ΔΗΜΕΑΣ

[

ΚΡΑΤΕΙΑ

655 ἀλλά, πάτερ, ε[ἰσίωμεν
ἄπαντ’ α[......]υκ[...].[..].[......].
(256) βουλευτέον νῦν ἐστ[ιν]· ἀλλ’ ἦ κἄ[μ]ε δ[εῖ
ζῆν, .. πρέπει μετο..[.]υ[.]...[   ].[

ΔΗΜΕΑΣ

ὦ τοῦ παραδόξου καὶ ταλαιπ[ώρ]ου [βίου.

ΘΡΑΣΩΝΙΔΗΣ

660 πατὴρ Κρατείας, φής, ἐλήλ[υ]θ’ ἀρ[τίως;
νῦν ἢ μακάριον ἢ τρισαθλιώτατον
(261) δείξεις με τῶν ζώντων ἁπάντων γεγονότα.
εἰ μὴ γὰρ οὗτος δοκιμάσει με, κυρίως

654 Paragraphus under the line in O.3, O.10.   655 ε[ἰσίωμεν
suppl. Webster.   657 ἦ κἄ[μ]ε suppl. and interpreted by
Sandbach, δ[εῖ suppl. Arnott (Sandbach ἔδ[ει).   658 Para-
graphus under the line in O.3, traces of note in left margin of
O.10. In O.3 Hunt reads ζηνεῦπρε[, Turner ζην..πρε[:
just [.]ζ[O.10.   659 θρ in left margin O.3, misplaced a line
too early; traces of note in left margin and paragraphus under
the line in O.10. βίου suppl. Handley.   660 φής Turner:
φησ O.10, word omitted by O.3. ἀρ[τίως suppl. Austin, Mette.
661 τρισαθλιώτατον deciphered by Jacques.

DEMEAS

Krateia, why [

KRATEIA

The man who did this[a] [   ]

DEMEAS

[

KRATEIA

But, father, [let's go in   655
All [
We must consider now, but how in fact [I must]
Now live, that's what [we] ought [

DEMEAS

That's [life]—rich in surprises, rich in woe!

(*Demeas, Krateia and her nurse now leave the stage, presumably back into Kleinias' house. Directly after their departure Getas enters, bringing Thrasonides with him, as he promised; they are imagined to be in mid-conversation, although only Thrasonides is heard to speak during the brief time that they are now on stage.*[b])

THRASONIDES

You say Krateia's father's [just] arrived?   660
You'll either make me happy now, or quite
The most heartbroken of all living creatures.
Suppose he doesn't approve of me, or give

[a] Presumably a reference to Thrasonides as the man believed to have killed Krateia's brother.

[b] Since only three actors with speaking roles were available to the playwright, Getas' part in this scene has to be taken by a mute.

315

δώσει τε ταύτην, οἴχεται Θρασωνίδης·
665   ὃ μὴ γένοιτ'. ἀλλ' εἰσίωμεν· [οὐ]κέτι
τὸ τοιοῦτον εἰκάζειν γάρ, εἰδέναι δὲ δεῖ
(266)   ἡμᾶς. ὀκνηρῶς καὶ τρέμων εἰσ[έρ]χομ[αι.
μαντεύεθ' ἡ ψυχή τί μου, Γέτα, κακόν·
δέδοικα. βέλτιον δ' ἀπαξάπ[αν γε τ]ῆς
670   οἰήσεώς πως· ταῦτα θαυμάσαιμι δ' ἄν.

ΚΛΕΙΝΙΑΣ

ξένος ἐστὶν εἷς, μάγειρε, κἀγὼ καὶ τρίτη
(271)   ἐμή τις, εἴπερ νὴ Δί' εἰσελήλυθεν·
ἀγωνιῶ γὰρ καὐτός. εἰ δὲ μή, μόνος
ὁ ξένος· ἐγὼ γὰρ περιδραμοῦμαι τὴν π[όλιν,
675   ζητῶν ἐκείνην, πᾶσαν. ἀλλὰ πάραγε [σὺ
καὶ τοῦ ταχέως, μάγειρε, φρόντισ[ο]ν πάνυ.

665 Suppl. Webster.
666–676 O.10.
667 οκνηιρως O.10.
669 Suppl. Arnott (ἀπαξάπ[αν also Lloyd-Jones).
670 Paragraphus under the line, dicolon after οιησεωσ, and γετ written over πωσ in O.10; but this would mean a speaking part for a fourth actor, and Sandbach rightly makes Thrasonides continue speaking. At the end of the line εισιον[τ]ι appears to have been added in O.10.
673 δὲ Handley: γε O.10.
676 πάνυ deciphered by Rea.

Her formally in marriage. Then Thrasonides
Is done for—God forbid! Well, let's go in.   665
There's [no] more room for speculation on
Such topics—we must *know*. I go in trembling
And nervous. Getas, my whole being senses
Failure. I'm scared. But anything is better
Than vaguish notions. Life's amazing, though!   670

(*Thrasonides and Getas go off into Thrasonides' house.
Immediately afterwards Kleinias enters by the side-
entrance on the right, bringing with him a cook whom he
has hired in town to prepare a meal for him and two
guests, one male and the other a female whom Kleinias
calls 'a girl of mine' (672); the former must be Demeas, the
latter presumably an unidentified friend of Kleinias. We
must assume that the invitations were given in a lost scene
earlier in the play, which doubtless identified the girl as
part of a now unknown sub-plot. One possibility is that
she was a hetaira owned by the fat-faced man of 560, if he
was a brothel-keeper (see on 576 ff.), and that Kleinias
was in love with her.*)

KLEINIAS

There's just one guest, cook, then there's me, and third
A girl of mine, if she has come indeed.
I too, you see, am in a torment! If she hasn't,
The guest must dine alone, for I'll be dashing
All round the town in search of her. But, cook,   675
In you go, and make speed your prime concern!

(*Exit Kleinias into his house. When the stage is empty, the
chorus give their third entr'acte performance.*)

ΧΟΡΟΥ

ΜΕΡΟΣ Δ´

ΚΛΕΙΝΙΑΣ

(276)   τί φής; ἐπιγνοὺς τὴν σπάθην τὴν κειμέν[ην
  ἔνδον παρ᾽ ἡμῖν ᾤχεθ᾽ ὡς τοὺς γείτονας,
  τούτων ἀκούσας οὖσαν αὐτ[ήν]; πηνίκα
680   ἔθεντο δ᾽ οὗτοι δεῦρο τα[ύτ]ην ἢ τίνος
  ἕνεκα πρὸς ἡμᾶς, γραῦ; [.].[.]ειστων....[
(281)   μόνης τι λήψεων .[
  εὔδηλος εἶ. ψοφεῖν [δὲ προ]ϊὼν φαίν[ε]ται
  αὐτῶν τις· ὥστε πάντ᾽ ἀκούσομαι σαφῶ[ς.

ΓΕΤΑΣ

685   ὦ Ζεῦ πολυτίμητ᾽, ὠμότητος ἐκτόπου
  ἀμφοῖν ἀπανθρώπου τε, νὴ τὸν Ἥλιον.

ΚΛΕΙΝΙΑΣ

(286)   ξένος τις εἰσελήλυθ᾽ ἀρτίως, Γέτα,
  ἔνθαδε πρὸς ὑμᾶς;

ΓΕΤΑΣ

              Ἡράκλεις, αὐθαδίας
.[ἀν]θ[ρ]ώπου λαβεῖν

677–680 O.3, O.10.   681–682 O.10.   681 ειστων deciphered by Coles.   682 O.10 has μονωνεπειλη.ο.[with all except the first three letters deleted and ηστιλημψεων.[written as a correction above the line (corrected further to λήψεων by Sandbach).   683–700 O.3, O.10.   683]οσιων O.3,]ιων O.10. 685 Speaker identified as γε^τ in left margin of O.10. πολυτειμητ᾽ O.10.   686 τε deciphered by Handley.   687 εισεληλυθεν O.10 (this part of the verse torn off in O.3).   689 Suppl. Hunt.

ACT IV

(After the chorus' performance, Kleinias re-enters from his house in conversation with his old female slave, who comes out with him.)

KLEINIAS

What's that you say? He recognised the sword
Lying in our house? And rushed next door when he
Learned it belonged to them? When did they bring
It here to us, old woman? And what was   680
Their reason? Clearly you [
Alone [   ] of captures (?) [ª
But one of them is coming [out], it seems—there's
The creaking^b! So I'll hear the full tale clearly.

(Thrasonides' door opens, and out comes Getas. He is so absorbed by his description of Thrasonides' meeting with Demeas and Krateia that he does not notice Kleinias. As Getas speaks, he paces up and down the stage.)

GETAS

O honoured Zeus, what inhumanity   685
Both showed, I swear—abnormal and cold-blooded!

KLEINIAS

O Getas, has a stranger called on you
Here recently?

GETAS

(Still not hearing Kleinias)
                    My god! What mulishness!
[Surely] a man's [the right to ask] to take

ª The gaps in the text here defy coherent supplementation.
^b The noise of a door being opened from the inside. The pivots and hinges of ancient doors creaked loudly.

690   γυναικ[   ]

ΚΛΕΙΝΙΑΣ
πῶς του]τὶ λάβω;

ΓΕΤΑΣ

φ.[

ΚΛΕΙΝΙΑΣ
                              ] Δημεας

(291)   .[   ].[..]

ΓΕΤΑΣ
                    ἐκεῖ]νος οὐδὲ γρῦ
.].[.   "   ]σα [κ]αὶ γ[ά]ρ, Δημέα,
φιλῶ Κράτεια]ν αὐτός, [ὡς] ὁρᾷς, ἐγώ·
695   σὺ δ' εἶ πατ]ὴρ <καὶ> κύριος." ταυτὶ λέγει
ἅ[παν]τα κλάων, ἀντιβολῶν· ὄνος λύρας.

ΚΛΕΙΝΙΑΣ
(296)   σ]υμπεριπατήσω καὐτός, ὡς ἐμοὶ δοκῶ.

ΓΕΤΑΣ
ἓν τοῦτο δ' εὕρει· "τὴν ἐμαυτοῦ σ' ἀξιῶ

690 πῶς suppl. Arnott, του]τὶ Jensen:]τὶλαβῶ O.3,]ιλαλω
O.10.   690, 691 Speaker twice identified as κλει^ν in right
margin of O.3.   691 Dicolon before δημεασ in O.3.
692 ἐκεῖ]νος suppl. Arnott, this part of the line assigned to Getas
by Sandbach. ουδεγρῦ O.3: μ[.]δεγρν O.10.   693 κ]αὶ suppl.
Handley, γ[ὰ]ρ Hunt.   694 [φιλῶ Κράτεια]ν and [ὡς]
suppl. Sandbach.]ρας O.10,]ερᾶς O.3.   695 [σὺ δ' εἶ] suppl.
exempli gratia Sandbach.]ηρκυριοσταντι O.10,]τησ·ρ[.]..[.]-
ταυτι apparently O.3.   696 ἅ[παν]τα suppl. Sudhaus.
Dicolon at end of line in O.3, omitted by O.10.   697 Suppl.

320

A wife? [They snubbed him!]

KLEINIAS

(aside)

                    [How] am I to take   690
This?

GETAS

[   ]

KLEINIAS
            Demeas

[   ]

GETAS

(still pacing up and down)
            [He] answered not a word!
           ] [a] "Really, Demeas, I [love]
[Krateia], as you see, myself. [You are]
Her father [and] her guardian." All this he said   695
Pleading, in tears! But a donkey's deaf to music[b]!

KLEINIAS
I think I'll walk about with him myself.

(He now walks alongside Getas, trying to attract his
attention, but Getas either ignores or does not see him.)

GETAS
He's harping on this one theme: "I'm here claiming

[a] The gaps in the text hereabouts defy supplementation.
[b] A Greek proverb: literally, 'a donkey (listening) to a lyre',
implying a total absence of response.

Wilamowitz (from O.3's περιπατησω). δοκω O.10: δοκεῖ O.3
(equally possible).   698 ειρει O.10: εἴρειμε O.3.

ἥκων ἀπολυτροῦν ὧν πατήρ." "ἐγὼ δέ γε
700 αἰτῶ γυναῖκά σ' ἐντετυχηκώς, Δημέα."

ΚΛΕΙΝΙΑΣ

ἔνδ[ο]ν μέν ἐσθ' ἄνθρωπος εἰσεληλυθώς·
(301) τοὔν[ομ]α λέγει γὰρ οὑτοσὶ τὸν Δημέαν.

ΓΕΤΑΣ

ὦ ['Ηρ]άκλεις, ἀνθρωπίνως ἂν οὐ λάβοι
τὸ συμβεβηκός; ὗς ὄρει, τὸ τοῦ λόγου.
705 ἀλλ' οὐχὶ τοῦτο δεινόν, ἀλλ' αὕτη πάλιν
ἀφ[ο]ρᾷ λέγοντος· "ἀντιβολῶ, Κράτεια, σε,
(306) μὴ μ' ἐ[γκ]αταλίπῃς. παρθένον σ' εἴ[λ]ηφ' ἐγ[ώ,
ἀνήρ ἐκλήθην πρῶτος, ἠγάπησά σε,
ἀγ]απῶ, φιλῶ, Κράτεια φιλτάτη· τί σοι
710 λυπηρόν ἐστι τῶν παρ' ἐμοί; τεθνηκότα
πεύσει μ', ἐάν μ' ἐγκαταλίπῃς." οὐδ' ἀπόκρισις.

699 απολυτρουν O.10: απολυτρουνθ' O.3.   700 εντετυχως
with omitted ηκ written above χως O.3, εντετυχηκω[O.10.
701–781 O.10.   702 Suppl. Rea. λεγειτουουτησι O.10 origi-
nally, with correcting γαρ above του, ο above η added by second
hand.   703 Speaker wrongly identified as]μα or]ρα (i.e.
γ]ρα(ῦς) ?) in left margin of O.10.   δουκανλαβοι O.10 origi-
nally, with correcting ανου added above λαβοι by second hand.
ορει interpreted as ὄρει by Austin, Sandbach.   705 τουτο{.}δει-
νον deciphered by Coles. αλλαταυτη O.10.   706 ἀφ[ο]ρᾷ
suppl. Austin. κρατια O.10.   707]αταλειπησ and]ηφαεγ[
O.10.   708 Punctuated after πρῶτος by Sandbach.
709 Punctuated after φιλτάτη by Handley, Mette.
711 ενκαταλιπησ· O.10.

That you release[a] my girl. I am her father."
"Now I've met you, I beg you for her hand   700
In marriage, Demeas."[b]

KLEINIAS

(*aside*)
            The man's come, gone
Indoors! This slave has named him—Demeas!

GETAS

(*Still ignoring or not seeing Kleinias*)
Heavens, couldn't he accept what's happened with
Humanity? Pig-headed, that's the word.[c]
This wasn't so bad, though, but the girl then turned   705
Her back when he said "I beseech you, don't
Abandon me, Krateia. I took you,
A virgin still. I was first called your man.[d] I loved
You, love and cherish you, Krateia darling. What's
So painful for you in your life with me? You'll hear   710
I'm dead, if you abandon me." Not even one
Word in reply!

---

[a] The Greek word implies that Demeas would pay a ransom to Thrasonides for the release of his daughter.

[b] The absence here in Menander's text of names or other indications to identify the quoted speakers implies that the actor playing Getas would be required to imitate their different voices and gestures if he wished their identities to be readily understood by the audience.

[c] Literally 'Pig on the mountain, that's the saying.' The proverb was applied to a person behaving with apparently unreasonable stubbornness like Demeas here.

[d] This implies that Thrasonides and Krateia lived as man and wife, although their situations at the time (free man, slave woman apparently from abroad) prevented any formal marriage.

ΚΛΕΙΝΙΑΣ

(311) τί ποτ᾽ ἐστι τὸ κακόν;

ΓΕΤΑΣ

βάρβαρος, λ[έ]αινά τις

ἄν[θρωπος].

ΚΛΕΙΝΙΑΣ

οὐχ ὁρᾷς με, κακόδαιμον, πάλαι;

ΓΕΤΑΣ

ἀπροσδόκητον.

ΚΛΕΙΝΙΑΣ

οὐχ ὑγιαίνει παντελῶς.

ΓΕΤΑΣ

715   ἐγὼ μὲν [αὐτήν], μὰ τὸν Ἀπόλλω τουτονί,
οὐκ ἂν ἀπ[έ]λυσ᾽. Ἑλληνικὸν καὶ πανταχ[οῦ]

(316)   γινόμ[ε]νον ἴσμεν. ἀλλ᾽ ἐλεεῖν ὀρθῶς ἔχει
τὸν ἀ[ν]τελεοῦνθ᾽. ὅταν δὲ μηδ᾽ ὑμεῖ[ς ἐ]μέ,
οὐδὲ λόγον ὑμῶν οὐδ᾽ ἐπιστροφὴν ἔχω.

720   οὐ[κ ἔστι] σοι; τί δ᾽; οὐθὲν ἄτοπον, ὡς ἐγὼ
δο[κῶ]. βοήσεται δὲ καὶ βουλεύσεται

719 KT fr. 687

713 Suppl. Handley. γετα O.10 originally, with correcting παλαι added above τα by second hand. 714 ἀπροσδόκητον deciphered by Tsantsanoglou, assigned to Getas by Kraus (O.10 has paragraphus under, but no dicolon at the end of, 713). The rest of the line assigned to Kleinias by Sisti (O.10 has dicolon before ουχ, but no paragraphus under 714). 715 Suppl. Handley. 716 Suppl. Sandbach. 718 ἀ[ν]τελεοννθ᾽ suppl. and deciphered by Handley, ὑμεῖ[ς ἐ]μέ by Rea. 720 ατοπονωςεγω is correction written by second hand on top of O.10's indecipher-

324

KLEINIAS

(*beginning to lose his temper at Getas' failure to notice him*)

        Damn it, what's going on?

GETAS

                    The girl's

A beast, a savage!

KLEINIAS

(*facing Getas*)

        Haven't you seen me yet,

You wretch?

GETAS

(*still ignoring Kleinias*)

        So unexpected!

KLEINIAS

        He's[a] completely mad!

GETAS

Now I would never have released [her], by   715
Apollo here[b]! We know it's a Greek custom,
And goes on everywhere. But pity's only right if it's
Reciprocated. When you two[c] refuse,
I shan't heed or regard you, either! You
[Can't do] that? Why, there's nothing odd in this,   720
I think. Well, he will bellow and make up his mind

---

   [a] Getas presumably, if this remark is correctly assigned to
Kleinias.   [b] He points to the altar or pillar erected to Apollo
Agyieus by the door of his house. See the note on *Dyskolos*
659.   [c] Demeas and Krateia.

---

able original text.   721 Suppl. Mette. βουλευεται O.10 origi-
nally, with correcting σ written by first hand above second υ.

(321) κ[τα]νεῖν ἑαυτόν. στὰς βλέπει δὲ πῦρ ἅμα
       ου[. .]. . ἐκεῖ καὶ δράττεταί <γε> τῶν τριχῶν.

ΚΛΕΙΝΙΑΣ
ἄν[θρωπε], κατακόψεις με.

ΓΕΤΑΣ
                χ[α]ῖρε, Κλεινία.

725   π[όθεν πάρ]εσθ';

ΚΛΕΙΝΙΑΣ
οὑμός τι θορυβεῖν φαίνεται
. . .]. [. . . .ε]λθὼν δ[.]ε.ισ' ὡς ὁ ξένος

(The lines from 727 to 756 are severely holed and
abraded. They are printed below with the paragraphi as
written in O.10, and with those assignments to speakers
which are either given by O.10 or suggested by the textual
content.)

(326) . . [

                                    (?)
       . . [
           ]. . [
730   ]. .ι δευτερ.[
           ]νουκαλ. . .[
(331) τα. .[   ].[ ]. .[   ]. .[   ]ν
       .[. . . . .].γω. .

ΓΕΤΑΣ
ε.ε.εν[. . .], Κλεινία.

ΚΛΕΙΝΙΑΣ
ουκ[. . . . .]α. .υ.[. . . .].τρ. . θεῶν

326

To kill himself. He stands there, eyes aflame,
As well as (?) [   ], and tears his hair!

KLEINIAS

(*angrily, to Getas*)
Man, you'll provoke me!

GETAS

(*now noticing Kleinias now for the first time*)
                              Hello, Kleinias!

(*aside*)
[Where]'s he [sprung from]?

KLEINIAS

                              My friend's arrival seems   725
To be creating mayhem! [   ] My guest

(*From 727 to 756 abrasion, holes and tears in the papyrus
have wiped out virtually the whole text. Only occasional
words, names of characters, and marks to indicate the
ends of speeches are decipherable. Getas speaks in the
middle of 733 and at 741; Kleinias is addressed at 733,
Getas at 736; Demeas is mentioned at 735. Most of the
recognisable words are inconsequential:* not *and* gods

---

722 Suppl. Webster. Punctuated before στὰς by Arnott (στασ'
followed by short space in O.10).   723 <γε> Handley: δρατ-
τεταιτων O.10.   724 χα[ῖ]ρε suppl. Handley, κατακόψεις
deciphered by Webster.   725 Before initial π two letters
deleted by second hand in O.10. π[όθεν πάρ]εσθ' suppl. Hand-
ley. τι deciphered by Rea.   728 Indecipherable traces of
speaker's name in O.10's left margin.   733 After].γω..
dicolon, with suprascript γετ identifying speaker of what follows,
in O.10.   734 Speaker identified as .ε (? = γε) in O.10's left
margin.

735   εὐεργ[ετ..]..ηρ.[..]. [Δ]ημέα[..]

ΓΕΤΑΣ (?)

.η.αρ..

..ε.ρ[....]..εξ..[....]. Γέτα

ΚΛΕΙΝΙΑΣ (?)

(336)   ....].[....]με[...]...μεν..[
..........]...[   ].....
    ε.[..].[   ].επ[...]..γ'[..].νοσ[
740   ἐγὼ [...]..[.....].ηρ[...]..ηκε γὰρ

ΓΕΤΑΣ

.ε.ινα[........].[.....]ζεται

ΚΛΕΙΝΙΑΣ

(341)   εἰσέρχο[μαι .....]..[....].ον σφ[ό]δρα [

ΓΕΤΑΣ

τὸ μὲν [...... γέ]γονεν [..].ριστα.ο[
.....[........]..[.....].. βίο[ς
745   οὔ φησι [..].[....]δια[
..]λασ[.].[.......].σλα[.....].[
(346)   .]..a[.].[..]..[.......]..ασ[..].[
..]..τ[..].[.....]...a.τ. κατὰ τὸν [

ΚΛΕΙΝΙΑΣ

πό[ει] δὲ τ[οῦ]το· .ρ[..].εσ[...] ἐμπειρία[

ΓΕΤΑΣ

750   γα[.]λ[.....]a[.]τ[..]τ[.] καὶ πλάνης γεν[

735 εὐεργ[ετ Austin, Turner. Over η.αρ indecipherable traces
of speaker's name.   737, 743 Indecipherable traces of
speaker's name in O.10's left margin.   741 Speaker identified
as]τ (? = γε]τ) in O.10's left margin.

734, I *and* for 740, very much 742, has *or* have become 743, life 744, says . . . that not 745, according to the 748, do *or* does this *and* experience 749, and 753, when *or* whenever 755, *perhaps* daughter 756. *Two snippets may be tentatively related to incidents in the plot:* benefit *or* benefactor *(735) to Thrasonides' return of Krateia to her father,* and wanderer *or* wandering *(750) to Demeas' travels in search of his family. Two further words may help to elucidate movements on and off stage. At 742 one of the two characters on stage says* I'm going in, *and at 751, if the papyrus is correctly deciphered, a character is addressed as* slave. *We may assume that Kleinias and Getas talk with each other at least up to 742, presumably focusing their attention on Thrasonides' release of Krateia and her father's and her total rejection of him. If the 'slave' of 751 is addressed in person and not apostrophised, he is most likely to be Getas, still on stage, and so the person who announces his intention to depart at 742 must be Kleinias. The most plausible scenario is that after Kleinias makes his announcement, he stays chatting with Getas until 750,*[a] *when he goes off into his own house. Directly afterwards a new character enters; the content of his subsequent remarks, together with his entitlement to address Getas as 'slave', identifies him as Thrasonides,*

[a] Note in the papyrus the paragraphi under lines 742, perhaps 749 and 750, and the traces of speakers' names in the left margin of lines 743 and perhaps 750.

---

742 Suppl. Austin, Turner.   749, 750 Traces of paragraphi are uncertain.   749 Suppl. Turner (with πο[εῖ: πό[ει Arnott).
750 Coles detects traces of ink in O.10's left margin (speaker's name?) and deciphered καὶ πλάνης. γεν[written as a correction over an erased . .εδ. .[in O.10.

ΘΡΑΣΩΝΙΔΗΣ

.]..ι[.]..[.....].η.[.....].ανα..σ.ε παῖ·

(351) ....]σα[....].........[....]περι[

καὶ .α[.........]..ε...ι.[....].ε.[

.].[.].....α[....]..[.]αι[........].α..[

ΓΕΤΑΣ

755 .]..[...........]...... ὁπόταν δ[

εγκ[......]........[..]ο [θυ]γάτριο[ν.

ΘΡΑΣΩΝΙΔΗΣ

(356) ..].. με μικρόψ[υ]χον εἶπέ τι[ς] τυχὸν

..].ηλ....νθ'.[..] πολλὰ πρ[ά]γματ[α

εἰ δ' εἰς μέσον ....φερ...[

760 ἕτερον .. τουτ..αυ.....ελ.[

ἔστ' ὥστ' ἔ[χ]ειν με καὶ λίθον ψυχὴν φερ[.]..

(361) ποεῖ<ν> τ' ἄδηλον τοῖς συνοῦσι τὴν νόσ[ο]ν

δυνήσ[ομ.]..[.....].....[...]..[.] τίνα [?

τρόπον [κα]θέξ[ω τ]οῦτο καὶ ῥᾷον φέρω.

765 ἀπαμφιεῖ γὰρ τὸ κατάπλαστον τοῦτό μου

καὶ λανθάνειν βουλόμενον ἡ μέθη ποτέ.

765–766 *Mis.* fr. 8 Kö.

752 περι deciphered by Coles, perhaps at verse end.
752–756 Portions of these lines may be preserved in O.26 (printed below as fr. 3), whose text appears not to match that of O.10 at all significant points.   754, 756 Coles detects traces of ink under the beginnings of these two lines (paragraphi ?). 755 ὁπόταν tentatively deciphered by Turner. 756 Deciphered by Austin.   757 Indecipherable traces perhaps of speaker's name in O.10's left margin. μεικροψ[.]χον O.10.   761 Tentatively suppl. and deciphered by Handley.   762 Corr. Handley:

now emerging from his house. It is likely that Thra-
sonides' speech to Getas at 751 ff. is briefly answered
before the slave departs at 756. Thrasonides is now alone
and launches into the long monologue that continues right
until the end of the fourth act.)

THRASONIDES

] Maybe a man called me small-minded—	757
] many things.	

But if in public [
This other (?) [   ] is [760
    ], to own and [wear] a heart of stone (?).
[I] shall be able to conceal my pain
From those I'm with [   ], how [I']ll
Control and bear this burden with less toil—
For drink will one day tear away this bandage which   765
I wear, though I should seek to hide the wound.   766

(Despite some holes and abrasions in the papyrus, the
opening of this monologue presents a speaker who
appears to reject any accusation of small-mindedness
(based presumably on his willingness to restore Krateia to
her father without a struggle), and is determined to steel
himself and not to sink (like other unhappy lovers in
Greco-Roman comedy) into either maudlin self-pity or an
alcoholic haze. In the more seriously damaged lines after
766 (767, 768, 778, 779, 783–786 are too indecipherable
for any word to be translated) Thrasonides seems to begin
by reviewing his past relationship with Krateia: he loved
her, but the two 'didn't fix it' (771)—perhaps a reference
to their failure to put the union on a more formal footing.)

ποει O.10.   764 Corr. (φερων apparently O.10), suppl. and
deciphered by Turner.

(366)   ....]κ.[.......].[
        ...[..].[..].[..]..[
        ἐ[γ]ὼ γὰρ ἂν τοῦτ' οὐ..' ο[

770   ἀγαπωμένη παρ...[
        οὐχ ἡρμόσαμεν αὐτὸ.[

(371)   οδυν[..]...νκα[.]..θ'[....].[
        εἴπῃ προσελθὼν .π....[.].λη.[..].[
        ἐστιν Κράτειά σοι· καθέζετα[ι

775   λυπρὰ κα....ματα[

(375a)   ἐγὼ τετ..[.....].....[

(375b)   εἴπα[ς] ἔκλα[ον .]....[
        ...ψατ' ..[..]...[...]αβ....[
        ει..β...[

780   ἄπασι[.].[
        ἀλλ' ὥσπ[ε]ρ .[ἀ]λλὰ τί;

(380a)   ....[   ]έχει[

769 Suppl. and deciphered by Handley.
773 ειπηι or ειζηι (i.e. εἰ ζῇ) O.10.
776 and 782 are written intralineally between 775 and 777, 781 and 783 respectively, either as corrections of the lines immediately following or more probably because they had been originally omitted by error.
777 Suppl. Arnott.
781 Suppl. Austin.
782–806 O.10, O.23.

You see, I'd [ ] this [	769
She being loved	770
We didn't fix it (?) [	
Pain (?) [	
He come and say [	
Krateia is to you. She sits [	
Painful [	775
I [	
I said, and broke down (?) [	777
To all [	780
But as [ ] But what *or* why?	
] has *or* have [	

(*The lines that follow are much better preserved, partly because of the recent identification of a second papyrus containing the central portions of lines 782 to 806, partly because re-examination of the previously known papyrus has shed substantial new light on these lines.*

In addition to solving old problems, however, that illumination produces a paradoxical new one. At 790 Thrasonides says 'Simiche's come out' (cf. the contextless 'came out' in 789). Simiche is likely to have been an old female slave (cf. her namesake in the Dyskolos), and since she cannot be identified with either Kleinias' old female slave (apparently named Syra) or Krateia's nurse (apparently named Chrysis: see note on line 555), she must in all probability be considered an additional member of Thrasonides' household. She may not now be entering for the first time in the play (her ownership or links with any of the other characters are not described here, so it seems likely that she was already familiar to the audience), and the reason for her presence on stage at this point (? to

(380b)   .].. .[   ]σδυ.[
          8–10 letters]υπροτ[8 letters?].[. . . .].α[
785   8–10 letters].τοκ. .[. . . . . . .]. .[. .]ιαν[
          . . . . . .]ειπωσειρ[.].π[. . . .]. . . .[
          . . .]κρινεῖ τὴν α[ἰτί]αν [. .].ε.ι[
(385)   . .]α γὰρ φρασαι . . . .ον. .ο.ωτ.[.].[
          ἐ]ξῆλθεν ἔνεχ' . .[. . . . . .]. . . . . .[
790   ὀργῇ σ', ἐλεεινός. Σιμίχη 'ξελήλυ[θ]εν.
          τ]ί φής; πέπονθ' ἄπα[ν]θ'; ὑπὲρ ταύτης λαλε[ῖς;

786]ειπω[O.23,]ιπωσειρ[O.10.
787 Suppl. and corr. tentatively M(argaret) (]κρινεῖ: ? or κρινεῖ
uncompounded, Arnott) and H(erwig) (α[ἰτί]αν) Maehler:]κρι-
νητηνα[O.10,].ε[ ]τηνα[. . .]αν[O.23.
788 γα[O.23,]αρ O.10.   789]ξηλθενενεχ O.10 with χ
corrected from κ.
790 'ξελήλυ[θ]εν M. Maehler after Turner (]ελήλυ[θε]ν):
ελ[. .]ινοσσειμιχη (or κη) εξελην λυ[.]εν O.10, ελεειν[. .]σιμιχ[
O.23.
791]ιφησπεπονθαπα[.]θ'υπερταυτας (with α deleted after θ'
and η written as correction above second α of ταυτασ),]ησπε-
πονθ'[.]π[. .]ταθ'υ.[(= ? [α]π[αν]τα θ') O.23. τ]ί and λαλε[ῖς
suppl. Turner.

*console or advise Thrasonides) is not made clear. All the
available evidence indicates that she was played now by a
mute; neither of the two papyri gives any clear indication
of change of speaker between 776 and 816, and the struc-
ture and contexts of the text itself make it difficult to
organise the lines as a dialogue between Thrasonides and
Simiche. We must accordingly assume that when she
comes out, she mimes her conversation with Thrasonides,
so that Thrasonides is compelled to repeat her words
aloud for the benefit of an audience accustomed to this
convention (see in this play already 660, 677–679).*

*But why should this artificial convention be employed
here? Elsewhere it is normally forced on the playwright
by the contemporary limitation on the number of speak-
ing actors available to him. At this point of the play, how-
ever, such a restriction is not a problem. Thrasonides is
the one speaker from 757 to 816, and the actor who left
the stage as Kleinias at 750 had plenty of time to change
costume and re-emerge as Simiche at 781 or 782.*

*Translation of Thrasonides' monologue becomes feasi-
ble again at line 787. The following passage combines
imagined repetition of Simiche's mimed words with self-
address, and so 'you' at times means Simiche, at times
Thrasonides. This may confuse a reader, but an actor's
use of voice and gesture would easily remove any prob-
lems in performance.)*

      ] will judge the cause (*or* blame) [787
For [   ] to show [
Came out because of [   ] you
In anger. Poor man! Simiche's come out. What's that   790
You say? She's suffered everything? You're taking her

335

MENANDER

με[λ]ει τ' ἐμοὶ ταύτης δι' ἐμαυτόν; μὴ λέγε.

(390)   ἐμόν τ' ἀτύχημα τοῦτ'· ἐκεῖ[νον μὴ] ψέγω;
οὔκουν ἔν ἐστι τοῦτό σοι, τὸ κωλύε[ι]ν

795   ταύτην ἀπολαβεῖν τοῦτο[ν; <ἀλλὰ> παντ]αχοῦ
οὕτως ἔχει. τὰ πρόσθε γενό[μεν' ἀ]νατ[ρέπει
τὸ ζῆν. ἀφήσεις; ἀλλ' ἐρεῖ "θέλξ[εις] ἄ[π]αν

(395)   οἴκτῳ τὸ μισοῦν ὡς σεαυτόν; ἀσχα[λᾷς."
καὶ τίς ὁ βίος σοι; ποῦ τὸ τῆ[ς] σ[ω]τηρίας

800   ἐπίσημον; εἴ τις ὁμ[ό]σε ταῖ[ς ὀ]ργαῖς τρέχοι—
πλεονεξία τοῦτ', εἴπερ; ἁρπάσαι βλέπων
ἴσως ἰταμὸς εἶ. τῷ λογισμῷ νῦν γενοῦ

(400)   εὔψυχος. ἀ[π]όρως ζῆθ', ὀδυνηρῶς, ἀσθενῶ[ς.
ὄν[ε]ιδος αὐτῇ τοῦτο καταλιπεῖν σε δεῖ

805   ἀθάνατον. εὖ παθοῦσ' ἐτιμωρήσατο

792 με[λ]ει suppl. M. Maehler: με[.]ειτεμοιταυτησδιε[.]αυ-
τονμη (or μοι) λεγε O.10,]ειτεμοιτα[..]ησδιεμ[O.23.
793 ἐ]μόν suppl. H. Maehler, ἐκεῖ[νον suppl. M. Maehler, μὴ
Handley:]μοντατυχηματουτελε[......]ψεγω O.10 (perhaps
with λ corrected to κ),]νατυχηματ..τεκε.[O.23.   794 ἔν ἐστι
so articulated by Handley. το or τι O.23. κωλύε[ι]ν suppl. and
deciphered by M. Maehler.   795 ταυτην in O.10 glossed by
suprascript κρ[ατε]ιαν (suppl. M. Maehler). τουτ[.....]αχου
O.10: τοῦτο[ν suppl. M. Maehler, <ἀλλὰ> H. Maehler (metre
and the length of O.10's gap compel the assumption of a scribal
omission), παντ]αχοῦ Austin.   796 πρόσθε Handley: εχει-
προσθεν O.10, ταπροσσεν or -σθεν O.23. γενό[μενα suppl. M.
Maehler, ἀ]νατ[ρέπει Handley.   797 αλλερει O.10: αλερει
O.23. θέλξ[εις suppl. H. Maehler, ἄ[π]αν Handley.   798 οικτω
O.10:]ρω (i.e. from οικτ]ρω ?) O.23. ἀσχα[O.10: suppl. M.
Maehler.   799 Suppl. M. Maehler: τη[..].[.]ηρ.ια[O.10,

Side? I care for her selfishly? Don't say so!
And this is my bad luck? [Can't] I blame him?
Well then, prevent him taking her—can't you
Do this one thing? But that's the rule, all over!   795
Those past events [turn] my life [topsy-turvy]!
You'll let her go? But will she then say "You'll
Charm all my hate away by pity for you? You're
Upset." What life's before you? Where's your badge
Of Safety[a]? Yet if one could fight these rages (?) —   800
Too much to hope for, that, perhaps! You've plunder in
Your look, maybe you're reckless! Now, be logical.
Be brave! Make your life futile, painful, feeble.
You must bequeath her this as her eternal
Reproach: 'She was well-treated. In return   805

---

[a] The allusion is puzzling. Thrasonides is a soldier, and one
possibility is that he is referring to a device emblazoned on his
shield of a god (Zeus?) or goddess (Artemis, Athena, Demeter?)
who familiarly had the title of 'Saviour'. If the shield had been
described in a lost earlier scene, Thrasonides would now be
wryly asking himself 'What's the point of your Safety badge, if
you can sink so easily into despair?'

τη[....]ρ.ασ O.23.   800 Suppl. and deciphered by Handley
(ὀργαῖς already M. Maehler): ...σεται[..]ργαιστ[..]ει O.10
with o written above the ε of ει: .τα[...]..αισ[O.23.
801 εἴπερ tentatively deciphered by Handley.   802 τῷ tenta-
tively M. Maehler: τοτε O.10 (torn off in O.23).   803 ἀ[π]ό-
ρως suppl. Turner, ζῆθ' deciphered by Handley, ἀσθενῶ[ς
suppl. M. Maehler.   804 ὄν[ε]ιδος suppl. Turner. αυτη (with
η written above and slightly in front of the α) O.10. καταλιπειν
O.23: κατ[α]λε[ι]πειν presumably O.10.   805 παθουσ'ετι-
μωρησατο O.10:]σαστιμ[(? error for -σα ετιμ-) O.23.

(403)	τὸν τἀγάθ᾽ αὐτῇ δόντα. πῶς ο[ὐ]κ ἔ[σ]τι μοι
(404*)	].ειν με προσποου[μεν
(405*)	π]έμψαι τοῦτον εἰ[ς
	]εν.δ[..]ησθαι[.]εσ[
810	] γὰρ [.. ἐσ]τιν οὕτω[
	].[ ]ωτηκ...[
	τ]ύχοις ἂν εἰ [
(410*)	]τίς πά[θ]η[
	] ἀνοσιωτ[
815	]ησιν τινα[
	κ]αὶ τρισαθλ[ι

ΧΟ Ρ ΟΥ

ΜΕΡΟΣ Ε´

ΓΕΤΑΣ (?)

ἐ]μαυτὸν ν[

	]νη που τ[
(415*)	] τὸ φάρμ[ακον
820	]εστ[
(418*)	]ρ.[

806 ο[ὐ]κ suppl. Austin, ἔ[σ]τι Turner.
807–821 O.23.
807–808 κτα]νεῖν με προσποου[μένῳ / τὸν παῖδα π]έμψαι
τοῦτον εἰ[ς τὴν οἰκίαν *exempli gratia* suppl. M. Maehler.
810 Traces of ink above the ρ of γὰρ in O.23.
812 Or τ]υχοῦσαν εἰ.
813, 816, 817, 819 Suppl. M. Maehler.

She abused her benefactor.' Perhaps I may
[Wreak some revenge] by feigning [suicide,]
[Then] send this [slave of mine] into [their house]   808

*(From line 807 to the end of the act the papyrus preserves
only small fragments of each line. The supplements
printed above for 807 and 808 are very uncertain; if cor-
rect, they would provide advance warning of one possible
development in the fifth act. From 809 to 816 only a few
words can be deciphered (for and thus 810, you might
happen or be lucky if (?) 812, unholy 814, and thrice
wretched 816); these words and phrases match the tone
of, but add nothing to, what Thrasonides had said before.
At the end of 816 Thrasonides presumably retired into his
own house; whether Simiche accompanied him, or had
departed earlier during the monologue, is unknown.
When the stage is empty, the chorus gives their fourth
entr'acte performance.)*

ACT V

*(After the chorus's performance, a few words are pre-
served from the opening five lines of the final act: a male
myself 817, where or somewhere or somewhat 818, the
drug 819). The speaker and his subject are uncertain; one
possibility is that Getas has emerged from Thrasonides'
house with the information that his master is taking or has
taken a drug in order to put himself to sleep and thus sim-
ulate suicide. There is then a gap in our text of 99 lines or
so, about whose contents we can only speculate. If the
previous hints (cf. 722, 807, 819) that Thrasonides after
his rejection by Krateia was contemplating, or planning to
simulate, suicide were intended to prepare for events in
the fifth act, the gap after line 821 would be an obvious*

(After 821 there is a lacuna of about 99 lines.)

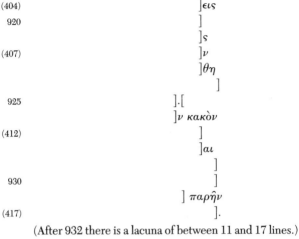

(404)	] εις
920	]
	]ς
(407)	]ν
	]θη
	]
925	].[
	]ν κακὸν
(412)	]
	]αι
	]
930	]
	] παρῆν
(417)	].

(After 932 there is a lacuna of between 11 and 17 lines.)

ΚΡΑΤΕΙΑΣ ΑΔΕΛΦΟΣ (?)

(418)	οὐκέτι [
	Θρασω[νίδ
950	τί τανα[
	καλῶς [
(422)	οὐ παιδ[
	ζηλοτυπ[ο
	ἃ νῦν λε[γ

919–932, 948–958 O.7.   948 ff. Speaker uncertain: tentative
identification as Krateia's brother by Guidorizzi.   949, 953,
954 Suppl. Grenfell and Hunt.

340

*place for them; one interpretation of the Mytilene mosaic
(see my introduction to Misoumenos) suggests a way in
which they could have been staged, with Getas demon-
strating to Demeas and Krateia how his master had
attempted to strangle (not drug!) himself. During this
gap too Krateia's brother is likely to have returned, and
thus removed the grounds for Krateia's hatred of Thra-
sonides.*

*After the gap we have only the very ends of lines
919–932, yielding just two decipherable words (bad 926, I
or he or she was there 931); neither speaker(s) nor situa-
tion(s) can be gauged. There follows another gap, of
between 11 and 17 lines, before we come to the final 49
lines of the play, which are rather more informative
although only partially preserved. From 948 to 957 we
have the line-beginning of a speech by an unidentified
character: No longer 948, Thrasonides 949, What 950,
Well 951, Not a child (?) 952, Jealous 953, What [   ] now
says 954, To the work or action 955, Two hundred 956, By
Zeus 957, Withdraw 958. At the end of 958 he appears to
have withdrawn from the stage, and Getas enters (proba-
bly from Kleinias' house), apparently addressing the
departing figure brusquely as 'man' (959). This implies
that he was a stranger to Getas, and the likeliest candidate
for such an address would be Krateia's brother newly
arrived on the scene and so far unknown to Getas.
Although the lines after 958 are still incompletely pre-
served, they often yield enough information about what is
going on to justify a translation with more speculative,
though (I trust) no less plausible, supplementation than is
normal in this edition of Menander.*

As the speaker of lines 948–958 departs, Getas enters,

955   εἰς τοὔρ[γον
    διακοσι[

(427)   νὴ Δία τ[
    ἀναγε[.].[

ΓΕΤΑΣ

ἀπὸ τῆς θύρας, ἄνθρ[ωπ', ἄπιθι].

ΘΡΑΣΩΝΙΔΗΣ

[τί τοῦτο, παῖ;

960   φαίνει γὰρ ἀγαθὸν ν..[

ΓΕΤΑΣ

διδόασί σοι γυναῖκα ..[

ΘΡΑΣΩΝΙΔΗΣ

(432)   προσευξάμην ..αυ...[

ΓΕΤΑΣ

οὕτως ἀγαθὸ[ν] γέ[νοιτο

ΘΡΑΣΩΝΙΔΗΣ

οὐκ ἐξα[π]ατᾷς δε[(?)]

ΓΕΤΑΣ

[   ]

955 Suppl. Grenfell and Hunt.   958–959 O.7 has the speaker's name γε(τας) in the left margin between these two lines, but its paragraphus is under 959, not 958.
959–974 O.7, O.10.   959 ἄνθρ[ωπ' suppl. Turner, ἄπιθι *exempli gratia* Arnott, τί τοῦτο, παῖ; (with attribution to Thrasonides) Sisti.   960 φαίνει γὰρ deciphered by Handley: φαινε[O.7,]..γ.ραγαθ.νν..[O.10.   961 σοι O.10: ν[or μ[O.7.   962 Assigned to Thrasonides by Arnott: no paragraphus under the line in O.7.   963, 964 Suppl. Turner.

probably from Kleinias' house. Thrasonides is there to meet him; he either left his house at the same time as Getas left Kleinias', or was already on stage. In the latter event he must have seen or talked with the man provisionally identified as Krateia's brother.)

GETAS

(to the man departing)
[Move off], man, from the doorway!

THRASONIDES

       [Hey, what's this?] 959

(to Getas)
You seem [to have] good [news   960

GETAS

They're[a] offering you [the girl you love] in marriage!

THRASONIDES

I prayed [for this, but how can I believe you?]

GETAS

As [I] do hope to prosper, [that's the truth!]

THRASONIDES

You're not deceiving me?

GETAS

     [Of course I'm not!]

[a] Presumably Demeas and Krateia's brother, whose arrival removed the major obstacle to Krateia's marriage to Thrasonides: her belief that her brother had been killed by Thrasonides.

ΘΡΑΣΩΝΙΔΗΣ

965 πῶς εἶπεν;

ΓΕΤΑΣ

Ἡρ[άκλεις,

ΘΡΑΣΩΝΙΔΗΣ

τὰ ῥήματ' αὐτά μοι [φράσον

(437) λέγων τάχα τρέχ', εἰ [

ΓΕΤΑΣ

ἔλεγεν· "θυγατρίον, [τοῦτον ἂν βούλοι' ἔχειν;"
"ναί," φησί, "πάππα, βούλ[ομαι

970 ἤκουσ'· ἃ δ' ἤκουσα.ε[χαρᾶς (?)
ἔκπλεα γελω.άγ'ηπ.[

ΘΡΑΣΩΝΙΔΗΣ

(442) ἀγαθὰ λέγεις.

ΓΕΤΑΣ

ἐφήδομ'· ἀ[λλὰ τὴν θύραν
ψοφεῖ τις αὐτῶν.

ΔΗΜΕΑΣ

πρ[ός σε νῦν ἐξέρχομαι.

ΘΡΑΣΩΝΙΔΗΣ

καλῶς ποῶν.

965 Traces of speaker's name in O.10 above ηρ[.   965, 966,
969 Suppl. Turner.   967 τρέχ', εἰ [tentatively Arnott, but
τρέχει[ς (Turner) is equally possible.   968 Suppl. *exempli
gratia* Arnott.   969 πάππα Turner: παπα O.10, but see appa-
ratus on 614.   970 ηκουσα[O.7: εκουσ. O.10.   χαρᾶς suppl.
exempli gratia Turner.   971 εκπλεαγελω.αγ' O.10 (γέλωτά
γ' or γελῶσά γ' are both possible): εκπλει.[O.7.   972 ἀ[λλὰ

THRASONIDES

How did he speak?

GETAS

I swear [965

THRASONIDES

[Tell] me the exact words [her father said],
Hurry up and say them, if [

GETAS

His words were "Daughter, [would you wish to marry
    him?"]
She said, "Yes, daddy, I do wish." [That's what]
I heard, and what I heard fills [me with joy] —   970
[She too] laughed (?) [

THRASONIDES

Your news is wonderful.

GETAS

                              I'm pleased—[but] one of them's
Rattling[a] [the door].

(Kleinias' door opens, and Demeas emerges. He is proba-
bly alone, since in Athens the presence of the future bride
was not required at the ceremony of betrothal.)

DEMEAS

(to Thrasonides)

                              [I've come to see you now.]

THRASONIDES

That's kind of you.

---

[a] By opening it from the inside: see the note on line 684.

---

suppl. Austin, τὴν θύραν Turner.   973 Speaker's name
δη(μεας) written above πρ[in O.10. Suppl. *exempli gratia*
Sandbach.   974 O.10 has the spelling ποιων.

ΔΗΜΕΑΣ

παίδ[ων ἐπ᾽ ἀρότῳ γνησίων
975 δίδωμι τὴν ἐμὴν θυγ[ατέρα σοί γ᾽ ἔχειν,
καὶ δύο τάλαντα προῖκ᾽ [ἐπ᾽ αὐτῇ].

ΘΡΑΣΩΝΙΔΗΣ

[λαμβάνω·
(447) μόνον ἀπόδος σύ, Δημέ[α, τὴν θυγατέρα.
πάντας γὰρ .ντ.σ[
ἀπὸ ταὐτομάτου [..]ε.[
980 δεῖπνον ξένια κ[αὶ
ἀλλ᾽ εἰσί[ωμ]εν ...[
(452) γε[.]...[......]..[
πα.[
ἐπ᾽ αὔρ[ιον
985 .].[.]οπ[......]α[
ἔστ᾽ ἔνδο[ν

ΔΗΜΕΑΣ

(457) οὐ πρ[ο]φ[έρε]τε ..υν.[
εἶ[έ]ν· μετέμελ᾽ αὐτ[ῇ

974 Suppl. Webster.   975–996 O.10.   975 θυγ[ατέρα σοι
suppl. Webster, γ᾽ ἔχειν Arnott.   976 Suppl. and assigned to
speakers by Borgogno.   977 Suppl. *exempli gratia* Sandbach.
978 γὰρ deciphered by Sandbach.   980, 984, 987, 988 Suppl.
Turner.   981, 986 Suppl. Handley.

[a] On the dowry and quaint formula of betrothal see the note
on *Dyskolos* 843.

[b] Presumably all the others who would be involved in the
wedding ceremonies: Krateia, her brother, perhaps Kleinias.

346

DEMEAS

(*formally*)

> I give [to you] my daughter,
> [To have and hold, to harvest lawful] children, and   975
> [With her] a dowry of two talents.[a]

THRASONIDES

>   [I accept—]
> But just restore to me [your daughter], Demeas!
> For all [
> By chance [
> A dinner—the host's gift—and [980
> But let's go in [
> [
> [
> Tomorrow [
> [985
> [Krateia] is inside [

(*Although the papyrus text hereabouts is badly damaged,
the final exchanges are easy to understand. After the for-
mal betrothal, Thrasonides appears to reflect on the influ-
ence of chance on events, and then promises to host a cele-
bratory dinner that evening inside his house. Tomorrow
will be the wedding, when Thrasonides formally takes his
bride from her father and escorts her to his house.*)

DEMEAS

(*to Thrasonides as he turns to go into his house along
with Getas*)

Don't bring [them] out now[b] [

(*to the audience*)

So be it. She regretted [her past conduct

παιδάριον, ἄψας δᾷ[δας ἡμῖν ἐκδίδου,

990   στεφάνους τ᾽ ἔ[χο]ντε[ς

καὶ μηδέπω δειπν[

(462)   προσμείνατ᾽ ἐπ..[

ὑμᾶς ν...[..].λ · μ[ειράκια, παῖδες καλοί,

ἄνδρες, πρεπόν[τω]ς πά[ντες ἐπικροτήσατε.

995   ἡ δ᾽ εὐπάτειρα φιλόγε[λως τε παρθένος

(466)   Νίκη μεθ᾽ ἡμῶν εὐ[μενὴς ἔποιτ᾽ ἀεί.

989 Suppl. *exempli gratia* Turner.   990 Suppl. Turner.
991 μηδεπο O.10 before correction.   993 Suppl. Austin.
994 πρεπόν[τω]ς πά[ντες suppl. and deciphered by Austin, ἐπι-
κροτήσατε suppl. Arnott.   995, 996 Suppl. Turner.
996 νεικη O.10. Under the last line in O.10 is a colophon
Μενάνδ[ρου] / Θρασων[ίδης· / εὔνοια τῷ ἀναγ[ιγνώσκοντι
καὶ] / τῷ γράψ[α]ντι .[(Θρασων[ίδης suppl. several, γρά-
ψ[α]ντι Austin, the rest Turner).

*Three small papyrus fragments which do not overlap
any otherwise known part of the play*

1 (Fr. 3 of O.11 = fr. 2 Sisti)

].[1,]δεκ[2,]ων[3,]νκ[4,]...[5,].φ.[6,]...[7,
]ειν[8,]το.σ[9,]...[10,]ψ.[11,]συν[12,].εδ[13,
]φοι[14,]μ[15,]εισν[16,]χοι[17.

---

[a] The emblems of celebration and revelry: cf. *Dysk.* 963 f.
(with Sandbach's note in his Commentary, *ad loc.*) and *Sik.* 418 f.

(to a slave emerging from Kleinias' house)

Slave, light the torch[es, hand them out to us,]
And with the garlands[a] [990
Don't yet [let's have the] dinner, [but
Wait for [
You [   ]

(to the audience again)

          [Youths, pretty boys,] men, all of you —
Give us our due applause! May Victory,
That merry [virgin], born of noble line,   995
[Attend] us with her favour [all our days]![b]

*(At the end of the text, the scribe has added a personal
colophon:[c] Menander's Thrasonides.[d] Best wishes to the
reader and the scribe.)*

> *From Misoumenos three further small scraps of
> papyrus survive, but their original position in
> the play is uncertain.*

1

*A tiny scrap of O.11, containing fewer than five letters
from each of seventeen lines of the play. Not a single word
here can be deciphered.*

[b] A conventional formula that also ends Menander's *Dysk.*
(968 f.) and *Sik.* (422 f.).

[c] E. G. Turner, *Bulletin of the Institute of Classical Studies,*
Suppl. 17 (1965), 73, cites some parallels.

[d] The scribe's title is *Thrasonides*, not *Misoumenos*: see my
introduction to the play, and E. G. Turner, *Greek Papyri: An
Introduction* (Oxford 1968), 65 f.

2 (Fr. 3 of O.23)

].[
]οση.[
].οιν.[
]σδυ.[
(?)   σπ]άθην[
(?)   νο]μίζω[

5

3 (O.26)

This scrap of papyrus was plausibly attributed by its first editor, P. J. Parsons, to *Misoumenos* because in lines 2–4 parts of the names of three characters (Krateia, Demeas, Kleinias) from the play can be recognised, while line 6 seems to preserve the first syllable of θυγάτηρ or a related diminutive ('daughter'), and this relationship of Krateia to Demeas is a stressed feature of the plot (968, 975, cf. 613 ff.).

A possible match of lines 5 (ονταλ.[) and 6 (οθυγ[) in this scrap was suggested by Austin (see ed. pr. p. 47); unfortunately the three preceding lines in O.10 are so badly abraded that it is impossible to detect any matching in these lines also. If O.26 did contain portions of 752–756, however, the text of O.10 in lines 752–754 was either misread by its first and subsequent editors, or differed from that offered by O.26.

]...[....].[
Κρά]τειαν ἐξαγε[
δ]ακρύει Δημέ[ας
]ν οὐχὶ μικρὰ Κλε[ινι
]. ἑαυτόν, ταλ.[
].α. δεῦρο θυγ[
]....[

5

2

A tiny scrap of O.23, containing fewer than six letters from each of six lines of the play. Line 5 may contain the word sword, *line 6* think *or* think[ing].

5, 6 Suppl. M. Maehler. Over the ω traces of ink (? name of speaker or correction). Although line 4 matches 783, lines 1 to 3 and 5 to 6 cannot be fitted into corresponding positions in 780–782 and 784–785.

3

*O.26, preserving one or two words in each of six successive lines (*bring *or* brings out [Kra]teia 2, Deme[as] *is* weeping 3, not small things, Kle[inias] 4, himself *or* yourself 5, here dau[ghter] 6), *has been attributed to Misoumenos because successive lines contain the admittedly mutilated names of three of its characters, together with a possible reference to a daughter.*

2–6 Suppl. Parsons.   5 Or σεαυτόν, then τἄλλα or part of τάλας.   6 θυγ[ατέρα (Parsons) or θυγ[άτριον (Arnott). Although lines 5 and 6 seem at first sight to match the abraded remains towards the ends of lines 755 (ταλ.δ[) and 756 (].ατρι.[), it is difficult to match line 2 with 752 (]περι[near line-end).

MENANDER

* * *

Eight fragments of Μισούμενος,
quoted by ancient authors

4 (Fr. 3 Körte and Sisti, 2 Sandbach)

Arrian, *Discourses of Epictetus* 4. 1. 19: ἀλλ' εἰ σὺ αἰσχύνῃ
τὰ σαυτοῦ ὁμολογεῖν, ὅρα ἃ λέγει καὶ ποιεῖ ὁ Θρασωνί-
δης, ὃς τοσαῦτα στρατευόμενος ὅσα τάχα οὐδὲ σύ, πρῶ-
τον μὲν ἐξελήλυθε νυκτός, ὅτε ὁ Γέτας οὐ τολμᾷ ἐξελθεῖν,
ἀλλ' εἰ προσηναγκάζετο ὑπ' αὐτοῦ, πόλλ' ἂν ἐπικραυγά-
σας καὶ τὴν πικρὰν δουλείαν ἀπολοφυράμενος ἐξῆλθεν.
εἶτα τί λέγει; Here the two-line fragment is quoted (with
φησίν added after με in v.1); shortly afterwards Epictetus
adds: εἶτα ξίφος αἰτεῖ καὶ πρὸς τὸν ὑπ' εὐνοίας μὴ διδόντα
χαλεπαίνει καὶ δῶρα τῇ μισούσῃ πέμπει καὶ δεῖται καὶ
κλαίει, πάλιν δὲ μικρὰ εὐημερήσας ἐπαίρεται.

Line one of the fragment is quoted less accurately by
Clement of Alexandria, Strom. 2. 15. 64. 2 (2 p. 147. 16 ff.
Stählin) τὸν γὰρ κωμικὸν ἐκεῖνον Θρασωνίδην ἄλλῃ
σκηνῇ παιδισκάριόν με, φησίν, εὐτελὲς καταδεδούλωκεν.

> παιδισκάριόν με καταδεδούλωκ' εὐτελές,
> ὃν οὐδὲ εἷς τῶν πολεμίων <οὐ> πώποτε.

1 καταδεδούλωκ' Salmasius: καταδεδούλωκεν Arrian.
2 οὐδὲ εἷς Koraïs: οὐδεὶς ms. <οὐ> πώποτε Meineke: πώποτε
ms.

MISOUMENOS

*   *   *

*Eight fragments of Misoumenos,
quoted by ancient authors*

4

Arrian's version of Epictetus' discourses: But if you're ashamed to admit to your own actions, just see what Thrasonides says and does! After going on so many campaigns—more perhaps than even you!—first he's come outside during the night, when Getas can't face coming out, and if he had been forced out of doors by Thrasonides, he'd have emerged making a great number of loud protests and lamenting his bitter enslavement. Then what does Thrasonides say?

> By a cheap little slave-girl I'm enslaved,
> Who've not been by a single foe before!

. . . Then he asks for a sword and is furious with the man who out of kindness refuses to give him one. He sends presents to the girl who hates him; he pleads and weeps; then, after gaining a little success, he becomes elated again.

Epictetus' description of Thrasonides' actions, when verifiable, seems reasonably accurate. The soldier does emerge in the dark of a stormy night (line 1) and is not joined by an irritated Getas until 15; the request for, and refusal of, a sword may come in the context of 509, where the text is badly damaged; his tearful entreaties to Krateia are described by Getas at 696. His gifts to Krateia and 'the little success' that he gained thereby, if accurately attributed to the play by Epictetus, must have been staged or described in a lost section of the play. The two lines cited by Epictetus were most probably uttered by Thrasonides at an early stage in the play, perhaps in a lost part of his opening conversation with Getas (e.g. 59–63, 69–77, 101 ff.)

MENANDER

5 (7 Kö, 5 Sa, 4 Si)

Scholiast on Homer, *Odyssey* 17.442: ὅτι ἀεὶ πολλοὺς εἶχεν ἡ Κύπρος βασιλεῖς ἐν ταὐτῷ φησι καὶ Μένανδρος ἐν Μισουμένῳ ὡς ἐν παρεκβάσει (corr. Heath: παραβάσει mss.):

> ἐκ Κύπρου λαμπρῶς πάνυ
> πράττων· ἐκεῖ γὰρ ὑπό τιν᾽ ἦν τῶν βασιλέων.

1 Corr. Meineke: λαμπρῶς πάνυ λαμπρὰ mss.

6 (12 Kö, 6 Sa, 5 Si)

Pollux 10. 145 f.: ὅτι δὲ καὶ τὴν σπάθην ἐπὶ τοῦ ξίφους εἰρήκασιν, εὕροις ἂν . . . καὶ ἐν τῷ Μισουμένῳ Μένανδρος ὅταν λέγῃ·

> ἀφανεῖς γεγόνασιν αἱ σπάθαι

7 (4 Kö, 7 Sa, 6 Si)

[Justin Martyr], *De monarchia* 5 (p. 142 in Otto's second edition): ἐν Μισουμένῳ δὲ πάλιν ἀποφαίνων περὶ τῶν εἰς θεοὺς παραλαμβανομένων τὰς γνώμας, μᾶλλον δὲ ἐλέγχων ὡς οὐκ ὄντας ὁ αὐτὸς Μένανδρος·

> εἰ γὰρ ἐπίδοιμι τοῦτο καὶ ψυχὴν <πάλιν>
> λάβοιμ᾽ ἐγώ· νυνὶ γὰρ—ἀλλὰ ποῦ θεοὺς
> οὕτω δικαίους ἐστὶν εὑρεῖν, ὦ Γέτα;

1 <πάλιν> added by Bentley.

---

[a] See my introduction to *Misoumenos*.

Clement of Alexandria inserts line 1 of the fragment into a comment: 'Another scene has the comic character Thrasonides saying "By a little slave girl cheap I'm enslaved."'

5

A scholiast on Homer's *Odyssey*: Menander too says parenthetically in *Misoumenos* that Cyprus always had many kings at one and the same time (?):

> From Cyprus, with most glorious
> Achievements. There he (*or* I) served one of their
>   kings.[a]

Possibly from the lost prologue, describing Thrasonides' success on his last campaign, or (with 'I served') from a boast by Thrasonides himself at any stage of the play.

6

Pollux: As evidence that they have also used the word σπάθη in the sense of "sword", ... you will find it also in the *Misoumenos* when Menander says:

> The blades (σπάθαι) have disappeared.

Presumably a remark by Thrasonides, after Getas moved all the lethal weapons in Thrasonides' house to that of Kleinias. See my discussion of lines 502–531.

7

An anonymous essay, falsely attributed to Justin the Martyr: The same Menander, revealing again in *Misoumenos* his views on those accepted as gods, or rather rejecting them as not gods at all, (writes):

> If I could only see this and revive
> My spirits once [again], for now—but where, Getas,
> Can one find gods with principles so honest?

8 (10 Kö, 8 Sa, 7 Si)

A scholiast on Aristophanes, *Thesmophoriazusae* 423, and
the *Suda* s.v. Λακωνικαὶ κλεῖδες (λ 64 Adler): Μένανδρος
Μισουμένῳ (so correctly the scholiast: Μισουμέναις *Suda*):

> Λακωνικὴ κλείς ἐστιν, ὡς ἔοικέ, μοι
> περιοιστέα.

καί φασιν (καί φασιν omitted by *Suda*) ὅτι ἔξωθεν περι-
κλείεται, μοχλοῦ περιτιθεμένου ἤ τινος τοιούτου, ὥστε
τοῖς ἔνδον μὴ εἶναι ἀνοῖξαι.

1 Correctly punctuated after ἔοικέ by Sandbach.

9 (13 Kö, 9 Sa, 8 Si)

The Συναγωγὴ λέξεων χρησίμων (Bekker, *Anecdota
Graeca* 1. 429. 27 ff.) and the *Suda* s.v. ἀποκτιννύναι (α 3372
Adler): καὶ ἀπεκτόνασιν, οὐκ ἀπεκτάγκασι. Μισουμένῳ
(so correctly the Συναγωγή: μισοῦσι μέν, ὦ mss. of the
Suda)·

> πάτερ, †μὲν θρασωνι†, ἀπεκτάγκασι δ' οὔ.

Presumably a depressed Thrasonides talking to his slave, but there is no way of identifying the context with any confidence. Perhaps early in the fifth act, after Thrasonides' total and (in his view) unreasonable rejection by Krateia and Demeas in the fourth.

8

A scholiast on Aristophanes' *Thesmophoriazusae*, and the *Suda*, under the heading 'Spartan keys': Menander in *Misoumenos*,

Apparently I've got to haul around
A Spartan key.

They say that the lock works from outside, with a bar or something similar being attached, preventing those inside from being able to open it.

Spartan keys had a high reputation for security; those mentioned by Aristophanes in the passage from which this scholion derives had three wards. Was Menander's speaker Thrasonides, seeking to lock Krateia up in her part of his house, or was he Kleinias, realising the importance of keeping safe all the swords stored in his house? We have no means of knowing.

9

The anonymous *Lexicon of Useful Terms* s.v. ἀποκτίννυσιν (a variant form of a verb meaning 'he kills'), and the *Suda* s.v. ἀποκτιννύναι (a related variant form meaning 'to kill'): And (they say) ἀπεκτόνασιν (the normal Attic word for 'they have killed'), not ἀπεκτάγκασι (a variant form with the same meaning). In *Misoumenos*:

Father, Thrasonides (?)—they haven't killed him!

10 (14 Kö, 10 Sa, 9 Si)

Photius (2. 169 Naber) s.v. σπαθᾶν· Μένανδρος Μισου-
μένῳ· τὸ ἀλαζονεύεσθαι.

11 (11 Sa, 10 Si)

Photius (K. Tsantsanoglou, *New Fragments of Greek Litera-
ture from the Lexicon of Photius*, Athens 1984, 129) s.v.
ἐνερόχρως· νεκρόχρως. Μένανδρος Μισουμένῳ.

*A quotation from an unnamed play in an ancient author,
doubtfully attributed to* Μισούμενος

12 (12 Sa, 11 Si)

Hermias' commentary on Plato, *Phaedrus* 230e (p. 33. 11 ff.
Couvreur): οἱ μὲν γὰρ ὑπέλαβον ἁπλῶς φαῦλον τὸ ἐρᾶν,
ὡς ... ὁ εἰπὼν "πλήρει γὰρ ὄγκῳ γαστρὸς αὔξεται
Κύπρις" (*TrGF* 2. 67 F186), καὶ "οὐπώποτε {φησίν} (del.
Couvreur) ἠράσθης, Γέτα;" "οὐ γὰρ ἐνεπλήσθην", φησίν.

ᵃ See the note on fr. 10 of *Heros*.

A puzzling remark, presumably made by Krateia to Demeas,
most probably in the fifth act after her brother had arrived
safe and well. The precise point of the reference to Thra-
sonides (if the corrupt Greek text is rightly interpreted as, or
emended to, his name) remains uncertain so long as we lack
the preceding context.

10

Photius s.v. σπαθᾶν (literally: to strike the woof in an upright
loom with the σπάθη, a flat wooden blade used to bring the
threads together): Menander in *Misoumenos* (used the word
in the sense) 'to boast falsely'.

Since soldiers in ancient comedy were often portrayed as
lying braggarts, it is probable that the verb was used about
Thrasonides.

11

Photius s.v. ἐνερόχρως: 'with the complexion of a corpse'.
Menander in *Misoumenos*.

Perhaps a description (by Getas ?) of Thrasonides' appear-
ance after he had pretended in the fifth act to commit suicide.

A quotation from an unnamed play in an ancient author,
doubtfully attributed to Misoumenos

12

Hermias of Alexandria's commentary on Plato's *Phaedrus*:
Some assumed that being in love was simply vulgar, like . . .
the man who said "The bulk of a full maw makes passion
grow",[a] and

MENANDER

(ΘΡΑΣΩΝΙΔΗΣ ?)

οὐπώποτ' ἠράσθης, Γέτα;

ΓΕΤΑΣ

οὐ γὰρ ἐνεπλήσθην.

Fragment 12 was tentatively assigned to Misoumenos by
Meineke. Characters named Getas, however, appear in other
comedies by Menander (e.g. Dyskolos, Heros, Perinthia), and
Leo's suggestion that this fr. might derive from the opening scene
of Heros, where a slave in love addresses a Getas, is equally plau-
sible (see fr. 10 there).

Five testimonia about Μισούμενος

I (Fr. 1 Kö and Sa, Test. 1 Si)

Choricius XLII = declamation 12 (p. 509. 8 ff. Foerster-
Richsteig): ἔχεις ἐκ τῆς κωμῳδίας παραλαβών, ὡς ὑπέρ-
ογκόν τι καὶ σοβαρὸν καὶ πολλή τις ἀλαζονεία στρατιώ-
της ἀνήρ. εἴ τις ὑμῶν τὸν Μενάνδρου φαντάζεται Θρα-
σωνίδην, οἶδεν ὃ λέγω. στρατιωτικὴν γάρ φησιν ἀηδίαν
νοσοῦντα τὸν ἄνθρωπον εἰς ἀπέχθειαν αὐτῷ (corr.
Meineke: αὐτῶ mss.) κινῆσαι τὴν ἐρωμένην· καὶ γέγονεν
ἀμέλει προσηγορία τῷ δράματι τοῦ Θρασωνίδου τὸ
μῖσος.

II (Test. 2 Si)

Diogenes Laertius 7. 130: τὸν γοῦν Θρασωνίδην καίπερ ἐν
ἐξουσίᾳ ἔχοντα τὴν ἐρωμένην διὰ τὸ μισεῖσθαι ἀπέχ-
εσθαι αὐτῆς.

MISOUMENOS

(THRASONIDES ?)
Were you never in love, Getas?

GETAS
No, for I never ate my fill.

So he says.

Hermias does not name the author of the second passage quoted, and its attribution to Misoumenos is uncertain. It could derive from a lost portion of the initial dialogue between Getas and Daos, or from another play (see also Heros fr. 10).

Five testimonia about Misoumenos

I

Choricius of Gaza: Having the evidence of comedy you know that a soldier is a larger-than-life, swashbuckling creature, with a great deal of false pretension. Any of you who can form a picture of Menander's Thrasonides knows what I mean. He says that this fellow, suffering from the disease of a soldier's disagreeable character, drove the girl he loved to loathe him. In fact this hatred of Thrasonides has come to be the play's title.

This passage is the main source of information about the presentation of Thrasonides (in some parts of the play at least) as the type of braggart soldier so familiar in ancient comedy.

II

Diogenes Laertius: (Stoic writers say that) although Thrasonides at any rate had the girl he loved in his power, he kept his hands off her because of the hatred he inspired.

MENANDER

III (Test. 3 Si)

Irenaeus, *Aduersus haereses* 2. 18. 5 (2. 2, p. 180 in the edition of Adelin Rousseau and Louis Doutreleau, Paris 1982): Sed mihi uidentur eius passionem qui est apud comicum Menandrum ualde amans (animas *CV*) et odibilis (hodibilia *C*, odibilia *V*) Aeoni suo circumdedisse.

IV (Test. 4 Si)

Plutarch, *Moralia* 1095d (*Non posse suauiter uiui secundum Epicurum* 13): καὶ Θρασωνίδας τινὰς καὶ Θρασυλέοντας, ὀλολυγμοὺς καὶ κροτοθορύβους ποιοῦντας.

V (Fr. 2 Kö)

Simplicius, commentary on Aristotle's *Physics* 2. 8, 199[b] 18 (p. 384. 13 Diels): καὶ ἐν τοῖς ἀπὸ τύχης εἶναι δοκεῖ τὸ οὗ ἕνεκα καὶ τὸ ἕνεκά του, ὅταν λέγωμεν ὅτι ἀπὸ τύχης ἦλθεν ὁ ξένος καὶ λυτρωσάμενος τὴν αἰχμάλωτον, ὡς ὁ παρὰ Μενάνδρῳ Δημέας τὴν Κράτειαν, ἀπῆλθεν ἢ ἀφῆκε. The reference here to Menander's *Misoumenos* was first noted by Hunt.

Less informative references to the play can be found in Alciphron's letter 4.19.19, Agathias' and Fronto's epigrams in the Palatine Anthology 5. 218 v. 11 and 12. 233 v. 3 respectively, and Martial's epigram 14. 214: see F. Sisti's edition of the play (Genoa 1985), 16 f. (his testimonia 5–8).

III

Irenaeus: (The heretics) seem to have endowed their Aeon[a] with the passion of the man who in Menander, the comic poet, is very much in love and odious.

IV

Plutarch: The likes of Thrasonides and Thrasyleon,[b] who break out in 'wild jubilations' and 'uproarious applause'.[c]

V

Simplicius' commentary on Aristotle's *Physics*: Even in things that happen 'by chance', there appears to be an identifiable or unidentified purpose, as for instance when we say that the stranger arrived by chance and went away after releasing the captive or sent him away, like Demeas in Menander with Krateia.[d]

[a] One of a complement of thirty divinities with this name in a form of Gnostic belief formulated by Valentinus and attacked here as heretical by Irenaeus. See especially F.-M.-M. Sagnard, *La gnose valentinienne et le témoignage de Saint Irénée* (Paris 1947), and the Rousseau-Doutreleau edition of Irenaeus' *Aduersus haereses* 2.1 (Paris 1982), 138–156.

[b] The title of another play by Menander.

[c] Plutarch is here quoting Epicurus (cf. fr. 143 Usener = 71 Arrighetti); cf. also Plutarch, *Moralia* 1117a (*Aduersus Colotem* 17).

[d] On this passage see especially G. Vogt-Spira, *Dramaturgie des Zufalls* (Zetemata 88, Munich 1992), 39.

PERIKEIROMENE

(THE GIRL WITH
HER HAIR CUT SHORT)

INTRODUCTION

Manuscripts

C = *P. Cairensis* 43227, part of a papyrus codex from Aphroditopolis written in the fifth century A.D. The codex originally contained at least five plays written by Menander; *Perikeiromene* was fourth in order (between *Epitrepontes* and an unknown play). Extant in C are lines 121–190, 261–406, 480–550, 708–725, 742–760. First edition: G. Lefebvre, *Fragments d'un manuscrit de Ménandre*, Cairo 1907, incorporating many suggestions by M. Croiset (cf. *Fragments* p. xii f.); Lefebvre's *Papyrus de Ménandre*, Cairo 1911, with a revised text, includes photographs of the papyrus. New photographs of C were published in 1978 by the Institute of Classical Studies, London (see my bibliographical supplement, printed after the preface).

H = *P. Heidelberg* 219, a scrap of papyrus dating from the second century A.D., contains the end portions of lines 162–179. First edition: G. A. Gerhard, *Sitzungsberichte Heidelberg*, 1911, section 4, with a photograph.

L = *P.* (or more correctly *Membr.*) *Leipzig* 613, two damaged pages from a parchment codex dated to the third century A.D. This codex originally contained several plays, in which *Perikeiromene* came second. Extant in L are lines 467–529, 768–827. First edition: A. Körte, *Sitzungsberichte Leipzig*, 60 (1908), 147–175, with photographs.

O = (i) *P. Oxyrhynchus* 211, a fragment of a papyrus roll written at the end of the first or beginning of the second century A.D. It contains one whole column (lines 976–1026) and the ends of a few lines in the preceding column (? 925–928, ? 930–931, ? 951, ? 962, ? 966, ? 969–970). First edition: B. P. Grenfell and A. S. Hunt, *The Oxyrhynchus Papyri*, 2 (1899), 11–20, with a plate showing only lines 976–1008; the papyrus was re-edited by G. M. Browne, *Bulletin of the Institute of Classical Studies*, 21 (1974), 43–54, with a better and complete photograph; see also the plates in W. E. H. Cockle, *Quaderni Urbinati*, 23 (1976), between pp. 48 and 49.

(ii) *P. Oxyrhynchus* 2830, a scrap of papyrus roll dating to the third century A.D. It contains the beginnings of lines 473–492 and decipherable endings of three lines in the previous column which come somewhere in the lacuna between 406 and 467, either before or after the end of the second act. First edition: E. G. Turner, *The Oxyrhynchus Papyri*, 38 (1971), 27–29, with a photograph.

(iii) *P. Oxyrhynchus* 3705, a scrap of papyrus first published by M. W. Haslam, *The Oxyrhynchus Papyri*, 53 (1986), 47 f., and dated by him to the third century A.D. Preserved is the first half of an iambic trimeter which is repeated three times with varied musical settings. M. Huys, *Zeitschrift für Papyrologie und Epigraphik*, 99 (1993), 30–32, noted that its text (τοῦ δὴ τόπου τι μνη[) was identical with *Perikeiromene* 796. From the third century B.C. onwards it was common for professional entertainers to set to music extracts even from previously spoken parts of earlier Greek drama for their performances.[1]

Fragments 1 and 2 are quotations from different sources. See Introduction to Volume I, pp. xxiv–xxv.

Pictorial Evidence

(i) A wall-painting of the second century A.D. from a house in the centre of Ephesus. It is inscribed ΠΕΡΙ-ΚΕΙΠΟΜΕΝΗ (*Perikeiromene*) and shows three figures. On the left stands a woman whose long cloak has been raised at the back so that it conceals her hair. She has turned away from the seated figure of a young, unbearded man in the centre who wears a military-style cloak knotted over the right shoulder. He seems to be gazing gloomily into the distance. To his right stands the third figure, badly faded and of indeterminate sex, but with the right arm raised in an emotional gesture. Although these characters are not identified by name on the painting, the first two are clearly Glykera concealing her savaged hair, and a disconsolate Polemon; the third may be Sosias, Polemon's slave. None of the extant portions of the play brings these three figures on stage together, and the most likely assumption is that the artist painted one of the play's more memorable but now lost scenes, perhaps the play's opening (see my comments on that opening below). Authoritative publication of the painting: V. M. Strocka, *Die Wandmalerei der Hanghäuser in Ephesus (Forsch-*

---

[1] Some surviving examples are listed by B. Gentili, *Theatrical Performances in the Ancient World* (Amsterdam and Uithoorn 1979), 19 f.

ungen in Ephesus VIII/1, Vienna 1977), 48, 55 f. and colour plate 66; cf. also my paper in *Zeitschrift für Papyrologie und Epigraphik*, 71 (1988), 11–15.

(ii) Two amateurish ink-drawings of the second or third century A.D. on scraps of papyrus. One (*P. Oxyrhynchus* 2652) shows a woman in full face wearing a knee-length tunic buckled over the right shoulder and belted at the waist. Her hair drops in ringlets to her neck. Her right arm is bent across her breast, and her left clasps by her waist a scarf or cloak dropping from her left shoulder. The identification ΑΓΝΟΙΑ (Misconception) has been written above her head. The other scrap (*P. Oxyrhynchus* 2653) preserves only the head and shoulder of an unbearded young man, also in full face, wearing a soldier's helmet with cheek-pieces. Here there is no identity tag in the clear space above the head. The two scraps of papyrus were found in Oxyrhynchus not far from each other, and the most plausible hypothesis is that originally they formed part of an illustrated manuscript of Menander's *Perikeiromene* (perhaps the one from which either *P. Oxyrhynchus* 211 or 2830 derives). In that case the illustrations portray the prologue figure and the soldier Polemon. They are published by E. G. Turner, *The Oxyrhynchus Papyri*, 32 (1967), 180 f., with photographs; the photographs are reproduced in M. Lamagna's edition of the play (Naples 1994), pp. 83, 84.

Some 450 lines of *Perikeiromene* are preserved (121–190, 261–406, 467–550, 708–725, 742–760, 768–827, 976–1026, and the two verses of frs. 1 and 2), probably 40–45 per cent of the play, although its original length is impossible to compute with certainty because of gaps in our knowledge at crucial points. In his commentary F. H. Sandbach (p. 44 f.) suggests a length of about 1040 lines, basing the figure on a combination of verifiable evidence (lines per page in the extant portions of C) and reasonable but hazardous assumptions (that *Perikeiromene* began on p. 95 of C, prefaced by cast-list and hypothesis like *Heros*, and ended on p. 124). However, even if Sandbach's presuppositions are correct, his computations contain two minor inaccuracies: they assume that the missing pages of C contained 35 lines per page, when the average for C as a whole is 35.765 lines and in extant pages of *Perikeiromene* 36.378; and that the final page of the play in C had a full 35 lines. A more correct estimate, accepting the Sandbach assumptions, would be 1030–1064 lines.

A similar figure can be achieved by a different but equally hazardous argument. The lengths of acts 2 to 5 seem normally (act 2 of *Epitrepontes* is a rare exception) to be roughly equal in individual plays by Menander, with opening acts longer but not disproportionately so. The last extant page of C for *Perikeiromene* has reached somewhere around line 760 of the play, which seems to be between one third and a half of the way through the fourth act. The *Dyskolos*, which is 969 lines long, reaches a similar stage between lines 674 and 701. If the proportions of *Perikeiromene* corresponded, the play would have had a length between 1051 and 1091 lines.

For the reader's convenience the line-numbering of this edition agrees with that devised by Gomme and adopted by Sandbach in his Oxford Text (*Menandri Reliquiae Selectae*, 1972[1], 1990[2]); this attempts thereby to gauge the original position of each papyrus fragment in the play. The numbering given in Körte's third Teubner edition (*Menandri quae supersunt* I, Leipzig 1945) is added in brackets.

No hypothesis, didascalic notice, or cast-list is preserved for *Perikeiromene*. Its production date is not recorded, although one certain and one possible reference to historical events of the time may offer clues to the time of composition. At line 125 the prologue mentions 'the war and the Corinthian troubles'. In 315/4 B.C. Cassander attacked Corinth and laid waste some of its territory; in 313 his opponent Antigonus sent an army against several cities in the Peloponnese, but it failed to occupy Corinth; in 308 Ptolemy won Corinth, either by force or by clandestine negotiation; some time after 306 the city was regained by Cassander, who held it until 303, when Demetrius Poliorcetes seized it. Line 125 could refer to any of these assaults.

In the opening scene of act 2 Moschion facetiously offers to make his slave Daos 'an overlord of Greek affairs and a marshal of land forces' (279–280), but Daos appears to reject the proposal because it would lead to his immediate murder (281). E. Schwartz (*Hermes* 64, 1929, 3 f.) suggested that this exchange was inspired by the murder in 314/3 of Alexander son of Polyperchon by a group of Sicyonians shortly after he had been appointed 'general of the Peloponnese' by Cassander, and that Menander must have written the play in that year or immediately afterwards. Schwartz's idea is ingenious and persuasive.

Dramatis personae, so far as they are known

Glykera, Polemon's mistress
Polemon, a Corinthian soldier

PERIKEIROMENE

Sosias, a slave of Polemon

Doris, a slave of Polemon who acts as Glykera's maid

Moschion, Glykera's twin brother

Daos, the slave of Moschion and of Moschion's foster-
father

Pataikos, an old Corinthian, father of Glykera and Mos-
chion

Misconception, a goddess, speaker of the prologue

Myrrhine, Moschion's foster-mother and married to an
unidentified husband,[1] does not appear in the extant por-
tions of the play, but she is likely to have had a role, speak-
ing rather than mute, in the play; one of the stage houses
belonged to her. A cook may also have had a speaking
role (see the note on line 995). In Polemon's 'army' (act
III, 467 ff.) there would be three or more mute charac-
ters, at least two male slaves and the female piper
Habrotonon. There is a conventional chorus of tipsy rev-
ellers, to perform the entr'actes.

[1] Misconception mentions only her in the story of Moschion's
adoption (121–123, cf. 795); if Myrrhine had had a husband alive
at that time, he presumably would have been named as the
adopter. She must have married subsequently, for two obscure
references in the text imply a husband: to Moschion's '(fos-
ter-)father' (713 f.) and to Daos' (senior) master (364). He does
not appear in the extant portions of the play, but there is no way
of knowing whether he did in one or more of the lost scenes. If
he was the Philinos mentioned (1026) as having a marriageable
daughter, that daughter would have come from an earlier mar-
riage.

ΠΕΡΙΚΕΙΡΟΜΕΝΗ

(SCENE: not specified in the preserved portions of the play, but almost certainly a street in Corinth; Misconception's reference to 'the Corinthian troubles' (125) would thus provide a plausible reason for an old woman's distress in or near Corinth, and Polemon, a Corinthian by birth (129), is most likely to have bought property (145 f.) and married a fellow-Corinthian (1013–1015) in his native city. Two houses are certainly visible; one belongs to Polemon (145 f.), the one next to it to Myrrhine and her husband (122 f., 147). Pataikos lives nearby, but there is no evidence in the surviving text that he occupied a third stage house.)

(If Perikeiromene began on p. 95 of C, as seems likely,[a] *with introductory matter of some 20 lines' length (hypothesis, cast-list) prefixed as it is to Heros in C and Dyskolos in B (but not to Aspis in B), then between 116 and 132 lines must have been lost at the beginning of Perikeiromene before C returns with its p. 99 (line 121 of the play in the Gomme-Sandbach numbering). What*

---

[a] This would require *Epitrepontes* to have ended on p. 94 of C, that is (given the fact that extant pages of C contain between 34 and 38 lines per page) between 35 and 76 lines after 1131; cf. volume I, pp. 519–521.

PERIKEIROMENE

(The Girl with Her Hair Cut Short)

*happened in these lost lines, covering one or two scenes
and the opening of Misconception's prologue speech? We
can only guess, but we have one certain, one probable and
two possible clues, in the following order.*

*In the prologue speech (127 f.) it is clearly stated that
Glykera had already been seen by the audience. Directly
afterwards (129) the soldier Polemon is described as 'this
(τούτου) young impetuous blood', and οὗτος in prologues
sometimes means that a character was recently on stage
(e.g. Aspis 97, 110, 117), sometimes merely that the char-
acter had just been mentioned (e.g. Dyskolos 8, 17, 24).
When Sosias appears at 172, he neither identifies himself
nor is identified by the character he meets; in Menander
this normally indicates that the audience had seen him
previously. The Ephesus wall-painting is the final clue; it
portrays a polled Glykera, a gloomy Polemon and a third
figure tentatively identified above as Sosias, possibly in
the opening or second scene of the play.*

*These clues tentatively suggest an opening in which
Glykera rushed out of Polemon's house at or just before
daybreak directly after Polemon had cut off her hair;
there is no need to assume that this action was performed
on stage, since the title of Apollodorus' Epidikazomenos,*

375

*which is also a present participle, refers to an off-stage
action completed before the play began, as Terence's
Phormio, modelled on Apollodorus' play, clearly shows.
Such an opening, with the silent entry of a distraught
character in an unusual situation (possibly attempting to
conceal the loss of her locks), would provide the audience
with puzzling circumstances designed to grasp their
attention even before a word was spoken, as commonly in
Greek comedy.[a] Glykera would have been followed on to
the stage, either immediately or at some interval, by Pole-
mon and Sosias.*

*We cannot gauge what was then said, but doubtless
expository information would have been included. The
audience might have learnt that Polemon and Sosias had
just returned from campaigning abroad (499 f.; cf. 182,
implying that the slave too had been away), that Sosias
had been sent ahead by Polemon yesterday evening to
inform Glykera of her lover's return, had surprised Gly-*

ΑΓΝΟΙΑ

[τὸ μὲν τρέφειν

121   αὐτὴ] προθυμηθεῖσα θῆλυ, τὸ δ' ἕτερον
       γυναικὶ] δοῦναι πλουσίᾳ τὴν οἰκίαν

In the apparatus to this play, those corrections and supplements
whose author is not identified were made by the first editors of
the various papyri: 121–760 G. Lefebvre with M. Croiset (C),
768–827 A. Körte (L), 976–1026 B. Grenfell, A. Hunt, F. Blass
(O = P.Oxy. 211). New conjectures and supplements of my own
are discussed at length in ZPE, 109 (1995), 17 ff.   120 Suppl.
here *exempli gratia* by Jensen, and 121 by Sudhaus, after Croiset
suggested these words elsewhere in the sentence.

kera in Moschion's arms, and returned post-haste to Pole-
mon with the news. Polemon would have angrily stormed
into his house that same night and cut off Glykera's hair.

At the end of the introductory scene Glykera would
have returned into Polemon's house, and the soldier and
his slave would have left by the parodos to the house of
one of his friends. Misconception would then have
entered an empty stage to deliver her prologue. It is
unlikely that much of her speech has been lost; 51 lines of
it survive, and comparable divine prologues in Menander
number only 48 (Dyskolos) or 52 (Aspis) lines, although
Moschion's (human) prologue speech in Samia goes on for
more than 90. All that Misconception needs to have said
before line 121 is that twin children had been born to
Pataikos, whose wife died at their birth (cf. 802–804) and
the babies were then exposed; if Menander followed his
usual custom in prologues of describing rather than nam-
ing characters, he would have identified at the most only
one of these three (Pataikos?) by name.)

(Page 99 of the Cairo codex begins with Misconception
delivering her prologue, postponed to the second or third
scene; the opening lines of her speech are lost.)

MISCONCEPTION
[to rear]
The] girl [herself] most eager, and to give   121
The other to a wealthy [lady] who

[a] See my paper in *Drama*, 2 (1993), 14–32.

(3)   ταύτην] κατοικούσῃ, δεομένῃ παιδίου.

        γέγον]ε δέ τα[ῦτ'. ἐγγενο]μένων δ' ἐτῶν τινων

125   καὶ τ]οῦ πολέμου καὶ τῶν Κορινθιακῶν κακῶν

        αὐξ]ανομένων, ἡ γραῦς ἀπορουμένη σφόδρα,

(7)   τεθραμμένης τῆς παιδός, ἣν νῦν εἴδετε

        ὑμεῖς, ἐραστοῦ γενομένου τε τοῦ σφοδροῦ

        τούτου νεανίσκου γένει Κορινθίου

130   ὄντος, δίδωσι τὴν κόρην ὡς θυγατέρα

        αὑτῆς ἔχειν. ἤδη δ' ἀπειρηκυῖα καὶ

(12)   προορωμένη τοῦ ζῆν καταστροφήν τινα

        αὑτῇ παροῦσαν, οὐκ ἔκρυψε τὴν τύχην,

        λέγει δὲ πρὸς τὴν μείραχ' ὡς ἀνείλετο

135   αὐτήν, ἐν οἷς τε σπαργάνοις διδοῦσ' ἅμα,

        τὸν ἀγνοούμενόν τ' ἀδελφὸν τῇ φύσει

(17)   φράζει, προνοουμένη τι τῶν ἀνθρωπίνων,

        εἴ ποτε δεηθείη βοηθείας τινός,

        ὁρῶσα τοῦτον ὄντ' ἀναγκαῖον μόνον

140   αὑτῇ, φυλακήν τε λαμβάνουσα μή ποτε

        δι' ἐμέ τι τὴν Ἄγνοιαν αὐτοῖς συμπέσῃ

(22)   ἀκούσιον, πλουτοῦντα καὶ μεθύοντ' ἀεὶ

        ὁρῶσ' ἐκεῖνον, εὐπρεπῆ [δ]ὲ κα[ὶ] νέαν

        ταύτην, βέβαιον δ' οὐθὲν ᾧ κ[ατ]ελε[ί]πετο

145   αὕτη μὲν οὖν ἀπέθανεν, ὁ δὲ τὴν οἰκίαν

        ἐπρίατο ταύτην ὁ στρατιώτης οὐ πάλαι.

(27)   ἐν γειτόνων δ' οἰκοῦσα τ[ἀ]δελφοῦ τὸ μὲν

124 γέγον]ε suppl. Weissmann, τα[ῦτ' Körte, ἐγγενο]μένων Leo.   125 Suppl. several.   135 διδοῦσ' Croenert, van Herwerden: διδωσ' C.   144 δ' van Leeuwen: θ' C.

Wanted a child. She lives there, in [that] house.
(*She points to Myrrhine's house.*)
This [has been done]. Some years [went by]. The war
And the Corinthian troubles[a] grew much worse,   125
Reducing the old woman[b] to the direst
Of straits. The baby girl's grown up—just now
You saw her—and this young impetuous blood,
Whose family hails from Corinth, fell in love
With her. The woman let him have the girl,   130
Treating her as her daughter. Frail in health
Now, and aware that life's last hour for her
Was near, she didn't keep that episode
A secret, but informed the girl of how
She took her in, giving her as she spoke   135
The baby clothes in which she'd found her. She
Mentioned the unknown blood-brother, as precaution
Against some human tragedy, in case
She ever needed help. She knew he was the girl's
One relative, and wished to guard against   140
Some unintended hurt befalling them
Through me—I'm Misconception. She could see
The boy was wealthy, always drinking, and the girl
Was young and pretty, while the man to whom
The girl was promised never looked reliable.   145
And so she died. Now he—the soldier—has
Just bought that house.

(*Here she points to the second stage house, that of Pole-mon.*)

The girl lives next door to

---

[a] Compare 532–534, and see the introduction to this play.
[b] The woman who had originally found the exposed babies.

MENANDER

πράγμ' οὐ μεμήνυκ' οὐδ' ἐκεῖνον βούλεται
εἶναι δοκοῦντα λαμπρὸν εἰς μεταλλαγὴν
150 ἀγαγεῖν, ὄνασθαι δ' ὧν δέδωκεν ἡ τύχη.
ἀπὸ ταὐτομάτου δ' ὀφθεῖσ' ὑπ' αὐτοῦ, θρασυτέρου
(32) ὥσπερ προείρηκ' ὄντος ἐπιμελῶς τ' ἀεὶ
φοιτῶντος ἐπὶ τὴν οἰκίαν, ἔτυχ' ἑσπέρας
π[έ]μπουσά ποι θεράπαιναν, ὡς δ' ἐπὶ ταῖς θύραις
155 α[ὐ]τὴν γενομένην εἶδεν, εὐθὺ προσδραμὼν
ἐφίλει, περιέβ[α]λλ', ἡ δὲ τῷ προειδέ[ναι
(37) ἀδελφὸν ὄντ' οὐκ ἔφυγε, προσιὼν δ' [ὁ θεράπων
ὁρᾷ. τὰ λοιπὰ δ' αὐτὸς ε[ἴρηχ'], ὃν τρ[όπον
ὁ μὲν ᾤχετ', εἰπὼ[ν] ὅτι κατὰ σχολὴν ἰδ[εῖν
160 αὐτήν τι βούλεθ', [ἡ δ'] ἐδάκρυ' ἑστῶσα καὶ
ὠδύρεθ' ὅτι ταῦτ' οὐκ ἐλευθέρως ποεῖν
(42) ἔξεστιν αὐτῇ. πάντα δ' ἐξεκάετο
ταῦθ' ἕνεκα τοῦ μέλλοντος, εἰς ὀργήν θ' ἵνα
οὗτος ἀφίκητ'—ἐγὼ γὰρ ἦγον οὐ φύσει
165 τοιοῦτον ὄντα τοῦτον—ἀρχὴν δ' ἵνα λάβῃ
μηνύσεως τὰ λοιπά, τούς θ' αὑτῶν ποτε
(47) εὕροιεν· ὥστ' εἰ τοῦτ' ἐδυσχεραινέ τις
ἀτιμίαν τ' ἐνόμισε, μεταθέσθω πάλιν.
διὰ γὰρ θεοῦ καὶ τὸ κακὸν εἰς ἀγαθὸν ῥέπει

148 μεμήνυκ' several: μεμενηκεν C.   151 ὑπ' αὐτοῦ Croenert: υπατου rather than υποτου C.   154 π[.]μποισα C.   155 Suppl. van Leeuwen.   157 Suppl. Kuiper.   158 ε[ἴρηχ'] and τρ[όπον deciph. and suppl. Jensen (ε[ἴρηκ'] Leo).   159 ἰδ[εῖν suppl. Sudhaus.   162–179 The later part of these lines is preserved also in H.   162 εξεκαετο C: εξεκαιετο H.   163 θ' om. H.   164 ἀφίκητ' several: αφικετ' C.   167 εδυσχεραινε C: εδυσχερανε H.

Her brother, but she's not divulged her secret, she's
No wish to blight the young man's prospects, which
Appear so bright, she wants him to enjoy   150
The gifts of fortune. He's quite hasty, as I said
Before, and always hanging with intent
About the house. At dusk he chanced to spot
Her sending off her maid upon some errand,
And when he saw her by the door, he ran   155
Straight up, he kissed and hugged her. She didn't try
Escaping, for she knew he was her brother.
[That slave][a] appeared and saw it. He himself['s]
[Described] the outcome—how the youth[b] went off
Saying he'd like to see her when convenient,   160
While she stood there in tears and sobbed "She wasn't
At liberty to act like that." This all
Blazed up to spark off future incidents,
To goad him into rage—I spurred him on,
He's not like that by nature, but I aimed to launch   165
Revelations from the outcome—and at last
To make them find their families. So, if this
Shocks anyone and seems disgraceful,[c] he must change
His views. With god's help evil turns to good,

[a] She means Sosias, if this supplement is correct.

[b] The 'youth' of course is Moschion, 'she' (161) is Glykera,
then 'him' (164) Polemon. Prologue-speakers rarely name the
characters they are describing.

[c] Athenian audiences at times protested so vociferously
against 'unacceptable' incidents and ideas in the plays staged
before them that performances could be disrupted or halted; see
A. Pickard-Cambridge, *Dramatic Festivals of Athens* (2nd edi-
tion, revised by J. Gould and D. M. Lewis, Oxford 1968), 272 f.

170   γινόμενον. ἔρρωσθ' εὐμενεῖς τε γενόμενοι
ἡμῖν, θεαταί, καὶ τὰ λοιπὰ σῴζετε.

ΣΩΣΙΑΣ

(52)   ὁ σοβαρὸς ἡμῖν ἀρτίως καὶ πολεμικός,
ὁ τὰς γυναῖκας οὐκ ἐῶν ἔχειν τρίχας,
κλάει κατακλινείς. κατέλαβον ποούμενον
175   ἄριστον αὐτοῖς ἄρτι, καὶ συνηγμένοι
εἰς ταὐτόν εἰσιν οἱ συνηθεῖς, τοῦ φέρειν
(57)   αὐτὸν τὸ π[ρ]ᾶγμα ῥᾷον. οὐκ ἔχων δ' ὅπως
τἀνταῦθ' ἀκο[ύσ]ῃ γινόμεν', ἐκπέπομφέ με
ἱμάτιον οἴσοντ' ἐξεπίτηδες, οὐδὲ ἓν
180   δεόμενος· ἀλλ' ἢ περιπατεῖν με βούλεται;

ΔΩΡΙΣ

ἐγὼ προελθο[ῦ]σ' ὄψομαι, κεκτημένη.

ΣΩΣΙΑΣ

(62)   ἡ Δωρίς. οἷα γέγονεν, ὡς δ' ἐρρωμένη.
ζῶσιν τρόπον τιν', ὡς ἐμοὶ καταφαίνεται,
αὗται. πορεύσομαι δέ.

171 σωζετε C: σωσατε H.
174 κατελαβον H: κατελιπον C.
175 αρτι C: γαρτι H.
178 γινομεν' C: γε[H.
180 ἀλλ' ἢ Meister: αλλη C.
181 Deciph. and suppl. Jensen.

Right from conception. Audience, good-bye,   170
And smile on us, support the coming scenes.

(*Exit the goddess Misconception, either by a side-entrance
(if she delivered her prologue on the stage itself) or down
from the roof of the stage-building (if she spoke from
there). After her departure Polemon's slave Sosias enters
from the side by which he had previously left. He has
come from the house where Polemon has taken up tempo-
rary residence since his breach with Glykera.*)

SOSIAS

Our swaggering soldier of an hour ago—
The one who won't let ladies keep their hair—
Now lies upon his couch in tears. Just now
I found some lunch being fixed for them, his friends   175
Have mustered there together, just to help
Him soldier through this business with less pain.
He had no means of learning what was going on
Here, so he's sent me out on purpose just to get
A cloak, though he needs nothing. Can he just   180
Want me to run around?

(*Doris now enters from Polemon's house. Her first words
are addressed back into the house to Glykera, who must
be imagined there inside. She does not see Sosias.*)

DORIS
           Mistress, I'll go out there
And see.

SOSIAS
(*aside*)
      It's Doris—how she's grown! How well
She looks! It's clear to me these women live
In style. I'm off now.

MENANDER

ΔΩΡΙΣ

κόψω τὴν θύραν.

185 οὐδεὶς γὰρ αὐτῶν ἐστιν ἔξω. δυστυχής,
ἥτις στρατιώτην ἔλαβεν ἄνδρα. παράνομοι

(67) ἅπαντες, οὐδὲν πιστόν. ὦ κεκτημένη,
ὡς ἄδικα πάσχεις. παῖδες.

ΣΩΣΙΑΣ

εὐφρανθήσεται

κλάουσαν αὐτὴν πυθόμενος νῦν. τοῦτο γὰρ

190 ἐβουλετ' αὐτός.

ΔΩΡΙΣ

παιδίον, κέλευέ μοι

(Here two pages of C have been lost, producing a lacuna
of between 70 and 76 lines.)

184 Kock fr. 860

184 κόψω τὴν θύραν is cited from Menander also by a scholion
on Ar. *Nub.* 132.
188–190 This speech (εὐφρανθήσεται—αὐτός) rightly assigned
to ὁ δοῦλος by ed. pr. (dicola after παῖδες 188 and αυτος 190 in
C).

384

(*Sosias goes off into Polemon's house, and then quickly returns with the cloak for which he has been sent, in time to overhear what Doris says about her mistress in her next speech.*)

DORIS

(*moving to the door of Myrrhine's house*)
                    I'll knock at the door,
For none of them's outside.
                    (*She knocks.*)
                    Unlucky girl!   185
She took a soldier for her partner—they're
All hooligans, quite unreliable—
Oh mistress, how unfair your treatment is!
                    (*She knocks again.*)
Slaves!

SOSIAS

(*aside*)
       He'll be glad to hear she's now in tears,
That's what he wanted.

DORIS

(*knocking once more*)
                    Slave!

(*The door opens, and she addresses the slave—perhaps Daos—who has come to the door.*)

                    Give orders, please   190

(*In the gap that follows Doris must have asked Myrrhine, either directly or through her slave, to allow Glykera to move from Polemon's hosue and stay with Myrrhine after Polemon's assault on her. Myrrhine must have agreed to the request, and Glykera have completed the move, since*)

385

ΔΑΟΣ

261 παῖδες. μεθύοντα μειράκια προσέρχεται
(72) π[ά]μπολλ'. ἐπαινῶ διαφόρως κεκτημένην·
εἴσω πρὸς ἡμᾶς εἰσάγει τὴν μείρακα.
τοῦτ' ἔστι μήτηρ. ὁ [τρ]όφιμος ζητητέος·
265 ἥ]κει[ν] γὰρ αὐτὸν [τὴν τα]χίστην ἐνθάδε
εὔκαιρον εἶναι φαίνεθ', ὡς ἐμοὶ δοκεῖ.

XO P OY

ΜΕΡΟΣ Β΄

263 ἡμᾶς Leo: υμας C.
265 ἥ]κειν deciph. and suppl. Jensen.

*when we next hear of Glykera (273 f.) she is already in
Myrrhine's house. We do not know whether Sosias stayed
and witnessed the move; he could have left the stage
directly after his comment at 190 in order to return to
Polemon (cf. 354). When the Cairo papyrus resumes,
Daos, the slave in Myrrhine's household assigned to look
after Moschion, is on stage. The first word preserved in
his speech appears to end a sentence with a reference to
some 'slaves'; these could have been addressed either
unseen inside Myrrhine's house (cf. Doris' remark at 181)
by Daos as he came on stage, or (more probably) seen
along with Daos on stage conveying Glykera's luggage to
Myrrhine's house.)*

DAOS

[   ]

Slaves. There's a horde of rather drunk young men   261
Approaching. I applaud my mistress highly
For taking in this girl into our house—
There's a real mother for you! I must find
My master—clearly now's the time for him   265
To be here at the double, that's my view.

*(Exit Daos, probably off right, in search of Moschion. We
do not know why Moschion is not at home; one possibility
is that he left during the gap between lines 190 and 261 to
go carousing in town. The approaching horde is the cho-
rus, who now enter after the conventional cue for their
first entr'acte performance.)*

ACT II

*(After the choral entr'acte Daos and Moschion enter,
probably from the right, in mid-conversation. Daos has
evidently just told Moschion about Glykera's move into*

387

MENANDER

ΜΟΣΧΙΩΝ

(77) Δᾶε, π[ολλ]άκις μὲν ἤδη πρός μ' ἀπήγγελκας
        λόγο[υ]ς
    ο]ὐκ ἀληθεῖς, ἀλλ' ἀλαζὼν καὶ θεοῖσιν ἐχθρὸς εἶ.
    εἰ δὲ καὶ [νυ]νὶ πλανᾷς με—

                        ΔΑΟΣ
                    κρέμασον εὐθύς, εἰ [πλανῶ.

                    ΜΟΣΧΙΩΝ
270 ἥμερον λέγεις τι.

                        ΔΑΟΣ
                    χρῆσαι πολεμίου τοίνυν [τρόποις.
    ἂ]ν δ' ἀληθὲς ᾖ κ[ατα]λάβῃς τ' ἔνδον αὐτὴν
        ἐν[θά]δε,
(82) ὁ δεδιωκηκ[ὼς ἐγώ] σ[ο]ι ταῦτα [πά]ντα, Μοσχίων,
    καὶ πεπεικ[ὼς τὴ[ν] μὲν ἐλθεῖ[ν] δεῦρ', ἀναλώσας
        [λ]όγους
    μυρίους, τὴν σ[ὴν δὲ] μητέρ' [ὑποδέχ]εσθαι καὶ
        ποε[ῖν
275 πάνθ' ἅ σο[ι] δοκεῖ, τίς ἔσομ[αι];

                    ΜΟΣΧΙΩΝ
                    [τίς] βίος μάλισθ', [ὅρα,

267 (πρός με) Kock fr. 978;   268 Kock fr. 875

267 λόγο[υ]ς deciph. and suppl. Jensen.   269 Suppl. Körte,
Leo.   270 Suppl. Arnott.   271 Up to ᾖ deciph. and suppl.
Wilamowitz, the rest Leo.   272 [πα]ντα deciph. and suppl.
several, the rest Sudhaus.   273 τὴ[ν] μὲν deciph. and suppl.
Sudhaus (πεπεικ[ὼς]), Schmidt (τὴ[ν] μὲν), Leo ([λ]όγους).

388

their house, and is claiming total credit for bringing it
about. Their rumbustious conversation is in trochaic
tetrameters throughout; the first 27 lines are hard to read,
supplement and interpret.)

MOSCHION

Daos, you have often brought me tales before now that
were not

True! You are a loud-mouthed charlatan, detested by
the gods!

If in fact you're fooling me now . . .

DAOS

You can thrash me if [I am].

MOSCHION

That's a mild suggestion.

DAOS

Then behave [just like] an enemy.   270

If it's true, though, and you find her in the house here,
Moschion,

[I'm] the man who's engineered it all on your behalf,
the man

Who's persuaded her to come here, drafting countless
arguments,

And who's got your mother now to [grant her refuge],
and [to] meet

All your wishes. So what's to become of me?

MOSCHION

[What] sort of life,   275

---

274 Deciph. and suppl. Körte.   275 πάνθ' Croenert, who
with several others deciph. and suppl. up to ἔσομ[αι]: απανθ' C.
[τίς] suppl. Leo, [ὅρα] Wilamowitz.

Δᾶε, τῶν πάντων ἀρέσκει; [τοῦ]τ᾽ ἐπίβλεψ[ον.

ΔΑΟΣ

[βλέπω.

(87) ἆρα τὸ μυλωθρεῖν κράτιστον;

ΜΟΣΧΙΩΝ

εἰς μυλῶν᾽ ἀ[φίξεται

οὑτοσὶ φερόμενος.

ΔΑΟΣ

ἡ[μ]ῖν μηδ[α]μῶς τέχνη[ν λ]έγ[ε.

ΜΟΣΧΙΩΝ

βούλομαι δὲ προστάτην σε πραγμάτων Ἑλλη[νι]κ[ῶν

280 κα]ὶ διοικήτην στρατοπέδων . . .

ΔΑΟΣ

[οὐ μ]έλε[ι μοι τῶν ξένων,

οἵ μ᾽] ἀποσφά[τ]τουσιν εὐθύς, ἂ[ν τύ]χῃ,

[κ]λέ[ψαντά τι.

276 [τοῦ]τ᾽ suppl. Guéraud, the rest Sandbach, who also sug-
gested change of speaker.   The lower part of C's page con-
taining 277–293 is so badly worn, rubbed and mutilated
that often decipherment is uncertain and supplementation
speculative.   277 C has κράτιστον:, but no paragraphus
under the line. μυλων᾽ deciph. Sudhaus, ἀ[φίξεται suppl.
Lowe.   278 ἡ[μ]ῖν with following dicolon deciph. and suppl.
several, but it makes better sense if taken as the opening word of
Daos' speech, cf. ZPE 109 (1995) 16. μηδ[α]μῶς τέχνη[ν]
deciph. and suppl. Jensen, [λ]έγ[ε Schmidt.   279 Suppl.

[See now,] Daos, most of all attracts you? Ponder [that].

DAOS

[I do.]

Is it best to be a miller?

MOSCHION

(*aside*)

Daos here [will make his way]
Any day now to the mill!^a

DAOS

Don't [name] an art or craft to us!

MOSCHION

I should like to see you as an overlord of Greek affairs
And a marshal of land forces . . .

DAOS

[I] [don't] care [for mercenaries],   280
[Who] will promptly cut [my] throat [for any theft], if
[given the chance.^b

---

^a Moschion predicts that Daos' misdemeanours will cause him to be sent for punishment to work in a flour mill. See the note on *Heros* 3.

^b Possibly a reference to the murder in 314/3 of Alexander son of Polyperchon by a group of Sicyonians shortly after he had been appointed 'general of the Peloponnese' by Cassander: see the introduction to this play.

Ricci.   280 κα]ὶ deciph. and suppl. Körte, [οὐ μ]έλε[ι Sudhaus, Jensen. μοι τῶν ξένων suppl. Jensen.   281 οἵ μ'] suppl. Sudhaus, ἂ[ν τύ]χῃ deciph. and suppl. Schwartz, [κ]λέ[ψαντά τι Jensen.

MENANDER

ΜΟΣΧΙΩΝ

(92) ἀλλὰ [.......] ἐκδότης <ὤν>· ἐκδόσει [λήσ]ει λαβὼ[ν
ἑπτὰ [τῶν ὀκτὼ] τάλαντα.

ΔΑΟΣ

πavτοπωλεῖν [βούλομαι,
Μοσχίων, ἢ [τυρ]οπ[ω]λεῖν ἐ[ν ἀ]γορᾷ καθήμεν[ος.
285 ὀμνύω μ[ηδὲν μέλειν μοι πλου]σίῳ καθεσ[τάναι.
κατ' ἐμὲ ταῦτ', ἐ[μοί τ' ἀρέσκει] μᾶλλον.

ΜΟΣΧΙΩΝ

ἀν[όσιον λέγεις·
(97) οἶδ' ἐκ[ε]ῖνο· μὴ γένοιτο μελ[ιτόπ]ωλις εὐ]σεβὴς
γραῦς.

ΔΑΟΣ

τὸ γαστρίζεσθ' ἀρέ[σ]κε[ι, γ]εγ[ογέναι δέ
γ' ἄξιος
φήμ' ἐφ' οἷς εἴρηκα τούτοις.

ΜΟΣΧΙΩΝ

μὰ [Δία, παῖ, σύ γ' οὐκ ἄφρων

282 Corr., deciph. and suppl. Sudhaus, with ἀλλὰ [κλέψεις] at
the beginning, good sense but not fitting the traces.   283 [τῶν
ὀκτὼ] suppl. Sudhaus. βούλομαι suppl. Jensen.   284 Deciph.
and suppl. Jensen (for [τυρ]οπ[ω]λεῖν compare 290).
285 [πλου]σίῳ deciph. and suppl. Körte, the rest Sudhaus.
286 ἐ[μοί τ' ἀρέσκει] suppl. Sudhaus, the rest *exempli gratia*
Jensen.   287 Suppl. Sudhaus provisionally.
288 ἀρέ[σκ]ε[ι deciph. and suppl. Jensen, the rest suppl. provi-
sionally Sandbach.   289 Suppl. Körte, van Herwerden.

MOSCHION

But [you'll thieve (?)] by farming contracts, that's the way
　　　you'll [secretly]
Pocket seven talents [out of every eight]![a]

DAOS

　　　　　　　　　　　　A general store,
Moschion, is what [I'd like], or in the market on a stool
Selling [cheese]. I swear [I've no desire] to be [a million-　　285
　　　aire].
That's my line, [I find it] more [attractive].

MOSCHION

　　　　　　　　　　　　[It's a wicked plan].
[I recall that proverb], "let me [never] meet a [pious] hag
Selling honey" (?).[b]

DAOS

　　　　A full belly—that's attractive, [and] I claim
[I deserve it], after what I've told you.

MOSCHION

　　　　　　　　　By [Zeus], you're [no fool],

[a] The text here is hard to make out, but the general meaning
seems to be that as an 'overlord' or 'marshal' Daos would be able
to make vast profits by farming out contracts.

[b] The text of this line is uncertain. The translation here pre-
supposes that Moschion is quoting a proverb claiming that all
shopkeepers were dishonest. Unfortunately there is no trace
elsewhere in Greek of this particular wording, although contem-
porary comedians accused many kinds of retail trader—fish-
mongers (see Athenaeus 6. 224c–228b) and wine-sellers (for
instance Alexis fr. 9, Nicostratus fr. 22; compare Theophrastus,
Characters 30) in particular—of cheating their customers.

290 ἦσθας· ἀλλὰ τυροπώλει καὶ ταλ[α]ι[πώρει.

ΔΑΟΣ

[καλῶς·
τ]αῦτα μὲ[ν δ]ή, φ[α]σίν, εὔχθω· δ[εῦρο πάραγε τήν
τε σὴν

(102) ο]ἰκίαν ἄνοι[γε], τρόφιμε.

ΜΟΣΧΙΩΝ

δεῖ μ[ὲν οὖν· ὀρθῶς λέγεις.
ἐ[μὲ δε] παραμυθεῖσθ᾽ [ἐκεί]ν[ην νῦν προσήκει καὶ
γελᾶν
ἐπὶ θεοῖς ἐχθρῷ πτεροφόρα χιλιάρχῳ.

ΔΑΟΣ

καὶ μάλα.

ΜΟΣΧΙΩΝ

295 εἰσιὼν δέ μοι σύ, Δᾶε, τῶν ὅλων κατάσκοπος
πραγμάτων γενοῦ, τί ποιεῖ, π[ο]ῦ ᾽στιν ἡ μήτηρ, ἐμὲ
(107) εἰς τὸ προσδοκᾶν ἔχουσι πῶς. τὸ τοιουτὶ μέρος
οὐκ ἀκριβῶς δεῖ φρά[σαι] σοι· κομψὸς εἶ.

290 Suppl. Sudhaus, who suggested also the part-division.
291 τ]αῦτα μὲ[ν δ]ή, φ[α]σίν deciph. and suppl. Sudhaus, not-
ing that the phrase was copied by [Aristaenetus] 2. 1. δ[εῦρο
πάραγε, τήν τε σὴν suppl. Arnott (τὴν δὲ σὴν van Leeuwen).
292 ο]ἰκίαν ἄνοι[γε] suppl. Sudhaus, the rest Arnott after
Sudhaus.   293 Suppl. Sudhaus.

---

[a] This proverb is cited also by [Aristaenetus] 2. 1 and Diony-
sius the Areopagite, *De mystica theologia* 1 (*Patrologia Graeca* 3
col. 997).

[Daos]! Sell your cheese, and work your fingers to the bone.

DAOS

(*approaching Myrrhine's door*)

[That's fine.] 290

As the proverb goes, "Let's say amen to that."[a] [Come
  over here],
Master, [and] unlatch [your] door![b]

MOSCHION

(*following Daos, and unlocking the door*)

[Yes, you're right,] I ought to. [It's]
[In my interest now] to coax [her], reassure [her, and to
  gloat]
Over a god-damned commander—with a feather in his
  cap![c]

DAOS

Yes indeed.

MOSCHION

Go in, please, Daos, and investigate for me 295
All their actions—what she's[d] doing, where my mother is,
  how they're
Planning to receive me. There's no need [to] spell this
  kind of thing
Out to you in detail—you're not stupid.

[b] Hereabouts supplementation is very speculative, but Daos'
request for his master to open the door may imply that it had
been locked (perhaps just before 261, at the approach of the cho-
rus of revellers), with Moschion having a key.

[c] Polemon is literally described as χιλίαρχος, an officer in
charge of a unit of 1000 men, and πτεροφόρας, wearing a plume
in his helmet to indicate his rank.

[d] Glykera.

ΔΑΟΣ

πορεύσο[μ]αι.

ΜΟΣΧΙΩΝ

περιπατῶν δὲ προσ[με]νῶ σε, <Δᾶε>, πρόσθε τῶν
θυρῶν.

300 ἀλλ' ἔδειξεν μέν τι τοι[ο]ῦθ', ὡς προσῆλθον
ἑ[σπ]έρας·
προσδραμόντ' οὐκ ἔφυγεν, ἀλλὰ περιβαλοῦσ'
ἐ[πέσπα]σε.

(112) οὐκ ἀηδής, ὡς ἔοι[κε]ν, εἴμ' ἰδεῖν οὐδ' ἐντ[υχεῖν,
οἴομαι, μὰ τὴν Ἀθηνᾶν, ἀλλ' ἑταίρ[α]ι[ς προσφιλής.
τὴν δ' Ἀδράστειαν μάλιστα νῦν ἄρ' [ὥρα]
προ[σκυνεῖ]ν.

ΔΑΟΣ

305 Μοσχίων, ἡ μὲν λέλουται καὶ κάθηται.

ΜΟΣΧΙΩΝ

φιλτάτη.

ΔΑΟΣ

ἡ δὲ μήτηρ σου διοικεῖ περιπα[τοῦ]σ' οὐκ οἶδ' ὅ τι.
(117) εὐτρεπὲς δ' ἄριστόν ἐστ<ιν>, ἐκ δὲ τῶν πο[ο]υμένω[ν
περιμένειν δοκοῦσί μ[οί σ]ε.

ΜΟΣΧΙΩΝ

κ[αὶ] πάλαι [μένο]υ[σί μ']; οὐκ

298 πορεύσο[μ]αι decipher. and suppl. Körte.   299 <Δᾶε>
added by Jensen.   300 ἑ[σπ]έρας suppl. Leo.   301 ἐ[πέ-
σπα]σε suppl. Leo.   302 ἐντ[υχεῖν suppl. several.   303 Suppl.
Sudhaus.   304 [ὥρα] suppl. Capps, προ[σκυνεῖ]ν Wilamowitz.
306 εστ' C.   308 κ[αὶ] suppl. Jensen, [μένο]υ[σί μ'] Sandbach
after Capps. οὐκ misplaced at the beginning of 309 by C.

DAOS

I'll be on my way.

MOSCHION

While I'm waiting for you, I shall take a stroll outside the
    door,

(*Daos goes off into Myrrhine's house.*)

[Daos]. — Well, she gave a sort of hint on my approach   300
    last night.

When I sprinted up, she didn't run away, she hugged and
    [pulled]

[Me to her]. I'm not bad-looking, by Athena, so it seems,

Nor bad [company], I fancy—no, the ladies[a] [fall for me].

— For that boast [I must] this instant make [amends] to
    Nemesis![b]

(*Daos comes on again from Myrrhine's house.*)

DAOS

Moschion, she's[c] had a bath, she's sitting there.

MOSCHION

The darling girl! 305

DAOS

And your mother's marching round and organising some-
    thing or

Other. Lunch is ready, and from their activities, it's [you]

That they're waiting for, [I] guess.

MOSCHION

[Have they been waiting] long [for me]?

---

  [a] Courtesans, specifically.   [b] The goddess of retribution, to
whom one customarily made obeisance after conceited remarks
like the one just made by Moschion.   [c] Again, Glykera.

εἴμ' ἀηδής. [ε]ἶπας αὐ[τ]αῖς [νῦν π]αρόντα μ' ἐνθάδε;

ΔΑΟΣ

310 μὰ] Δί[α].

ΜΟΣΧΙΩΝ

νῦν [τ]οί[ν]υν [λ]έγ' ἐλθών.

ΔΑΟΣ

ὡς ὁρᾷς, ἀναστρέφω.

ΜΟΣΧΙΩΝ

ἡ μὲν αὐσχ[υν]ε[ῖτ' ἐ]πειδὰ[ν] εἰσίωμεν δηλαδή,
(122) παρακαλύ[ψεταί τ', ἔθο]ς γὰρ τ[ο]ῦ[τ]ο· τὴν δὲ
μητέρα
εἰσιόντ' εὐθ[ὺς] φιλῆσαι δεῖ μ', ἀνακτήσασθ' ὅλως,
εἰς τὸ κολακεύειν τραπέσθαι, ζῆν τε πρὸς ταύτην
ἁπλῶς·
315 ὡς γὰρ οἰκείῳ κέχρηται τῷ παρόντι πράγματι.
ἀλλὰ τὴν θύραν ψοφεῖ τις ἐξιών. τί τοῦτο, παῖ;
(127) ὡς ὀκνηρῶς μοι προσέρχε[ι], Δᾶε.

ΔΑΟΣ

ναὶ μὰ τὸν Δία·
πάνυ γὰρ ἄτοπον. ὡς γὰρ ἐλθὼν εἶπα πρὸς τὴν
μητέρα

309 [ε]ἶπας Leo:]ιπαις C. [νῦν π]αρόντα suppl. Meister.
310 Suppl. Jensen, but after Δί[α] there hardly seems room for
a dicolon.   311 αἰσχ[υν]ε[ῖτ' suppl. Sudhaus, the rest Jensen.
312 Deciph. and suppl. Körte from comparison with [Aristaene-
tus] 2. 2.   315 οἰκείῳ Sudhaus: οικειως C.   318 ἄτοπον
Sudhaus: ατοπως C.

I'm not unattractive! Did you let them know I've [just]
    arrived?

DAOS

[No,] I didn't.

MOSCHION
So go and tell them now!

DAOS

(*going off into Myrrhine's house*)

                    I'm on my way back, as   310
You can see.

MOSCHION
(*musing alone to himself*)
    She'[ll] be embarrassed when we go in, that is clear,
And she'[ll] hide her face, for that's [quite normal]. First
    though I must kiss
Mother right on entry, and secure her absolute support,
Try to show her some attention, simply live for her alone.
She's dealt with this present trouble just as if it were her   315
    own.
But the door is creaking—someone's coming out.

(*Moschion turns to Daos as he re-enters from Myrrhine's
house.*)

                    Oh! What's up? How
Timidly you're walking to me, Daos!

DAOS

                    Yes indeed, by Zeus.
It's all very strange. When I approached your mother with
    the news

ὅτι πάρει, "μηδὲν ἔτι τούτων," φησ[ί, "πῶς δ᾽
 ἀ]κήκοεν;
320 ἢ σὺ λελάληκας πρὸς αὐτ[όν], ὅτι φοβηθεῖσ᾽
 ἐνθάδε
 κα]ταπέφευγ᾽ αὔ[τ]η πρ[ὸς ἡμᾶς; πάνυ] γε. μὴ
 ὥρας σύ γε,"
(132) φή]σ᾽, "ἵκοι᾽, ἀλλ᾽ [ὡς τάχιστα νῦ]ν βάδιζε,
 παιδίον,
 ἐκ]ποδὼν [ἐνθένδ᾽." Ἀπ]ολλ[ον], πάντ᾽ [ἀν]ήρ-
 παστ᾽ ἐκ μέσου.
 οὐ σφό]δρ᾽ [ἤκ]ουσεν παρόντα σ᾽ ἡδέ[ως].

MOΣXIΩN

μαστιγία,

325 κατακέχρη]σαί μοι.

ΔΑΟΣ

γέλοιον. ἡ μὲν οὖν μήτηρ—

MOΣXIΩN

τί φής;
 οὐ λαβεῖν ἑ]κοῦσαν αὐ[τ]ήν, ἢ τί πρᾶγμ᾽; οὐχ ἕνεκ᾽
 ἐμοῦ;
(137) εἶπας ὡ]ς πέπεικας ἐλθεῖν πρός μ᾽.

ΔΑΟΣ

ἐγὼ δ᾽ εἴρηκά σοι

319 Suppl. Sudhaus. μηκετι C with δεν written above κετ as
correction.   320 ηκαισυ C: corr. several.   321 αὔ[τ]η
πρ[ὸς ἡμᾶς] suppl. Housman, Sudhaus, [πάνυ] Housman.
ωρασσυγε C perhaps correctly, but Schwartz's conjecture ὥρασί

400

You were here, she answered "None of that—[how]'s he
    found out? Or are
You the blabbermouth who's told him that she's taken   320
    refuge here
[With us] now in fear and trembling. Yes, [that's it]—be
    damned to you!"
[So she said], "And [now], my boy, move off [from here]
    out of my way
[At top speed!" Ap]ollo, everything's been snatched
    right from our grasp!
She was[n't over]joyed to hear that you were on the
    scene.

MOSCHION

    Blackguard!
You've [destroyed] me!

DAOS

    That's absurd. Your mother though . . .

MOSCHION

(interrupting)

                What's that you say?   325
[Didn't take] her in by choice? Or why then? Not
    on my behalf?
[You said] you persuaded her to come to my house!

DAOS

                 Have I said

γε is also possible, cf. *ZPE*, 109 (1995), 17 f.   322 φή]σ'
suppl. Headlam, Wilamowitz, the rest Körte.   323 ἐκ]ποδῶν
suppl. Lefebvre, [ἀν]ήρπαστ' Körte, the rest *exempli gratia*
Arnott.   324 Suppl. Sudhaus.   325 Suppl. Robert.   326 οὐ
λαβειν] suppl. Arnott, the rest Lefebvre.   327 Suppl.
van Leeuwen.

ὡς πέπει]κ' ἐλθεῖν ἐκείνην; μὰ τὸν Ἀπόλλω, 'γὼ μὲν
    οὔ.
.... ψε]ῦδό[ς <με>, τρ]όφ[ι]με, σοῦ καταψεύ-
    δεσθ' [

330 ...... οὐ τὴν] μ[ητέρ' αὐτὸ]ς ταῦτα συμπε[π]ε[ικ]έ-
    ναι
ἀρτίως ἔφησθα ταύτην ἐνθάδ' ὑποδέξασθ' ἐμοῦ
(142) ἕνεκα;

ΔΑΟΣ
    τοῦθ', ὁρᾷς, ἔφην· ναί, μνημονεύω.

ΜΟΣΧΙΩΝ
                καὶ δοκεῖν

ἕνεκ' ἐμοῦ σοι τ[ο]ῦτο πράττειν;

ΔΑΟΣ
               οὐκ ἔχω τουτὶ φράσαι,

ἀλλ' ἔγωγ' ἔπειθον.

ΜΟΣΧΙΩΝ
εἰέν· δεῦρο δὴ βάδιζε.

ΔΑΟΣ
                ποῖ;

ΜΟΣΧΙΩΝ
335 μ[ὴ] μακράν· εἴσει.

328 Suppl. Körte.   329 <με> add. Arnott deleting μου
before σοῦ, the rest suppl. and corr. Sudhaus:]μεμουσουκατα-
ψευδεσθ[with μουσου corrected from μεπολυ C.   330 Suppl.
Sudhaus.   331 C wrongly gives this line to Daos (δα΄ in right
margin).   335 μ[ὴ] suppl. Körte, μακράν deciph. Körte,
Jensen (in C μικρον corrected to μακραν). Assignment of parts

[I persuaded] her to come here? By Apollo I did not—
[You're accusing me] of telling lies about you, master,
    [now].

MOSCHION

[   ]^a Did[n't] you just now allege that you [yourself]   330
    had helped
To persuade [my mother] to allow the girl to stay with us
All for *my* sake?

DAOS

(*edging away from Moschion*)

                    Look, I said that. Yes, I do remember.

MOSCHION

                                        And

That you thought she did this all for me?

DAOS

                            I can't say that, but I

Did try to persuade her.

MOSCHION

            Well then, you come over here.

DAOS

                                Where to?

MOSCHION

No long distance—you'll find out!

---

^a The beginning of this line, which could have been spoken
by either Moschion or Daos, has been torn off the papyrus and so
far no plausible supplement has been suggested.

---

first indicated by van Leeuwen (C has paragraphus under 335,
dicolon after ϵυσϵι 335 but not after ποι 334); see J. C. B. Lowe,
Bulletin of the Institute of Classical Studies, 20 (1973), 100–102.

ΔΑΟΣ

τὸ δεῖνα, Μοσχίων· ἐγὼ τότε—

μ[ικ]ρ[ὸ]ν ἔτι μεῖνον.

ΜΟΣΧΙΩΝ

φλυαρεῖς πρός με.

ΔΑΟΣ

μὰ τὸν Ἀσκληπιόν,

(147) οὐ[κ ἔγ]ωγ', ἐὰν ἀκούσῃς. τυχὸν ἴσως οὐ βούλεται,

μ[ανθ]ά[ν]εις, ἐξ [ἐ]πιδρομῆς ταῦθ', ὡς ἔτυχεν, ἀλλ'
ἀξιοῖ,

π[ρὶν τάδ'] εἰδέναι σ', ἀκοῦσαι τὰ παρὰ σοῦ γε, νὴ
Δία.

340 οὐ [γὰρ ὡς αὐ]λ[ητρ]ὶς οὐδ' ὡς πορνίδιον τρισ-
άθλιον

ἦλθε].

ΜΟΣΧΙΩΝ

[νῦν δοκ]εῖς λέγειν μοι, Δᾶέ, τι πάλιν.

ΔΑΟΣ

δοκί[μασον·

(152) οἶσθας] οἷ[όν ἐ]στιν, οἶμαι. καταλέλοιπεν οἰκίαν,

οὐ φλυαρ[ία γ'], ἐραστήν. εἰ σὺ τρεῖς ἢ τέτταρας

ἡμ]έρας βο[ύ]λει, προσέξει σοί τις· ἀνεκοινοῦτό μοι

336 Suppl. Jensen.   337 Suppl. Körte.   338 Suppl. Sudhaus.
339 Suppl. Wilamowitz.   340 Suppl. Sudhaus.   341 Up to
δοκ]εῖς suppl. Sudhaus, δοκί[μασον Leo.   342 Suppl. Wila-
mowitz.   343 Suppl. Schwartz.   344 ἡμ]έρας suppl. Leo,
Sudhaus, βο[ύ]λει Körte.

DAOS

It's like this, Moschion, then I— 335
(*Moschion approaches Daos threateningly*)
Wait a little longer . . .

MOSCHION
You are talking nonsense!

DAOS

No, I'm not,
By Asclepius, if you'll just attend! Maybe she doesn't
    want
This event—you [understand]—to be a blitz, a
    shambles—no,
She requires to hear your story, yes, [before] you learn
    [the facts].
She's no [call-girl],[a] no pathetic prostitute [who's come, 340
    you see]!

MOSCHION
Daos, [now] I [think] you're talking sense again.

DAOS

Just test me out!
[You know] what it's like, I fancy. She has given up a
    house—
I'm not kidding—and a lover. If you want a three or
    four
Days' encounter, somebody will dance attendance.[b]
    She conveyed

[a] Literally 'female piper', but these professional musicians
(like Habrotonon in *Epitrepontes*) were expected additionally to
provide sexual favours at the parties for which they were hired.
[b] Daos is in fact lying when he coyly implies that Glykera is
ready to have a short affair with Moschion.

405

345 το]ῦτ'· ἀκοῦσαι γάρ σ[ε δ]εῖ νῦν.

ΜΟΣΧΙΩΝ

ποῦ σε δήσας κατα[λίπω,
Δ]ᾶε; περιπατεῖν [πο]εῖς με περίπ[α]τον π[ο]λύν
τινα.

(157) ἀρτίως μὲν οὖ[ν ἔπε]ιθες, [νῦ]ν δὲ λελά[λη]κας
πάλιν.

ΔΑΟΣ

οὐκ ἐᾷς φρονεῖν [μ' ἀ]θορύβ[ως. πα]ρ[α]βαλοῦ
τρόπον τινὰ
κοσμίως τ' εἴσω πάρ[ε]λθε.

ΜΟΣΧΙΩΝ

σ[ὺ δ' ἀποδ]ράσει;

ΔΑΟΣ

καὶ μάλα·

350 ἐφόδι' οὐχ ὁρᾷς μ' ἔχοντα;

ΜΟΣΧΙΩΝ

π[άνυ γε· πά]ραγε, παι[δίον.

ΔΑΟΣ

εἰσιὼν δὲ κἄ[ν] τι τούτων συνδιορθώσαις.

ΜΟΣΧΙΩΝ

ἐκ[ών·

(162) ὁμολογῶ νικᾶν σε.

345 το]ῦτ' suppl. Lefebvre, the rest Leo.   346 Δ]ᾶε suppl.
Sudhaus, [πο]εῖς Leo.   347 οὖ[ν and λελά[λη]κας suppl.
Körte, ἔπε]ιθες Arnott, [νῦ]ν Sudhaus.   348 [μ' ἀ]θορύβ[ως
suppl. Sudhaus, πα]ρ[α]βαλοῦ Post.   349 Suppl. Körte.
350 Suppl. Sudhaus. C has no dicolon after ἔχοντα nor para-

That to me. Now you must be informed.

MOSCHION

(*pretending to threaten Daos*)

                Where can I [leave] you, tied   345
Up securely, Daos? You've given me a lengthy runaround!
Just before you [were convincing, now] you're blathering
      again!

DAOS

You won't let [me] think in peace and quiet! Bring your
      ship to port,
Something like—behave when you go in!

MOSCHION

(*jokingly*)

               And you'll [de]camp?

DAOS

(*responding to Moschion's joke*)

                      Oh yes —
Don't you see I've got provisions?

MOSCHION

(*serious again*)

          [Quite]. But come [along], my boy.   350

DAOS

You go in—you might then make some progress in this.

MOSCHION

                   Happily:
I agree, you win.
    (*Moschion now goes off into Myrrhine's house.*)

---

graphus under the line.   351 εἰσιὼν δὲ κἂ[ν] Sudhaus:
δ'εισιωνκα[C. ἐκ[ών suppl. Jensen.

MENANDER

ΔΑΟΣ

μικροῦ γ᾽, Ἡράκλεις, καὶ νῦ[ν δέει
αὖός εἰμ᾽· οὐκ [ἔ]στι γὰρ ταῦθ᾽, ὡς τότ᾽ ᾤμην,
εὐκρι[νῆ.

ΣΩΣΙΑΣ

πάλιν πέπομφε τὴν χλαμύδα φέροντά με
355 καὶ τὴν σπάθην, ἵν᾽ ἴδω τί ποιεῖ καὶ λέγω
ἐλθών. ἀκαρὲς δέω δὲ φάσκειν καταλαβεῖν
(167) τὸν μοιχὸν [ἔ]νδον, ἵν᾽ ἀναπηδήσας τρέχῃ,
εἰ μή γε παν[τά]πασιν αὐτὸν ἠλέουν.
κακοδαίμον᾽ οὕτω δε[σπ]ότην οὐδ᾽ ἐνύπνι[ον
360 ἰδὼν γὰρ οἶδ᾽. ὦ τῆς π[ικρᾶ]ς ἐπιδημίας.

ΔΑΟΣ

ὁ ξένος ἀφῖκται. χαλεπὰ ταῦτα παντελ[ῶς
(172) τὰ πράγματ᾽ ἐστί, νὴ τὸν Ἀπόλλω τουτο[νί.
καὶ τὸ κεφάλαιον οὐδέπω λογίζομαι,
τὸν δεσπότην, [ἂ]ν ἐξ ἀγροῦ θᾶττον π[άλιν
365 ἔλθῃ, ταραχὴν οἵαν ποήσει παραφ[ανείς.

352 Suppl. Schmidt.
353 Suppl. Wilamowitz.   356 ἀκαρὲς deciph. Jensen.
359 Suppl. Headlam.   360 Suppl. Croenert, Headlam.
362 τουτο[νί Leo: ταυτο[C.   364 Suppl. several.
365 Suppl. Leo.

---

[a] Polemon.

[b] Daos points to an altar or pillar of Apollo Agyieus set up by Myrrhine's front door. See the note on *Dyskolos* 659.

[c] Myrrhine's husband. See the introduction to this play.

PERIKEIROMENE

DAOS

(*alone on stage*)

A close call! Heracles, I'm petrified
Now [with fear], for the prognosis isn't as good as I once
    thought!

(*Sosias now enters, probably by the side-entrance on the spectators' right: see the comment after 172. He is carrying Polemon's sword and military cloak. As yet he fails to notice Daos.*)

SOSIAS

He's sent me back again with cloak and sword,
To see what she is doing, then to go and tell   355
Him. I'm well-nigh inclined to claim I found
The fancy man indoors, to get him to jump up
And rush here—yet I pity him with all my heart!
I'm sure I've never seen or even dreamed
Of master being so wretched. What a [bitter] home-   360
Coming!

(*Exit Sosias into Polemon's house.*)

DAOS

The mercenary's[a] arrived! These problems are
Extremely difficult, by Apollo here.[b]
And I've not yet considered the main point—
If master[c] comes [back] from the farm too soon,   365
What chaos his appearance will create!

(*Sosias now emerges from Polemon's house, shouting to slaves inside. One of these was Doris, who probably followed Sosias to the open door and stayed there visible to the audience as a silent observer of the following exchange.*)

MENANDER

ΣΩΣΙΑΣ

ὑμεῖς δ' ἀφήκαθ', ἱερόσυλα θηρία,

(177)   ἀφή]κατ' ἔξω τῆς θύρ[α]ς;

ΔΑΟΣ

[ἀ]νασ[τρέ]φ[ει

ἄνθ]ρωπος ὀργιζόμ[εν]ος· [ὑπα]πο[στήσομαι.

ΣΩΣΙΑΣ

ἡ δ' οἶχεθ' ὡς τὸν γείτον' εὐθὺς δηλαδὴ

370   τὸν μοιχόν, οἰμώζειν φράσασ' ἡμῖν μακρὰ

καὶ μεγάλα.

ΔΑΟΣ

μάντιν ὁ στρατιώτης [πε]ρι[άγει

(182)   τοῦτον· ἐπιτυγχάνει τι.

ΣΩΣΙΑΣ

κόψω τὴν θύραν.

ΔΑΟΣ

ἄνθρωπε κακόδαιμον, τί βο[ύ]λει; ποῖ φέ[ρ]ει;

ΣΩΣΙΑΣ

ἐντεῦθεν εἶ;

ΔΑΟΣ

τυχόν. ἀλλὰ τί [π]ολυπρα[γμ]ο[νεῖς;

367 ἀφή]κατ' suppl. van Leeuwen, [ἀ]νασ[τρέ]φ[ει Sudhaus.
368 ἄνθ]ρωπος and [ὑπα]πο[στήσομαι suppl. Sudhaus, ὀργι-
ζόμ[εν]ος deciph. and suppl. Wilamowitz.   371 Suppl.
Sudhaus.   373 Deciph. and suppl. Jensen.   374 Suppl.
Jensen.

SOSIAS

You've let her go, you wicked brutes? You've let
Her go outside?

DAOS

(*still unseen by Sosias*)

        That fellow['s here] again,
In a foul temper! [I'll step] back.
(*Daos moves further into the background.*)

SOSIAS

          And like
A shot she's moved in with her fancy man
Next door, that's plain, telling us loud and long   370
To go to hell!

DAOS

(*aside*)

        That solder'[s got] him [on his staff]
As a clairvoyant—he's hit the target!

SOSIAS

(*moving to Myrrhine's door*)

             I'll knock on
The door.
(*At this point Daos comes forward and intercepts
Sosias.*)

DAOS

      You wretch, what do you want? Where are
You going?

SOSIAS

     Are you from there?

DAOS

          Perhaps. But why are [you]
Intruding?

411

ΣΩΣΙΑΣ

375 ἀπονενόησθε, πρὸς θεῶν; [ἐλ]ευθέραν
ἔχειν γυναῖκα πρὸς β[ία]ν τοῦ κυρί[ου
(187) τολμᾶτε κατακλείσαντες;

ΔΑΟΣ

ὡς πο[νηρὸς εἶ
καὶ συκοφάντης, ὃς το[ιαῦθ᾽ ὑπολαμβάνεις.

ΣΩΣΙΑΣ

πότερα νομίζετ᾽ οὐκ ἔχειν ἡ[μᾶς χολὴν
380 οὐδ᾽ ἄνδρας εἶναι;

ΔΑΟΣ

ναὶ μὰ Δία, τε[τρω]βό[λους.
ὅταν δὲ τετράδραχμος τοιούτ[ους ἀνα]λάβ[ῃ,
(192) ἢ ῥᾳδίως μαχούμεθ᾽ ὑμῖν.

ΣΩΣΙΑΣ

Ἡ[ράκλ]ε[ις,
πράγματος [ἀ]σελγοῦ[ς· ὁ]μολ[ο]γεῖτε δ᾽, εἰπέ
μ[οι,
ἔχειν; πρόσ]ελθ᾽, ἄνθρ[ω]φ᾽ [ὁ π]αριών· οἴχετ[αι

375 Deciph. and suppl. Wilamowitz. 376 β[ία]ν suppl.
Körte, κυρί[ου Leo, Wilamowitz. 377, 378 Suppl. Jensen.
379 ἡ[μᾶς suppl. Körte, χολὴν Wilamowitz. 380 Suppl. Sud-
haus. 381 τετραδραχμοις with ι scored out C. τοιούτ[ους
suppl. Schmidt, ἀνα]λάβ[ῃ Arnott. 382 Suppl. Jensen.
383 [ἀ]σελγοῦ[ς deciph. and suppl. Jensen, the rest Sudhaus.
384 ἔχειν and οἴχετ[αι suppl. Sudhaus, πρόσ]ελθ᾽ Koenen,
ἄνθρ[ω]φ᾽ [ὁ π]αριών Rea (ἄνθρ[ω]π᾽ already Sudhaus).

SOSIAS

Heavens, are you insane? You dare   375
To hold a girl who's free behind locked doors, against
Her guardian's[a] [will]?

DAOS

What a [scoundrel you are],
And filthy liar, with [assumptions of that sort]!

SOSIAS

Do you think [we]'re not [hot-blooded], or
Real men?

DAOS

By Zeus, yes—worth [four]pence a day.[b]   380
And when a tinpot[c] officer leads men like that,
We'll fight you without trouble!

SOSIAS

[Heracles], what an
Outrageous business! Tell me though, do you admit
You've got her?

(*Sosias now addresses an unidentified free man who
either walks across the stage at this point as a mute or is
imagined to pass nearby.*)

---

[a] Under Athenian law a free woman had no legal independence; before marriage she was under the control of her nearest relative (her father if still alive), after marriage under that of her husband. Sosias here, perhaps improperly, assigns the rights of an Athenian husband to Glykera's Corinthian lover.

[b] Literally 4 obols (2/3 of a drachma), apparently the lowest rate of daily pay for a mercenary at that time.

[c] Literally one who was paid 4 drachmas a day, implying that Polemon was an officer of the lowest rank.

385   φυ[γὼ]ν ὃς ἦλ[θ]ε μάρτυ[ς. ὁμ]ολογεῖτ᾽ ἔχειν;

ΔΑΟΣ

οὐκ [ἔχομεν.]

ΣΩΣΙΑΣ

[ἀλλ᾽ ἔ]στ᾽ ἔν[δον. ὄ]ψ[ο]μαί τινας
(197)   ὑμῶν [στένον]τας. πρὸς τίν᾽ οἴεσθ᾽, εἰπέ μοι,
παίζειν; [τίς] ὁ λῆρος; κατὰ κράτος τὸ δυστυχὲς
οἰκίδιον τ[ο]ῦτ᾽ αὐτίκ᾽ ἐξαιρ[ήσ]ομεν.
390   ὅπλιζε τὸν μοιχόν.

ΔΑΟΣ

πονηρόν, ἄθλιε.
ὥσπερ παρ᾽ ἡμῖν οὖσαν ἐπι[μ]ένεις πάλαι.

ΣΩΣΙΑΣ

(202)   οἱ παῖδες οἱ τὰ πελτί᾽ οὗτοι πρὶν πτύσαι
διαρπάσονται πάντα, κἂν τετρωβόλους
καλῇς.

ΔΑΟΣ

ἔπαιζον· σκατοφάγ[ο]ς γὰρ εἶ.

385 φυ[γὼ]ν ὃς ἦλ[θ]ε deciph. and suppl. Koenen, μάρτυ[ς
Jensen.   386 ἔχομεν suppl. Jensen, [ἀλλ᾽ ἔ]στ᾽ ἔν[δον
Arnott, ὄ]ψ[ο]μαι deciph. and suppl. Lefebvre.   387 Suppl.
van Leeuwen.   388 Suppl. Leo.   391 Suppl. Körte.
392 οὗτοι deciph. Guéraud.

---

[a] Such an appeal for a passer-by to act as witness of an illegal
act (as alleged in 376 f.) was a common practice in Athenian law;

414

You sir, you who're passing! A
Witness[a]—he's come and rushed away!
(*He turns to address Daos again.*)

                              Do you admit you've got   385
Her?

DAOS

No, [we haven't.]

SOSIAS

         [But] she's in there! I'll see that some
Of you'll [be sorry]! Tell me, who do you think
You're playing with? [What]'s this foolery? We'll take
This wretched shack by storm in a few seconds!
So arm the fancy man!

DAOS

              A bad case, you   390
Poor fellow! You've been here so long, believing
She's in our house.

SOSIAS

         These young commandos[b] will
Smash everything before you can spit, even though
You call them fourpenny men.

DAOS

                That was a joke. You are
A shit!

see J. R. Rea, *ZPE*, 16 (1975), 128 f. On the staging here see
K. B. Frost, *Exits and Entrances in Menander* (Oxford 1988), 94.

[b] Literally 'light-shield boys', i.e. peltasts, the best contempo-
rary soldiers, who were armed with light shields, a sword and
either two javelins or the long pike with a heavy point and metal
foot which is mentioned in 396.

ΣΩΣΙΑΣ

πόλιν

395   οἰκοῦντες—

ΔΑΟΣ

ἀλλ' οὐκ ἔχομε[ν].

ΣΩΣΙΑΣ

[α]ἰ[β]οῖ, λήψομαι

σάρισαν.

ΔΑΟΣ

ἄπαγ' ἐς κόρακας· [ὡ]ς εἴσειμ' ἐγώ,

(207)   ἕως ἔοικας α[ὐθεκάσ]τῳ.

ΔΩΡΙΣ

Σωσία.

ΔΑΟΣ

σὺ] μὲν εἶ πρό[σει μ]οι, Δωρί, μέγα τί σοι κακὸν

δ]ώσω· σὺ τ[ού]των γέγονας α[ἰ]τιωτάτη.

ΔΩΡΙΣ

400   οὕ]τως ὄναιο, λέγ' ὅτι πρὸς γυναικά ποι

δεί]σασα κατ[α]πέφευγε.

ΣΩΣΙΑΣ

πρὸς γυναικά ποι

(212)   δει]σασα;

ΔΩΡΙΣ

καὶ γὰρ οἴχεθ' ὡς τὴν Μυρρίν[η]ν,

395 [α]ἰ[β]οῖ suppl. Sudhaus.   396 [ὡ]ς suppl. Körte, Wilamo-
witz.   397 Suppl. Jensen.   398 Suppl. Sudhaus.   399 δ]ώσω

SOSIAS

So civilised!

DAOS

We haven't got   395

Her!

SOSIAS

Huh! I'll get a pike.

DAOS

You go to hell! You are

Behaving like [a lout]. I'm off in.

(Exit Daos into Myrrhine's house. Doris now either enters from Polemon's house or more probably comes forward from the doorway where she has been standing since 365.)

DORIS

Sosias!

SOSIAS

If you come near me, Doris, I'll give you
What for! You've been responsible for this!

DORIS

Bless you, tell him she's run off [in a fright]   400
To a lady somewhere.

SOSIAS

[In a fright], to a lady

Somewhere?

DORIS

In fact—so may my dreams come true! —

---

suppl. von Arnim, Körte.   400, 401 Suppl. Housman.   402
δεί]σασα suppl. several. Μυρρίν[η]ν Lefebvre: μυρρην[.]ν C.

τὴν] γείτον', οὕτω μο[ι] γένοιθ' ἃ βούλομαι.

ΣΩΣΙΑΣ

ὁρᾷ]ς ἵν' οἴχεθ'; οὗ τὸ μέλημ' ἐστ', ἐνθά[δ]ε.

ΔΩΡΙΣ

405   οὐ]δὲ[ν π]οεῖ [ν]ῦν [ὧ]ν σύ βούλει, Σ[ωσία.

ΣΩΣΙΑΣ

406   ἄπ[αγ]ε σε[αυτή]ν, ἀ[πα]γ', [ἐπεὶ ψ]ευδῆ λ[έγεις

(After 406 one leaf of the Cairo papyrus is missing; this
would have contained between 66 and 74 lines of text,
most probably 68 or 69, as well as the normal indication
for a choral intermission between acts II and III. *P.Oxy.*
2830 preserves the final letters of three unplaced lines in
that gap:]οπως,].ν:,].σ.

The final 13 of the lines lost in the Cairo papyrus, how-
ever, are preserved at the beginning of the Leipzig parch-
ment (L), which overlaps the next extant leaf of that
papyrus. Hence the lacuna between 406 and 467 can be
computed more accurately as between 53 and 61 lines,
most probably 55 or 56.)

ΜΕΡΟΣ Γ´

(The opening lines of the act are lost.)

404 ὁρᾷ]ς suppl. Sudhaus.   405 οὐ]δὲ[ν π]οεῖ suppl. Sand-
bach, [ν]ῦν [ὧ]ν Sudhaus, Σ[ωσία Jensen.   406 [ἐπεὶ] suppl.
Sudhaus, ψ]ευδῆ Jensen, λ[έγεις Sandbach.

She's gone to Myrrhine, who lives next door.

SOSIAS

(*pointing to Myrrhine's door*)
You [notice] where she's gone—there, where her dar-
ling
Lives!

DORIS

Sosias, she's doing none of what you have   405
In mind!

SOSIAS

Away with you, away! [You're telling] lies . . .

(*At 406 Sosias and Doris are still arguing; it is unlikely
that their quarrel went on much longer—perhaps 20 to 30
verses—or that it was resolved satisfactorily. At its close
Sosias would have departed by the left parodos in order to
tell Polemon about Glykera's move into Myrrhine's house
and possibly also to suggest that Polemon and he should
return immediately with an 'army' intended to bring Gly-
kera back into Polemon's house by force. Doris would
either have re-entered Polemon's house or more probably
have gone off to seek help from Pataikos, who had already
befriended Glykera (see 508 f.). Then would have come
the choral entr'acte.*)

(*An Oxyrhynchus papyrus seems to preserve the word
how as the last word of a line in the lacuna between lines
406 and 467.*)

ACT III

(*In the lost opening lines of Act III—perhaps 26 to 36
verses—Polemon and Sosias would have entered with*)

ΣΩΣΙΑΣ

467 ἐκ]εῖθεν ἥκει χρήματ' εἰληφώς, ἐμοὶ
(218) πίστευε· προδίδωσίν σε καὶ τὸ στρατ[ό]πεδον.

ΠΑΤΑΙΚΟΣ

κάθευδ' ἀπελθών, ὦ μακάριε, τὰς μά[χ]ας
470 τ]αύτας ἐάσας· [οὐ]χ ὑγιαίνεις. σοὶ λαλῶ·
ἧττον μεθύεις γά[ρ].

ΠΟΛΕΜΩΝ

ἧττον; ὃς πέπωκ' ἴσως
(222) κοτύλην, προειδὼς πάντα ταῦθ' ὁ δυστυχὴς
τηρῶν τ' ἐμαυτὸν εἰς τὸ μέλλον.

ΠΑΤΑΙΚΟΣ

εὖ λέγεις·

πείσθητί μοι.

467–527 preserved in L (467–479 lost in C). 467–474 Suppl.
Körte. 471 ως corr. to ος L. 473–492 O preserves the
beginnings of these lines.

ᵃ 'He' clearly = Pataikos, and 'from there' probably = from
Myrrhine's house. In the previous scene, however, Sosias' allega-
tions are sometimes wild and unreliable (e.g. 392–394, 399), and
we cannot infer from his words here that Pataikos has now
entered from Myrrhine's house, only that he appears to have
been on good terms with Myrrhine and her family as well as with
Polemon and Glykera.

their 'army', consisting in all probability of no more than
a couple more male slaves, the female piper Habrotonon,
all of them mutes and presumably belonging or invited to
the household where Polemon had been staying after he
had cut off Glykera's hair; a possibility that a hired cook
with his pig was in the party is discussed below in the note
on 995 f. When the text resumes at 467 Pataikos is on
stage with them, attempting to persuade this ragtag army
to substitute reasoned argument for drunken violence.
We do not know why Pataikos intervened at this stage. He
may have entered with the 'army' at the beginning of the
act, or come on later in answer to a summons from Doris.)

SOSIAS

(*to Polemon*)
He's come from there; believe me, he's been bribed![a]   467
He'll be a traitor to the army and yourself.

PATAIKOS

(*to Sosias*)
My friend, you'd better leave, and drop these raids.
Go and lie down. You're mad.
(*turning now to Polemon*)
                                    I'm talking to   470
You —you're less drunk!

POLEMON
                        Less? Half a pint or so
Is all I've drunk! Oh dear, I knew all this
Would happen. I was keeping tabs upon
Myself, in case.

PATAIKOS
Good. Follow my advice.

MENANDER

ΠΟΛΕΜΩΝ

τί δ' ἐστὶν ὃ κελεύεις ἐμοί;

ΠΑΤΑΙΚΟΣ

475　ὀρθῶς μ' ἐρωτᾷς· νῦν ἐγὼ δὴ τἆλλ' ἐρῶ.

ΣΩΣΙΑΣ

Ἀβρότονον, ἐπισήμηνον.

ΠΑΤΑΙΚΟΣ

εἴσω τουτονὶ

(227)　πρῶτον ἀπόπεμψον τούς τε παῖδας οὓς ἄγει.

ΣΩΣΙΑΣ

κακῶς γε πολεμεῖς· τὸν πόλεμον διαλύσεται,
ἐξὸν λαβεῖν κατὰ κράτος.

ΠΟΛΕΜΩΝ

οὑτοσί με γὰρ

480　ὁ Πάταικος ἐξόλλυσιν.

ΣΩΣΙΑΣ

οὐκ ἔσθ' ἡγεμών.

ΠΑΤΑΙΚΟΣ

πρὸς τῶν θεῶν, ἄνθρωπ', ἄπελθ'.

476 Kock fr. 1011

475 μ' om. L, νῦν om. O. τἆλλ' deciph. Gomme.　476 Para-
graphus in L, om. O.　478 Paragraphus wrongly inserted by
O.　γεπολεμεις O, γε{ι}πολεμεις above the line L[2]: διοικεις
L[1].　διαλυσεται L[1]: -λυεται L[2], -λυετε L[3].　479 Para-
graphus in L, om. O.　εξον O: δεον L, deciph. D. Müller.
479–481 Attribution and division of parts uncertain.
480 Here C resumes. ο[.]αταικος L: παταικος without article
O, ...]κος C.　481–486 Line openings torn off in C, end-
ings often torn or illegible in L.

POLEMON

What will you have me do?

PATAIKOS

            Good question. I'll   475

Say now what still needs saying —

SOSIAS

(*interrupting*)

                  Sound the attack,

Habrotonon.

PATAIKOS

(*addressing Polemon, and attempting to stop Habro-*
tonon as she prepares to play her pipes in obedience to
this command.)

            Get rid of him indoors

First, and the crew he's brought.

SOSIAS

               You're wrecking our

Campaign. He'll end the war, when we could force

A capture!

POLEMON

      Yes, because Pataikos here   480

Is sabotaging —

SOSIAS

(*interrupting*)

           He's not our commander![a]

PATAIKOS

In gods' name, man, be off!

---

[a] Division and assignment of parts here are uncertain.

MENANDER

ΣΩΣΙΑΣ

ἀπέρχομαι.

(232) ᾤμην σε ποιήσειν τι. καὶ γάρ, Ἁβρότονον,
ἔχεις τι πρὸς πολιορκίαν σὺ χρήσιμον,
δύνασαί τ᾽ ἀναβαίνειν, περικαθῆσθαι. ποῖ στρέφει,

485 λαικάστρι᾽; ᾐσχύνθης; μέλει τούτων τί σοι;

ΠΑΤΑΙΚΟΣ

εἰ μέν τι τοιοῦτ᾽ ἦν, Πολέμων, οἷόν φατε
(237) ὑμεῖς τὸ γεγονός, καὶ γαμετὴν γυναῖκά σου—

ΠΟΛΕΜΩΝ

οἷον λέγεις, Πάταικε.

ΠΑΤΑΙΚΟΣ

διαφέρει δέ τι.

ΠΟΛΕΜΩΝ

ἐγὼ γαμετὴν νενόμικα ταύτην.

ΠΑΤΑΙΚΟΣ

μὴ βόα.

490 τίς δ᾽ ἔσθ᾽ ὁ δούς;

ΠΟΛΕΜΩΝ

ἐμοὶ τίς; αὐτή.

---

486 τι om. O.   πολεμων L: ωπολεμων C.   488 L omits para-
graphus.   490 δ᾽ om. CL.

---

[a] Jokes involving a sexual *double entendre* are rare in Menan-
der: see the Gomme–Sandbach commentary *ad loc.* Here ἀνα-
βαίνειν combines the meanings 'to climb (a wall)' and 'to mount
(a sexual partner)', περικαθῆσαι 'to besiege' and 'to embrace'.

424

SOSIAS
I'm off.

(*Sosias now turns first to address Polemon, then Habro-tonon.*)

I thought
You'd manage something. Look, Habrotonon —
You're handy in blockades—can climb erections,
And squeeze . . .[a] You tart, where are you going?　　　485
　　　Embarrassed?
Something I've said offends you?

(*At this Habrotonon flounces off into Polemon's house, fol-lowed by Sosias and the other slaves, leaving Polemon and Pataikos alone on stage together.*)

PATAIKOS
If the event
At all resembled your description, Polemon,
With her being married to you —

POLEMON
What a thing
To say, Pataikos!

PATAIKOS
It's important.

POLEMON
(*angrily*)
I've
Treated her as my wife.

PATAIKOS
Don't shout. Who gave　　　490
Her?

POLEMON
Who? To me? *She* did, herself.

425

ΠΑΤΑΙΚΟΣ

πάνυ καλῶς.

ἤρεσκες αὐτῇ τυχὸν ἴσως, νῦν δ' οὐκέτι.

(242) ἀπελήλυθε[ν δ'] οὐ κατὰ τρόπον σοῦ χρωμένου
αὐτῇ.

ΠΟΛΕΜΩΝ

τί φής; οὐ κατὰ τρόπον; τουτί με τῶν
πάντων λελύπηκας μάλιστ' εἰπών.

ΠΑΤΑΙΚΟΣ

ἐρᾷς,

495 τοῦτ' οἶδ' ἀκριβῶς, ὥσθ' ὃ μὲν νυνὶ ποεῖς
ἀπόπληκτόν ἐστιν. ποῖ φέρει γάρ; ἢ τίνα

(247) ἄξων; ἑαυτῆς ἐστ' ἐκείνη κυρία.
λοιπὸν τὸ πείθειν τῷ κακῶς διακειμένῳ
ἐρῶντί τ' ἐστίν.

ΠΟΛΕΜΩΝ

ὁ δὲ διεφθαρκὼς ἐμοῦ

500 ἀπόντος αὐτὴν οὐκ ἀδικεῖ μ';

ΠΑΤΑΙΚΟΣ

ὥστ' ἐγκαλεῖν
ἀδικεῖ σ' ἐκεῖνος, ἄν ποτ' ἔλθῃς εἰς λόγους.

(252) εἰ δ' ἐκβιάσει, δίκην δ' ὀφλήσεις· οὐκ ἔχει
τιμωρίαν γὰρ τἀδίκημ', ἔγκλημα δέ.

---

492 απεληλυθ'ου C, απεληλυθε....κατ. L: suppl. van Leeuwen.
At 492 O breaks off.   494 ερεις CL: corr. van Leeuwen.   496 ποι
L: που C. C wrongly has a paragraphus under this line.

PATAIKOS

All right. Perhaps
She liked you—now she doesn't any more.
She's left because you've treated her so badly!

POLEMON

What's that? So badly? With those words you've hurt
Me most of all.

PATAIKOS

You are in love, of that   495
I'm certain, so your present conduct's crazy.

(*Here Polemon turns away and makes for Myrrhine's
house, where Glykera has taken refuge.*)

Where *are* you going? Who for? She's her own mistress!
Unhappy men in love have only got
One remedy—persuasion.

POLEMON

Her seducer in
My absence, though—he's wronged me, hasn't he?   500

PATAIKOS

He's wronged you, so lodge a complaint, if you
Can meet and talk. Use force, though, and you'll lose
Your case! This wrong doesn't call for a reprisal,
But a complaint.[a]

---

[a] Such a 'complaint' could involve a private law-suit (see
A. R. W. Harrison, *The Law of Athens: Procedure* (Oxford 1971),
88), informal discussion with the alleged wrongdoer, or even
private retaliation within the law (cf. the Gomme–Sandbach
commentary *ad loc.*).

ΠΟΛΕΜΩΝ

οὐδ' ἄρα νῦν;

ΠΑΤΑΙΚΟΣ

οὐδ' ἄρα νῦν.

ΠΟΛΕΜΩΝ

οὐκ οἶδ' ὅ τι

505   λέγω, μὰ τὴν Δήμητρα, πλὴν ἀπάγξομαι.
Γλυκέρα με καταλέλοιπε, καταλέλοιπέ με
(257)   Γλυκέρα, Πάταικ'. ἀλλ' εἴπερ οὕτω σοι δοκεῖ
πράττειν—συνήθης ἦσθα γὰρ καὶ πολλάκις
λελάληκας αὐτῇ πρότερον—ἐλθὼν διαλέγου,
510   πρέσβευσον, ἱκετεύω σε.

ΠΑΤΑΙΚΟΣ

τοῦτό μοι δοκεῖ,

ὁρᾷς, ποεῖν.

ΠΟΛΕΜΩΝ

δύνασαι δὲ δήπουθεν λέγειν,

(262)   Πάταικε.

ΠΑΤΑΙΚΟΣ

μετρίως.

ΠΟΛΕΜΩΝ

ἀλλὰ μήν, Πάταικε, δεῖ.
αὕτη 'στιν ἡ σωτηρία τοῦ πράγματος.
ἐγὼ γὰρ εἴ τι πώποτ' ἠδίκηχ' ὅλως,
515   εἰ μὴ διατελῶ πάντα φιλοτιμούμενος,
τὸν κόσμον αὐτῆς εἰ θεωρήσαις—

POLEMON

Not even now?

PATAIKOS

                Not even now.

POLEMON

I don't know, by Demeter, what to say, except   505
I'll choke! Pataikos, Glykera has left
Me, left me—Glykera! But if you settle
On action—you were friendly, in the past
You've often talked to her—well, go and talk
To her, be my ambassador, I beg   510
You!

PATAIKOS

That's a good idea, you know.

POLEMON

                  Of course you're good

With words, Pataikos.

PATAIKOS

Fairly.

POLEMON

             It's so vital,

Pataikos. All success in this attempt
Depends on it! You see, if I have ever
At all wronged her . . . if I don't keep on trying   515
My best, in every way . . . if you could see her things . . .

---

510 δοκεις C with ς crossed out.   515 L wrongly puts a dicolon after φιλοτιμουμενος.

MENANDER

ΠΑΤΑΙΚΟΣ

καλῶς

(267)   ἔχει.

ΠΟΛΕΜΩΝ

θεώρησον, Πάταικε, πρὸς θεῶν·
μᾶλλον μ' ἐλεήσεις.

ΠΑΤΑΙΚΟΣ

ὦ Πόσειδο[ν].

ΠΟΛΕΜΩΝ

[δ]εῦρ' ἴθι.

ἐνδύμαθ' οἶ'· οἷα δὲ φαίνεθ' ἡνίκ' ἂν
520   λάβῃ τι τούτων. οὐ γὰρ ἑοράκεις ἴσως.

ΠΑΤΑΙΚΟΣ

ἔγωγε.

ΠΟΛΕΜΩΝ

καὶ γὰρ τὸ μέγεθος δήπουθεν ἦν
(272)   ἄξιον ἰδεῖν. ἀλλὰ τί φέρω νῦν εἰς μέσον
τὸ μέγεθος, ἐμβρόντητος, ὑπὲρ ἄλλων λαλῶν—

ΠΑΤΑΙΚΟΣ

μὰ Δί', οὐδέν.

ΠΟΛΕΜΩΝ

οὐ γάρ; ἀλλὰ δεῖ, Πάταικέ, σε
525   ἰδεῖν. βάδιζε δεῦρο.

---

518 ποσιδ[C, ποσιδο[...]ευρ'ιθι L: suppl. Körte.   520 εορα-
κεις with ω written above ο L, εωρακεις C.   521 εγωγε: L,
εγωσ: corrected to εγωγ: C.   523 λαλῶ L (= -ων): λαλω C

430

PATAIKOS

No need for that!

POLEMON

Just look, Pataikos, *please* —
You'll pity me the more!

PATAIKOS

In heaven's name!

POLEMON

(*walking towards his door*)

Do
Come here—such dresses! How she looks when she
Slips one of these on! Perhaps you won't have seen . . .   520

PATAIKOS

I have.

POLEMON

Of course her height's remarkable—but why
Should I now introduce her height? I'm crazy,
Going on about irrelevances!

PATAIKOS

No,
Heavens, no!

POLEMON

No? Yet, Pataikos, you should see
Them. Walk this way!

(see F. H. Sandbach, *ZPE*, 40 (1981), 51).   524 ματονδιουδεν-
ουγαρ LC, then αλ[...]ειγεσε L, αλλαδειπαταικεσε C: corr.
Sudhaus.

MENANDER

ΠΑΤΑΙΚΟΣ

πάραγ'· εἰσέρχομαι.

ΜΟΣΧΙΩΝ

οὐκ εἰσφθερεῖσθε θᾶττον ὑμεῖς ἐκποδών;
(277) λόγχας ἔχοντες ἐκπεπηδήκασί μοι.
οὐκ ἂν δύναιντο δ' ἐξελεῖν νεοττιὰν
χελιδόνων· οἷοι γάρ εἰσ' οἱ βάσκανοι.
530 ἀλλὰ ξένους, φήσ', εἶχον· εἰσὶ δ' οἱ ξένοι
οἱ περιβόητοι Σωσίας εἷς οὑτοσί.
(282) πολλῶν γεγονότων ἀθλίων κατὰ τὸν χρόνον
τὸν νῦν—φορὰ γὰρ γέγονε τούτου νῦν καλὴ
ἐν ἅπασι τοῖς Ἕλλησι δι' ὅ τι δή ποτε—
535 οὐδένα νομίζω τῶν τοσούτων ἄθλιον
ἄνθρωπον οὕτως ὡς ἐμαυτὸν ζῆν ἐγώ.
(287) ὡς γὰρ τάχιστ' εἰσῆλθον, οὐδὲν ὧν ἀεὶ
εἴωθ' [ἐ]ποίου[ν], οὐδὲ πρὸς τὴν μητέρα
εἰσῆλθ[ο]ν, οὐ τῶν ἔνδον ἐκάλεσ' οὐδένα

533 Kock fr. 872

525 :παραγ: C, :παρα[. . .]σερχομαι L with no space for dicolon
in the gap. After 527 L ceases.   528 δ'ανεξελειν C: corr.
several.   529 γαρεὶσ' (rather than παρεὶσ') C: see J. R. Rea,
ZPE, 16 (1975), 131.   533–534 Philoponus' commentary on
Arist. *Meteor.* p. 94 Hayduck quotes inaccurately with φορὰ γὰρ
νῦν τούτου γέγονε καλή, δι'ὅτι δή ποτε.

PATAIKOS
Move on, I'm coming in.   525

(*Polemon and Pataikos go off into Polemon's house. Moschion now enters from Myrrhine's house and observes their departure. Although his opening remarks are ostensibly addressed to them, he probably waits until they are out of earshot before he opens his mouth.*)

MOSCHION
You get to hell in there! Out of my way,
And hurry! Armed with pikes they were, and yet
I've made them scuttle off. *They* couldn't wipe
A nest of swallows out—what pansies these
Devils are! They'd got mercenaries, he[a] said—   530
These celebrated mercenaries amount
To Sosias here[b] and no one else! Of all
The many creatures born to misery
These days—of *that* there is a noble crop
All over Greece now, from some cause or other[c]—   535
In my view, no one out of all that number
Endures a life as miserable as mine.
You see, as soon as I went in, I didn't
Do any of my usual things, I didn't
Go up to mother, or call one of the   540

[a] Daos presumably, who left the stage and departed into Myrrhine's house at 397, and there described to Moschion the attack on Myrrhine's house by Polemon's 'army' which he had witnessed.

[b] Here presumably the speaker points to Polemon's house; see J. R. Rea, *ZPE*, 16 (1975), 131, and K. B. Frost, *Exits and Entrances in Menander* (Oxford 1988), 96 n. 17.

[c] Compare vv. 124 f. and see the introduction to this play.

540 πρὸς ἐμαυτόν, ἀλλ' εἰς οἶκον ἐλθὼν ἐκποδὼν
ἐνταῦθα κ[α]τεκ[ε]ίμην συνεστηκὼς πάνυ.

(292) τὸν Δᾶον εἰσπέμπω δὲ δηλώσονθ' ὅτι
ἥκω, τοσοῦτον αὐτό, πρὸς τὴν μητέρα.
οὗτος μὲν οὖν μικρόν τι φροντίσας ἐμοῦ

545 ἄριστον αὐτοῖς καταλαβὼν παρακείμενον
ἐγέμιζεν αὐτόν. ἐν δὲ τούτῳ τῷ χρόνῳ

(297) κατακείμενος πρὸς ἐμαυτὸν ἔλεγον· "αὐτίκα
πρόσεισιν ἡ μήτηρ <ἀπ>αγγελοῦσά μοι
παρὰ τῆς ἐρωμένης ἐφ' οἷς ἄν φησί μοι

550 εἰς ταὐτὸν ἐλθεῖν." αὐτὸς ἐμελέτων λόγον

(After line 550 four and a half pages of the Cairo papyrus
have been lost, producing a gap in the text of between 153
and 172 lines, in which the third act ended and the fourth
began.)

ΜΕΡΟΣ Δ´

(The opening of the act is lost.)

540 αλλ'εισοικοντιν'ελθων C: τιν' del. Lefebvre.
548 αγγελουσα C: corr. Croenert, Sudhaus.

---

[a] On this translation of συνεστηκώς see M. Gronewald, ZPE,
107 (1995), 58.

House servants—no, I found a room away
From everyone, I lay there all on edge,[a]
And sent in Daos to my mother to
Say I was home, just that. But little heed
Paid he to me—on finding lunch out on   545
The tables for the family, he stuffed
Himself, and all this time I lay there, telling
Myself "Soon mother will be here to bring
A message from my love with her terms for
A rendezvous." I practised what I'd say . . .   550

(It is impossible to work out in detail what the following lacuna contained, but a few hints are provided by references in extant passages of the play. Moschion's monologue must have gone on to explain why 'no one . . . endures a life as miserable' (537) as his. Either Glykera or (more probably) Myrrhine must have told Moschion that an affair with Glykera was out of the question, but we do not know how far the truth about Glykera and his parentage was then divulged as a reason to prevent it. When Moschion reappears at line 774 he now knows that Myrrhine was only his foster mother and that he and a previously unknown twin-sister were foundlings, and he suspects that Glykera may be that twin-sister, but it is uncertain what he has been told directly, and what he has worked out for himself.)

ACT IV

(When the text resumes at line 708, Glykera is talking to Pataikos and defending herself from the charge that infatuation for Moschion led to her move from Polemon's to Myrrhine's house. She goes on to say that in Polemon's house she has evidence about the identity of her true

MENANDER

ΓΛΥΚΕΡΑ

(in mid-speech)

708
πρὸς τὴν μ]ητέρ' αὐτοῦ, φί[λτ]ατε,

(302)
κα]ταφυγοῦσ' ἐδυνάμην, οὐ σκοπεῖς;

710
ἵν]α με λ[άβῃ] γυναῖκα; κατ' ἐμὲ γὰρ πάνυ
γέγ]ον' οὗ[τος]. ἀλλ' οὐ τοῦθ', ἑταίραν δ' ἵνα μ'
ἔχῃ;

(305)
εἶτ' οὐ λαθεῖν τούτους ἂν ἔσπευδον, τάλαν,
αὐτός [τ'] ἐκεῖνος, ἀλλ' ἰταμῶς εἰς ταὐτό με
τῷ πατρὶ κατέστησ'; εἱλόμην δ' οὕτως ἐγ[ὼ

715
ἀφρόνως ἔχειν ἔχθραν τε πράτ[τειν Μυρρίνη,
ὑμῖν θ' ὑπόνοιαν καταλιπεῖν [ἀκοσμίας,

(310)
ἣν οὐκέτ' ἐξαλείψατ', οὐδ' αἰσχ[ύνομαι,
Πάταικε; καὶ σὺ ταῦτα συμπεπ[εισμένος
ἦλθες τ[ο]ιαύτην θ' ὑπέλαβές [με γεγονέναι;

708 πρὸς τὴν μ]ητέρ' suppl. Sudhaus, φί[λτ]ατε deciph. and
suppl. Jensen.   709 Suppl. Leo.   710–711 Suppl. Sudhaus.
τουτ' C.   713 Suppl. Leo.   715 πράτ[τειν suppl. Wila-
mowitz and Schmidt, Μυρρίνη Meister.   716 Suppl. Körte.
717 εξαλειψαιτ'ουκετ' C: ἐξαλείψετ' Gomme, transposition by
Sandbach. αἰσχ[ύνομαι suppl. Leo.   718 Suppl. Sudhaus.
719 Suppl. Körte.

parents (742–744). At this point Pataikos is unaware that
he is Glykera's and Moschion's father. When he left the
stage with Polemon at 525 he had agreed to enter the lat-
ter's house in order to see Glykera's wardrobe; he is likely
to have emerged again, perhaps at or very near the end of
the third act, having offered (or been persuaded by Pole-
mon) to visit Myrrhine and/or Glykera and seek on Pole-
mon's behalf a reconciliation. In that event Pataikos and
Glykera could have entered from Myrrhine's house in
mid-conversation at the beginning of the fourth act, an
indeterminate number of lines before 708.)

GLYKERA

(*in mid-speech*)
— [and what] could I [have done], my dear,   708
By running [to his] mother? Ask yourself—
Was it [to make him] marry me? His standing's just   710
Like mine, of course![a] No. Was it, though, to make me
His mistress? Wouldn't I then have sought, along with
     him,
To hide it from his people? Would he recklessly
Have lodged me with his father[b]? Wouldn't this mean
I chose to be a fool, turn [Myrrhine]   715
Against me, plant in you suspicions [of]
[Misconduct] that you'll never drop? Nor [I]
Feel any shame, Pataikos? And you came
Believ[ing] this, assuming [I'm] like that?

[a] A subtle irony. Glykera sarcastically pretends that she,
brought up in poverty (cf. 125 f.) and lately a soldier's concubine,
has the same status as Moschion, raised in a wealthy household
(122), but behind that pretence there is the reality of their being
twins.   [b] She means Myrrhine's husband. See the introduc-
tion to the play.

ΠΑΤΑΙΚΟΣ

720　μὴ δὴ [γ]ένοιτ', ὦ Ζεῦ πολυ[τίμηθ'· ἃ δὲ λέγεις
　　 δείξαις ἀληθῶς ὄντ'· ἐγὼ [δὲ πείθομαι.

ΓΛΥΚΕΡΑ

(315)　ἀλλ' ἄπιθι μηδὲν ἧττον. [εἰς ἑτέραν τινὰ
　　 ὑβριζέτω τὸ λοιπόν.

ΠΑΤΑΙΚΟΣ
　　　　　　　οὐχ [ἑκούσιον
　　 γέγ[ο]νε τὸ δεινόν.

ΓΛΥΚΕΡΑ
　　　　　　ἀνόσιο[ν
725　ο[　　, τά]λαν, θεράπαιναν [

(After line 725 there is a lacuna of most probably 15 to 18
verses, covering the top half of the other side of the sheet
which contained 708–725. When the text returns, Glykera
is still conversing with Pataikos.)

ΓΛΥΚΕΡΑ
(in mid-speech?)

742　ἐγ[ὼ δ' ἐκεῖν' ἐ]λάμβα[νον· γνωρίσματ' ἦν
(320)　τοὐμοῦ πατρὸς καὶ μητρός. εἴ[θισμαι δ' ἔχειν
　　 ἀεὶ παρ' ἐμαυτῇ ταῦτα καὶ τηρ[εῖν.

ΠΑΤΑΙΚΟΣ
　　　　　　　　　　　　τ]ί οὖν
745　βούλει;

720 πολυ[τίμητ' originally suppl. Lefebvre, ἃ δὲ λέγεις
Schwartz.　　721 δὲ suppl. Schwartz, πείθομαι Wilamowitz,
Schwartz.　722–723 Suppl. Sudhaus.　724–725 Suppl. Sudhaus,

PATAIKOS

O [blessed] Zeus, not that! I'd like you to   720
Prove [what you say] is true. I [do believe you.]

GLYKERA

Well, all the same, you must go back. Let him
Assault [another girl] in future.

PATAIKOS

           This
Outrage was not [deliberate].   724

*(The last fragment of text on this page is too broken to
provide continuous sense. In replying to Pataikos' last
remark Glykera uses the word* wicked, *probably with ref-
erence to the outrage, and in the next line she says some-
thing about a* servant girl, poor me. *Then there is a lacuna
of probably 15 to 18 lines, during which Glykera passes
from a defence of her recent behaviour to a discussion of
her parentage.)*

GLYKERA

(perhaps in mid-speech)
[These] I received. [They were mementoes] of   742
My father and mother. [I've] always kept
Them by me [as a rule], looked after them.

PATAIKOS

So what do you want?

---

van Leeuwen.   742 ἐ[γὼ δ' ἐκεῖν' ἐ]λάμβα[νον suppl. Körte
(but ἐγὼ δ' ἐκεῖνα also Sudhaus). γνωρίσματ' ἦν suppl. Arnott
(γνωρίσματα van Leeuwen).   743 Suppl. Sudhaus (δ' ἔχειν
also Wilamowitz).   744 Suppl. Lefebvre.

ΓΛΥΚΕΡΑ

κομίσασθαι ταῦτ'.

ΠΑΤΑΙΚΟΣ

[ἀπέγν]ωκας σ[ὺ γὰρ
κομιδῇ τὸν ἄνθρωπον; τί βούλει;

ΓΛΥΚΕΡΑ

φίλτατε,

διὰ σοῦ γενέσθω τοῦτό μ[ο]ι.

ΠΑΤΑΙΚΟΣ

[π]ραχθ[ή]σεται

(325)   τοῦτό <γε>· γελοῖον. ἀλλ' ὑπὲρ πάντων [ἐ]χρῆν
ὁρᾶ]ν σ' —

ΓΛΥΚΕΡΑ

ἐγῷδα τἄμ' ἄρισθ'.

ΠΑΤΑΙΚΟΣ

οὕτως ἔχεις;

750   τίς τῶν θ]εραπαινῶν οἶδε ταῦθ' ὅπου 'στί σοι;

ΓΛΥΚΕΡΑ

ἡ Δωρὶ]ς οἶδε.

ΠΑΤΑΙΚΟΣ

καλεσάτω τὴν Δωρίδα
ἔξω τι]ς. ἀλλ' ὅμως, Γλυκέρα, πρὸς τῶν θεῶν,

745 Suppl. Capps. There is no paragraphus under this line in
C.   746 [:]φίλτατε in C deciphered and supplemented by
Guéraud.   747 [π]ραχθ[ή]σεται suppl. Eitrem, Richards.
748 <γε> add. Headlam, Leo, with punctuation after it by
Arnott.   749 Suppl. Ellis, Headlam.   750 Suppl. Leo.
751–752 Suppl. Leo.

GLYKERA
To fetch them.

PATAIKOS
[Why,] have you   745
Entirely broken with the fellow? What do you want?

GLYKERA
My dear, please do this for me.

PATAIKOS
It shall be
Done. It's absurd—you should have [looked at] all
The angles . . .

GLYKERA
(*interrupting*)
I know my own business best.

PATAIKOS
That's how
You feel? [Which] of [the] maids knows where these   750
    things
Of yours are?

GLYKERA
[Doris] knows.

PATAIKOS
Call Doris [out],
[Somebody].

(*The text here provides no clues to the stage action, but one possibility is that Pataikos himself eventually knocks on Polemon's door, and when it opens mimes a request for Doris to come out. Pataikos then returns to Glykera.*)

Still, in heaven's name, Glykera,

(330)   πείσ]θητ' ἐφ' οἷς νυνὶ λόγοις ἐγὼ λέγω,

                     ] δός.

ΔΩΡΙΣ

          ὦ κεκτημένη.

ΓΛΥΚΕΡΑ

755   τί ποτ' ἔστιν;]

ΔΩΡΙΣ

    [ο]ἷον τὸ κακόν.

ΓΛΥΚΕΡΑ

                    ἐξένεγκέ μοι

τὴν κιστίδ'] ἔξω, Δωρί, τὴν τὰ ποικίλα

ἔχουσαν· οἶσθα, ν]ὴ Δί'· ἣν δέδωκά σοι

(335) τηρεῖν. τί κ]λαίεις, ἀθλία;

ΠΑΤΑΙΚΟΣ

                  πέπονθά τι,

νὴ τὸν Δία τὸ]ν Σωτῆρα, [θαυμαστὸν π]άνυ.

760   ] πρᾶγμ' οὐδέν. ἠκ[

(At line 760 the final portion of the play preserved in the Cairo papyrus comes to an end, but the two sides of the second sheet of the Leipzig parchment (L) contain a further 60 lines, beginning only between 5 and 7 verses after 760.)

753 πείσ]θητ' suppl. Rea. λόγοις Arnott (after Sudhaus, Capps): λογοσδ' C.   755 Suppl. Arnott (τί ἔστιν; already Jensen).   756 Suppl. Croiset.   757 ἔχουσαν suppl. Leo, the rest Croiset.   758 τηρεῖν suppl. van Leeuwen, τί κ]λαίεις Headlam.   759 νὴ τὸν Δία τ]ὸν suppl. Croiset, [θαυμαστὸν] Klaus, π]άνυ several.

Take [my advice, and] grant [him pardon] on
The terms I now propose.

(*Doris now enters and makes for Glykera. She is upset.*)

DORIS
O mistress!

GLYKERA

[What's]

[The matter?]

DORIS
What a tragedy!

GLYKERA

Bring me   755
[The box] out, Doris, that [with] needlework inside —
In heaven's name, [you know] — the one I gave
You [to look after! Why] the tears, you wretch?

PATAIKOS
[By Zeus our] Saviour, it's a quite [amazing]
Experience. Nothing['s impossible. I']ve come   760

(*In a short lacuna—no more than 7 lines—Doris' tears
may or may not have been explained, but the box contain-
ing Glykera's recognition tokens was produced, either by
Doris after fetching it from Polemon's house, or by
Pataikos who had picked it up on his earlier visit with
Polemon to view Glykera's wardrobe. In the latter event
Doris' tears would have been caused by her discovery that
the box was missing. Doris returned to Polemon's house
before the text returns at 768, with Pataikos and Glykera
examining one of the tokens, a child's embroidered gar-
ment.*)

443

MENANDER

ΠΑΤΑΙΚΟΣ

(in mid-speech)

768   ὃν] καὶ τότ' εἶδον. οὐ παρ' αὐτὸν οὑτοσὶ

(339)   τ]ράγος τις ἢ βοῦς ἢ τοιουτὶ θηρ[ί]ον

770   ἔ]στηκεν;

ΓΛΥΚΕΡΑ

ἔλαφος, φίλτατ', ἐστίν, οὐ τράγος.

ΠΑΤΑΙΚΟΣ

κέρ]ατ' ἔχει, τοῦτ' οἶδα. καὶ τουτὶ τρίτον

(342)   πετ]εινὸς ἵππος. τῆς [γ]υναικὸς τῆς ἐμῆς

ποικίλ]ματ' ἐστὶ ταῦτα καὶ μάλ' ἀθλίας.

ΜΟΣΧΙΩΝ

οὐ τῶν] ἀδυνάτων ἐστί, τουτί μοι δοκεῖ

775   σκοποῦν]τι, τὴν ἐμὴν τεκοῦσαν μητέρα

ἅμ' ἐμοὶ προ]έσθαι θυγατέρ' αὐτῇ γενομένην·

(347)   εἰ δὲ γεγένητ]αι τοῦτ', ἀδελφὴ δ' ἔστ' ἐμή,

πρόρριζος ἐξέ]φθαρμ' ὁ δυστυχὴς ἐγώ.

ΠΑΤΑΙΚΟΣ

ὦ Ζε]ῦ, τίν' ἤδη τἀπίλοιπα τῶν ἐμῶν;

768–827 are preserved only in L; supplements and corrections not otherwise identified were made by the ed. pr., A. Körte. 768 ουτοσει L.   770 η with ου correction suprascript L. 771 Suppl. Wilamowitz, van Leeuwen. L wrongly has a dicolon after τουτι.   773 Suppl. Dedoussi.   775, 777 Suppl. Sudhaus. 776 ἅμ' ἐμοὶ suppl. Gomme, προ]έσθαι Körte. αὐτῇ Arnott: αυτη L.   778 Suppl. Arnott (or κάκιστά γ' ἐξ-).   779 Suppl. Sudhaus.

444

PATAIKOS

(*in mid-speech*)
[Which] I then saw.[a] And by its side—isn't that   768
A goat or bull or some such animal?

GLYKERA

My dear, that is a stag, and not a goat.   770

PATAIKOS

It's got [horns], that I know! And here's a third—
A horse with wings. These are my own poor wife's
[Embroideries].

(*Enter Moschion from Myrrhine's house. He makes his
opening speech before noticing the presence of Glykera
and Pataikos. Then, after spotting them, he retires into the
background and becomes an unobserved witness of their
actions and listener to their words, which now ape the
rhythms and diction of tragedy.*)

MOSCHION

On reflection, I don't feel
It is impossible that at my birth
Along with me my mother then abandoned   775
A daughter born to her too. But if that's
What happened, and she is my sister, then
My wretched life is totally destroyed!

PATAIKOS

[O Zeus], what shred now of my destiny awaits?

[a] Pataikos is referring to some article (the loss of the preced-
ing context makes it impossible to identify it) which Pataikos had
seen either when he inspected Glykera's clothes with Polemon
just now, or when Glykera was exposed as a baby.

445

ΓΛΥΚΕΡΑ

780 πέραι]ν' ὃ βούλει, τοῦτο πυνθάνου τ' ἐμοῦ.

ΠΑΤΑΙΚΟΣ

πόθεν] λαβοῦσα ταῦτα κέκτησαι φράσον.

ΓΛΥΚΕΡΑ

(352) ἐν τ]οῖσδ' ἀνηρέθην ποτ' οὖσα παιδίον.

ΜΟΣΧΙΩΝ

ἐπ]άναγε σαυτὸν μικρόν· ὡς ῥόθ[ῳ] τ[ινὶ
ἤ[κ]ω τύχης εἰς καιρὸν οἰκείας [ἐγώ.

ΠΑΤΑΙΚΟΣ

785 μόνη δ' ἔκεισο; τοῦτο γὰρ σήμ[α]ινέ μο[ι.

ΓΛΥΚΕΡΑ

οὐ δῆτ'· ἀδελφὸν δ' ἐξέθ[ηκ]ε κἀμέ τις.

ΜΟΣΧΙΩΝ

(357) τουτὶ μὲν ἕν μοι τῶ[ν πάλ]αι ζητουμένων.

ΠΑΤΑΙΚΟΣ

πῶς οὖν ἐχ[ω]ρί[σθη]τ' ἀπ' [ἀ]λλήλων δ[ίχα;

ΓΛΥΚΕΡΑ

ἔ]χοιμ' ἂν ε[ἰπεῖ]ν πάντ' ἀκηκουῖά σοι.
790 τἀμὰ δ<έ μ'> ἐρώτα· ῥητὰ γ[ὰ]ρ ταῦτ' ἐστί μοι·
ἐκεῖνα δ' αὐτῇ μὴ φράσειν ὀμώμοκα.

780 Suppl. Schwartz.   783 ῥόθ[ῳ] suppl. von Arnim and van
Leeuwen, τ[ινὶ Wilamowitz.   787 [πάλ]αι suppl. Lloyd-Jones.
790 Suppl. Robert: ταμαδ'ερωτα L.

GLYKERA

[Satisfy] your craving, and learn that from me.   780

PATAIKOS

Tell me [where] you obtained these things you own.

GLYKERA

I wore] these when once rescued as a baby.

MOSCHION

(*aside*)
Draw back a step! See, on a surging wave
I reach a turning in my destiny!

PATAIKOS

Tell me, were you abandoned on your own?   785

GLYKERA

No, no — my brother was exposed with me.

MOSCHION

(*aside*)
That answers for me one of my [old] queries.

PATAIKOS

How [were you parted] from each other, then?

GLYKERA

I've heard the full tale, and could [tell] it you.
Ask me my part, though—that's no secret, but   790
I swore to her[a] I'd not reveal the rest.

---

[a] Myrrhine, as Moschion's interpretation in 793 confirms. We must accordingly assume that when Glykera moved into Myrrhine's house, she told Myrrhine all that she knew about her and Moschion's origins, with a promise on oath that she would say nothing to anybody else about those of Moschion.

MENANDER

ΜΟΣΧΙΩΝ

(362) κ]αὶ τ[οῦ]τό μοι σύσσημον εἴρηκεν σαφές·
ὁ]μώμοκεν τῇ μ[ητρί. πο]ῦ ποτ᾽ [ἐ]ιμὶ γῆς;

ΠΑΤΑΙΚΟΣ

ὁ δὴ λαβών σε [καὶ τ]ρέφων τίς ἦν ποτε;

ΓΛΥΚΕΡΑ

795 γυνή μ᾽ ἔθρε[ψεν, ἣ] τότ᾽ εἶδε κειμένην.

ΠΑΤΑΙΚΟΣ

τοῦ δὴ τόπου τί μνημόνευμά σοι λέγει;

ΓΛΥΚΕΡΑ

(367) κρή[νην] τιν᾽ ε[ἶπε κ]αὶ τόπον <γ᾽> ὑπόσκιον.

ΠΑΤΑΙΚΟΣ

τὸν αὐ[τ]ὸν ὅνπερ χὠ τιθεὶς εἴρηκέ μοι.

ΓΛΥΚΕΡΑ

τίς δ᾽ οὗτός ἐστιν; εἰ θέμις, κἀμοὶ φράσον.

ΠΑΤΑΙΚΟΣ

800 ὁ μὲν τιθεὶς παῖς, ὁ δὲ τρέφειν ὀκνῶν ἐγώ.

ΓΛΥΚΕΡΑ

σὺ δ᾽ ἐξέθηκας ὢν πατήρ; τίνος χάριν;

ΠΑΤΑΙΚΟΣ

(372) πόλλ᾽ ἐστὶν ἔργ᾽ ἄπιστα, παιδίον, τύχ[ης·
ἡ μὲν τεκοῦσ᾽ ὑμᾶς γὰρ ἐκλείπει βί[ον
εὐθύς, μιᾷ δ᾽ ἔμπροσθεν ἡμέρᾳ, τέκνο[ν—

792 (σύσσημον) Kock fr. 1073

793 πο]ῦ suppl. Wilamowitz.　　　795 Over τοτ᾽ L has και
suprascript.　　796 τοῦ δὴ τόπου τί μνη[or μν[is cited three

448

MOSCHION

(*aside*)

Those words provide a clear endorsement too:
"She swore to [mother." Where] does that leave me?

PATAIKOS

Who was the man who took you in [and] raised you?

GLYKERA

A woman did, [who] saw me then abandoned.   795

PATAIKOS

What memory of the [spot] did she pass on to you?

GLYKERA

She [named] a spring and—yes—a shady spot.

PATAIKOS

Exactly what the man who left you told me.

GLYKERA

Who was that man? Tell me, if that's allowed.

PATAIKOS

A slave, but it was I who shrank from raising you!   800

GLYKERA

You cast me off, though you're my father? Why?

PATAIKOS

Actions [of] fate are often strange, my child.
Your mother died directly when you both
Were born, and just one day before, my girl . . .

---

times with musical notation in *P. Oxyrhynchus* 3705; see
M. Huys, *ZPE*, 99 (1993), 30–32.   798 κοτιθεισ L with the
omitted αι added above κοτ.   804 επροσθεν L with the omit-
ted μ added above the π. τέκνο[ν deciph. and suppl. Sudhaus.

MENANDER

ΓΛΥΚΕΡΑ

805   τί γίνεταί ποθ'; ὡς τρέμω τάλαιν' [ἐγώ.

ΠΑΤΑΙΚΟΣ

πένης ἐγενόμην, βίον ἔχειν [εἰθισμένος.

ΓΛΥΚΕΡΑ

(377)   ἐν ἡμέρᾳ; πῶς; ὦ θεοί, δεινοῦ πό[τμου.

ΠΑΤΑΙΚΟΣ

ἤ]κουσα τὴν ναῦν ἢ παρεῖχ' ἡμῖν τροφ[ὴν
ἄ[γρ]ιον καλύψαι πέλαγος Αἰγαίας ἁλός.

ΓΛΥΚΕΡΑ

810   τάλαιν' ἔγωγε τῆς τύχης.

ΠΑΤΑΙΚΟΣ

                ἐφόλκια
ἡ[γησ]άμην δὴ πτω[χ]ὸν ὄντα παιδία
(382)   τ[ρέφ]ειν ἀ[βού]λου παντελῶς ἀνδρὸς τρόπ[ον.
      ]τ[. . . . .]α τῶν πάντων, τέκ[νον.

ΓΛΥΚΕΡΑ

τὸ ποῖ[ον;

ΠΑΤΑΙΚΟΣ

[. . .]λ.[. . .].ε.

ΓΛΥΚΕΡΑ

μηνυθήσεται·

805 τάλαιν' deciph. Wilcken.   806, 809 Suppl. Wilamowitz.
810 Dicolon after τυχης deciph. Jensen.   813–827 are badly
torn and abraded.   813 τέκ[νον suppl. several.   814 ποῖ[ον
suppl. Sudhaus.

GLYKERA
Whatever happened? Poor [me], how I tremble! 805

PATAIKOS
Ruined, I was! I'd [always] been well off.

GLYKERA
In one day? How? O gods, what awful [luck]!

PATAIKOS
I heard the ship that made our livelihood
Had sunk beneath a wild Aegean sea.

GLYKERA
Your tragedy grieves me.

PATAIKOS
                        I thought that in 810
My poverty raising dependent children
Was acting like a total scatterbrain!
                    ] of them all, my girl.[a]

GLYKERA
Which one?

PATAIKOS
        [   ]

GLYKERA
            That (?) will be made known. There were

---

[a] In this and the next line, too badly damaged for plausible
supplementation, Pataikos and Glykera return to discussing the
recognition tokens exposed with Glykera and Moschion as
babies.

815 ἦν καὶ δέραια καὶ β[ρ]άχυς τις [δι]άλιθ[ος
κόσμος προσὼν γ[νώ]ρισμα τοῖς [ἐκκε]ιμένοις.

ΠΑΤΑΙΚΟΣ
(387) ἐκεῖ[νον] ἀναθεώμ[εθ'].

ΓΛΥΚΕΡΑ
[ἀλλ' οὐκ] ἔ[στ'] ἔτι.

ΠΑΤΑΙΚΟΣ
τί [φής;]

ΓΛΥΚΕΡΑ
[τὰ λοῖφ' ἀδελφὸς ἔλαχε δη]λαδή.

ΜΟΣΧΙΩΝ
ἀλ]λ' ἐ[στὶν] οὗτ[ος, ὡς ἔοιχ', οὑ]μὸς πατήρ.

ΠΑΤΑΙΚΟΣ
820 ἔ]χοις ἂν εἰπεῖν;

ΓΛΥΚΕΡΑ
[πορφυρ]ᾶ ζώνη τις ἦν.

ΠΑΤΑΙΚΟΣ
ἦν γάρ.

ΓΛΥΚΕΡΑ
χορός τε παρθέ[νω]ν ἐνταυθά τις—

ΜΟΣΧΙΩΝ
(392) οὔκουν συνῆκας;

815 δι]άλιθ[ος suppl. Jensen.   816 Suppl. Sudhaus.
817 ἐκεῖ[νον] ἀναθεώμ[εθ'] suppl. Wilamowitz, the rest Sud-
haus.   818–819 Suppl. Sudhaus.   820 [πορφυρ]ᾶ suppl.
Sudhaus.   822 It is uncertain whether there is a dicolon after

Necklaces, and a small charm set with stones —   815
Put in to identify the castaways.

PATAIKOS

[Let's] look at it.

GLYKERA
[But it's no] longer here.

PATAIKOS

What's [that]?

GLYKERA
Presumably [my brother took the rest].

MOSCHION

(*aside*)
But] he['s] my father, [it appears!]

PATAIKOS

Could you

Say what they were?

GLYKERA
There was a [crimson] belt.   820

PATAIKOS

There was.

GLYKERA
With dancing girls embroidered on it.

MOSCHION

(*aside*)
Doesn't that clinch it?

συνῆκας; the first two words in the line were assigned to Moschion by Sudhaus.   οὔκουν Sandbach: L has neither accent nor breathing.

MENANDER

ΓΛΥΚΕΡΑ

δ[ιαφαν]ές τε χλ[ανί]διο[ν
μίτρα τε χρυσῆ. πάντα [καθ' ἓ]ν εἴρηκά σ[ο]ι.

ΠΑΤΑΙΚΟΣ

οὐκέτι καθέξω. φιλτάτη, χ[αῖρ'.]

ΜΟΣΧΙΩΝ

            εἰ δ' ἐγὼ
825   πρόειμ]ι, "τί προσέχεσθ';" ἐρ[ῶ, "τὸν διά]λο[γον
πάρειμι τοῦτον πά[ντα παρακούσ]α[ς] ἐγώ."

ΠΑΤΑΙΚΟΣ

827   ὦ θεοί, τίς ἐστιν οὗτος;

ΜΟΣΧΙΩΝ

            ὅστ[ις εἰ]μ'· ὁ σ[ὸς
[υἱὸς]

822 Suppl. Sudhaus.   823 χρυσητεμιτρα L.: corr. van Her-
werden.   [καθ' ἓ]ν suppl. Petersen, Sudhaus.   εἴρηκά σ[ο]ι
deciph. and suppl. Jensen.   824 Suppl. Sandbach.
825 [πρόειμ]ι and ἐρ[ῶ suppl. Arnott exempli gratia, τὸν
διά]λο[γον Jensen; L has at the end of the line νο with a correct-
ing λ above the ν.   826–828 Suppl. Körte.

(827 is the final line in L, and we have a gap of probably
between 100 and 200 lines before a different papyrus
(P. Oxyrhynchus 207 = O) provides us with 52 end-
damaged lines from a closing scene of the play, in which
Polemon and Glykera are reconciled and—now that
Glykera has been shown to be a free Corinthian girl—
formally betrothed. The lacuna between 827 and this later
scene contained the end of Act IV and most of Act V. It is

GLYKERA

A [see-through] cloak, a golden
Frontal. I've listed every single one for you.

PATAIKOS

(*taking Glykera in his arms*)
I can't hold back, my dearest, any more!

MOSCHION

(*aside*)

If I
[Go forward, I can say] "Why are you hugging? I   825
Was here, [and overheard] all [that was said"].

(*Moschion now comes forward.*)

PATAIKOS

(*still embracing Glykera, and hearing but not seeing
Moschion*)
In heaven's name, who is that?

MOSCHION

Who [am I]?
Your [son]!

difficult to guess what may have happened in the gap. At
826 Moschion emerges from the shadows to accost
Pataikos and Glykera, and a scene in which he was con-
firmed as Pataikos' son and Glykera's brother will have
followed. It is unlikely to have been as elaborate, emo-
tional and serious as the previous one identifying Glykera
as Pataikos' daughter; Moschion has already overheard
most of the relevant facts, and Menander avoids unneces-
sary repetition, as for instance Dyskolos 821ff. shows. The
new scene could have been written either in iambic trime-

MENANDER

ters—with θεοί *in 827 scanning as one long syllable by tragic synizesis—or, perhaps more effectively, in trochaic tetrameters—with 827 then perhaps ending with* ὁ σ[ὸς, πάτερ]; *a lively trochaic scene would suit the intervention of the ridiculously self-centred Moschion and provide a welcome contrast with the relatively serious scene preced-*

ΜΕΡΟΣ Ε΄

(The opening of this act is lost.)

ΠΟΛΕΜΩΝ

(in mid-speech)

976   ἵν᾽ ἐμαυτὸν ἀποπνίξαιμι.

ΔΩΡΙΣ

                    μὴ δῆτ[᾽, ὦ τάλαν.

ΠΟΛΕΜΩΝ

ἀλλὰ τί [π]οήσω, Δωρί; πῶς βιώ[σομαι

(400)   ὁ τρισκακοδαίμων χωρὶς ὦ[ν αὐτῆς;

ΔΩΡΙΣ

                            [πάλιν

ἄπεισιν εἰς σέ—

ΠΟΛΕΜΩΝ

πρὸς θεῶν, οἷ[ον λέγεις.

ΔΩΡΙΣ

980   ἐὰν προθυμήθῃς ἀκάκως—

976–1026 Supplements and conjectures not otherwise identified were made by edd. prr. of O, B. P. Grenfell and A. S. Hunt (*The Oxyrhynchus Papyri*, 2, 1899, 11–20).   976 Suppl. Browne.

ing it, as the Gomme-Sandbach commentary well notes.
This scene may have been quite short and may have con-
cluded Act IV.

A more or less continuous text resumes at 976, with
Polemon and Doris on stage. They both now know that
Moschion and Glykera are Pataikos' twin children, but
Polemon believes that he has now lost Glykera for ever.
However, before 976 P.Oxy. 207 preserves the final letters
of a few lines in the previous column: 925]ν:, 926]μοι,
927]σμενο[.], 928].ο.ους, 930]λέγεις = 'you say', 931
]ων, 951].ι, 962]ν, 966].ασ:, 969].ωσ, 970]τα.)

ACT V

POLEMON

(*in mid-speech*)
So as to kill myself.

DORIS

[Oh dear], not that!   976

POLEMON

But what can I do, Doris? How [shall I]
Survive in all my misery without [her]?

DORIS

She will come [back] to you . . .

POLEMON

(*interrupting*)

What [a suggestion]!

DORIS

. . . If you try to behave well in the future.   980

---

978 αὐτῆς suppl. Sudhaus, πάλιν van Leeuwen.

ΠΟΛΕΜΩΝ

[προθυμίας
οὐκ ἐλλίποιμ' ἂν οὐθέν· εὖ τοῦ[τ' ἴσθι.

ΔΩΡΙΣ

[δεῖ.

ΠΟΛΕΜΩΝ

ὑπέρευ λέγεις. βάδιζ'· ἐγὼ σ' ἐλ[ευθέραν
(405) αὔριον ἀφήσω, Δωρί. ἀλλ' ὃ δε[ῖ λέγειν
ἄκουσον. εἰσελήλυθ'. οἴμοι· [φιλτάτη,
985 ὡς κ[α]τὰ κράτος μ' εἴληφας. ἐ[φίλησάς γ' ἄρα
ἀδελφόν, οὐχὶ μοιχόν· ὁ δ' ἀλάστωρ ἐγὼ
καὶ ζηλότυπος ἄνθρωπος ἀ[δικεῖσθαι δοκῶν
(410) εὐθὺς ἐπαρῴνουν. τοιγαροῦ[ν ἀπηγχόμην
καλῶς ποῶν. τί ἐστι, Δωρὶ φιλ[τάτη;

ΔΩΡΙΣ

990 ἀγαθά· πορεύσεθ' ὡς σέ.

ΠΟΛΕΜΩΝ

κατεγέλα [δέ μου;

986–987 Kock fr. 862

980 προθυμίας suppl. Gronewald.   981 ενλιπομ' O. δεῖ
suppl. Arnott.   982 γωσ' O with the omitted ε suprascript.
984 φιλτάτη suppl. Sudhaus.   985 Suppl. Arnott.
986–987 ὁ δ'—ἄνθρωπος cited from Menander by several lex-
ica (Photius I p. 97 (α 899) Theodoridis, *Etymologicum Magnum*
57.35, anon. rhetorical lexicon p. 374 Bekker). It is disputed
whether O here has ζηλοτυπος or ζηνοτυπος.
987, 988 Suppl. Wilamowitz.   989 εξερχ(εται) δωρις added
by a second hand in left margin of O.
990 Suppl. Arnott (after δ' ἐμοῦ Capps).

458

POLEMON

I'll not stop trying, [be sure of] that!

DORIS

[You mustn't].

POLEMON

Well spoken. Now go in.

(*Polemon turns away as Doris goes off to Myrrhine's house. When he turns back to address her further, he finds that she has already disappeared.*)

I'll make you [free]
Tomorrow, Doris. Listen though to what
I need [to say]. She's gone in! Oh, [my darling],[a]
How powerfully you have conquered me! [You kissed]   985
A brother, not a lover! [Thinking I]
[Was wronged], straight off I played the jealous
      scourge,
In drunken rage. [I planned to hang myself] —
Quite right, too!

(*Doris re-enters.*)
    Dear[est] Doris, what is it?

DORIS

Good news—she's coming back to you!

POLEMON

        She's not   990

Teasing [me]?

---

[a] Alone on stage now, he apostrophises Glykera.

MENANDER

ΔΩΡΙΣ

μὰ τὴν Ἀφροδ[ί]την, ἀλλ' ἐνεδύετο [στολήν·
ὁ πατὴρ ἐπεσκ[εύ]αζ'. ἐχρῆν σε νῦν τα[χὺ
(415) εὐαγγέλια τῶν γεγονότων ποθ' [ἡδέως
θ[ύε]ι[ν] ἐκ[ε]ίνης εὐτυχηκυίας [τόδε.

ΠΟΛΕΜΩΝ

995 νὴ τὸν Δί', ὀρθῶς γὰρ λέγεις. ὁ δ' [ἀπ' ἀγορᾶς
μάγειρος ἔνδον ἐστί· τὴν ὗν θ[υέτω.

ΔΩΡΙΣ

κανοῦν δὲ ποῦ, καὶ τἄλλ' ἃ δεῖ;

ΠΟΛΕΜΩΝ

κα[νοῦν μὲν οὖν
(420) ὕστερον ἐνάρξετ', ἀλλὰ ταύτην σφ[αττέτω·
μᾶλλον δὲ κἀγώ. στέφανον ἀπὸ βω[μοῦ τινα
1000 ἀφελὼν ἐπιθέσθαι βούλομα[ι].

ΔΩΡΙΣ

πιθα[νώτερος
πολλῷ φανεῖ γοῦν.

ΠΟΛΕΜΩΝ

ἄγετέ [γ' ἔ]ξ[ω Γλυκέριον.

991 στολήν suppl. Kretschmar.   992 ἐπεσκ[εύ]αζ' deciph.
and suppl. Browne, τα[χὺ suppl. van Herwerden.
993 ευαγελια O. ἡδέως suppl. Arnott.   995 Suppl. Wila-
mowitz.   999 τινα suppl. Robert.   1001 O has suprascript
ν over the φ and ησ over the ιγ, implying an alternative (but
incorrect) reading πολλῶν φανείης. [γ' ἔ]ξ[ω] suppl. Browne,
Γλυκέριον Arnott.

460

DORIS

Heavens, no! She's slipping on [a dress]
Provided by her father. Hurry! You
Should now be celebrating her good fortune with
A sacrifice to mark [with joy] news of the event!

POLEMON

By Zeus, you're right. The cook [we hired in town[a]]   995
Is in my house — [let's have him kill] the pig!

DORIS

But where's the basket, and our other needs?[b]

POLEMON

The bas[ket] will do later—[let him kill] this pig!
No—better me! I'd like to take [a] garland from
The al[tar] and wear that.

DORIS

That way you'll look   1000

Far [more] convincing.

POLEMON

Bring [out Glykera.]

---

[a] The supplement here may be speculative, but Menander's practice elsewhere makes it likely that this cook was a character in the play, entering at some point earlier with his pig and going into Polemon's house. One possibility (see the Gomme–Sandbach commentary on 995) is that he arrived with Polemon's 'army' early in Act III and departed with Sosias and the other slaves at line 485 into the house.

[b] The cook doubled as a butcher and normally cut the throat of the animal to be sacrificed. All participants in sacrifices wore garlands; the ceremony began with sprinkling grains of barley from a basket over the head of the still living victim.

ΔΩΡΙΣ

καὶ μὴν ἔμελλεν ἐξιέναι δ[ὴ χὠ πατήρ.

ΠΟΛΕΜΩΝ

(425) αὐτός; τί γὰρ πάθῃ τις;

ΔΩΡΙΣ

ὦ τά[λαιν᾽ ἐγώ·
ἔ[φυγ]εν. [κ]ακὸν τοσ[οῦτο]ν ἦν θ[ύ]ραν [ψοφεῖν;
1005 εἴσειμι καὐτὴ σ[υ]μπόησουσ᾽, [εἴ τι δεῖ.

ΠΑΤΑΙΚΟΣ

πάνυ σου φιλῶ τὸ "[ν]ῦν διαλλαχ[θήσομαι".
ὅτ᾽ εὐτύχηκας, τότε δέ[χεσθ]αι τὴν δίκ[ην
(430) τεκμήριον τοῦτ᾽ ἐστ[ὶν Ἕλλ]ηνος τρ[όπου.
ἀλ[λ᾽ ἐκκ]αλείτω τις δ[ραμὼ]ν αὐτ[ὸν ταχύ.

ΠΟΛΕΜΩΝ

1010 ἐ[ξέρχομ᾽· ἀ]λλ᾽ ἔθυον [ὑ]περευ[δαιμονῶν.
Γ[λυκέραν γ]ὰρ εὕρηκ[υ]ῖαν οὓς [εἶχ᾽ ἐν γένει
π[υθό]με[νο]ς—

1002 Suppl. van Leeuwen.   1003 εισερχ(εται) [? πολεμων]
written by a second hand above the line after τις in O. τά[λαιν᾽
ἐγώ suppl. Papabasileios.   1004 Suppl. Sudhaus.   1006 [ν]ῦν
deciph. and suppl. Handley.   1007 Suppl. Dziatzko.
1009 δ[ραμὼ]ν suppl. Weil, αὐτ[ὸν ταχύ van Herwerden.
1010 πο]λεμ(ων) O in left margin. ἐ[ξέρχομ᾽] suppl. van
Leeuwen, [ὑ]περευ[δαιμονῶν Arnott.
1011 [εἶχ᾽ ἐν γένει suppl. exempli gratia Arnott.

DORIS

Well, she was going to come out [with her father].

POLEMON

With him? What's one to do?

(At this point the door of Myrrhine's house begins to open, and Polemon panics at the thought of facing Pataikos now no longer as just a friend but as Glykera's father. He rushes off into his house.)

DORIS

De[ar me], he's [fled]!
The nuisance of a [creaking] door — so terrible!
I'll go in too, to help, [if help's required].   1005

(Doris goes off into Polemon's house, and Pataikos enters from Myrrhine's house, probably talking back through the open door to Glykera, who is still inside. Pataikos may be accompanied by a mute slave.)

PATAIKOS

(to Glykera)
I greatly like your "[I'll] now make it up".
Accepting a fair settlement when you've
Been lucky — that's a mark of [Greek] beha[viour]!
[Quick], somebody should [run] and call him [out]!

(Pataikos' slave, if one is present, or perhaps even Pataikos himself—compare the situation at line 751—goes towards Polemon's door to summon him, but Polemon is already at his door and enters forthwith.)

POLEMON

[I'm coming]. I was sacrificing in   1010
My great [joy]. [Hear]ing [Glykera] had found
[Her kin] . . .

ΠΑΤΑΙΚΟΣ

ὀρθῶς γὰρ λέγεις. ἃ [δ' οὖν ἐγὼ

(435) μέλλω λέγειν ἄκουε. ταύτην γν[ησίων
παιδῶν ἐπ' ἀρότῳ σοι δίδωμι.

ΠΟΛΕΜΩΝ

λ[αμβάνω.

ΠΑΤΑΙΚΟΣ

1015 καὶ προῖκα τρία τάλαντα.

ΠΟΛΕΜΩΝ

καὶ καλῶ[ς ποεῖς.

ΠΑΤΑΙΚΟΣ

τὸ λοιπὸν ἐπιλαθοῦ στρατιώτης ὤν, [ἵνα
προπετὲς ποήσῃς μ[η]δὲ ἕν, [Πολέμων, πάλιν.

ΠΟΛΕΜΩΝ

(440) Ἄπολλον· ὃς καὶ νῦν ἀπ[ό]λωλα πα[ρ' ὀλίγον,
πάλιν τι πράξω προπετ[έ]ς; οὐδὲ μ[έμψομαι
1020 Γλυκέρᾳ. διαλλάγηθι, φιλτάτη, μό[νον.

ΓΛΥΚΕΡΑ

νῦν μὲν γὰρ ἡμῖν γέγονεν ἀρχὴ [πραγμάτων
ἀγαθῶν τὸ σὸν πάροινον.

ΠΟΛΕΜΩΝ

ὀρθῶ[ς γὰρ λέγεις.

1012 παταικ(ος) written above ορθωσγ in O.
1015 ποεῖς suppl. Sandbach.   1016 ἵνα suppl. Sandbach.
1017 Suppl. Gronewald.   1019 Suppl. Wilamowitz.
1022 λέγεις suppl. Sudhaus.

(*Either during or at the end of this speech Glykera makes
her entrance from Myrrhine's house.*)

PATAIKOS

(*interrupting Polemon*)
        That's right. [However], listen to
What I'm going to say. This girl I give to you
To harvest [lawful] children.[a]

POLEMON
        [I accept].

PATAIKOS

I add three talents dowry.

POLEMON
        [You're] generous.   1015

PATAIKOS

From now on, [Polemon], forget your soldiering —
[So then] you'll never act too hastily [again]!

POLEMON

O god, can I, who've [nearly] died the death,
Again behave too hastily? But Glykera [is not]
[To blame]. My darling, just be reconciled!   1020

GLYKERA

Your monstrous act has now become for us
The start of good [experiences].

POLEMON
        [Yes, that's] right.

---

[a] On the formula of betrothal, the dowry and its size see the
note on *Dyskolos* 842–843.

ΓΛΥΚΕΡΑ

(445) διὰ ταῦτα συγγνώμης τετύχηκα[ς.

ΠΟΛΕΜΩΝ

[εὖ λέγεις.

σύνθυε δή, Πάταικ'.

ΠΑΤΑΙΚΟΣ

ἑτέρους ζη[τητέον

1025 ἐστὶν γάμους μοι· τῷ γὰρ ὑῷ λαμβάν[ω

1026 τὴν τοῦ Φιλίνου θυγατέρ'.

ΜΟΣΧΙΩΝ

ὦ Γῆ [καὶ θεοί,

(Here the papyrus breaks off, with probably only a very few lines remaining before the play comes to an end.)

1023 εὖ λέγεις suppl. Sandbach.   1024 Above ετερους in O another hand writes πολεμ^μ(ων) εισ<ε>ισι.   1026 In O there seems to be the upper dot of a dicolon before the ω. Kauer identified the new speaker as Moschion.

*   *   *

GLYKERA

That's why you are forgiven.

POLEMON
[You're a saint.]

Pataikos, share my sacrifice.

(*Polemon goes back into his house, possibly accompanied by Glykera.*)

PATAIKOS
[I've now to] fix

A second wedding. For my son [I]'ll get   1025
Philinos' daughter.

(*At this point Moschion bursts on to the stage from Myrrhine's house.*)

MOSCHION
[Gods of heaven], and Earth . . .   1026

(*The papyrus breaks off at this point, with very little of the play still to run, in all probability. Pataikos may have announced a party to celebrate the family reunion and the betrothal(s?), thus providing an appropriate context for a conventional dramatic coda with its final prayer for Victory, perhaps identical in wording with that preserved in the closing lines of the Dyskolos, 968–969.*)

*   *   *

MENANDER

Two fragments of Περικειρομένη,
quoted by ancient authors

1 (1 Sandbach and Körte, 391 Kock)

Stobaeus, *Eclogae* 2. 33. 6 (ὅτι ἡ ὁμοιότης τῶν τρόπων
φιλίαν ἀπεργάζεται): Μενάνδρου Περικειρομένη·

οὕτω ποθεινόν ἐστιν ὁμότροπος φίλος.

2 (2 S and Kö, 392 K)

The Συναγωγὴ λέξεων χρησίμων (Bekker, *Anecdota
Graeca* 1. 427. 23) s.v. ἀποδεῖξαι, οὐ παραδεῖξαι·

ὅμως δ᾽ ἀπόδειξον ταῦτα τῇ γυναικὶ καί . . .

Περικειρομένη Μένανδρος.

PERIKEIROMENE

Two fragments of Perikeiromene,
quoted by ancient authors

1

Stobaeus ('That likeness of character creates friendship'): in
Menander's *Perikeiromene*

A friend in harmony is so desirable.

These words were perhaps spoken by Polemon in praise of
Pataikos.

2

The anonymous *Lexicon of Useful Terms* s.v. ἀποδεῖξαι,
advising the use of ἀποδεῖξαι, not παραδεῖξαι, in the sense
'to indicate/show':

Yet show them to the woman and . . .

Menander in *Perikeiromene*.

Was this Pataikos addressing Glykera somewhere after line
827 and encouraging her to show her recognition tokens to
Myrrhine and have her compare them with Moschion's?

PERINTHIA
(THE GIRL FROM PERINTHUS)

INTRODUCTION

Manuscript

O = *P. Oxyrhynchus* 855, a scrap of papyrus from the third century A.D., containing 23 lines in one column and the end of one in the column that precedes. It is now in Oxford: Bodleian Library, Gr. Class. e 99 (P). First edition: B. P. Grenfell and A. S. Hunt, *The Oxyrhynchus Papyri*, 6 (1908), 150–155; no photograph is published, but I am grateful to the Bodleian Library for supplying one to me.

Fragments 1 to 10 are quotations in later authors (see the introduction to Volume I, pp. xxiv f.), numbered here in the order of their conjectured appearance in the original play; they are printed after the papyrus text, together with four testimonia that provide information from antiquity about the play.

Perinthus was a town on the north side of the Propontis (now the Sea of Marmara) near to the modern Marmaraeğlisi, and a girl who had moved from there to Athens gave Menander's play its title, although it is possible that she never spoke a word in it nor even appeared on stage. Although only one small piece of papyrus and ten ancient quotations survive from *Perinthia*, the play has attracted a great deal of scholarly interest, owing mainly to Terence's confession in the prologue to his *Andria* that he had been able to blend material from both the *Andria* and the *Perinthia* of Menander in his Latin comedy because the two Greek plays 'are not so different in plot' (*non ita dissimili sunt argumento* v. 11: see testimonium I).

The precise meaning and trustworthiness of this confession are both disputed; Terence's prologues are adversarial and point-scoring defences of his methods, not statements sworn on oath. Even so, such evidence as is preserved tends to indicate that here Terence sticks closer to the truth than sometimes he does elsewhere. The plot of his *Andria* centres on the love affair of Pamphilus, a young Athenian, and Glycerium, a girl apparently hailing from the island of Andros; their baby is born during the play. Simo, the young man's father, had meanwhile arranged for his son to marry Chremes' daughter, but Chremes renegued when he learnt about Pamphilus' affair. Simo still pressed on with the arrangements for the marriage, hoping thereby to test Pamphilus' loyalty to him and to foil in advance any tricks that might be devised by Davos, a house slave and Pamphilus' abettor, to prevent it. When Davos advised Pamphilus to call his father's bluff by now agreeing to the marriage, the results at first were disastrous for both Pamphilus and another young man named Charinus who wanted to marry Chremes' daughter; Simo was able to persuade Chremes to agree once again to the marriage. In the end, after a series of misadventures and misunderstandings, the arrival of a new character called Crito made possible a solution that the two young men desired. Glycerium had originally

473

come to Athens with a girl from Andros who had exchanged her job as a spinner and weaver for the more lucrative one of *hetaira* before she died, and Crito was that girl's cousin and heir. Crito was able to prove that Glycerium was a long-lost daughter of Chremes, and so she was free, being Athenian, to marry her Pamphilus, while the other young man could ask Chremes for the hand of his other daughter.

The fragments of *Perinthia* on papyrus and in ancient quotations point to a plot similar to that of Terence's *Andria* at various points. Some character names are different (thus the Greek counterpart to Simo is named Laches), some are identical (Terence's Davos is certainly Menander's Daos, and another slave in Terence's play named Byrrhia may reappear as Pyrrhias, if a plausible supplement at v. 8 of the papyrus is accepted: but see below). In the scene partly preserved on the papyrus Daos has taken refuge at the stage altar in order presumably to escape punishment for some serious misdeed, while Laches and several slaves prepare a bonfire to force him out of his place of sanctuary. In Terence's *Andria* Simo first threatens (196–201) and then proceeds (860–867) to chastise Daos, but there the punishment (along presumably with the crime) is much less brutal.

Several of the Greek quotations from *Perinthia* show points of contact with the Terentian comedy. Fragment 4 mentions a woman who drinks heavily; if this is Terence's Lesbia, the midwife called in to deliver Glycerium's baby (*Andria* 228–230, 459–488), we must presume that the delivery of a baby to Glycerium's counterpart was also part of the *Perinthia*'s plot. Fragment 6 mentions a slave carrying cheap fish into a house; this corresponds closely with *Andria* 368 f., where Davos describes the absence of any preparations for a wedding at Chremes' house, and implies that in *Perinthia* too Simo's counterpart had used the pretence of a wedding as a subterfuge. These two fragments provide the closest contacts; several others fit well if less precisely into the Terentian structure. Thus fragment 2 is possibly a comment by Sosia's Greek counterpart (Laches' wife: see below) on the funeral of Glycerium's associate at the beginning of the play (*Andria* 107–141), 7 and 8 may be advice to Crito's counterpart when he arrives in Athens as heir to the deceased girl of Andros (*Andria* 799), and 9 can be interpreted as the same character's claim to have an honest heart as well as a becoming exterior (see *Andria* 856).

A little more information about *Perinthia* and its relation to the *Andria* plays of Menander and Terence is provided by the commentaries of Donatus, garbled though these often are now. Writing on vv. 10 and 14 (testimonia II and III) Donatus tells us that the opening scenes of the two Menander plays were virtually identical, although in his *Andria* the old man was alone while in *Perinthia* he conversed with his wife; Terence's *Andria* retained the dialogue form, but substituted a freedman for the wife. On v. 301 of Terence's play (testimonium IV) Donatus says that Charinus and his slave Byrrhia were not *apud Menandrum*, 'in Menander', but does that mean that they were not in either Menandrean play (and so added by Terence as a personal invention), or that they did not exist in Menander's *Andria* (but were taken by Terence from Menander's *Perinthia*)? We cannot be sure of the correct answer here; the plausible supplementation of the name Pyrrhias (the Greek form of Byrrhia) at v. 8 of the *Perin-*

thia papyrus is no real help to a solution, since here
Pyrrhias is far more likely to be a slave of Laches helping
to start the bonfire than the attendant of Charinus'
counterpart.[1]

The first editors of *P. Oxyrhynchus* 855 called it an
'unidentified New Attic comedy' of uncertain authorship,
although they noted that the close similarity of its vv.
13–15 to fragment 3 of *Perinthia* seemed to 'point to
Menander'. A year later Körte (*Hermes*, 44, 1909,
309–313) firmly identified both author and play by show-
ing that the similarity noted by Grenfell and Hunt was
due simply to Laches at vv. 13–15 of the papyrus throwing
back in Daos' teeth an insult which the slave had made
earlier at fragment 3 of *Perinthia*; it is unclear whether
Laches had himself overheard that insult, or had only had
it reported to him.

Since 1908 two other papyri have tentatively but with
less success been attributed to Menander's *Perinthia*.
Adelmo Barigazzi (*Hermes*, 88, 1960, 379–382) drew at-
tention to a note added by a second hand below line 36 of
fr. 3 of *P. Hibeh* 181.[2] That note referred to a προστά-
τ[η]ν, 'protector' or 'patron', and Barigazzi attributed the
three mutilated scraps of comic trimeters in *P. Hibeh* 181
to Menander's *Perinthia* because of the attested use of
this word at the beginning of this play (see *Perinthia* fr. 1

---

[1] See now S. M. Goldberg, *Understanding Terence* (Prince-
ton 1986), 126–135 (with brief bibliography at 127 n. 6).

[2] First published by E. G. Turner, *The Hibeh Papyri*, 2
(London 1985), 18, 24 f.; see also Colin Austin, *Comicorum
Graecorum Fragmenta in Papyris Reperta* (Berlin and New York
1973), pp. 295 f., no. 262.

below). The argument is not compelling in itself; although the word is not elsewhere found with this sense in identified passages of Menander,[1] it is likely to have occurred in plays where the need for a protector or patron of a resident alien (such as a *hetaira*) in Athens was relevant to the plot, and Terence's *Eunuchus* 1039 f. is not the only passage in Latin where the word προστάτης in that sense is likely to have occurred in the Menandrean original. In any event the three fragments of *P. Hibeh* 181, which all derive apparently from the same section of the play, include a list of food (fr. 1) which has no place at the beginning of a play known to have closely resembled that of Terence's *Andria*.

The other papyrus is *P. Berlin* 11771,[2] which I myself (*Zeitschrift für Papyrologie und Epigraphik*, 102, 1994, 61–70) hesitantly identified as an earlier part of that scene to which the *Perinthia* papyrus belongs. In it a slave rushes in and seeks asylum at the stage altar, and I drew attention to three points of contact between the Berlin papyrus and Menander's *Perinthia*. There is a character named Sosias in both *P. Berlin* (v. 10) and the *Perinthia* papyrus (v. 21: Σω]σίας as speaker). An 'heir' is mentioned in *P. Berlin* v. 9, an 'inheritance' in the *Perinthia* papyrus (v. 18), while Crito is the dead *hetaira*'s heir in Terence's *Andria* 799. Finally v. 57 of *P. Berlin* seems to echo Laches' reference to τὸν μὲν ἀπράγμονα ('the

---

[1] It does, however, occur with this sense in anonymous fragments of New Comedy which *may* be by Menander: e.g. (in addition to the passage cited by Barigazzi) fr. 269.5 Austin.

[2] First published by Wilamowitz, *Sitzungsberichte der Deutschen Akademie der Wissenschaften zu Berlin*, 1918, 743–747; cf. Austin, *op. cit.*, pp. 239–241, no. 239.

easy-going' master) in v. 13 of the *Perinthia* papyrus. It is, however, very difficult to see how some events that loom large in the comedy on the Berlin papyrus—a wealthy man's death, a slave pursued to his asylum by somebody who accuses him of kidnapping, for instance—could be incorporated in a plot basically similar at so many points to that of Terence's *Andria*.

Accordingly, neither the Hibeh nor the Berlin papyrus fragments are printed here.

No hypothesis, didascalic notice, or cast list is preserved for this play. Its production date is unknown; some have suggested that *Perinthia* was an early work of Menander's, with his *Andria* providing a more mature and less violent version of the plot, but such a view is not supported by any evidence (see volume I of the Loeb Menander, p. 384).

Dramatis personae, so far as they are known (the names of their counterparts in Terence's *Andria* are added in brackets):

(i) those whose presence is confirmed by the Greek fragments or the *testimonia*:

Laches, an old man (Simo)

Laches' wife

Daos, a slave in Laches' household (Davos)

[So]sias, a slave or freedman whose owner is unknown (and so not necessarily to be equated with Terence's Sosia, the freedman in Simo's household)

A midwife (Lesbia)

(ii) those whose presence can be assumed from the plot of Terence's *Andria*:

The Perinthian girl's maid (Mysis)

Laches' son (Pamphilus)

A second old man (Chremes)

A Perinthian relative of the *hetaira* who died in Athens (Crito)

It is possible, but not certain, that counterparts to Terence's Charinus (a second young man) and his slave Byrrhia were characters in the play. Other slaves in Laches' household seem to have appeared as mutes: Tibeios, Getas and (unless he was the second young man's slave named Byrrhia in Terence) Pyrrhias. There is no evidence that the title figure appeared on the stage in Menander's play. There was presumably also a chorus to perform the entr'actes.

The scene was presumably Athens, and if it corresponded to that in Terence's *Andria*, two houses would have been visible: one belonging to Laches, the other to the girl of Perinthus.

ΠΕΡΙΝΘΙΑ

(The main papyrus fragment)

ΛΑΧΗΣ (?)
. . . .]· σὺ δ' ἀκολούθει, [Πυρρία.

ΔΑΟΣ (?)
κληματίδ]ας ἔξεισιν φέρων.

ΛΑΧΗΣ (?)
                    τὸ πῦρ [ἔχεις;

ΔΑΟΣ
καὶ πῦρ; πρόδηλον. ὦ Τίβειε καὶ Γέτα,

In the apparatus to this play, those conjectures and supplements
whose author is not named were made by the edd. prr. of O,
Grenfell and Hunt.

1 Suppl. Leo.

2 κληματίδ]ας suppl. Wilamowitz, ἔχεις Sudhaus. Change of
speaker after φέρων suggested by Körte (O appears to have no
dicolon).

ᵃ Presumably Pyrrhias.

PERINTHIA

(The Girl from Perinthus)

(Three characters with speaking roles appear to be involved in this extract: Laches, his slave Daos, and a second slave Sosias of unknown ownership. Laches, with the help of three other slaves (Tibeios, Getas and Pyrrhias) played here by mutes, prepares a bonfire to be lit around the stage altar. The aim is to punish or at least dislodge Daos, who has sought sanctuary there, presumably after some serious misdemeanour which may have been connected with the inheritance mentioned in v. 18. At the beginning of the extract it seems likely that Laches speaks as he enters from his house and gives orders back to an unseen slave inside.)

LACHES (?)
[Pyrrhias,] you follow me.

DAOS (?)
He'll[a] come out with the [brushwood].

LACHES (?)
(still addressing Pyrrhias inside)

[Have you got] the fire?

DAOS
(terrified)
Fire too? It's clear. Tibeios and Getas,

481

ἔπειτα κατακαύσει μ'· ἀφείητ' ἄν, Γέτα,
5 σύν]δουλον ὄντα, καὶ διασώσαι[τ'· ε]ὖ πάνυ·
οὐκ] ἄν μ' ἀφείητ', ἀλλὰ περιόψεσθέ με;
οὕτ]ω πρὸς ἀλλήλους ἔχομεν; προσέρχεται
ὁ Πυρ]ρίας, ὅσον γε φορτίον φέρων.
ἀπό]λωλα. καὶ δᾷδ' αὐτὸς ἡμμένην ἔχων
10 . . . . . ἀκ]ολουθεῖ.

ΛΑΧΗΣ

περίθετ' ἐ[ν] κύκλῳ ταχύ.
νυνί γ' ἐπ]ίδειξαι, Δᾶε, τὴν πανουργίαν,
τέχνην τιν' εὑρὼν διαφυγών τ' ἐνθένδε με.

ΔΑΟΣ

τέχνην ἐγώ;

ΛΑΧΗΣ

ναί, Δᾶε, τὸν μὲν ἀπράγμονα
καὶ κοῦφον ἐξαπατᾶν γάρ ἐστι δεσπότην
15 φλύαρος.

ΔΑΟΣ

ἤήν.

5 διασώσαι[τ' suppl. van Herwerden, ε]ὖ Leo.
6 Suppl. Leo.
7 οὕτ]ω suppl. Leo (pace Grenfell and Hunt p. 154).
8 Suppl. Wilamowitz.
11 Suppl. Leo.

[a] See fragment 3 below and the introduction to *Perinthia*.

Will he then burn me alive? Please, let me go,
Getas—your [fellow] slave—and save me? Very 5
   [good]—
[Not] let me go? And turn your back on me?

(The text of lines 4 to 7 has four small lacunae, whose sup-
plementation remains uncertain. The translation given
above implies a series of visual gestures from the partici-
pants in the scene: desperate pleas by Daos to Tibeios and
Getas, then initial support from Getas at least, followed—
under threat from Laches?—by a repudiation. Pyrrhias
now enters and carries his load of sticks to the altar.
Laches follows him, holding a lighted torch.)

Is [that the way] we treat each other? Here
Comes [Pyr]rhias—what an enormous load
He has. I'm finished. Master's there, behind
Him [   ] with a blazing torch.

LACHES

                 Quick, put them round. 10

(While Pyrrhias scatters the brushwood around the altar,
Laches turns to address Daos.)

[Now,] Daos, demonstrate your wicked stunts —
Devise a scheme, give me the slip from here!

DAOS

Scheme? Me?

LACHES

        Yes, Daos—it's a joke, you see,
To trick your easy-going, bird-brained master![a]

DAOS

Oh no!

483

MENANDER

ΛΑΧΗΣ

εἰ δέ τις τὴν τῶν φρενῶν
στακτήν—ἐκνίσθης;

ΔΑΟΣ

οὐχὶ πρὸς σοῦ, δέσποτα.

ΣΩΣΙΑΣ (?)

ὁ μὲν πονηρός, ὁ θρασὺς ἐνθάδ' ἀρτίως
κατὰ τῶν σκελῶν—τὴν κληρονομίαν φι[λ]τάτο[υ
                                          ]οδων.

(?)

                              ἕξειν χάριν
20   ]s ὑφ' ἡμῶν.

ΛΑΧΗΣ

                          κάετ[ε].

ΣΩΣΙΑΣ

                    ].ως ἀφίκετο
]φερόμενος γὰρ κἂν κύκλῳ
23   ]ρτων τ' ἐστὶ τὸ [

17 The name σω^σ clearly written in the left margin of O.
19 ? :εξειν O, but the lower point of the dicolon is uncertain.
21 σω]σιας written above]ωσαφικετο in O to indicate speaker.

---

^a This reference, literally to 'the inheritance', remains a puz-
zle; if it concerns a part of the plot involving Sosias, it might
imply a major deviation from the plot of Terence's *Andria*, where

484

LACHES

If one should find your precious brains—   15
Did *that* sting you?

DAOS

But that's not like you, master!

(Sosias, previously a silent witness of events, now enters the conversation, after noticing that Daos' terror has impaired control of his bowels.)

SOSIAS

This cunning rogue, this man so reckless here
Just now—look down his legs! The legacy[a]
Of (?) dearest [   ] out.

(?)

[

Will thank [   ] by us.

LACHES

Light the fire!   20

SOSIAS

] he came [
Taken [to market] and there in the rings[b]
] and is the [23

(Here the papyrus breaks off. We may surmise that Daos was released before being seriously injured, but we cannot

the problem of inheritance is of minor importance (799, 807–816) and does not affect any slave.

[b] In Athens 'the rings' were normally that part of the Athenian market where slaves were sold. The broken text in *Perinthia* here may imply that after his punishment Daos will be put up for sale.

MENANDER

Two further minute scraps of the papyrus

(a) *End of line in previous column, level with line 14 above*

(b) *Separate scrap, not certainly placed*

]χοι

]τιβ]

Scrap (b) could be fitted into Leo's tentative supplements before the extant part of v. 1, ὧ] Τίβ[ειε καὶ Γέτα, / φυλάττετ᾿ αὐτον]·.

* * *

Ten fragments of Περινθία,
quoted by ancient authors

1 (1a Körte, 1 Sandbach)

Harpocration s.v. προστάτης (π 105, p. 223 Keaney) οἱ τῶν μετοίκων Ἀθήνησι προεστηκότες προστάται ἐκαλοῦντο· ἀναγκαῖον γὰρ ἦν ἕκαστον τῶν μετοίκων πολίτην τινὰ τῶν Ἀθηναίων (so mss. of fuller version: Ἀθηναῖον in epitome) νέμειν προστάτην. ... μέμνηται καὶ Μένανδρος ἐν ἀρχῇ τῆς Περινθίας (-είας mss. of fuller version: first corrected in a printed edition (Paris 1614) by P. J. Maussacus).

*be certain that this was due to the arrival of a man from
Perinthus acting as the counterpart of Crito in Terence's
Andria. Two other tiny fragments of text survive from this
papyrus. One is an incomprehensible group of three let-
ters from the end of a line in the previous column; the
other may be the first part of Tibeios's name, perhaps
from the line lost before v. 1: e.g. 'Tib[eios and Getas, /
Guard him, and Pyrrhias,] you follow me'.)*

*   *   *

*Ten fragments of Perinthia,
quoted by ancient authors*

1

Harpocration s.v. προστάτης ('protector' or 'patron'): Those
protecting resident aliens in Athens were called προστάται,
for each of the resident aliens was obliged to have an Athe-
nian citizen as a προστάτης . . . Menander too mentions
this at the beginning of his *Perinthia*.

*The word does not occur elsewhere with this sense in what
survives of Menander, but as the recognised term for an offi-
cial important to many characters in Menander's plays—his
hetairai for example were typically resident aliens in the
cities where the events of the plot were set—it is likely to have
appeared more than once in his lost works. Harpocration's
statement makes it likely that Laches or his wife referred in
the opening scene of the play to the necessity for Menander's
counterparts to Terence's Chrysis and/or Glycerium to
acquire a προστάτης when they settled in Athens (note
Andria 71, and see 813). See especially A. R. W. Harrison,
The Law of Athens, I (Oxford 1968), 189–199, and D. M.
MacDowell, The Law in Classical Athens (London 1978),
77 f.*

MENANDER

2 (2 Kö, 5 S)

Stobaeus, *Eclogae* 4. 55. 2 (περὶ ταφῆς), with the heading
Μενάνδρου Περινθίας (-θείας ms. A). Line 1 is also cited in
the monostichs attributed to Menander (601 Jäkel).

ΛΑΧΗΤΟΣ ΓΥΝΗ (?)
οὐπώποτ᾽ ἐζήλωσα πολυτελῆ νεκρόν·
εἰς τὸν ἴσον ὄγκον τῷ σφόδρ᾽ ἔρχετ᾽ εὐτελεῖ.

2 Corr. Bentley: ἴσον δ᾽ mss. SA, ἶσον δ᾽ M.

3 (1b Kö, 3 S)

Aelius Dionysius (α 4 Erbse), Photius (α 36, I p. 11 Theodor-
idis) and the *Suda* (α 32 Adler) s.v. ἀβέλτερος· οὐ μὰ Δία οὐχ
ὁ πλεονέκτης καὶ ἀγνώμων, ἀλλ᾽ ὁ ἀνόητος καὶ εὐήθης
μετὰ χαυνότητος. Μένανδρος Περινθίᾳ·

ΔΑΟΣ
ὅστις παραλαβὼν δεσπότην ἀπράγμονα
καὶ κοῦφον ἐξαπατᾷ θεράπων, οὐκ οἶδ᾽ ὅ τι
οὗτος μεγαλεῖόν ἐστι διαπεπραγμένος
ἐπαβελτερώσας τὸν πάλαι <γ᾽> ἀβέλτερον.

4 πάλαι Photius: ποτε *Suda*. γ᾽ added by Reitzenstein.

4 (5 Kö, 4 S)

Athenaeus 11. 504a: (ὁ Πλούταρχος) ἔδωκε (τὴν φιάλην)
τῷ παιδὶ περισοβεῖν ἐν κύκλῳ κελεύσας, τὸ κύκλῳ πίνειν
τοῦτ᾽ εἶναι λέγων, παρατιθέμενος Μενάνδρου ἐκ Περιν-
θίας·

---

[a] On this character see my note on *Theophoroumene* fr. 3.

2

Stobaeus ('On burial'): from Menander's *Perinthia*,

LACHES' WIFE (?)
I've never envied an expensive corpse —
It and the cheapest end with equal bulk!

*Presumably a comment on the funeral of the counterpart to
Terence's Chrysis (Andria 107–136). See also the introduc-
tion to Perinthia.*

3

Three lexica s.v. ἀβέλτερος ('stupid'): On my oath, not the
man who is grasping or unfeeling, but one who is mindless
and foolish combined with frivolity. Menander in *Perinthia*,

DAOS
I don't know what remarkable achievement's
Accomplished by a servant who takes on
And tricks an easy-going, bird-brained master —
He's fooling one who's been a fool for years!

*Daos' complacent boast is later quoted back at him (see vv.
13–15 of the papyrus fragment) by his master, who accord-
ingly must have either overheard it here or had it reported to
him: see the introduction to Perinthia. The boast could have
been inserted in a monologue comparable to that in Terence,
Andria 206–227, for example.*

4

Athenaeus: Plutarch (of Alexandria[a]) gave (the cup) to the
slave with an order 'to whizz it around', explaining that this
meant 'drinking (from one beaker passed) around the whole
circle', producing as evidence a passage from Menander's
Perinthia,

MENANDER

οὐδεμίαν ἡ γραῦς ὅλως
κύλικα παρῆκεν, ἀλλ' ἔπιε τὴν ἐν κύκλῳ.

1 Corr. Musurus: ἤγρευσ' A (omitted in Epitome).　　2 Corr.
Arnott tentatively: ἀλλὰ πίνει τὴν κύκλῳ A (πίνει τὴν κύκλῳ
also mss. of Epitome).

5 (4 Kö, 8 S)

Harpocration (π 80 p. 217 Kearney), Photius (p. 381 Porson)
and the *Suda* π 2032 Adler) s.v. πομπείας καὶ πομπεύειν·
ἀντὶ τοῦ λοιδορίας καὶ λοιδορεῖν … ἡ μεταφορὰ δὲ
(μεταφέρει δὲ mss. of Harpocration apart from D) ἀπὸ τῶν
ἐν ταῖς (ταῖς omitted by some mss. of Harpocration) Διονυ-
σιακαῖς πομπαῖς ἐπὶ τῶν ἁμαξῶν λοιδορουμένων ἀλλή-
λοις· Μένανδρος Περινθίᾳ (Περινθίῳ ms. D of *Suda*)·

ἐπὶ τῶν ἁμαξῶν εἰσι πομπεῖαί τινες
σφόδρα λοίδοροι.

6 (6 Kö, 2 S)

Athenaeus 7. 301ab: ἑψητός· ἐπὶ τῶν λεπτῶν ἰχθυδίων …
Μένανδρος Περινθίᾳ·

490

PERINTHIA

> The old hag never once
> Missed out a cup, but drank the circling beaker.

Presumably a description of an alcoholic midwife, Menander's counterpart to the Lesbia of Terence's Andria, who is called a drunkard at 228–232. See also the introduction to Perinthia.

5

Three lexica, s.vv. πομπείας καὶ πομπεύειν ('ribaldries and to utter ribaldries'): in place of 'abuse' and 'to abuse' ... the new sense comes from those in the Dionysiac processions abusing each other on their wagons. Menander in *Perinthia*,

> There's some very abusive ribaldry
> Upon the wagons.

Speaker and situation are unidentified. One possibility is that a speaker such as Daos is referring to the kind of behaviour expected in wedding processions, when the bride was driven by the bridegroom to the latter's house in a wagon, and obscene comments were made by participants and spectators (cf. Hans Licht, Sexual Life in Ancient Greece, translated by J. H. Freese (London 1932), 41–53, and Walter Erdmann, Die Ehe im alten Griechenland (Munich 1934), 250–261). A dramatic context could be provided by Davos' question after he had noted the absence of wedding preparations around Chremes' house, from which the bride would have had to be collected (Andria 366): num uidentur conuenire haec nuptiis? ('Does this look like a wedding?').

6

Athenaeus, under the heading ἑψητός (boiled fish): With reference to tiny little fish ... Menander in *Perinthia*,

ΔΑΟΣ

τὸ παιδίον

εἰσῆλθεν ἑψητοὺς φέρον.

2 φέρον ms. A and Epitome ms. C: φέρων Epitome ms. E. The fragment is usually (but unnecessarily) printed as a single iambic trimeter, with δ᾽ added (first by Musurus) after τὸ παιδίον.

7 (3 Kö, 6 S)

Pollux 10. 12: ἐκαλεῖτο δὲ ταῦτα (sc. τὰ κατ᾽ οἰκίαν χρήσιμα) ὑπὸ τῶν νεωτέρων καὶ μαλακά, οἷον εὐμεταχείριστα, ὡς εἶπε Μένανδρος ἐν τῇ Περινθίᾳ·

ὅσ᾽ ἐστὶ μαλακὰ συλλαβὼν
ἐκ τῆς πόλεως τὸ σύνολον ἐκπήδα, < ∪ – >,
θᾶττον.

1 ὅσ᾽ Bentley: ὡς mss. FS, ὃ CL. ἐστὶ CL: ἐπὶ FS.
2 ἐκπήδα θᾶττον FS, ἐκπήδα φίλος CL: where φίλος looks like a feeble stopgap introduced after the original word (e.g. a vocative such as Κρίτων) had been omitted from the quotation.

PERINTHIA

DAOS
The slave
Went in, bringing some tiny fish.

This fragment closely matches one of Davos' comments after his scouting expedition to Chremes' house (Andria 368 f.): etiam puerum inde abiens conueni Chremi: / holera et pisciculos minutos ferre obolo in cenam seni, 'Furthermore, I met a slave of Chremes as I left, / Bringing for the old man's dinner greens and tiny fish bought cheap.' It appears that in Menander's Perinthia too at the equivalent stage Daos visited the house of the Greek counterpart to Chremes and found that no preparations were being made there for the wedding of the daughter of the house to Laches' son. See the introduction to Perinthia.

7

Pollux: These things (sc. items useful in a house) were described by later authors as μαλακά ('soft', presumably a colloquial substitute for 'movable'), that is easy to handle, as Menander said in the *Perinthia*,

Assemble all
That you can handle, and leave town, [⌣ –],
Quickly!

In Terence's Andria Crito was officially Chrysis' heir (799), but he faced practical and legal difficulties now that Glycerium had come into possession of the estate (809–816). Could this fragment have been advice proffered in Menander's play to Crito's counterpart, to make a quick raid on the house? The suspected omission in the text at the end of v. 2 could most conveniently be filled by a vocative naming the dead girl's cousin (not necessarily called the Greek equivalent of Crito). See the introduction to Perinthia.

MENANDER

8 (8 Kö, 7 S)

The *Suda* s.v. ἀνέπαφον (α 2289 Adler)· ἀνεύθυνον, καθα-
ρόν, ἀθιγές, ἀψηλάφητον. Μένανδρος Περινθίᾳ·

> τὰ δ' ἄλλ' ἀνέπαφα σώματ', οὐδ' ἔλη.

οὐδ' ἔλη ms. S (first printed in L. Kuster's edition, Cambridge
1705): οὐδέλη other mss. Mss. IM add a note ἴσως βδέλλη.
On the text, punctuation, and possible relation to fr. 7 see my
paper in *ZPE* 111 (1996), 5 f.

9 (7 Kö, 9 S)

Maximus Planudes, *Scholia in Hermogenem*, περὶ ἰδέων I
(*Rhetores Graeci* 5. 486 Walz): κεῖται δὲ (sc. τὸ ὑπόξυλος)
ἐπὶ τῶν λαμπρῶν μὲν ἔξωθεν καὶ ἐπιεικῶν, πονηρῶν δὲ τὰ
ἔνδον· καὶ Μένανδρος ἐν τῇ Περινθίᾳ φησίν·

> οὐδ' αὐτός εἰμι σὺν θεοῖς ὑπόξυλος.

See also the anonymous scholion on Hermogenes in *codex
Parisinus* 1938 fol. 186 (cited by Johann von Borries, *Phryn-
ichi sophistae Praeparatio sophistica*, Leipzig 1911, p. 116):
Μένανδρος ἐν τῇ Περινθίᾳ φησίν· οὐδ'—ὑπόξυλος· οἷον
κίβδηλος καὶ οὐ γνήσιος οὐδὲ ἀληθής, ἀπὸ τῶν ξυλίνων
καὶ περιηργυρωμένων σκευῶν.

8

The *Suda* s.v. ἀνέπαφον ('not for seizing'): not accountable, clear, inviolate, untouched. Menander in *Perinthia*,

> The rest are bodies[a] not for seizing, you'll
> Not take them!

In the absence of context the reference is uncertain, but one possibility is that this is a warning by the speaker of fragment 7, not to seize any of the house slaves. If so, fragment 8 could be a continuation of 7. See also the introduction to Perinthia.

9

A scholion of Planudes on Hermogenes: The word (sc. ὑπό-ξυλος: literally 'wooden underneath') is applied to those who have dazzling and fine exteriors, but are rotten inside. Menander says in the *Perinthia*,

> And I'm not rotten underneath, god willing!

An anonymous scholion on the same passage in a Paris manuscript introduces the same fragment with: 'Menander in the *Perinthia* says: And I'm not—willing', continuing with the explanation: 'false, not genuine or true, from articles made of wood and silver-plated'.

Crito is presented in Terence's Andria as a man of impressive appearance (856 f.) and good character (915), and this fragment could be a rejoinder to doubts expressed about his behaviour by either Daos or more probably Laches (cf. Andria 909–925). See the introduction to Perinthia.

[a] I.e. slaves: see especially W. K. Pritchett, *The Greek State at War* 5 (Berkeley, Los Angeles, Oxford 1991), 182–185, and A. M. Belardinelli's edition of Men. *Sik.* (Bari 1994), commentary on line 3.

MENANDER

10 (9 Kö, 10 S)

A compilation of proverbs based on Zenobius (1. 60:
Emmanuel Miller, *Mélanges de littérature grecque* (Paris
1868) 355): Αἰάντειος γέλως· μέμνηται ταύτης (sc. τῆς
παροιμίας) Μένανδρος ἐν τῇ Περινθίᾳ τῇ πρώτῃ. λέγουσι
δὲ ὅτι Πλεισθένης ὁ ὑποκριτὴς (= in their lists of actors no.
400 O'Connor, 2069 Stefanis, p. 351 Ghiron-Bistagne) τὸν
Καρκίνου Αἴαντα (probably Carcinus II: *TGrF* I² p. 211 F
1a) ὑποκρινόμενος εὐκαίρως ἐγέλασε· τοῦ γὰρ Ὀδυσσέως
εἰπόντος ὅτι τὰ δίκαια χρὴ ποιεῖν, μετὰ εἰρωνείας ὁ Αἴας
τῷ γέλωτι ἐχρήσατο.

10

[Zenobius]: Ajax laughter: Menander mentions this (proverb) in his first *Perinthia*. Men say that the actor Pleisthenes when acting the role of Ajax in Carcinus' play laughed at an appropriate moment. When Odysseus said that "one must do the honest thing", Ajax interposed an ironic laugh.

The paroemiographer's words imply that the proverb 'Ajax laughter' originated in a historical event. A tragic actor named Pleisthenes is known to have won a victory in the Greater Dionysia at Athens probably in the late fourth century B.C. (IG ii² 2325.36 = V A 2 col. 4.15 Mette), but we cannot be certain whether (i) this Pleisthenes was identical with the one mentioned above, (ii) the author of the Ajax tragedy was the elder Carcinus (who was a contemporary of Aristophanes), or his very productive and successful grandson (who flourished in the middle of the fourth century B.C.). It is possible that the event which gave rise to the proverb did not antedate Menander's Perinthia by many years, but the relevance of the proverb to the tragic plot, where doubtless Carcinus presented Odysseus as a man bent on securing his own ends by dishonest means if necessary, just as Sophocles had done in Philoctetes (for instance 79–85, 108 f., 1047–1053), is far clearer than its application in Menander's play.

The reference here to a 'first' Perinthia is not supported by other known evidence; if correct, it must imply that either one play was produced twice in two different versions, or two different plays shared the same title, like Menander's two Adelphoi.

MENANDER

Four testimonia about Περινθία

I

Terence, *Andria* 9–14:

9   Menander fecit Andriam et Perinthiam;
10   qui utramuis recte norit, ambas nouerit:
       non ita dissimili sunt argumento, et tamen
       dissimili oratione sunt factae et stilo.
       quae conuenere in Andriam ex Perinthia
14   fatetur transtulisse atque usum pro suis.

10 utrumuis *G*.   11 et *Eugraphius*: sed *all mss. except G*
(set).   12 factae *om. G*.   14 transtulisse se *DL*.

II

Donatus (1. 44 Wessner) commenting on Terence, *Andria* 10
VTRAMVIS: prima scaena Perinthiae fere isdem uerbis
quibus Andria scripta est, cetera dissimilia sunt exceptis
duobus locis, altero ad uersus XI, altera ad XX (.XX.*a. A*,
.XXa (*with a deleted and* uicesimum *added above the line by
a second hand*) *C*, XXOI *T*, XX^ti *V*), qui in utraque fabula
positi sunt.

III

Donatus (1. 45 Wessner) commenting on Terence, *Andria* 14
FATETVR TRANSTVLISSE: sed quare ergo se onerat Teren-
tius, cum possit uideri de una transtulisse? sic soluitur: quia
conscius sibi est primam scaenam de Perinthia esse trans-
latam, ubi senex ita cum uxore loquitur, ut apud Terentium
cum liberto. at in Andria Menandri solus est senex.

PERINTHIA

Four testimonia about Perinthia

I

From the prologue to Terence's *Andria*:

> Menander wrote an *Andria* and a   9
> *Perinthia*; if either is known well,   10
> Both are. Their plots are not so different;
> The language, though, and style do differ. He
> Admits he took what fitted from *Perinthia*
> And used it as his own in *Andria*.   14

*The implications of this admission are discussed in the intro-
duction to Perinthia.*

II

Donatus' commentary on Terence's *Andria* 10: EITHER: The
first scene of (Menander's) *Perinthia* uses virtually the same
words as the *Andria*, but the rest of the play is different
except for two passages, one of up to 11 verses, the other up
to 20, which occur in both plays.

*See the introduction to Perinthia. There is no way of identify-
ing the two short passages which are alleged to occur in both
plays.*

III

Donatus' commentary on Terence, *Andria* 14: HE ADMITS
HE TOOK: But why then does Terence burden himself, when
he could appear to have used one source? This is the answer:
because he is aware that the first scene is adapted from the
Perinthia, where an old man converses in this way with his
wife, just as in Terence he converses with his freedman. But

499

IV

Donatus (1. 118 Wessner) commenting on Terence, *Andria*
301/2 QVID AIS BYRRIA: has personas (Charinum, Byrrhiam)
Terentius addidit fabulae—nam non sunt apud Menan-
drum—ne †οπιθελτον† (*so A*: παθητικὸν *Rabbow*, ἀπίθανον
Nencini) fieret Philumenam spretam relinquere (relinquere
sanc ti *A*, relinquere sane *TC*) sine sponso, Pamphilo aliam
ducente.

in Menander's *Andria* the old man is alone.

See the introduction to Perinthia.

IV

Donatus' commentary on Terence, *Andria* 301/1: WHAT DO YOU SAY, BYRRHIA: Terence has added these characters (sc. Charinus, Byrrhia) to the play—they are not in Menander—in order to prevent it being implausible (?) that Philumena should be left rejected without a husband when Pamphilus marries somebody else.

Donatus' words here are ambiguous; they may imply that the two characters Charinus and Byrrhia (and the subplot that they introduce) occurred in neither the Andria nor the Perinthia of Menander, but were invented by Terence; or alternatively that they did not figure in Menander's Andria, but were taken from his Perinthia. See the introduction to Perinthia.